Learnability and Cognition

Learning, Development, and Conceptual Change

LD&CC

Lila Gleitman, Susan Carey, Elissa Newport, and Elizabeth Spelke, editors

Learnability and Cognition   Steven Pinker

The Acquisition of Argument
Structure

A Bradford Book

The MIT Press
Cambridge, Massachusetts
London, England

This book was set in Times Roman by The MIT Press and printed and bound by Halliday Lithograph Corporation in the United States of America.

Library of Congress Cataloging in Publication Data

Pinker, Steven, 1954–
  Learnability and cognition: the acqisition of argument structure
  /Steven Pinker.
    p. cm.—(Learning, development, and conceptual change)
  Bibliography: p.
  ISBN 0-262-16111-7
  1. Language acquisition. 2. Grammar, Comparative and general.
3. Semantics. 4. Learning ability. 5. Child psychology.
I. Title. II. Series: MIT Press series in learning, development, and conceptual change.
P118.P555 1989
401'.9—dc19   88-39989
                                                                CIP

To the memory of
Clara Daly Wiesenfeld
(1902–1988),
who would have tried to read
this book

Contents

ix

Series Foreword

This series in learning, development, and conceptual change will include state-of-the-art reference works, seminal book-length monographs, and texts on the development of concepts and mental structures. It will span learning in all domains of knowledge, from syntax to geometry to the social world, and will be concerned with all phases of development, from infancy through adulthood.

The series intends to engage such fundamental questions as

The nature and limits of learning and maturation: the influence of the environment, of initial structures, and of maturational changes in the nervous system on human development; learnability theory; the problem of induction; domain-specific constraints on development.

The nature of conceptual change: conceptual organization and conceptual change in child development, in the acquisition of expertise, and in the history of science.

Lila Gleitman
Susan Carey
Elissa Newport
Elizabeth Spelke

Acknowledgments

In developing the ideas presented in this book, I was lucky to have encountered audiences who refused to believe them, students who refused to pretend to understand them, and children who refused to behave in accordance with them. Facing these challenges led me to discoveries that provided the most satisfying moments of this research.

Jess Gropen has shared my enthusiasm for this topic during the entire time I have worked on the book, and I have benefited greatly from our discussions on every aspect. His independent proposals on how to grapple with various problems were invariably of great help, and the ingenious experiments he developed and executed are a crucial part of the research. I am happy to be able to thank him for these invaluable contributions. Among other graduate students at MIT, Paul Bloom and Karin Stromswold also provided helpful comments and discussions.

Jill Gaulding and Marc Light took on as their senior research projects the task of implementing parts of the theory as a computer simulation. Their penetrating analysis of the representational formalism and learning algorithms led to countless improvements in the precision, economy, and accuracy of these mechanisms and in the clarity of the exposition.

Michelle Hollander and Richard Goldberg assisted in the developmental research with dedication, intelligence, and skill. Loren Ann Frost, Ronald Wilson, and Larry Rosen deserve thanks for their work on earlier experiments. I am also very grateful to the child-care centers in the Boston area that invited us in to conduct the research.

I am in debt to a number of researchers who have shared their findings and disagreements. Melissa Bowerman has doubted whether constraints on lexical rules could get the child out of the learnability paradox I have addressed. Lila Gleitman has questioned how much of a verb's meaning a child could learn from the situations in which it is used. Jane Grimshaw and Janet Randall have warned against neglecting properties of the grammatical representation of argument structure as a source of learning constraints. Janet Fodor has been skeptical about how productive children's use of rules really is. Kenneth Wexler has argued against assuming that the biological mechanisms of language acquisition remain unchanged through childhood. I think that all of these people are right about something, and I have strived toward a theory that is eclectic enough to encompass all of their insights in some form, though naturally these people can be expected to continue to find its weaknesses. What makes the topic so much fun to work on is that it is clear that the ultimate best theory, though eclectic, will not be a banal resignation to the effect that "anything can happen." There are striking regularities in argument structure and its acquisition, and I am glad to be part of a research community that is working toward discovering them.

I also have been fortunate to have worked on this project at MIT during a time when the Lexicon Project at the Center for Cognitive Science was in full swing. Beth Levin, director of the project through 1987, has offered many helpful comments on this work, and the theory owes a great deal to her research. Levin, Jay Keyser, and Kenneth Hale created a stimulating environment with a seminar series and technical reports that were an important catalyst in the research. A visiting position in the Department of Psychology at Brandeis University gave an official status to my very helpful discussions with Jane Grimshaw, Ray Jackendoff, Alan Prince, and Jerry Samet.

Lila Gleitman, Jane Grimshaw, Ray Jackendoff, Barbara Landau, Beth Levin, and several anonymous reviewers read portions of the manuscript and offered many invaluable suggestions. Katarina Rice edited the manuscript masterfully. Michael Tarr, David Plotkin, and Kyle Cave gave me generous advice on computer-related matters, including what to do with a blazing Sun. I am grateful to all of them.

I thank my parents, Harry and Roslyn, and my brother and sister, Robert and Susan, for their interest and encouragement.

Although Nancy Etcoff does not share my obsession with verbs, her interests encompass all aspects of mind, and I have benefited from her insights on countless matters. For these "ninsights" and for her support, I thank her.

This research was funded by NIH grant HD 18381 and by a grant from the Alfred P. Sloan Foundation to the MIT Center for Cognitive Science.

Learnability and Cognition

Chapter 1
A Learnability Paradox

Some of the most rewarding scientific pursuits begin with the discovery of a paradox. Nature does not go out of its way to befuddle us, and if some phenomenon seems to make no sense no matter how we look at it, we are probably in ignorance of deep and far-ranging principles. For anyone interested in the human mind, language offers many such opportunities for discovery. Language is created anew each generation, so details of grammar, even subtle and intricate ones, are products of the minds of children and bear the stamp of their learning abilities.

This book is about a paradox in language acquisition. The paradox begins with a small linguistic puzzle: Why does *He gave them a book* sound natural, but *He donated them a book* sound odd? It is complicated by a fact about children's environment —that they are not corrected for speaking ungrammatically —and a fact about their behavior —that they do not confine themselves to the verb phrase structures they have heard other people use. In trying to resolve this paradox, we must face fundamental questions about language and cognition: When do children generalize and when do they stick with what they hear? What is the rationale behind linguistic constraints? How is the syntax of predicates and arguments related to their semantics? What is a possible word meaning? Do languages force their speakers to construe the world in certain ways? Is there a difference between a word meaning and a concept? Why does children's language seem different from that of adults? The goal of this work is to resolve the learning paradox and to show how the solution leads to insight into these deep questions.

The strategy I will follow comes out of what is sometimes called the learnability approach to language acquisition (Hamburger and Wexler, 1975; Pinker, 1979; Wexler and Culicover, 1980; Baker and McCarthy, 1981). This approach focuses on the logical nature of the task facing the child as he or she tries to learn a language and on the mental representations and processes that make such learning successful. I will pursue the solution to the learning paradox relent-lessly, trying to create a trail that leads from the prelinguistic child to the adult's command of subtle discriminations of linguistic structure. Though parts of the trail may be rough going, what is most important is that each segment link up with the next to form an unbroken path of explanation from children's experience to adults' knowledge.

In this chapter I outline the problem: first, the specific domain of language and why it is important, then the logic of language learning in general, then the jux-taposition of the two that creates the learning puzzle. Then I consider some half-dozen simple ways in which the problem might be eliminated. All can be shown to be incorrect or unsatisfactory. In my mind this is what elevates the problem from a puzzle to a paradox, which the rest of the book attempts to solve.

Chapter 2 discusses phenomena that point to a way out of the paradox and presents evidence that that path is the right one. The next three chapters outline a theory of adult linguistic knowledge that is logically capable of resolving the paradox while providing an explanation for the form of that knowledge. Chapter 3 tries to make sense of the phenomena, making them fall out of more general principles. Chapter 4 extends those principles so that the original linguistic problems can be solved in detail. Chapter 5 deals with representation; it presents and justifies an explicit description of the representational structures for verb meanings and rules that the theory needs.

The next two chapters take up the psychological processes for acquiring the linguistic knowledge underlying the solution to the paradox. Chapter 6 is about learning; it discusses the computational problem of how the linguistic structures are acquired through interaction with the environment, and it outlines a proposal for how the child does this. Chapter 7 is about children's development; in it I compare the facts of child language with the acquisition problems and mecha-nisms discussed previously. In the concluding chapter I spell out some interest-ing implications that the solution of the paradox holds for language and cognition.

Much of this book is about words, and this calls for a special apology. People know tens of thousands of words, no two alike, making the mental lexicon a domain of immeasurable richness. Any theory that tries to find common organizing principles amongst this richness can be confronted with a huge number of empirical tests. While this makes for lively linguistic argumentation, at times it can be overwhelming. In the middle chapters (3, 4, and 5) I describe a theory of the mental representation of words and rules whose machinery is outlined explicitly and which is buttressed with many linguistic data. I have tried, however, to organize the material so that it can be absorbed by readers with varying degrees of expertise and interest, including those with little background in linguistics.

The key ideas of these middle chapters are presented in overview sections at the beginning and in summary sections at the end. The first section of chapter 3, section 3.1, is a capsule description of the theory discussed in that chapter, and similarly section 4.1 motivates and previews the claims of chapter 4. The final section of chapter 4 spells out the relationship between the two key parts of the theory, the one presented in chapter 3 and the one presented in chapter 4. The general justification for the theory of representation in chapter 5 is presented in sections 5.1 through 5.4, and the accomplishments of the theory are summarized at the end of the chapter. Finally, chapter 8 begins with a brief recapitulation of everything that went before.

The detailed linguistic discussions in the middle of chapters 3–5 are also modularly organized. In each one I begin with linguistic evidence that is independent of the problems I try to solve. These can be found in sections 3.2, 4.2, and 5.3–5.4. I present the theoretical claims explicitly in sections 3.3, 4.3 and 5.5. In the remaining sections I apply the theory to each of four linguistic phenomena, the dative, causative, locative, and passive alternations. Because the topic of this book is the psychology of language acquisition, I have chosen to organize the book around issues of representation and learning rather than around the linguistic phenomena, and this means that I discuss each of the four alternations a number of times. The sections in which the individual alternations are discussed are self-contained, labeled, and cross-referenced, and specialists with an interest in one alternation can skip or skim the others. Readers who want to see the theory applied in detail to one illustrative alternation are encouraged to track the discussions of the dative.

But let me get on with the paradox.

1.1 Argument Structure and the Lexicon

Human languages do not define straightforward mappings between thoughts and words. To get a sentence, it is not enough to select the appropriate words and string them together in an order that conveys the meaning relationships among them. Verbs are choosy; not all verbs can appear in all sentences, even when the combinations make perfect sense, as shown in (1.1).

(1.1) John fell.
   *John fell the floor.

   John dined.
   *John dined the pizza.

   John devoured the pizza.
   *John devoured.

John ate.

John ate the pizza.

John put something somewhere.

*John put something.

*John put somewhere.

*John put.

These facts demonstrate the phenomenon often referred to as subcategorization: different subcategories of verbs make different demands on which of their arguments must be expressed, which can be optionally expressed, and how the expressed arguments are encoded grammatically—that is, as subjects, objects, or oblique objects (objects of prepositions or oblique cases). The properties of verbs in different subcategories are specified by their entries in the mental lexicon, in data structures called *argument structures* (also called predicate argument structures, subcategorization frames, subcategorizations, case frames, lexical forms, and theta grids). Thus the argument structure of *fall*, *dine*, and the intransitive version of *eat* would specify that only a subject is permitted. The argument structures for *devour* and the transitive version of *eat* would specify that a subject and an object are required. The argument structure for *put* would call for no more and no less than a subject, an object, and an oblique object.

Lexical argument structures play an extremely important role in modern theories of language. Beginning with *Aspects of the Theory of Syntax* (Chomsky, 1965) and continuing to the present, it has become apparent that many of the facts of grammar are caused by properties of the particular lexical items that go into sentences. Recent theories of grammar specify rich collections of information in lexical entries and relatively impoverished rules or principles in other components of grammar (e.g., Chomsky, 1981; Bresnan, 1982a). Sentences conform to the demands of the words in them because of general principles (for example, Chomsky's Theta-Criterion and Bresnan's Coherence and Completeness Principles) that deem a sentence to be grammatical only if the arguments specified by the verb's argument structure are actually present as constituents in the sentence and vice versa. Chomsky's Projection Principle specifies further that the demands of verbs' argument structures must be satisfied at every level of sentence representation, not just deep structure.

Since verbs' argument structures assume such a large burden in explaining the facts of language, how argument structures are acquired is a correspondingly crucial part of the problem of explaining language acquisition. (In fact, Elliott and Wexler, in press, have gone so far as to suggest that language acquisition may be *nothing but* the acquisition of information about the words in the language.) How argument structures are acquired is intertwined with the question of why particular verbs are paired with particular argument structures—that is, with the question "What do verbs want?" What we need is a theory that answers those two questions simultaneously.

1.2 The Logical Problem of Language Acquisition

Language acquisition in general, and the acquisition of verb argument structures in particular, can be thought of in the following terms. The child hears a finite number of sentences from his or her parents during the language-learning years, which are symbolized by the X's in (1.2). But a language is an open-ended set, not a fixed list, so the child must generalize from these inputs to an infinite set of sentences that includes the input sample but goes beyond it. This is shown in (1.2) as the circle with the arrow pointing to it. As in all induction problems, the hard part is that an infinite number of hypotheses are consistent with the input sample but differ from each other and from the correct hypothesis (the actual target language) in ways that are not detectable given the input sample alone. Some of the incorrect hypotheses are depicted by the other circles in (1.2).

(1.2)

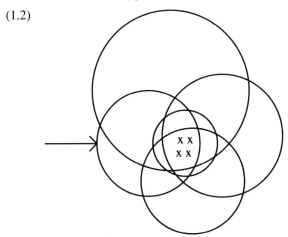

The solution to this (or any other) learning problem works as follows. Constraints on the learner force him to entertain a restricted set of hypotheses that includes the correct hypothesis but excludes many others. The learner can then compare the predictions of a hypothesis (which sentences it generates) with the input data so that incorrect hypotheses can be rejected.

There are four ways in which one of the the child's hypotheses can be incorrect before learning is successful. The child's language can be disjoint from the target language, as in (1.3a). In this case any sentence in the input is sufficient to inform the child that the hypothesis is wrong. Such sentences, called *positive evidence*, are depicted in the figure with a "+" symbol. Likewise, if the language generated by the child's hypothesis grammar intersects the target language, as in (1.3b), or is a subset of it, as in (1.3c), positive evidence consisting of input sentences in the nonoverlapping region of the target language suffices to impel the child to reject the hypothesis. However, if the child entertains a grammar generating a superset of the target language, as in (1.3d), no amount of positive evidence can strictly falsify the guess. What he or she needs is *negative evidence*: evidence about which word strings are ungrammatical (that is, not in the target language). This is shown as the "−" symbols in (1.3d). Explaining successful learning basically consists of showing that the learner can entertain and stick with a correct hypothesis and can falsify any incorrect ones (see, e.g., Osherson, Stob, and Weinstein, 1985; Pinker, 1979; Wexler and Culicover, 1980).

(1.3)

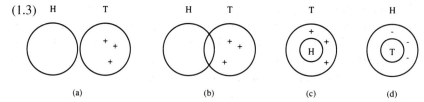

The first important question about child language acquisition is whether negative evidence is available. Obviously no one gives children a list of ungrammatical sentences tagged with asterisks. The most psychologically plausible kind of negative evidence would be some sort of parental feedback that children might receive related to whether their own utterances are grammatical or not, such as corrections or expressions of approval. The available evidence suggests that children are not provided with such information. Brown and Hanlon (1970) found that parents do not differentially express approval or disapproval contingent on whether the child's prior utterance was well formed; nor do they understand well-formed questions better than ill-formed ones. As a result it is commonly assumed that children do not depend on negative evidence to acquire a language. This means that they cannot engage in the sort of hypothesis falsification illustrated in figure (2d); either they never entertain any hypothesis that is a superset of the target language, or, if they do, some endogenous force must impel them to abandon it, because the world will never force them to. On the other hand, children cannot simply stick with the exact sentences they hear, because they must generalize to the infinite language of their community. This tension, between the need to generalize and the need not to generate supersets, characterizes many of the toughest problems in explaining human language acquisition. Some of these are discussed by Baker (1979), Berwick (1986), Bowerman (1987a, 1987b), Braine (1971), Chomsky and Lasnik (1977), Pinker (1982, 1984), and Wexler and Culicover (1980).

1.3 Baker's Paradox

Now we can juxtapose the facts of argument structure with the logic of the learning problem. The acquisition of the syntactic properties of verbs is one of the clearest cases in which the no-negative-evidence problem arises. Though Georgia Green (1974; pp. 3, 199) first pointed out a learning paradox based on it, C. Lee Baker (1979) discussed it in a larger context that drew more attention. Consider a child hearing sentence pairs such as those in (1.4) and forming the associated argument structures.

(1.4) John gave a dish to Sam.
give: NP_1 __ NP_2 to–NP_3
John gave Sam a dish.
give: NP_1 __ NP_3 NP_2
John passed the salami to Fred.
pass: NP_1 __ NP_2 to–NP_3
John passed Fred the Salami.
pass: NP_1 __ NP_3 NP_2
John told a joke to Mary.
tell: NP_1 __ NP_2 to–NP_3
John told Mary a joke.
tell: NP_1 __ NP_3 NP_2

It would seem to be a reasonable generalization that any verb with the NP_1 __ NP_2 to–NP_3 argument structure (prepositional dative) could also have a NP_1 __ NP_3 NP_2 argument structure (double-object dative). This generalization could be captured in, say, a lexical rule such as that in (1.5), which would allow the child to create a double-object dative corresponding to any prepositional one for some new verb (e.g., send), even if he or she had never heard the verb in the double-object form.

(1.5) NP_1 __ NP_2 to–NP_3 —> NP_1 __ NP_3 NP_2

The problem is that not all the verbs with the prepositional argument structure dativize (that is, appear in both versions of the alternation), as (1.6) shows.

(1.6) John donated a painting to the museum.
*John donated the museum a painting.

John reported the accident to the police.
*John reported the police the accident.

But the child has no way of knowing this, given the nonavailability of negative evidence. The fact that he or she hasn't heard the ungrammatical sentences in (1.6) could simply reflect adults' never having had an opportunity to utter them in the child's presence (after all, there are an infinite number of grammatical sentences that the child will never hear). Therefore, the child should speak ungrammatically all his life—or more accurately, the language should change in a single generation so that exceptional verbs such as those in (1.6) would become regular.

I will call this learning problem "Baker's paradox." It has attracted a great deal of attention among language acquisition researchers, for example, Berwick and Weinberg (1984), Bowerman (1983a, 1987a, 1987b), Clark (1987), Fodor (1985), Fodor and Crain (1987), Maratsos, Gudeman, Gerard-Ngo, and De Hart (1987), MacWhinney (1987), Mazurkewich and White (1984), Pinker (1981a, 1982, 1984, 1986, 1988), Pinker, Lebeaux and Frost (1987), Randall (1987), and Roeper (1981). In Pinker (1984) I considered several other lexicosyntactic alternations where the combination of widespread generalization and lexical exceptions creates the same learnability problem. Among them are the passive, shown in (1.7), the lexical causative alternation, in (1.8), and the locative alternation, in (1.9). I will return to these four alternations repeatedly in this book in discussing the resolution of Baker's paradox.[1]

(1.7)   John touched Fred.
        Fred was touched by John. (also hit, see, like, kick, etc.)

        John resembled Fred.
        *Fred was resembled by John.

(1.8)   The ball rolled.
        John rolled the ball. (also slide, melt, bounce, open, close, etc.)

        The baby cried.
        *John cried the baby.

(1.9)   Irv loaded eggs into the basket.
        Irv loaded the basket with eggs. (also spray, cram, splash, stuff, etc.)

        Irv poured water into the glass.
        *Irv poured the glass with water.

1.4   Attempted Solutions to Baker's Paradox

1.4.1   Components of the Paradox

Three aspects of the problem give it its sense of paradox. First is the lack of *negative evidence*: if children could count on being corrected or on being given some other signal for every ungrammatical utterance they made, then simply saying something like *I am resembled by Seth* and attending to the resulting feedback would suffice to expunge the passive lexical entry for *resemble*.

Second, *productivity*: if children simply stuck with the argument structures that were exemplified in parental speech, never forming a productive rule such as that in (1.5), then they would never make errors to begin with and hence would have no need to figure out how to avoid or expunge them. Third, *arbitrariness*: the fact that near-synonyms have different kinds of argument structures, such as *give* and *donate*, or *load* and *pour*, or *own* (which passivizes) and *have* (which does not), or *move* (which occurs in a lexical causative) and *go* (which does not) means that the child cannot use some simple semantic guideline indicating where productive rules can be applied and where they are blocked. But in combination these three factors make acquisition of argument structure alternations in the verb lexicon impossible to explain. Accordingly, the various solutions to the paradox that have been proposed have denied one or more of these three assumptions.

1.4.2 Solution #0: Nonsolutions
Language acquisition research has no shortage of vague general proposals about what language acquisition is like, and often it has been suggested to me that the problem disappears or is easily solved by one of these proposals. For example, Bowerman (1987b) suggests that Braine's (1971) "Discovery Procedures Model" might lead to a solution of Baker's paradox, and MacWhinney (1987) claims that his "Competition Model" solves it outright. It has also been suggested to me that processes that go by such names as "abduction algorithms" and "syntactic distributional analysis" would do the job. These suggestions are not necessarily wrong, but they are about as useful as saying that you can get rich by buying low and selling high. Since none of them provides any details as to how Baker's paradox might be solved in any concrete instance—the models cannot even represent the distinctions made in the adult state, let alone show how they are acquired—there is no need to discuss them further.

1.4.3 Solution #1: Variants of Negative Evidence

1.4.3.1 Subtle Negative Evidence   The idea that children have no access to negative evidence does not sit well with many people. As Michael Maratsos (1986) has put it, psychologists seem to want to take the difficult problem of language acquisition away from the helpless child and return it to the hands of responsible authorities. Thus several investigators have recently taken a closer look at the negative evidence question. These reexaminations have replicated Brown and Hanlon's finding that parental expressions of approval are independent of the grammaticality of the child's prior utterance. However, there have been found to be slight differences in the frequency with which some mothers repeat, alter, question, and follow up in various ways on their child's well-formed

versus ill-formed utterances (Hirsch-Pasek, Treiman, and Schneiderman, 1984; Demetras, Post, and Snow, 1986; Penner, 1987; Bohannon and Stanowicz, 1988). Nonetheless, this feedback is unlikely to solve the learnability problem we are faced with in this case, or probably any other one (see also Bowerman, 1987a, 1987b, Gordon, in press, Grimshaw and Pinker, in press, and Morgan and Travis, in press, for similar arguments). For Baker's problem to go away, the following things would have to be true:

1. *Negative evidence would have to exist.* One thing is certain: children do not receive negative evidence in the technical sense of the term. Negative evidence (see Gold, 1967; Pinker, 1979) is information about the ungrammaticality of every ungrammatical string composed of the language's vocabulary items. None of the new studies has shown that all the ungrammatical sentences of all children elicit reliable differences in parental behavior, only that some do sometimes.

In these studies, all forms of ill-formedness are lumped together in the analyses. Thus we do not know whether it is ungrammaticality in general that elicits differences in parental behavior, or a particular salient kind of ungrammaticality such as missing major constituents. In the Hirsch-Pasek et al. study, only children in the youngest age-group (2-year-olds) were found to receive partly diagnostic input in the form of more frequent repetitions of ungrammatical utterances (the analysis combined verbatim repetitions with those in which the error was corrected); for the 3-year-olds, 4-year-olds, and 5-year-olds, there was no difference. Penner (1987) also found that feedback rates declined precipitously after the age of two. But there is surely a lot of language left to be acquired at that age, including the structures relevant to Baker's paradox. In fact Gropen, Pinker, Hollander, Goldberg, and Wilson (1989) documented a number of examples of children uttering double-object sentences that were ungrammatical because of their verbs; in no case did the parents react with disapproval, correction, repetition, or recasting.

An equally serious problem is that it is unlikely that *all* children receive diagnostic parental feedback—but all children learn their native language. Except for the Demetras et al. paper, the new studies report aggregate data, rather than data from individual children. Nonetheless even the aggregate data from the Hirsh-Pasek study make it clear that not every mother of a 2-year-old in their middle-class sample (let alone mothers from other classes or cultures) differentially repeated ungrammatical utterances, and this is likely to be true of the Bohannon and Stanowicz and Penner studies as well. Note in this regard that the use of inferential statistics in an attempt to generalize to a population of mothers is highly misleading. It is not the psychology of the average mother that is in question here but the availability of certain kinds of information to *any* child who learns to speak.[2]

A third reason to doubt that children receive negative evidence is that much of the parental feedback that has been documented may not even be feedback about grammaticality. In the Demetras et al. study, the three kinds of feedback measures that had a probabilistic relationship to the utterances of all the children in the sample (clarification questions, signals to "move on" in the conversation, and verbatim repetitions) were not consistently related to whether the utterance was deviant for syntactic, phonological, semantic, or pragmatic reasons. Thus there was no information indicating to the children whether it was their grammar and lexicon that needed fixing or their pronunciation or conversational skills; a child who paid heed to parental feedback could needlessly mess up his rules of syntax or morphology when all he had done was pronounce *balloon* as *bawoon*. The same problem infects the Bohannon and Stanowicz (1988) study.

Finally, in no study was any of the forms of feedback uniformly contingent on properties of the child's utterance. For example, Hirsh-Pasek et al. found that 20% of the child's ungrammatical utterances were repeated; but so were 12% of their *grammatical* utterances. So any child who changed his or her grammar so as to rule out a repeated utterance would be making his grammar better a fifth of the time but making it *worse* an eighth of the time. The other studies of parental feedback also found that its relation to the well-formedness of children's speech was highly noisy at best; usually the mean difference between the frequency of a form of feedback following a well-formed utterance and following an ill-formed utterance was a few percentage points. Again, we must not be misled by the habit of trying to detect weak effects by looking at average tendencies in large samples. Although this might be appropriate for a study of the psychology of mothers, it is not appropriate for a study of the information available to every child.

The noisiness of parental feedback suggests that the child might be better off ignoring it altogether and changing his or her grammar only in response to positive evidence. According to some estimates (Newport, Gleitman, and Gleitman, 1977), parental speech is 99.93% free from speech errors (putting aside irrelevancies such as ellipses and casual speech forms that are "errors" only in a prescriptive sense). Relying on positive evidence alone, in contrast to relying on negative evidence as well, would thus make the child's grammar worse virtually never. Note also that the extremely high reliability of positive evidence shows that skepticism about the value of noisy and inconsistent negative evidence is not based on a naive faith in a pristine, noise-free world.

2. *Negative evidence, even if it exists, would have to be useful.* Although negative evidence in the technical sense surely does not exist, perhaps, it could be argued, the children that do receive probabilistic feedback could make use of it in some way. For example, children might be able to aggregate information

from the statistical tendencies of parental reactions, rejecting a sentence if it had been followed by a given type of feedback so often that the hypothesis that it was ungrammatical was very much more probable than the hypothesis that it was grammatical.

But how this would work is quite unclear. Children certainly cannot aggregate information about feedback to *tokens* of particular sentences; no sentence is used by a child often enough. So if they use feedback at all, they must lump "equivalent" kinds of sentences together for the tallies. How they hypothesize the right equivalence classes and assign sentences correctly to them simply re-raises all the questions about generalization that have to be answered under the assumptions that positive evidence alone is used.

The usefulness of the information that a kind of sentence is ungrammatical is highly questionable too. Sentences are generated by large numbers of rules and principles that vary crosslinguistically, not just one. So even a child who is able to make a binary good/bad decision faces a formidable example of what artificial intelligence researchers call the "blame-assignment" problem: figuring out which rule to single out for change or abandonment. (As mentioned in the preceding discussion, in practice the problem is even worse because the child may have no way of distinguishing "errors" that are due to syntax from those due to defective word meanings, bad pronunciation, or conversational maladroitness.)

3. *Negative evidence, even if present and useful, would have to be used.* Hirsh-Pasek et al. are careful to point out that their study does not establish that children were at all sensitive to the contingencies they tried to document. We have very little good evidence on this matter. But we do have a set of consistent observations of parent-child interaction suggesting that parental feedback, even in the form of maximally clear and informative overt corrections, may be fruitless in changing the grammar of the child. For example, McNeill (1966) reports the following dialogue:

(1.10) Child: Nobody don't like me.
          Mother: No, say "Nobody likes me."
          Child: Nobody don't like me.

          [dialogue repeated eight times]

          Mother: Now listen carefully, say "NOBODY LIKES ME."
          Child: Oh! Nobody don't likeS me.

Braine (1971) reports that he made several extensive efforts to change the syntax of his two children through feedback. Over a span of several weeks, for example, he repeatedly but unsuccessfully tried to persuade his daughter to substitute *other N* for *other one N*, in interchanges such as the following:

(1.11) Child: Want other one spoon, Daddy.
         Father: You mean, you want THE OTHER SPOON.
         Child: Yes, I want other one spoon, please, Daddy.
         Father: Can you say "the other spoon"?
         Child: Other ... one ... spoon.
         Father: Say ... "other."
         Child: Other.
         Father: "Spoon."
         Child: Spoon.
         Father: "Other ... spoon."
         Child: Other ... spoon. Now give me other one spoon?

Braine reports that "further tuition is ruled out by her protest, vigorously supported by my wife." Maratsos (1986) has reported similar exchanges from the speech of Stan Kuczaj's son, and I chanced upon the following dialogue from transcripts of the speech of Brian MacWhinney's sons (MacWhinney and Snow, 1985):

(1.12) Child: I turned the raining off.
         Parent: You mean you turned the sprinkler off?
         Child: I turned the raining off of the sprinkler.

Though isolated, the reports are consistent, and I know of no demonstrations in which overt correction or other immediate parental feedback has led to persistent changes in children's language.

Although it is possible that corrections or other forms of enriched interaction with children might in the future be shown to lead to measurable changes in the children's speech, such evidence would have to be interpreted cautiously. Any correction by its very nature also offers positive evidence, and positive evidence of a peculiarly relevant kind. So any study which purports to show that corrections are actually used by children can be given the more parsimonious explanation that this is just another case where relevant positive evidence is used. To make any kind of case for the role of corrections as negative evidence, it is necessary to distinguish the statistical correlation between partial corrections and ungrammatical utterances from the content of the corrections themselves, which is a form of positive evidence.

4. *Negative evidence, even if used, would have to be necessary to avoid or recover from overgeneration.* Even if the child were shown to learn faster by virtue of using negative evidence, it would have to be demonstrated that negative evidence was *necessary* to cause the change. If it simply sped up some change that was bound to happen because of other learning mechanisms, we would still have to explain how those other mechanisms worked. An analogy: It is

conceivable that explicit language drills, such as in high school "language laboratories," could affect the child's acquisition of some aspect of grammar. Unless that drill was the *only* way in which that learning accomplishment could take place, a theorist could not rely on it to explain that facet of language acquisition.

In fact, it seems quite unlikely that negative evidence is necessary for the child to learn which verbs take which argument structures. Virtually every adult speaker of standard American English would judge the sentences such as *I ladeled the floor with paint, Ten pounds was weighed by the boy, I murmured John the answer* and *He rejoiced the audience* to be ungrammatical. Is that because everyone has at some point uttered these verbs in these contexts and benefited from negative feedback? If someone's personal history had not included such events, would he or she find such sentences acceptable? The low frequency of these verbs, and of children's and adults errors with them, combined with the uniformity of adults' judgments that these sentences sound bad, makes that extremely unlikely. We must look elsewhere to explain how children turn into adults.

Two other ideas are often discussed in connection with negative evidence, each aimed at showing that some kind of information in the environment is sufficient to tell the child which strings are ungrammatical in the language, not directly via some physical cue or signal, but indirectly via a short inference.

1.4.3.2 Nonoccurrence: A Surrogate for Negative Evidence? Occasionally it is suggested that if the child noted that certain forms did not occur in the input, that could serve as a kind of evidence that such forms were ungrammatical (e.g., Chomsky, 1981). This is called indirect negative evidence. But on closer examination it turns out to be far from clear what indirect negative evidence could be. It can't be true that the child literally rules out any sentence he or she hasn't heard, because there is always an infinity of sentences that he or she hasn't heard that are grammatical (and the discussion of conservatism below will show that at no point in development does a speaker rule out all the verb-argument structure combinations that have not yet appeared in the input). And it is trivially true both that the child picks hypothesis grammars that rule out *some* of the sentences he or she hasn't heard, and that if a child hears a sentence he or she will often entertain a different hypothesis grammar than if he or she hasn't heard it. So the question is, under exactly what circumstances does a child conclude that a nonwitnessed sentence is ungrammatical? This is virtually a restatement of the original learning problem. Answering it requires specifying some detailed learning strategy. It takes the burden of explaining learning out of the environmental input and puts it back in the child. Use of indirect negative evidence, even if true in some sense, is thus not, strictly speaking, a feature of the child's learning environment (as subtle direct negative evidence would be) but rather a feature of his learning strategy, and hence it must be fleshed out according to a particular theory of these learning strategies. (Osherson, Stob, and Weinstein, 1985, discuss one theoretical possibility, though it is not plausible for the present problem.)

1.4.3.3   Uniqueness: Another Surrogate for Negative Evidence?   It is also occasionally suggested that the child hears sentences in perceptual contexts containing information about the meaning of the sentences rather than disembodied strings of words, and that this gives him or her a substitute for negative evidence (see Pinker, 1979, 1982; Wexler and Culicover, 1980; Osherson et al., 1985). There are two versions of this suggestion, and neither one of them can solve Baker's problem directly. On the one hand, a language can be construed as a set of pairs each consisting of a string and a semantic representation. The child's task is to learn the infinite set of legitimate pairs, and his or her input consists of a sample of such pairs (sentences, plus a representation of their meanings, inferred from their contexts). Negative evidence in this case would consist of information that certain meaning-sentence pairings were impossible. But it is clear that the child does not receive this kind of negative evidence either. For example, the child would have to know that *John donated the museum a painting* is not among the legitimate ways of expressing the proposition that John donated a painting to the museum, leading us back to the Brown and Hanlon findings that such information is probably not available.

On the second construal, the language would be treated as a set of strings and the child's input as a finite sample of those strings, but the child would assume that meanings and strings pair up in one-to-one fashion. Thus if a given string was heard paired with a particular meaning, the child could reject any hypothesis that paired a different string with that meaning. In this way any ungrammatical sentence (as long as it was given a determinate semantic interpretation) could be ruled out. The one-to-one or Uniqueness postulate (see Wexler and Culicover, 1980; Pinker, 1984; Clark, 1987) would be necessary because if a language allowed synonymous sentences, hearing one sentence paired with a meaning would not license the child to conclude that some other sentence with that meaning was ungrammatical. Once again, there is no straightforward way in which this solves Baker's problem. On the face of it, languages do contain synonymous sentences, such as *Give the book to me* and *Give me the book*. Thus if a child hears *Donate the book to me* he cannot justifiably infer that *Donate me the book* is ungrammatical. (If the child did erroneously assume that Uniqueness was the unmarked case, relaxing it for *give* and the scores of verbs like it under the pressure of witnessing both versions in the input, he would simply be adopting the conservatism strategy that I discuss in the next section.) Thus an appeal to Uniqueness will not resolve Baker's paradox. It's not that the logic of Uniqueness is faulty. For example, it works in principle in the case of recovering from overgeneralization of past-tense morphology, because virtually every verb has a unique past-tense form: hearing *broke* in a past tense context is evidence that *breaked* is ungrammatical. The problem for the case of argument structures is that there is unlikely to be a perceptually recoverable semantic representation that can be paired up uniquely with each alternative argument structure.

Before I reject this option too quickly, it is worth noting that Clark (1987) does review evidence suggesting that perfect synonymy is rare or nonexistent in natural languages. She points out that seemingly synonymous constructions can differ in discourse properties, entailments, speech register (e.g., formal versus casual), and other subtle factors. For example, Erteschik-Shir (1979) points out that the two forms of the dative differ in discourse focus. *Give the X to the Y* is most felicitous when *X* (the transferred object) is known background information and *Y* (the recipient) is the new information that attention is being called to; *Give the Y the X* is appropriate when *Y* is background and *X* is foreground. But how could the learner use this information to rule out **He donated the museum a painting*? Basically, each combination of a verb and a set of discourse roles for its arguments would have to be paired uniquely with an argument structure. In Pinker (1981a) I sketch the necessary kind of scenario. There would have to be a situation in which the recipient is background information and the transferred object is new information but the speaker insists on using the nonfelicitous prepositional-object form instead. For example, if a person were to ask, "What did John do with the museum that inspired its directors to make him a trustee?" and heard as an answer, "He donated a Vermeer to the museum," the listener could conclude that the double-object form of *donate* is ungrammatical. This scenario, of course, is highly implausible. Though children are demonstrably sensitive to discourse properties of the dative forms (Gropen et al., 1989), their sensitivity is statistical, not absolute. Furthermore, in ordinary discourse a host of focusing devices, such as pronominalization, contrastive stress, and clefting, can override the default differences in discourse focus between alternative argument structures. Thus, in my example, *He donated a VERMEER to it* is a perfectly felicitous reply to the hypothetical question. Unique discourse correlates of alternative argument structures would therefore be a tenuous basis for rejecting one of them.

1.4.4   Solution #2: Strict Lexical Conservatism

Baker (1979) and Fodor (1985; see also Fodor and Crain, 1987) have suggested that children add an argument structure to the lexical entry of a verb only when they hear the verb exemplified in parental speech in that argument structure. They do not deny that children record systematic generalizations among items (e.g., between actives and passives or between prepositional datives and double-object datives), but they believe that these generalizations would not be extended to new forms. The generalizations might be used to store existing lexical entries in memory more compactly, or to dictate the *form* of possible lexical items if positive evidence mandated adding them to the lexicon. For example, given an active verb, some version of a passive rule might dictate that the verb could have a passive participle that was related to it in a particular way (i.e., its object would correspond to the passive subject, and so on). But whether *in fact* it had a passive participle of this form could be ascertained only by observing whether adults had uttered that verb in the passive.

As Wasow (1981), Pinker (1984), and others have pointed out, this hypothesis is prima facie implausible for adults, given the sheer number of verbs in the adult lexicon and adults' apparent freedom in using verbs in passives, double-object datives, and other derived constructions. Verbs of arbitrarily low frequency, which most people have never heard passivized or dativized, are instantly recognizable as grammatical in their passive or dative forms (e.g., *The food was masticated; The matrix was diagonalized; Pierre flipped / slapped / kicked / shot / tapped / poked him the puck*). This is in stark contrast to the stubborn ungrammaticality of the passive of *have* or the double-object dative of *explain*. Furthermore, when new verbs enter the language, they seem to be passivizable or dativizable immediately. For example, Wasow notes that if one were to invent a verb *to satellite a message to Bob*, meaning to transmit a message to him via satellite, the variant *to satellite Bob a message* would sound perfectly fine. (Wasow was prophetic in spirit if not in detail: in 1988 no one is satelliting messages, but people are faxing each other documents with a vengeance.) Likewise, neologisms such as *to format* and *to xerox* rapidly become perfectly passivizable; in its manuscript form, this book was formatted and xeroxed more times than I care to remember.

The argument can be made more general. English has a number of mechanisms for converting nouns, including proper nouns, into new verbs (see Clark and Clark, 1979). Several kinds of these denominal verbs satisfy the conditions for application of a lexical rule. Thus an essentially unbounded set of new verbs potentially entering into argument structure alternations can be created. Though the denominal verbs in the (a) lines of (1.13) sound unfamiliar, once they are accepted by themselves the new, related argument structures created by the lexical rules and shown in (b) possess no increment of oddness or ungrammaticality over the original ones. This suggests that verbs are added to the mental lexicon in sets related by lexical rules; not every verb must be heard in every argument structure.

(1.13) *Dative: verbs derived from means of communication*
   (a) I arpanetted / kermitted / E-mailed / bitnetted / the message to him.
   (b) I arpanetted / kermitted / E-mailed / bitnetted / him the message.

Causative: verbs derived from means of transportation
   (a) She Chevy'd / Harley'd / Winnebago'd / Cessna'd to New York.
   (b) Harry Chevy'd / Harley'd / Winnebago'd / Cessna'd her to New York.

Passive: Verbs derived from names
   (a) Artis Gilmore out-Kareemed Kareem / out-Maloned Malone / out-Parished Parish last night.
   (b) Kareem was out-Kareemed / Malone was out-Maloned / Parish was out-Parished last night by Artis Gilmore.

Locative: verbs derived from instrument of removal
   (a) She Hoovered / Electroluxed / Hoky'd / Eureka'd ashes from the carpet.
   (b) She Hoovered / Electroluxed / Hoky'd / Eureka'd the carpet.

There is good evidence that children are not conservative either. This evidence, which I will review in the next two sections, comes in two forms: errors in spontaneous speech, and generalizations made in experiments involving the teaching of new forms.

1.4.4.1 Evidence Against Strict Lexical Conservatism in Children:

Spontaneous Speech   In chapter 7 I will examine in detail children's errors with argument structures; here it will suffice to show that children make the errors in spontaneous speech.

Passives can be extracted from on-line transcripts of spontaneous speech by searching for instances of *-ed*, *-en*, and a few irregular endings; once such a list has been extracted, one can check to see if any of them are unacceptable as adult forms and hence could not have been learned from adult speech models. We searched the corpora of speech of the children named Adam, Eve, and Sarah studied by Brown (1973), using the Child Language Data Exchange System (ChiLDES) database (MacWhinney and Snow, 1985). In addition, one can examine published accounts of children's creative invention of transitive verbs, such as verbs created from nouns (e.g., *Can you nut these?* from Clark, 1982), or transitive causatives created from intransitives (e.g., *Don't giggle me*, Bowerman, 1982a, b). If children are productive passivizers, some of these novel verbs should have been produced in the passive, again without benefit of an adult model.

Each of these searches yielded passives that for a variety of reasons could not have been based directly on parental speech. Some, such as *I don't want to be shooted*, gave evidence of a productive morphological process yielding passive participles, similar to classic morphological overregularizations such as *singed* or *foots* (Pinker, Lebeaux, and Frost, 1987, lists about twenty examples). A defender of strict lexical conservatism could reply that in these cases children could have noted the existence of passives in parental speech and simply forgotten their surface form, invoking a morphological rule to generate it. Therefore, the more relevant cases are those where not even the existence of the participle could have been inferred from adult speech because the verb was invented by the child to begin with. These are reproduced in (1.14), taken from Pinker, Lebeaux, and Frost (1987):

(1.14) Adam, 4;11: I'm gonna ask Mommy if she has any more grain ... more
        stuff that she needs grained.
        Adam, 4;11: All smoked up [referring to crackers he has crushed].
        Sarah, 3;8: He get died.

From Clark (1982):

        LA, 2;0: C'est déconstruit, c'est bulldozé. [It's unbuilt, it's
            bulldozered.]
        RN, 2;10: Da wird er glatt und dann wird er ausgeplatzelt. [Then
            it's getting smooth and then it's caked/made into cakes.]
        S, 3;2: Is it all needled?
        EB, 3;4: It was bandaided.
        HS, 3;6: Der Löffel ist besuppt. [The spoon is souped.]
        FS, 3;9: ... vollgeascht ... [well-ashed; talking about something
            covered in ashes]
        EG, 3;10: Elles ne sont pas encore grainées. [They (plants) haven't
            made seeds yet/are not seeded yet.]
        CB, 4;2: But I need it watered and soaped [talking about a rag for
            washing a car].
        CB, 4;4: How was it shoelaced?
        HS, 4;7: ... zugebändst ... [ribboned; talking about having ribbons
            on that needed tying]

CB, 5;6: I don't want to be dogeared today [asking for her hair not to be arranged in "dogears"].

DL, 5;6: Hier ist Gold angestreift. [This is gold-striped.]

EG, 6;8: ... pain enoeuffé ... [egged bread; talking about bread with egg on it]

CG, 7;0: ... pain enconfituré ... [jammed bread; talking about bread with jam on it]

CG, 7;4: Mon assiette est entartée. [My plate is covered with tart.]

MA, 9;3: ... une procession eautée ... [a watered procession; describing a procession on the water]

From Bowerman (1983a):

CB, 3;6: If you don't put them in for a very long time they won't get staled.

CB, 3;6: Until I'm four I don't have to be gone [= be taken to the dentist].

CB, 4;3: Why is the laundry place stayed open all night? [= kept].

CB, 5;1: I need to round this circle very much. I need to have this rounded very much [as she rotates knife tip in lump of clay to make a cut-out circle].

H, 4+: He's gonna die you, David. [Turns to mother] The tiger will come and eat David and then he will be died and I won't have a little brother any more.

From Tom Roeper (personal communication):

I don't want to get waded.

I don't want to get waved over.

(Note: The children referred to as "EB" and "CB" by Clark are Eva and Christy Bowerman, whose speech is also reproduced in several examples from Bowerman.)

Example (1.15) presents other passives that children could not have learned directly from their parents, either because a verb takes a preposition that cannot be stranded or because the phrase that the child promoted to subject position is not the direct object of the verb in its transitive form.

(1.15) Adam, 4;2: [Playing with a cord of a toy telephone] Oh, look it's ropted through here. [Past participle of "rope"]

Adam, 4;2: [Another child has put a bowl on Adam's mother's head.] You look like a crashed lady. [Mother: A crashed lady?] Yeah, like a crashed lady.

Sarah, 3;5: It was get burned on my thore fingeh.

Sarah, 4;2: We got all stucked on each other.

Sarah, 4;7: She's scribbled.

Sarah, 4;7: I'm making her picture scribbled.

From Wasow (1981):

4+: I don't like being falled down on!

From Bowerman (1983a and personal communication):

EB, 3;8: [Watching one child sit on a potty, another on a toilet] Both are going to be go-ened in!

CB, 3;3: [After putting small items into a jewelry box and a coin purse] Both of these things can be put things in.

Double-object datives cannot be found as easily, both because there are fewer potentially dativizable verbs than passivizable ones, and because they contain no distinctive affix that can be searched for in on-line transcripts. Nonetheless, there are recurring reports of them in the literature, and Jess Gropen, Michelle Hollander, Richard Goldberg, Ronald Wilson, and I (Gropen et al., 1989) turned up several more in searches of transcripts of the spontaneous speech of Adam, Eve, and Sarah and of Brian MacWhinney's two sons, Ross and Mark (MacWhinney and Snow, 1985).[3] These are reproduced in (1.16).

(1.16) Adam, 4;1: I gon' put me all dese rubber bands on.

      Adam, 4;11: You finished me lots of rings.

      Adam, 5;2: Mommy, fix me my tiger.

       Ursla, fix me a tiger.

       Ursla, fix me a tiger.

    Eve, 2;3: But I go write you a lady now.

      I go write you something.

      I go write you train.

      I writing you something.

      You please write me lady. You please write me lady.

      You can write me a lady on that page.

      Writing you someping.

      Write me another one right here.

      You please write me snowman.

      When Fraser come back he goin' to write me another snowman.

    Eva, 2;0: [Driving in the country. Mother: Oh, look at the horsies.] Where'd those horsies go? [Mother: We passed them.] Pass me some more horsies. [Repeated with "silos", "barns", and "houses"]

Ross, 2;8: Jay said me no.

Ross, 3;3: Don't say me that [asking adult not to tell him to put on his socks].

Ross, 3;3: You ate me my cracker.

Mark, 3;8: So don't please ... keep me a favor [asking brother not to throw up on a ride].

Mark, 4;0: Ross is gonna break into the TV and is gonna spend us money. [Father: What is he gonna do, Mark?] Spend us money [i.e. to fix it will cost us money, cause us to spend money].

From Mazurkewich and White (1984):
2;3: I'll brush him his hair.
5;2: Pick me up all these things.
6;0: Mummy, open Hadwen the door.

From Bowerman (1978, 1983a, 1987a):
C, 3;1: I said her no.
C, 3;3: You put me just bread and butter.
C, 3;4: Put Eva the yukky one first.
C, 3;6: Don't say me that or you'll make me cry.
C, 3;4: Button me the rest.
C, 3;9: I do what my horsie says me to do.
E, 2;4: Then put her some more.
E, 2;4: How come you're putting me that kind of juice?

From E. Clark, personal communication:
Damon, 8;0: Mattia demonstrated me that yesterday.

Although some of these errors might have been caused by the direct substitution of one verb stem for a semantically similar one (e.g., *write* for *draw*, *keep a favor* for *do a favor*) rather than by the application of a dative rule, most of them (e.g., *Fix me a tiger*) must have involved the use of a rule. Even Eve's use of *write* in the double-object form was probably created by the application of a dativization operation; she uttered prepositional-dative sentences with *for* (e.g., *Write a lady for me* four times in that session, but never used *draw* in the double-object form in any of her transcripts. This issue will be discussed in detail in chapter 7.

Causatives. Melissa Bowerman (1982a) lists over 150 examples of spontaneous causatives. Many of them are from her two daughters, Christy and Eva, but examples can be found in virtually any reasonably large sample of children's speech. They have also been found in other languages, including Hebrew (Berman, 1982), Hungarian (MacWhinney, 1985), Portuguese (Figueira, 1984), French, Polish, and Turkish (Slobin, 1985). Because I will be discussing these examples in detail in chapter 7, I reproduce in (1.17) all of the novel causatives involving intransitive verbs from Bowerman's paper.

(1.17) C, 2;9: I come it closer so it won't fall [= bring it closer].

C, 3;4: She came it over there. She brought it over there.

Rachel, 5;5: Come me out. [R in bathtub. Repeats several times.]

E, 5;5: Come back on the light. [= make it come back on]

C, 3;6: Until I'm four I don't have to be gone [= be taken to the dentist].

C, 3;10: Go me to the bathroom before you go to bed [= take me].

E, 4;3: Why didn't you want to go your head under? [= put].

E, 5;1: Go it over here so it will be more better.

E, 4;11: Do you have anything else you'd like to go to China? [= send].

C, 2;8: Daddy go me around [= spin, turn].

C, 2;9: You go it in [= push].

C, 3;2: How came she goes on the bathtub, Mommy? [= turns on the tap].

C, 2;6: Mommy, can you stay this open? [= keep].

C, 3;7: I want to stay this rubber band on [= keep, leave].

C, 4;3: Why is the laundry place stayed open all night? [= kept].

C, 4;5: Eva won't stay things where I want them to be [= leave].

E, 3;2: I'm staying it in the water [= keeping].

E, 5;0: I want to sleep with it 'cause they'll stay me warmer [= keep].

C, 2;9: I'm gonna just fall this on her.

E, 3;8: And the doggie had a head. And somebody fell it off.

Kendall, 2;3: Kendall fall that toy.

Stevie, 2;2: Tommy fall Stevie truck down.

Hilary, 4+: He's gonna die you, David. [Turns to mother] The tiger will come and eat David and then he will be died and I won't have a little brother any more.

C, 5;0: O.K. If you want it to die. Eva's gonna die it. She's gonna make it die.

C, 3;3: But I can't eat her! [= feed].

C, 3;8: No, Mommy, don't eat her yet, she's smelly! [= feed].

Rachel, 2;0: Don't eat it me [as M feeds Rachel].

C, 6;11: Will you please remember me what I came in for? [= remind].

E, 4;11: I keep have to remember you [= I keep having to remind you].

Mindy, 6;7: I have to remember my daddy ... Saturday Winnie the Pooh is on.

Marcy, 6;4: Why do we have to rise it? [re: crossbar of baby swing].

C, 6;8: It's rising me [C in tub, warm water making her float up].

C, 4;0: Will you have me a lesson? [= give].

C, 4;2: How do you write "Marc," 'cause I want to have it to Marc.

C, 4;6: Would you like me to ... have ... you some?

C, 3;8: You feed me. Take me little bites. Give me little bites.

Robert, 11+: We took him a bath yesterday and we took him one this morning.

Julie, 5+: When we go home I'm gonna take you a bath with cold water.

Hilary, 4+: C'mon, Mama, take me a bath. C'mon, David, Mama's gonna take us a bath.

C, 3;9: You better not take me a quiet time, you better take me a quiet time [= give].

C, 3;5: A nice nurse lady took me a ride.

Hilary, 4+: David, let's take Mama a ride. [M: Oh, you're gonna give me a ride?] Yes, we're gonna take you a ride, Mama.

Rachel, 4;6: I want you to take me a camel ride over your shoulders into my room.

Jaime, 5;10: I'm taking my babies a walk.

E, 5;0: Be a hand up your nose. [M: What?] Put a hand up your nose.

C, 3;1: I wanta be it off. I wanta put it off [= take].

C, 5;0: C: Why do you have to be it smooth before you put it in a pony tail? [M: What?] Why do you have to put it smooth before you put it in a pony tail?

C, 3;5: Be a picture of Emily and me [= take a picture].

C, 5;5: I meant to be it like this [= make it, have it be].

C, 2;1: [M: Close your eyes.] No! I want be my eyes open.

C, 3;1: I'm singing him. [Pulling string on cow-shaped music box]

E, 2;11: Do you want to come watch the mans sing their guitars?

E, 2;11: [M: How do you use a piano?] You sing it.

E, 2;2: I'm talking my birdie. [Pulling string on bird-shaped music box]

E, 4;0: Polly and Vicky aren't real. We just hold them up and talk them by themselves. We talk for them. [Re: her and C's dolls]

E, 3;0: Don't giggle me. [as D tickles E]

E, 5;3: You cried her! [After M drops E's doll and it squeals]

C, 4;6: Spell this "buy." Spell it "buy." [Wants M to rotate blocks on toy spelling device until word "buy" is formed]

C, 4;3: Andrea. I want you to watch this book. Andrea. I want to watch you this book. [Shortly] I just want you to watch this book. [C trying to get A's attention]

E, 2;11: Watch your faces! [Trying to get parents' attention so their faces will "watch" something]

E, 2;1: I wanta swim that. [Holding an object in the air and wiggling it as if it were swimming]

C, 3;4: [M: Do you think Daddy can guess that one?] [C turns toward D] I'm gonna guess it to him.

E, 3;7: Yawny Baby—you can push her mouth open to drink her.

C, 3;1: Drink me. Uh ... put it in. [Asking for an orange half to be squeezed into her mouth]

Jaime, 6+: It sounds you like a mouse. [When parent makes a noise]

E, 3;2: Will you climb me up there and hold me?

E, 3;7: I'm gonna put the washrag in and disappear something under the washrag.

C, 4;2: C: He disappeared himself. [A moment later] He just keeps disappearing himself in different places.

Jennifer, 6+: Do you want to see us disappear our heads?

Scott, 5;0: I disappeared a bear in the back of the car; that's why you can't see him.

C, 7;8: Did they vanish "knock-knock" cups? [Noticing Dixie cups in new pack no longer have knock-knock jokes on them]

C, 4;3: It always sweats me. That sweater is a sweaty hot sweater.

C, 3;6: Did she bleed it? [After E falls and hits head on edge of table]

E, 3;3: Carrie bleeded a tree and we put a bandaid on it. [After child at school makes sap ooze from tree]

Mindy, 5;8: These are nice beds. [M: Yes, they are.] Enough to wish me that I had one of those beds.

C, 2;3: Bottle feel my feets better [= makes them feel better].

E, 5;3: This is aching my legs. [As she climbs a long flight of stairs]

Rachel; 4:1: You ached me.

Locatives. Finally, Bowerman (1982b) reports persistent errors in children's use of verbs appearing in the locative alternation. Errors in *fill*-type verbs recorded by Bowerman and by Jess Gropen and me are reproduced in in (1.18); errors in *pour*-type verbs appear in (1.19). Gropen and I also found that children were quite prone to uttering sentences like *He's filling the water* or *He's filling water into the glass* when describing pictures in an experiment (Gropen, Pinker, and Goldberg, 1987; Gropen, 1989; Gropen, Pinker, Hollander, and Goldberg, in preparation). Such errors occurred 53% of the time in our 2-to-3-year-old group, 53% of the time in our 3-to-4-year-old group, and 34% of the time in our 4-to-5-year-old group. (Adults, by comparison, did so only 3% of the time.) Children also uttered sentences of the form *He's pouring the glass* or *He's pouring the glass with water*, though less often.

(1.18) Adam 4;2: [Another child has put a bowl on Adam's mother's head.] You look like a crashed lady. [M: A crashed lady?] Yeah, like a crashed lady.

Adam, 4;2: Oh, look it's ropted through here. [Playing with cord of toy telephone]

Adam, 4;11: See, it fills the grain in.

Adam, 4;11: I filled the grain up.

Sarah, 4;7: She's scribbled.

Sarah, 4;7: I'm making her picture scribbled.

Mark, 4;7: And fill the little sugars up in the bowl how much you should [= fill the bowl with as much cereal as you should].

From Bowerman (1981, 1982b):

E, 3;0: My other hand's not yukky. See? 'Cause I'm going to touch it on your pants [= touch your pants with it].

C, 4;3: [M: Simon says, "Touch your toes."] To what? [Interprets toes as theme, is looking now for goal. A moment later: M: Simon says, "Touch your knees."] To what?

C, 6;10: Feel your hand to that [= feel that with your hand].

E, 5;0: Can I fill some salt into the bear? [fill a bear-shaped salt shaker with some salt].

E, 4;5: I'm going to cover a screen over me.

C, 4;9: She's gonna pinch it on my foot.

E, 4;1: I didn't fill water up to drink it; I filled it up for the flowers to drink it [= filled the watering can up with water].

E, 4;11: And I'll give you these eggs you can fill up. [Giving M beads to put into cloth chicken-shaped container]

E, 5;3: Terri said if this were a diamond then people would be trying to rob the shirt [= rob me of a shirt with rhinestones].

C, 3;11: Eva is just touching gently on the plant.

C, 4;2: Pinch on the balloon [= pinch the balloon].

(1.19) E, 2;11: Pour, pour, pour. Mommy, I poured you. [Waving empty container near M. M: You poured me?] Yeah, with water.

E, 7;2: My belly holds water! Look, Mom, I'm gonna pour it with water, my belly.

E, 4;11: I don't want it because I spilled it of orange juice [spilled orange juice on her toast].

C, 6;5: Once the Partridge Family got stolen. [M, puzzled: The whole family?] No, all their stuff.

C, 3;4: I bumped this to me [= I bumped myself with this toy].

C, 3;8: I hitted this into my neck [= I hit my neck with this toy].

1.4.4.2   Evidence Against Strict Lexical Conservatism in Children:
Experiments   In collaboration with a number of students I have run a set of experiments based on the following logic: if children productively create new argument structures for verbs, then if we teach them made-up verbs presented only in a single argument structure, the children, given a suitable discourse context, should be willing to use those verbs productively in an alternative argument structure.

For the *passive* (Pinker, Lebeaux, and Frost, 1987), we invented verbs—using nonsense syllables such as *pilk* or *gump*—to describe physical interactions such as leapfrogging over, nuzzling the nose of, or backing into. Children learned the verbs by hearing them in active-voice sentences describing a particular event involving toy animals, such as *The bear is pilking the pig*. Then they saw a new pair of toys exemplifying the action, such as a tiger "pilking" a horse, and were asked, "What's happening to the horse?". Because the question focused the patient, the passive was the most felicitous form in which to answer.

For the *dative* (Gropen et al., 1989), we invented verbs for physical transfers involving toy instruments, such as sending an animal to a recipient in a toy gondola car or lazy Susan. Children would hear *The bear is pilking the pig to the giraffe* (or, in some conditions, simply *This is pilking*), while watching a bear putting the pig in the gondola car and sending it to a waiting giraffe. Then they would see a tiger "pilking" a horse to a cat, and would be asked, "What's the tiger doing with the cat?" Since the identity of the goal is already known and the theme is being focused in the question, the natural way to answer is using the double-object form: *Pilking him the horse*.

For the *causative* (Gropen, Pinker, and Roeper, in preparation), children would see a pig doing a headstand and hear *The pig is pilking*. Then they would see a bear upending a tiger and sending it into a headstand, and we asked, "What's the bear doing?" (Possible answer: *Pilking the tiger*.)

For the *locative* (Gropen, 1989; Gropen et al., in preparation), children in one experiment would see the experimenter rub a wet sponge against a wet cloth, causing it to change color, or would see the experimenter placing marbles into a small cloth hammock, causing it to sag, and would hear *This is mooping*. Similar actions were then performed, and the children were asked what the experimenter was doing. (Possible answers: *Mooping the towel (with water)*, *Mooping the cloth (with marbles)*.

In all the experiments, several actions, words, and sets of toys were used, all counterbalanced within an experiment.

Of course we could not guarantee that children would use the argument structure we were interested in even if it was available to them and even when we used questions that focused one or another participant, making the targeted form the most felicitous in the discourse context. To establish a baseline as to how successful the elicitation technique was, we also elicited passives, double-object datives, and causative versions of made-up verbs that we had actually taught to the children in the passive, double-object, or lexical causative. In some experiments we also tried to elicit passives and datives of real English verbs such as *kick* or *give*. Our success rate with these verbs established an upper limit on how successful we could hope to be with the made-up verbs taught only in the active, prepositional-object, or intransitive form, which should have been somewhat harder because of those verbs' unfamiliarity and the requirement that a productive rule be applied.

The table in (1.20) summarizes some of the results. Each line represents an experiment with a different group of subjects (there were several replications and a number of manipulations we can ignore for now). The first column of data displays the results of interest: how often the children produced passives, double-object datives, lexical causatives, or "container-object" locatives (like *Load the wagon with hay*) of verbs they had never heard in those forms. The second column of data shows, by comparison, how often the elicitation technique was successful at drawing out such forms when productivity was not at issue because the verbs had been taught in the targeted forms. The third column of data gives the other estimate of the limits of the technique by showing children's frequency of uttering the targeted form with existing English high-frequency verbs.

Clearly, children were not strictly conservative: they uttered productive passives anywhere from 19% to 81% of the available opportunities (depending on age, stimulus materials, and so on), which is consistently less frequent, but not by much, than their production of verbs that they actually heard in the passive or of existing English verbs. Similarly, children uttered double-object datives on 40%–53% of the opportunities (not much less than the 56% production rate when they had actually heard those forms); they uttered lexical causatives on 55%–66% of the available opportunities; and they uttered locative verbs with the container as direct object 78%–100% of the time.

One possible objection to this experiment is that the children could have been responding to experimental demand characteristics, stringing together ad hoc word sequences in order to please the experimenter or "play the game." This counterexplanation is quite unlikely. First of all, we have shown that the productive forms elicited in the experiment also show up in spontaneous speech in natural settings. Second, contrary to the suspicions of some, it is not possible to induce children to apply just any linguistic generalization in an experimental setting. Major (1974), for example, had children participate in a game in which they turned declaratives into questions. Children did not indiscriminately play along; for example, they would not reply to *You better go* by asking *Better you*

(1.20)

Age	Proportion of trials a productive form was elicited	Proportion of trials a nonproductive form was elicited	Proportion of trials an existing verb was elicited
Passive			
$3–4\frac{1}{2}$	.25	.38	.25
3–4	.19	.44	.38
4	.59	.62	
$4\frac{1}{2}–5$	.25	.50	.50
5–6	.56	.75	
5–6	.25	.50	.81
7–8	.8	.88	.69
7–8	.38	.69	
Dative			
6–8	.44	.56	.72
$5–7\frac{1}{2}$	.50	.78	
$7\frac{1}{2}–8$	.53		
Causative			
4	.55	.75	
6–7	.66	.56	
Locative: container as direct object			
3	.78		
5	1.00		
7	.84		

go?. This is exactly the kind of error that children never make in their spontaneous speech either (Kuczaj and Maratsos, 1979; Pinker, 1984). Thus spontaneous speech and elicitation experiments can yield consistent evidence both for the occurrence and for the nonoccurrence of productive generalizations by children. Third, in the Gropen et al. experiments, we used a control condition in which children were exposed to a pseudoargument structure, *I norped the mouse of a ball*, in contexts identical to those we had used for the double-object form. When we elicited such forms with novel verbs, we were successful only 4% of the time, as compared to our 50% success rate for the double-object form. We concluded that our technique could not be used to teach arbitrary verb-syntax combinations to children; it simply provided a context in which children's prior knowledge of grammar could be brought to bear on newly learned verbs.

In sum, this series of studies forces us to reject strict lexical conservatism—the hypothesis that children record which verbs appear in which argument structures and stick to those combinations—as a solution to Baker's paradox. We have now rejected the most obvious kinds of resolutions of the paradox: those that seek to find some kind of negative evidence to guide children, and those that deny that children are productive.

This leaves us with one option: rejecting arbitrariness. Perhaps the verbs that do or don't participate in these alternations do not belong to arbitrary lists after all. Lexical entries specify associations among semantic, syntactic, phonological, morphological, and pragmatic bits of information. These associations may not be completely arbitrary. Perhaps a verb's set of possible argument structures can be predicted from one of the other kinds of information in its entry. If so, the apparent arbitrariness of argument structure subcategorization is just an illusion stemming from naive first impressions or from a faulty theory of lexical entries. If learners could acquire and enforce criteria delineating the alternating and nonalternating classes of verbs, they could productively generalize an alternation to verbs that meet the criteria without overgeneralizing it to those that do not. In principle, any of the tiers of information associated with a verb could be used to determine whether a rule applies to it. I will first examine whether verbs' syntactic properties can delineate the range of rule application; in the next chapter I will examine morphological and semantic properties.

1.4.5 Solution #3: Syntactic Representations as Criteria for the Application of Lexical Rules

It might seem that the most elegant theory of how children solve Baker's paradox would be to discover some syntactic property of verbs that perfectly predicts whether they enter into a given alternation, where the predictive contingency would be a consequence of some theory of the nature of the alternation. After all, argument structures are syntactic entities, and the rules manipulating them should be subject to properties of the verbs' syntactic representations. There have been several proposals of this kind in the linguistic literature. We shall see, however, that all such proposals either *cannot* resolve Baker's paradox or *do not* resolve it. But before we examine such proposals, it is necessary to review very briefly the current theories about how the syntactic properties of verbs' argument structures are represented.

1.4.5.1 Representations for Argument Structures
Argument structures for a verb can be represented in a variety of ways, so long as there is a precise association between symbols that refer to grammatical entities and symbols that refer to the verb's semantic or logical arguments. The classical notation, shown in (1.21), is simply one or more ordered lists of the phrasal categories that may simultaneously appear with the verb in a verb phrase, perhaps annotated to indicate which argument they correspond to.

(1.21) dine: NP_1 ___
       devour: NP_1 ___ NP_2
       put: NP_1 ___ NP_2 PP_3

Since this notation duplicates information that is ordinarily stated in rules and principles governing phrase structure and otherwise hides a variety of generalizations, it is used mainly as a transparent mnemonic rather than as a hypothesis about the mental representation of argument structure information. A more theoretically motivated notation, based on Bresnan and Kaplan's Lexical Functional Grammar (LFG; Bresnan, 1982a, b; Kaplan and Bresnan, 1982) is shown in (1.22).

(1.22) fall (SUBJ)
           theme

        dine (SUBJ)
           agent

        devour (SUBJ, OBJ)
              agent   theme

        eat (SUBJ, OBJ)
           agent   theme

        eat (SUBJ)
           agent

        put (SUBJ, OBJ,   OBL)
           agent   theme location

Each argument structure in (1.22) indicates how many syntactically expressed arguments the verb takes: one for *dine* and the intransitive version of *eat*, two for *devour* and the transitive version of *eat*, three for *put*. It also indicates what thematic role, or "theta-role," each argument is an example of: an agent is the instigator of an action; a theme is the object asserted to have a particular location or to be changing location; a location, source, or goal corresponds to where the theme is, what it is moving from, and what it is moving to, respectively.

According to the Thematic Relations Hypothesis (TRH; Gruber, 1965; Jackendoff, 1972, 1978, 1983), thematic roles can apply not only to literal physical motion but also in a quasi-metaphorical way to changes of state or possession, including abstract "possession" of ideas, as if states, possessors, and minds were "places" in an abstract space (referred to as a semantic field) and objects, possessions, and ideas were movable things. Thus in *John bequeathed his house to Mary, John told a story to Mary*, and *John made the house red*, one can identify abstract themes and goals: *the house* and *a story* are themes, *Mary* and *red* are goals. The Thematic Relations Hypothesis is motivated by a host of parallelisms between expressions for physical location and expressions for abstract states, and between expressions for physical motion and expressions for abstract changes. Examples include *John went from Chicago to Boston, John went from being sick to being well*, and *The inheritance went to the oldest son*; *Bill kept the book on the shelf*, *Bill kept the money*, and *Bill kept his children in poverty*. It plays a prominent role in many theories of argument structure representation.

In addition to specifying the number and kind of arguments a verb takes, its argument structure specifies the grammatical device used to express each argument. In (1.22), this is done indirectly, by specifying the name of the grammatical function or grammatical relation used to express each argument. The function SUBJ (subject) expresses the theme argument of *fall* and the agent argument of *dine*, *eat*, *devour*, and *put*. OBJ (object) expresses the theme arguments of *devour*, *eat*, and *put*. OBL (oblique object) expresses the location argument of *put*. Other rules, in the phrase structure and morphological components, spell out how subjects, objects, and oblique objects are actually expressed by surface devices such as phrase structure position or case and agreement markers. For example, English grammar specifies that subjects are sentence-initial NPs, objects are postverbal NPs within the VP, and oblique arguments are the objects of prepositions.

By specifying the syntactic realizations of arguments indirectly, via grammatical functions, rather than directly in terms of surface positions or morphological markings, we factor out a range of problems such as word order variations, cliticization, interactions between case marking and word order, and so on, so verbs' lexical entries are spared from having to worry about these more or less independent phenomena. For example, if a language specifies that direct objects can appear postverbally in matrix clauses, or preverbally in embedded clauses, or attached to the verb as a clitic, and if the language has a complex inflectional case-marker paradigm involving gender and number, each of these facts can be stated once in the grammar where the symbol "OBJ" is cashed in, rather than replicated in every single verb that takes a direct object.

A similar effect is attained in a different way in theories of "transformational" grammar (Chomsky, 1965), in which the grammatical roles of arguments are encoded in terms of positions in a canonical, abstract phrase structure representation which is then mapped onto surface phrase structure by grammatical transformations and other devices. Though the theory has undergone significant changes leading to the Government-Binding formulation (GB; Chomsky, 1981, 1982), the assumption that verbs' argument structures are defined in terms of the positions of arguments in an underlying syntactic representation (originally called deep structure, now "d-structure") has remained in almost every version of the theory. In what is probably the most popular current formulation, arguments are syntactically distinguished in terms of whether they are *internal* or *external* (Williams, 1981). Roughly, an internal argument is in the same phrase as the head verb and corresponds to the verb's deep-structure objects and complements. An external argument is outside the phrase containing the head verb, and in single-clause sentences it will end up as the subject. The external argument is related to the combination of the verb and its other arguments by the relation of "predication." Internal arguments are further differentiated by Marantz (1984) and Levin and Rappaport (1986) as being either direct, that is, receiving a thematic role directly from the verb, or indirect, that is, receiving a thematic role from an intervening preposition.

There are various typographical conventions for distinguishing external, direct internal, and indirect internal arguments in a verb's argument structure. The one used by Levin and Rappaport and by Marantz lists the external argument outside of the bracketed argument list and italicizes the direct internal argument, as in (1.23).

(1.23) PUT: agent < *theme*, location >

An alternative notation eschews thematic role labels as a means of identifying a verb's arguments and simply uses arbitrary variables (x, y, z) for the arguments. An example of this kind of notation, used in Zubizaretta (1987), is shown in (1.24a), where the hyphen links the theta-role-assigning element to the argument that receives the role, and "loc P" stands for a locative preposition. A hybrid representation used by Rappaport and Levin (1986) is shown in (1.24b).

(1.24) a. PUT–y, x; loc P–z
        b. PUT: $x < y, P_{loc} z >$

In all these formulations, any phrase that is associated with a verb but is not one of its arguments (for example, "adjunct" phrases like *at three o'clock* or *in order to please his mother*) is simply not listed in the verb's argument structure. When a verb has an argument that can be expressed optionally, such as *John ate the meat* / *John ate*, the optional argument can be symbolized in any of these formulations using parentheses in the argument structure, as in *eat*: (SUBJ, (OBJ)) or EAT: $x, < (y) >$.

In the GB theory, some verbs can have direct objects in underlying d-structure but not in the surface structure, or "s-structure," which corresponds more closely to the spoken sentence. Passive participles and certain kinds of intransitive verbs called "unaccusatives" (like *arrive*) are the main examples. (I will discuss the difference between standard intransitives, or "unergatives," and intransitive verbs that are said to be transitive in underlying structure, or "unaccusatives," in more detail later.) These forms are represented as having a direct internal argument that receives a theta-role from the predicate but does not receive "abstract case" either from the predicate or from a preposition. Since Chomsky's Case Filter would generally disallow sentences with non-case-marked lexical NPs, the only way that such a sentence can become grammatical is if a transformation ("Move α") moves the argument into subject position, where it can be case-marked by an abstract tense element in the INFL (inflection) node. (Another mechanism that forces unaccusative intransitives and passives to get subjects is the Extended Projection Principle, which requires all verbs to have subjects.) For these verbs, the surface subject will correspond to the internal argument, not the external argument. The fact that the internal argument is caseless is predictable from the fact the verb does not assign a theta-role to an external argument; this is sometimes known as Burzio's Generalization (Burzio, 1986). A GB representation of the intransitive verb *fall* would be something like (1.25).

(1.25) fall $< x >$

The GB and LFG representations are fairly intertranslatable (see, e.g., B. Levin, 1985, L. Levin, 1985. and Jackendoff, 1987a, for discussion), and in most of the book I will use the LFG and GB terminology for grammatical roles interchangeably, except in those few cases where one makes a distinction ignored by the other. The main substantive difference between them is the GB differentiation between subjects that are external arguments and subjects that are moved internal arguments, though even here L. Levin has shown that the distinction can easily be captured in LFG. The table in (1.26) shows how the translation works for argument structures and grammatical functions. (There is no consensus among GB linguists as to how to represent the second object in double-object or ditransitive structures such as *Give me the book*. I will simply call them "second direct internal arguments.")

Another theory, Relational Grammar (RG; Perlmutter, 1980; Perlmutter and Rosen, 1984), combines features of both. As in LFG, the syntactic roles of arguments are specified in terms of grammatical relations such as "subject" rather than configurations in phrase structure. As in GB, the grammatical roles are assigned at an underlying level of representation that is mapped onto a surface representation by transformational rules during the derivation of a sentence. A fourth theory, Generalized Phrase Structure Grammar (GPSG; Gazdar, Klein, Pullum, and Sag, 1985), resembles LFG and GB in the opposite pair of respects: as in LFG, the representation in which the verb's subcategorization is stated is not transformed in the derivation of a sentence; as in GB, the representation is in terms of phrase configurations (specifically, in terms of a modified classical notation listing the categories of the phrasemates of the verb).

1.4.5.2 Using Properties of Syntactic Representations to Solve the Learning Problem
There have been a number of suggestions that certain general principles of grammar are sensitive to details of the syntactic representation of verbs, allowing some verbs to undergo a lexical rule while superficially

(1.26)

Traditional	LFG Representation	GB Representation
Transitive	(SUBJ, OBJ)	$x < y >$
Intransitive (unergative)	(SUBJ)	$< y >$
Intransitive (unaccusative)	(SUBJ)	$x < >$
Transitive/prepositional	(SUBJ, OBJ, OBL_{loc})	$x < y, P_{loc}-z >$
Double–object	(SUBJ, OBJ2, OBJ)	$x < z, y >$
Passive participle	(OBL_{by}, SUBJ)	$< y, P_{by}-x >$
Subject	SUBJ	external argument
		$x < >$
		direct internal argument (no external argument, no case)
		$< x >$
Object	OBJ	direct internal argument (with external argument, case–marked)
		$< x >$
Oblique object	OBL	indirect internal argument
		$< P-x >$
Second object	OBJ2	second direct internal argument
		$< w, x >$

similar ones with different representations are left untouched. For example, Randall (1987) suggests that dativizable verbs are represented as having two obligatory internal arguments, whereas for nondativizable verbs the goal argument is optional. A related suggestion is that the theme and goal phrases associated with dativizable verbs are both arguments of the verb, whereas nondativizable verbs have only a theme argument, the goal being an adjunct. Borer and Wexler (1987) suggest that the causativizability of an intransitive verb is predictable by whether it is unaccusative or unergative, that is, whether its sole argument is its object in d-structure or its subject. Often it is suggested that passivizability hinges on whether a verb and its object are adjacent in d-structure; it is also suggested that passivizability of NPs that are not objects of the verb depends on the verb and object being represented as parts of a single complex verb.

There is a problem with proposed solutions of this ilk: as usually stated, they are logically incapable of explaining Baker's paradox. Abstract syntactic representations are colorless, odorless, and tasteless. Saying that one verb alternates and a superficially similar one does not because the first has syntactic representation A whereas the second has syntactic representation B only pushes the question back a step: how does the child know which verbs have representation

A and which have representation B? Without an answer, the representational theory offers no advantage over saying that one kind of verb is represented with the abstract feature [+dativizable] and the other has the feature [−dativizable].

Two kinds of answers are possible. One is that there is some morphological, phonological, or semantic property of the verb that allows the child to predict which syntactic representation it has. This makes the learnability-theoretic aspect of the syntactic representation accounts reduce to the accounts I will discuss in the rest of this book, as far as solving Baker's paradox is concerned, and the configurations themselves have no direct role to play in the solution. That is not to say that proposals about the abstract syntactic representations are false or useless—they could enter into the explanation of a variety of linguistic regularities that ensue once the correct representation is identified by the child— it's just that they do not explain the learning problem at hand. I will say little about them, simply because it is the learning problem that I am confronting here.

The second possible answer is that each of the representations has *other* detectable syntactic effects in the behavior of the verbs. For example, all the verbs that alternate between argument structures X and Y could invariably appear in structure Z, while all the verbs that fail to alternate never appear in Z, or vice versa. This kind of solution *is* logically capable of resolving the paradox: the child could note which of the verbs appearing in X also appear in Z and could successfully predict that those verbs do (or don't) alternate between X and Y. (It is actually the vice versa case, where Z predicts not-Y, that is most interesting, because the Z-predicts-Y case would be similar to conservatism: the child would simply wait to hear Z before generalizing to Y, rather than waiting to hear Y before generalizing to Y.) Note, though, that there is a kernel of implausibility lying at the center of this kind of account. The reason we have a learning paradox is that some verbs appear in X and Y and some appear only in X. Presumably there is some set of factors yet to be discovered that prevents some of the verbs that appear in X from appearing in Y. But this account requires that whatever those choosy factors are, they are completely nullified when it comes to the alternation of X and Z—all verbs (or no verbs) that appear in X appear in Z, without exception. That is possible, of course, but if the X-Z alternation is even vaguely in the domain of phenomena encompassing the X-Y alternation, it is unlikely. In fact, I will show that none of the proposals hinging on abstract syntactic representations makes the right kind of predictions about the child's discovering those representations on the basis of independent inputs.

1.4.5.3 Obligatory Versus Optional Arguments

Janet Randall (1987) suggests that dativizable verbs specify both their objects as obligatory arguments, whereas nondativizable verbs specify only the theme as an obligatory argument. Since predicates and their obligatory arguments are adjacent within a phrase but optional arguments are generally outside the phrase (Jackendoff, 1977), two obligatory arguments can switch places in linear order whereas an optional argument cannot intrude between a verb and its obligatory argument without destroying the connectivity of the tree or violating other principles. The general principle is illustrated in (1.27), where the verb *get* has an obligatory argument for the received object and an optional argument for the sender.

(1.27)   John got an invitation from Mary.
       John got an invitation.
      *John got from Mary.
      *?John got from Mary an invitation.

In the case of dativization, Randall provides the lexical entries shown in (1.28) for the dativizable *give* and the undativizable *deliver*.

(1.28) give: __ NP PP
      deliver: __ NP (PP)

Randall therefore predicts that only nondativizable verbs can appear in simple transitive structures with theme objects. Hearing such structures would then be sufficient for the child to deduce that the verb is nondativizable. For example, the child, upon hearing *Connie reported the news*, would know that the goal argument of *report* is optional, hence that *report* cannot have a goal argument between itself and its (obligatory) theme argument, hence that *report* cannot be dativized. Positive evidence would suffice to avoid or unlearn double-object phrases with *report*: children should avoid dativizing *report* when and only when they hear *report* used without a goal argument. Randall supports her predictions with the data reproduced in (1.29).

(1.29) (a)   Agamemnon reported the news.
          Pablo explained his painting.
          Gertrude recited the recipe.
          Romeo delivered the posies.
          Cressida dictated the letter.
          Joan contributed six warriors.

    (b) *Agamemnon told the news.
        *Pablo gave his painting.
        *Gertrude showed the recipe.
        *Romeo brought the posies.
        *Cressida sent the book.
        *Joan lent six warriors.

Randall notes that these judgments are somewhat shaky and tries to show that the sentences in (1.29b) are acceptable only when the verb is elliptical, idiomatic, or ambiguous. However, the account does not work in general. *Bill told a story* is fully grammatical, unambiguous, and pragmatically neutral, as are *Sam asked a question* (cf. *Sam asked me a question*), *Irv wrote a letter* (cf. *Irv wrote her a letter*), and *John threw / kicked / rolled the ball* (cf. *John threw / kicked / rolled me the ball*). Conversely, the sentences containing *explain, contribute,* and *deliver* in (1.29a) seem fairly elliptical—no less so, in any case, than the sentences with *deliver, brought, sent* or *lent* in (1.29b). There are also nondativizable verbs with obligatory *to*-phrases; they should be unlearnable on Randall's hypothesis: *She entrusted her child to the daycare center / *She entrusted her child / *She entrusted the daycare center her child,* and *He credited the money to my account / *He credited the money / *He credited my account the money.* See Dowty (1979a) for a related set of phenomena.

The noncorrelation between the obligatoriness of an oblique argument and its ability to be promoted to direct object can be seen in other constructions, such as the locative alternation. Rappaport and Levin (1985) and Levin and Rappaport (1986) point out that among the verbs that alternate between *into/onto* and *with* forms, all logical possibilities for combinations of optional and obligatory arguments can be found (thus speaking against Randall's generalization regardless of which of the variants is thought to be derived from the other). Furthermore, verbs that do not alternate can also have their oblique phrases either obligatory or optional. Examples are given in (1.30).

(1.30)   *Alternating, Theme obligatory, Goal optional:*
         John piled books on the table / John piled the table with books.
         John piled the books.
         *John piled the table.

         Alternating, Theme optional, Goal obligatory:
         John stuffed feathers into the pillow / John stuffed the pillow with
             feathers.
         *John stuffed the feathers.
         John stuffed the pillow.

         Alternating, Theme obligatory, Goal obligatory:
         John heaped books on the shelf / John heaped the shelf with books.
         *?John heaped the books.
         *John heaped the shelf.

         Alternating, Theme optional, Goal optional:
         John packed books into the box / John packed the box with books.

John packed the books.
John packed the box.

(1.31)   *Nonalternating, Theme object, Goal optional:*
John spilled soup onto the table / *John spilled the table with soup.
John spilled soup.

Nonalternating, Theme object, Goal obligatory:
John slopped water onto the floor / *John slopped the floor with water.
*John slopped water.

Nonalternating, Goal object, Theme optional:
John filled the glass with water / *John filled water into the glass.
John filled the glass.

Nonalternating, Goal object, Theme obligatory:
John encrusted the cake with walnuts / *John encrusted walnuts onto
   the cake.
*John encrusted the cake.

Quite possibly Randall's generalization could be salvaged by differentiating
the verbs in (1.30) by various criteria, so that some of the examples would involve
not a single verb extended to a new surface argument structure but two quasi-
independent verbs. Of course, this just moves the resolution of Baker's paradox
to a discussion of what those criteria are, thereby collapsing Randall's solution
with those considered later in the book.

1.4.5.4 Arguments Versus Nonarguments   Randall's specific hypothesis
can be generalized to make dativizability hinge on a more fundamental distinction, that between arguments and nonarguments. Intuitively, there is a big
distinction between the uses of the prepositional phrase *near the store* in *John remained near the store* and *John sang near the store.* In the first case, the phrase
in some sense completes the meaning of the verb or combines with it to define
a single predicate; in the second, it is tacked on as a mere comment and the verb
would denote pretty much the same event without it. In the first sentence, the PP
is said to be an argument of the verb; in the second, it is an adjunct. Generally
arguments are thought to be represented syntactically as sisters of the verb within
the VP, whereas adjuncts are attached outside the VP in VP' or S. A phrase could
fail to be an argument of the verb for another reason: it could be an embedded
modifier of one of the verb's arguments rather than an argument of the verb itself.
For example, there is a clear difference between the *in*-phrases of *Bob put the hat
in the box* and *John patched the hole in the rug.* Some nonargument phrases can
have the prepositions *to* and *for.* This can lead to sentences that resemble
dativizable ones in terms of literal word-by-word composition but that quite

obviously do not meet the conditions for dativizability. For example, *John told the joke to death* (adjunct) does not yield **John told death the joke*; *John found the top to the jar* (embedded modifier) does not yield **John found the jar the top*. Similarly, *Sarah raced motorcycles for a thrill* (adjunct) does not license **Sarah raced a thrill motorcycles*; and *Sarah found the case for her flute* (embedded modifier) does not license **Sarah found her flute the case*.

Thus, for an alternation to apply, it is clearly a necessary condition that all the affected phrases be arguments of the verb. The question is, is it a sufficient condition as well? Perhaps one could argue that in *John threw the box to Mary*, the phrase *to Mary* is an argument of *throw*, whereas in *John pulled the box to Mary*, the phrase *to Mary* is merely an adjunct. That would account for the difference between *John threw Mary the box* and **John pulled Mary the box*. Grimshaw (1989) and others have made this suggestion.

To evaluate the suggestion, we must make sure that "argument" is not being defined in such a way that it is synonymous with "dativizable," thus begging the question once again. Fortunately, there are independent criteria in the linguistics literature for when a phrase may count as an argument (Bresnan, 1982c; Dowty, 1982; Gazdar et al., 1985). These criteria associate the argument/nonargument distinction with sentences and phrases that do not involve the dative alternation directly, and hence could be used by the child to acquire representations for the verbs that have predictive power with respect to dativizability. Unfortunately, when these independent criteria are invoked, they fail completely:

• *Compositionality.* In arguments, the preposition can be a meaningless syntactic marker; in adjuncts, the interpretation of the meaning of the phrase depends crucially on the inherent meaning of the preposition. A straightforward example is the contrast between *the king of France*, where *of* is meaningless and *of France* is an argument, and *the king from France*, where *from* is used as it always is, to denote a source, and *from France* is an adjunct. The problem is that in *John threw the ball to Mary*, we want *to Mary* to be an argument, but the preposition *to* has a clear independent meaning. Compare *John ran to / past / around the store* with *John threw the ball to / past / around Mary*.

• *Existential entailment.* The use of a verb entails that the referents of its arguments exist, even when the arguments are not expressed overtly. However, there need not be any definite thing that invariably corresponds to the referent of a phrase that can appear as an adjunct. For example, if Susan is a *sister*, she must be the sister of some specific person, so in *Susan is the sister of Steven*, the phrase *of Steven* is an argument of *sister*. However, a sister need not be near anything in particular, so in *Susan is the sister near the wall*, the phrase *near the wall* is not an argument. Similarly, *John ate* implies that there must be something that John ate, so *the apple* in *John ate the apple* must be an argument. The problem is that there is no clear sense in which *throwing* or *sliding* entails a definite goal to which the object must be thrown or slid at the same time that *pulling* or *lifting* does not entail a definite goal to which the object must be pulled or lifted. But such a difference must exist, according to the account appealing to argument-hood. Similarly, one can ask a question without there being anyone to whom the question is addressed (it can be rhetorical), yet *Ask him a question* is possible.

• *Uniqueness.* Adjuncts can be iterated; arguments must appear singly. For example, *Paul sang a song in the park near the tree across from the fence at 3 o'clock on a cloudy day to impress the townfolk* (iterated adjuncts) is possible, whereas **Paul sang a song a pretty ballad* (iterated arguments) is impossible. Another example: *Susan is the sister near the wall under the mistletoe* (iterated adjuncts), versus **Susan is the sister of Steven of Robert* (iterated arguments). The problem is that this criterion deems certain phrases to be arguments that the dativizability account wants as adjuncts, such as **Sam pulled the box to Mary to Sally*, which has iterated putative adjuncts. (*Sam pulled the box past Mary to Sally* is fine, but so is *Sam threw the ball past Mary to Sally.*) By this criterion, even the *for* argument of prepositional datives must be an argument: **I baked cakes for Susan for Mary*, with the meaning "I baked cakes intended both for Susan and for Mary." (If the action of baking a cake intended for Susan alone is done for Mary's benefit, the first *for*-phrase is uncontroversially an argument, the second an adjunct.)

• *Obligatoriness.* Arguments are often obligatory; adjuncts never are. For example, the verb *devour* takes an obligatory argument: *John devoured the steak / *John devoured.* No verb takes an obligatory adjunct such as those denoting time of day or the actor's intentions. The problem is that the empirical problems for Randall's hypothesis apply here exactly. For dativizable verbs, the *to*-phrase must be an argument, hence it should be obligatory, but for some verbs it is not: *John threw the ball; John asked a question.* Conversely, for nondativizable verbs, the *to*-phrase must be optional, but for some verbs it is not: *Babs credited the money to his account / *Babs credited the money / *Babs credited his account the money.*

Examples could be multiplied, especially when the similar locative alternation is examined; see (1.30, 1.31). Thus if we apply independent criteria for what an "argument" is, argumenthood is a necessary condition for dativizability, ruling out some blatant counterexamples, but not a sufficient condition, failing to make the right distinctions for the more subtle cases.

1.4.5.5 Unaccusativity Hagit Borer and Kenneth Wexler (1987) suggest that the difference between causativizable and uncausativizable intransitives corresponds to the difference between unaccusative and unergative verbs

.(Perlmutter, 1978), which in GB theory is captured by differences in whether they specify their arguments in deep subject or deep object position (Burzio, 1986; see also L. Levin, 1985, for an LFG treatment, and Grimshaw, 1987, for a review).[4] The difference is shown in (1.32).

(1.32) laugh (unergative):   x < >
        arrive (unaccusative) : < x >

Because *arrive* does not assign a thematic role to a subject, it does not assign case to its internal argument (Burzio's Generalization), so the argument would have to be moved into subject position, obscuring the difference between *arrive* and a verb like *laugh* in surface structure. Causativization would simply insert a new, agent argument into the empty subject position, obviating the need for movement. But in the unergative entry, no empty slot is available, so causativization is blocked.

According to Borer and Wexler, children are initially incapable of registering the possibility that an intransitive may have an object in underlying structure, because they lack the device that would link surface subjects with the trace of their deep object position. Only after neural maturation installs this device can they differentiate the two kinds of verbs, using the following criteria: "First, only the ergative verbs appear in the object position (in causative constructions). Second, only ergative verbs appear as passive participles, either in adjectival or in verbal constructions." The first of these possibilities, or course, is simply strict lexical conservatism, because the ability of a verb to take an object in the causative is just what the child is faced with determining. The second possibility is basically the same, since verbal passive participles of causative verbs are simply derived from causative verbs. (The use of adjectival participles to predict the existence of lexical causatives doesn't work: *upswept hair* / **Mary upswept her hair; a fallen sign* / **Bill fell the sign; an undescended testicle* / **The drug undescended the testicle* / **The drug descended the testicle.*)

In any case, the original proposal that causativization applies to unaccusative verbs is unsound. In (1.33a) there are verbs that are unaccusative (by the usual criteria; see Perlmutter, 1984) but do not causativize; in (1.33b) there are verbs that are unergative but do causativize. (In section 4.4.3, I explore these patterns systematically.)

(1.33) (a) The ball fell. / *John fell the ball.
             The boy came. / *Sam came the boy.
             The cloud appeared. / *The wind appeared the cloud.
             Sam arrived. / *Bob arrived Sam.
             A bug entered. / *Mary entered a bug.
             The smoke ascended. / *Sue ascended the smoke.

The cat died. / *John died the cat.
The dirt vanished. / *Josephine vanished the dirt.
A bad situation existed. / *Reagan existed a bad situation.

(b) John walked home. / I walked John home.
Cathy drove to Chicago. / I drove Cathy to Chicago.
The soldiers marched across the field. / The general marched the
soldiers across the field.
The horse raced past the barn. / The jockey raced the horse past the
barn.

1.4.5.6 Other Proposals There are many other proposals that are not even
as explicit as those of Randall and of Borer and Wexler, in that they attribute
some crucial abstract property to alternating or nonalternating verbs alone
without any suggestion whatsoever as to how the child could tell the difference.
For example, Larson (1988) suggests that *give* but not *donate* marks its second
object as having the thematic role "goal," so that the preposition *to* is semantically redundant when used with *give* but conveys information when used with
donate.   Therefore, applying the dative shift allows the role of the now-
prepositionless argument to be recovered for *give* but not for *donate*. *Donate* is
thus undativizable because the deletion of *to* is unrecoverable, violating the
general principle of recovery of deletion. However, if the notion of recoverability
of theta-roles is meant literally—could the speaker figure out which preposition
should go with the prepositional counterpart to a double-object sentence containing *donate*?—the hypothesis is simply false. The meaning of *donate* is so
close to that of *give* that one could easily infer that its third argument is a goal and
so it would have to have been *to* that was deleted. That is, no one could be in doubt
as to what role *them* would play in *donate them a book*. If the notion of assigning
a theta-role is more abstract, it only begs the question of why *donate* but not *give*
lacks the abstract property. Another suggestion comes from Larson and from
Belletti and Rizzi (1986), who argue that certain verbs that appear to have direct
objects on the surface may not actually be adjacent to these NPs in deep structure
but are separated from them by another phrase; this intervening phrase would be
moved into surface subject position in active sentences, creating the illusion of
a transitive verb. These verbs cannot passivize, because passivization is an
operation that moves the argument adjacent to the verb in deep structure.[5] But
there is a massive tendency in English to reanalyze postverbal surface NPs as
objects and hence to allow them to passivize (both synchronically and diachronically—see Bresnan, 1982b; Visser, 1963), resulting in such forms as *John was
thought well of*. This raises the question of how the child knows that the
postverbal NPs of some verbs, but not others, is an underlying object.

In sum, it is unlikely that children can use properties of strictly syntactic representations as criteria to determine the syntactic privileges of verbs. The reasons are twofold:

• If the syntactic criteria are completely abstract, then we are begging the question of how the child can predict which verbs possess them. This is a special case of the "bootstrapping problem": how children recognize tokens of abstract grammatical representations in the input (see Pinker, 1982, 1984, 1987).

• If the syntactic criteria have detectable consequences such as the ability of the verb to appear with some distinct set of arguments, those consequences would have to be perfectly correlated with the alterability of the verbs in question. Unfortunately, those cases do not exist; many so-called adjuncts, and many so-called optionally deleted arguments, are selective in the verbs they apply to in ways that cross-classify the selectivity with respect to the argument structures of interest (see, e.g., Atkins, Kegl, and Levin, 1986).[6]

The point of this section is not to criticize these proposals generally; many of them help capture other interesting linguistic generalizations and might be accepted in some version on those grounds.[7] The point is that they do not provide the crucial first step in resolving Baker's paradox: differentiating a priori the verbs that take different sets of argument structures. Once that step is taken, some of the theories I discussed could take over and explain a variety of consequences of the choice of representation, but how that choice is first made is the problem at hand.

Note also that by taking Baker's paradox seriously, a variety of traditional concepts concerning lexical representation must be called into question. One can easily see now why it is illegitimate to try to explain a phenomenon by calling a rule "partially productive" or "less than fully applicable" or having "idiosyncratic exceptions," or describing the lexicon as being "partially structured" or having "accidental gaps." In fact, this was the larger point of Baker's (1979) article: many devices commonly used in grammatical explanation raise major learnability problems.

Given the failure of subtle negative evidence, surrogates for negative evidence, and strict lexical conservatism to solve Baker's paradox, criteria distinguishing the alternators from the nonalternators is the only option standing. And since criteria pertaining to verbs' syntactic representations do not solve the problem either, the child is left with two possible kinds of cues for verbs' syntactic behavior: their sounds and their meanings. The next chapter explores this path.

Chapter 2
Constraints on Lexical Rules

For many years linguists have noted systematic semantic and morphological differences between the verbs that enter into a construction and those that are syntactically similar but fail to enter into it. Some of these differences are commonly noted in descriptive grammars of English; others have emerged in the literature of generative grammar as linguists have attempted to make grammars descriptively adequate. Let us consider whether any of these differences could serve as criteria governing a speaker's willingness to generalize.

2.1 Morphological and Phonological Constraints

It has often been pointed out that dativizable verbs tend to have native (Germanic), not Latinate stems (e.g., Green, 1974; Oehrle, 1976; Mazurkewich and White, 1984); examples are given in (2.1).

(2.1) John gave / donated / presented a painting to the museum.
John gave / *donated / *presented the museum a painting.

Bill told / reported / explained the story to them.
Bill told / *reported / *explained them the story.

Sue built / constructed / designed the house for us.
Sue built / *constructed / *designed us the house.

This correlation is the residue of one of the many peculiar developments in the history of English. In its earlier stages, English had case markers for accusative and dative cases (the latter corresponding to the goal) and had more word-order freedom than contemporary English. According to Visser (1963), in Old English the order "V NP-dat NP-acc" was more common than the order "V NP-acc NP-dat." In Middle English the case markers eroded, resulting in a "V NP_{goal} NP_{theme}" verb phrase similar to the double-object construction of contemporary English. Very few verbs appeared in the prepositional form "V *to* NP NP" in early Middle

English. But in the fourteenth and fifteenth centuries many new verbs entered the language as borrowings from French, which marked the goal phrase with the preposition à. When these verbs were assimilated into English, the French argument structure was translated, and thus the preposition *to* (the translation of à) was used to mark the goal argument. Native verbs were then allowed to take this argument structure as well, presumably via the application of a dative rule operating in what we now think of as the "backward" order, from the double-object form to the prepositional form. Thus the verbs that take the double-object form are the ones that were already in the language when that form came into being, and the verbs that fail to take that form came into the language more recently from French (and Latin as well), accompanied by a French-like argument structure.

Presumably children lack a collective racial memory for the history of the language, so the native/Latinate distinction would have to involve some audible synchronic property of verbs, not their etymology. It turns out that most often native stems are monosyllabic or, if polysyllabic, have stress only on the first syllable. And in fact Latinate verbs that have been assimilated to the native stress pattern do generally dativize, as (2.2) shows. Similarly, some speakers use otherwise undativizable verbs in the double-object form but shift the stress so as to conform to the native pattern when they do, as shown in (2.3).

(2.2)   Promise/Offer/Recommend/Describe anything to her, but give her Arp`ege.
        Promise/Offer/*Recommend/*Describe her anything, but give her Arp`ege.

(2.3)   IBM doNATED / DOnated some computers to them.
        *IBM doNATED them some computers.
        ?IBM DOnated them some computers.

Grimshaw (1985) and Grimshaw and Prince (1986) note that this definition of the native class corresponds to a phonological natural kind. The theory of metrical phonology picks out monosyllables, and polysyllables with stress only on the first syllable, as constituting a single metrical foot. At first it might appear that there are counterexamples in the form of dativizable verbs that do not match this definition, such as *assign him a seat*, *allot him a space*, *award him a prize*, or *allow him one phone call*. However, they begin with an unstressed schwa, which Grimshaw and Prince suggest is not a complete foot but an invisible or negligible residue of the metrical analysis of the word. When the verb begins with an unstressed syllable containing more than a schwa, such as *return*, *explain*, or *obtain*, dativization is blocked, as predicted. The constraint would then seem to be that dativization is restricted to verbs that have no more than one metrical foot (more precisely, "no more feet than one").[1]

There is an alternative formulation of the native/Latinate distinction: Latinate verbs could be those that are formed from any combination of a fixed set of largely meaningless stems and prefixes ("cranberry morphemes"), such as *re-, de-, pre-, in-, con-, trans-, sub-, ad-, ex-, per-, -fer, -mit, -sume, -ceive, -duce, -nounce, -pel, -plain,* and so on (Aronoff, 1976). This would be a morphological rather than a phonological definition of the class. Though I know of no proposals that it is the right definition for the dativizable class, it is consistent with the ungrammaticality of **I transferred him some money* and **I purchased him a jacket,* both of which have initial stress and hence would be "native" by strictly prosodic criteria. (*Promise,* on the other hand, is probably not analyzed as *pro + mise* by modern speakers.) There has been a proposal for a strictly morphological constraint on dativizability: Storm (1977) has suggested that dativizable verbs must be monomorphemic. This largely coincides with the proposal that dativizable verbs must be (morphologically) non-Latinate, since the morphological definition of Latinate is that it consist of combinations of Latinate prefixes and stems. However, it differs in cases where a verb is composed of two or more native morphemes. Unfortunately for any account based strictly on morphology, there seem to be multimorphemic verbs (both Latinate and native) that do dativize: *He bequeathed them his fortune; I telegraphed them the news; I reserved him a seat; She referred me a patient;* and others.

An experiment by Randall (1980) suggests that both morphological and phonological factors may be psychologically active, at least in other areas of the lexicon. She asked subjects to rate how good a nonsense word suffixed with *-ity* sounded. The suffix appears only with Latinate words in English. Subjects gave higher ratings to nouns formed from Latinate stems that were familiar in English than to nouns whose stems had Latinate stress patterns but were not familiar. This suggests that subjects were sensitive to a morphological distinction (whether or not a word is composed of a set of known morphemes) rather than a phonological one. However, subjects also gave higher ratings to nouns formed from unfamiliar Latinate stems than to nouns formed from familiar native stems. This suggests that the phonological properties of the native/Latinate distinction are attended to as well. Therefore, the distinction is probably "morphophonological," in that there is a morphological class whose members can be recognized partially by their phonological properties. I will return to this issue in section 4.4.1.

2.2 Semantic Constraints

Virtually all argument structure alternations interact with semantics in one way or another. In Pinker (1984), I reviewed some of the more prominent interactions that had been reported in the linguistics literature, and I suggested that a child who knew the morphological and semantic properties of words and the morphological and semantic constraints on the alternations could use the constraints as criteria in deciding how far to extend productive rules.

2.2.1 Dative

Dativizable verbs have a semantic property in common: they must be capable of denoting prospective possession of the referent of the second object by the referent of the first object (Green, 1974; Mazurkewich and White, 1984; Oehrle, 1976). In the case of verbs that appear in the prepositional form with *to*, such as *give* and *send*, the first object must be not only the goal to which the transferred thing goes as the result of its movement or transfer, but its possessor. In the case of verbs that appear in the prepositional form with *for*, the first object not only must be the beneficiary of an act but must come to possess a thing as the result of it. The "possessor effect," as I will call it, is illustrated in (2.4).

(2.4)   John sent a package to the border / boarder.
        John sent the boarder / *border a package.

        Rebecca drove her car to Chicago.
        *Rebecca drove Chicago her car.

        Bob made / got / stirred / tasted the cake for Phil.
        Bob made / got / *stirred / *tasted Phil the cake.

Possession need not be literal; in accordance with the Thematic Relations Hypothesis, verbs of communication are treated as denoting the transfer of messages or stimuli, which the recipient metaphorically possesses. This can be seen in sentences such as *He told her the story*, *He asked her a question*, and *She showed him the answer*.

2.2.2 Causative

A lexical causative is a transitive verb signifying causation that is identical in form to an intransitive verb signifying the caused event. It has often been noted that lexical causatives apply to cases of causation via direct or physical contact but not to extended chains of causation. Indirect causal chains can, by contrast, be expressed in a periphrastic causative, in which the intransitive verb is embedded as a complement of *make* or some other causal verb like *cause* or *let* (Fodor, 1970; McCawley, 1971; Shibatani, 1976; Gergely and Bever, 1986). The sentences in (2.5) show that lexical causatives are prohibited for causation mediated by the voluntary actions or psychological processes of the causee. We can call this the "directness effect."

(2.5) Sally made the ball bounce / the puck slide / the baby burp / the children laugh / the Red Sox triumph (by her enthusiastic cheers).

Sally bounced the ball / slid the puck / burped the baby / *laughed the children / *triumphed the Red Sox.

John made the glass break by startling the carpenter, who was installing it.

*John broke the glass by startling the carpenter, who was installing it.

In addition, Gergely and Bever, discussing examples from Fodor, Garrett, Walker, and Parkes (1980), suggest that stereotypy or conventionality of manner constrains the causative. Although *to paint* means something like "to cause to be covered with paint," one does not *paint a brush* when one dips it in the can, and it is hard to say with a straight face that *Michelangelo painted the ceiling* when he caused the ceiling of the Sistine Chapel to be covered with paint. This might be called the "stereotypy effect."

2.2.3 Locative

The locative, also known as the "spray/load" or "figure/ground" alternation, denotes a transfer of a substance or set of objects (the theme, content, or locatum) into or onto a container or surface (the goal, container, or location). It is often assumed that the standard member of this pair of constructions is the one taking the prepositions *into* or *onto*, which can be called the content-oriented or theme-object form, and that the locative rule converts it into a construction taking *with*, often called the container-oriented or goal-object form. The two forms are not synonymous. In the goal-object form, the goal must be completely filled or covered by the theme (see S. Anderson, 1971; Talmy, 1976; Bowerman, 1982b; Rappaport and Levin, 1985); if this is not a possible effect of the event denoted by the verb, the verb does not undergo the alternation, as (2.6) shows.

(2.6) (a) Irv loaded hay into the wagon.
Irv sprayed water onto the flowers.
Irv threw the cat into the room.
Irv pushed the car onto the road.

(b) Irv loaded the wagon with hay.
Irv sprayed the flowers with water.
*Irv threw the room with the cat.
*Irv pushed the road with the car.

There is a similar pair of constructions, shown in (2.7), involving an alternation of *from* with *of*, where the verb denotes that the surface or container (the source) contains some substance or objects that are then removed from it. In the *of* form (container-oriented or source-object), the source must be completely empty or stripped following the movement of the object or substance.

(2.7) (a)   Irv emptied water from the bucket.
            Irv drained mud from the pipes.
            Irv read a story from the book
            Irv threw the ball from the porch.

      (b)   Irv emptied the bucket of water.
            Irv drained the pipes of mud.
            *Irv read the book of a story.
            *Irv threw the porch of a ball.

This "holism effect" not only rules out the goal-object and source-object constructions for verbs like *push* and *read* where the action cannot result in complete filling or depletion, but alters the interpretation of sentences with verbs that do alternate: the grammatical sentences in (2.6b) and (2.7b), but not those in (2.6a) and (2.7a), entail that the wagon is completely full, the flowers totally wet, the bucket and pipes competely empty.

2.2.4 Passive

Passivization has long been noted to work best with verbs that are actional, with an agent subject and a patient object. None of these verbs (e.g., *cut*) fails to passivize; all the verbs that do fail to passivize are stative (Quirk, Greenbaum, Leech, and Svartvik, 1971). Examples are given in (2.8).

(2.8) *Two hundred pounds is weighed by John.
       *Five dollars is cost by this pen.
       *Amy is resembled by Sue.
       *Four is equaled by two plus two.

However, no simple distinction such as actional/nonactional or stative/non-stative completely distinguishes passivizable from nonpassivizable verbs. First, there are stative and abstract passives such as *This book is owned by the library; These drastic measures are justified by the situation;* and *The team was liked by the fans.* More dramatically, there are cases where the underlying object is an idiom chunk, pleonastic element, or nonargument, such as *The hatchet was buried; It was thought to be raining; The morning star was believed to be different from the evening star.* Thus, Jackendoff (1972) offers a more subtle constraint. He proposed that thematic relations are ordered in the hierarchy shown in (2.9).

(2.9) theme   source/goal/location   agent

In a passive, the surface subject must have a thematic role that is higher on the list in (2.9) than the object of *by* (or the argument that remains unexpressed in short passives like *John was hit*).

This Thematic Hierarchy Condition (THC) rules out the passives of "measure" verbs like those listed in (2.8), where a quality or quantity of one entity is compared with a standard, because in such verbs the entity acts as a theme and the standard acts as a metaphorical location. How do we know this? Because expressions for measurements use locative or goal prepositions in other constructions, such as *Grapes are selling AT a dollar a dozen; Bird weighed in AT 260 pounds; Jerry's resemblance TO Roger is uncanny; One and one is equal TO two*. In the passives in (2.8), we get a location or goal mapped onto the subject and a theme mapped onto the object of *by*, in violation of the constraint.

In addition, Jackendoff notes that verbs that are ambiguous between an agent-location reading and a theme-location reading in the active voice express only the agent-location reading when passivized, as (2.10) shows.

(2.10) John touched the wall (after he reached for it strenuously).
            [agent-location]
         John touched the wall (for two days, since his murderer had propped his lifeless body against it). [theme-location]

         The wall was touched by John (after he reached for it strenuously).
        *The wall was touched by John (for two days, since his murderer had propped his lifeless body against it).

The THC also rules out other examples of nonpassivizable verbs. In **John was resembled by Bill*, *John* is a goal, if we use prepositions in related constructions as our guide, because one can talk about *Bill's resemblance TO John*. Therefore the passive of *resemble* violates the THC. By similar arguments, one would treat *Bill* in *Bill's arguments escape me* as a source, because one also says *Mary escaped FROM Sue*. If so, the THC would correctly rule out **I am escaped by Bill's arguments*. See Jackendoff (1972), Pinker (1984), Pinker et al. (1987), and Grimshaw (in press) for other passives ruled out by this constraint.

2.3   How Semantic and Morphological Constraints Might Resolve Baker's Paradox

Mazurkewich and White (1984) and Pinker (1984) argued that the semantic and morphological constraints discussed in sections 2.1 and 2.2 might form the basis of how children solve Baker's learnability problem. If children could come to know the criteria distinguishing, say, dativizable from nondativizable verbs, they could append a condition onto a productive dative rule constraining it to apply only to verbs that meet the condition. Thereafter they would apply the rule productively only to the sets of verbs for which the alternation applies. If there are scattered positive exceptions (i.e., double-object verbs that violate the constraints), they could be learned on a conservative, verb-by-verb basis from positive evidence. The learning sequence proposed in Pinker (1984) was roughly as follows:

1. Record the argument structures of verbs heard in the input.

2. Note whether there are a large number of verbs that all occur in the same two argument structures. If so, create a productive lexical rule that would take as input the verb form with one argument structure and yield as output the corresponding form with the other argument structure.

3. Note whether there are also a large number of verbs that all *fail* to occur in one of the argument structure forms. If the verbs that occur in both forms have some property—either a morphological/phonological property of their stems, a semantic property of their predicates, or a thematic property of their arguments—in common, a property that is missing in the verbs that occur in only one form, bifurcate the verbs into two classes distinguished by that property and constrain the rule to apply productively only to the class defined by possession of that property. Apply the constraint retroactively so as to expunge nonwitnessed verb forms generated by the earlier unconstrained version of the rule if they violate the newly learned constraint.

4. If a hypothesized constraint becomes falsified because a large number of verbs violating it appear in the input, search for a new property that distinguishes the alternating from nonalternating verbs and replace the old criterial property with the new one.

This procedure might appear to be using a kind of indirect negative evidence: it is sensitive to the nonoccurrence of certain kinds of forms. It does so, though, only in the uninteresting sense of acting differently depending on whether it hears X or doesn't hear X, which is true of virtually any learning algorithm (see section 1.4.3.2). It is *not* sensitive to the nonoccurrence of particular sentences or even verb-argument structure combinations in parental speech; rather, it is several layers removed from the input, looking at broad statistical patterns across the lexicon.

This kind of solution to Baker's paradox I will call "criteria-governed productivity."

2.4 Evidence for Criteria-Governed Productivity

The set of procedures just described can, at least in principle, account for how the child can be a productive generalizer while speaking a language that maintains exceptions to the generalization. To support the theory of criteria-governed productivity, my students and I have attempted to show two things: that adults respect the criteria, even the seemingly obscure ones, and that children are in the process of coming to respect them. Of the criteria, the morphophonological constraint on the dative, being the result of an accident in the history of the English language, seems the least likely to be operative in the minds of present-day adult speakers. Jess Gropen and I (Gropen et al., 1989) invented eight new verbs whose meanings were exemplified in prepositional-dative sentences in terse written stories, one of which is presented in (2.11).

(2.11) Sue, who had wanted the deed to the house for twenty years, was very excited when her lawyer called with the good news. Her lawyer told her that Bob, the current owner, was ready to begin tonkation, the formal (and only legal) process by which she could obtain the house from him. After Bob had finally tonked the house to Sue, she tonked her duplex to Francis.

Half the verbs were monosyllabic (*norp, moop, pell, tonk*), and half were polysyllabic (*calimod, orgulate, repetrine, dorfinize*), counterbalanced across stories and subjects. After reading each story, subjects were shown eleven new sentences containing the verb and asked to rate how good each one sounded. One of the sentences was a double-object dative. In addition, we orthogonally varied whether the sentences involved a transfer of possession—(2.11) involves such a transfer; (2.12) and (2.13) do not—and whether the verb involved the preposition *to*, signifying an act of transfer, as in (2.12), or *for*, signifying an act done for someone's benefit, as in (2.13).

(2.12) Ron, who had promised Dave that he would try to help him make the flight, entered the garage with some regret. It had been a full month since he fired up the orgulator, and he was unsure how it would handle the rough atmosphere. Later, after having orgulated Dave to the hotel, Ron was quite relieved.

(2.13) Ned, a young but upcoming inventor, was eager to spring his latest idea on the unsuspecting world. He thought he'd begin with his neighbor, Cindy, by offering to do her ceiling with his new mooper. It is a profound understatement to say that Cindy was displeased after Ned had mooped the ceiling for her.

We found that subjects rated the double-object sentences in the questionnaire, such as *Fred tonked Mary the house*, as sounding much better if the verb signified a transfer of possession than if it did not. In addition, among the possession-transfer verbs involving the preposition *to*, those that were monosyllabic were rated as significantly better sounding than those that were polysyllabic.[2] As expected, no such differences were found for ratings of the prepositional-dative forms. Thus the phonological and semantic constraints on dativization are not mere historical residues but are active in the minds of adult speakers, affecting whether or not they judge novel verbs to be acceptable in the double-object construction. Similar effects occur when subjects judge the acceptability of nonce words suffixed with -*ity* (Randall, 1980) or prefixed with various negative affixes (Baldi, Broderick, and Palermo, 1985). Though we have not yet run analogous experiments for the other criteria and alternations I have discussed, the fact that adults are sensitive to the most puzzling of the criteria, the morphophonological constraint on the double-object dative, leads us to predict that other criteria are psychologically real as well.

Children, too, are sensitive to constraints on the dative, though they do not apply them consistently, as examples such as *Brush me my hair* and *Mattia demonstrated me that yesterday* from (1.16) attest. In the first experiment of Gropen et al. (1989), where children were taught new verbs of transfer, we used two monosyllabic and two polysyllabic nonsense words and found that children produced significantly more double-object datives with the monosyllabic than with the polysyllabic verbs (55% versus 39%) but showed no such preference with prepositional-object datives (36% versus 39%). Thus the effect is not an artifact of polysyllabic verbs' being generally harder to learn or pronounce. This difference was replicated, though at a nonsignificant level, in a second study (43% versus 38%). In that study we also varied whether the event referred to by the verb denoted a transfer of a thing to a toy animal, who could plausibly possess the thing, or simply to a location indicated by an inanimate object, which could not. Children produced double-object forms significantly less often when the goal was inanimate than when it was a toy animal (32% versus 38%). When the child himself or herself was the recipient of the thing, making the possibility of possession even more salient, even more double-object sentences (52%) were elicited.

Children occasionally disobey the adult constraint on the causative. Bowerman (1982a) gives examples such as *Those are nice beds ... Enough to wish me that I had one of those beds* and *I want to watch you this book*, which sound odd to adult ears because the causation involved is circuitous or nonphysical. However, though children do make such errors, our experiment on productive causativization in children (Gropen, Pinker, and Roeper, in preparation) showed that children are at least probabilistically sensitive to the directness constraint. In the conditions I described earlier, we had one toy animal directly manipulate a second into a posture or action. But in addition, we had a condition in which the causation was mediated by an intervening act: one animal threw a marble at the second, resulting in its assuming the posture or engaging in the motion expressed by the intransitive verb. Children used lexical causatives more often for direct causation than for mediated causation: 55% versus 0% for the 4-year-olds; 66% versus 22% for the 6-year-olds. However, they showed the opposite preference when producing periphrastic causatives with the verb *make*, seldom using them in trials with direct causation but using them fairly often in trials with mediated causation (10% versus 50% for the 4-year-olds, 0% versus 31% for the 6-year-olds). Likewise, when they simply used the intransitive form, omitting mention of the causal agent altogether, it was never in trials with direct causation (0% versus 20% for the 4-year-olds; 0% versus 25% for the 6-year-olds).

Finally, Pinker, Lebeaux, and Frost (1987) tested various possible constraints on passivization in children. Many experimenters have shown that children have difficulty comprehending the passives of perceptual and psychological verbs such as *see* and *know*, though they have no trouble with their corresponding actives or with the passives of actional verbs such as *kick* (Maratsos, Kuczaj, Fox and Chalkley, 1979; de Villiers, Phinney, and Avery, 1982; Maratsos, Fox, Becker, and Chalkley, 1985; Gordon and Chafetz, 1986; Borer and Wexler, 1987). Perhaps children are adhering to an actional-versus-stative criterion that approximates the distinction noted by descriptive grammarians to hold for adult English. Unfortunately, it turns out that adults show roughly the same pattern in their speech: passives of perception and psychological verbs are quite rare. Thus children may have simply recorded certain active and passive versions of actional and nonactional verbs conservatively from their parents' speech. Since input frequency was controlled exactly in our experiments, we could distinguish these possibilities. In one experiment we contrasted novel actional verbs with novel perceptual verbs meaning "to see through binoculars" and "to hear through an ear trumpet." In two others we contrasted actional verbs with verbs of spatial relationships, roughly, "to suspend" and "to contain." By using a variety of teaching and testing conditions we were able to determine whether any reluctance on the part of children to passivize these nonactional verbs was due to non-passivizability per se, not just to their being more difficult to learn across the board. We discovered in four separate groups of children a selective reluctance to passivize nonactional verbs involving spatial or perceptual relations productively (these differences, though consistent, did not result in statistical significance).

In two other experiments we tested Jackendoff's Thematic Hierarchy Condition directly. In one, actional verbs were taught, but for half the verbs the agent was expressed as the object and the patient was expressed as the subject. Thus for these verbs *The bear was pilking the cow* would mean that the cow was knocking over the bear. Such verbs can be learned by young school-age children, not without difficulty (Marantz, 1982), but they are as strong a violation of the THC as one could imagine. So if children are criterion-governed passivizers, they should fail to passivize these "anticanonical" verbs even if they can learn them in the active voice. And indeed, we found a strong and statistically significant reluctance to passivize these verbs when they had been taught in the active voice, above and beyond the inherent difficulty of using these anticanonical verbs and the overall difficulty of passivizing any verb. In the other experiment we taught verbs of spatial relationships (meaning "to hang from," "to be centered on," "to be at the end of," and "to be wrapped around") and varied whether the larger reference object, presumably perceived as a location, was subject or object. Thus the verbs could be either of the form *The penny is pilking the record* (theme subject, location object) or of the form *The record is pilking the penny* (location subject, theme object). The THC predicts that when the location is the subject of the active, and hence the theme is the surface subject of the passive, the passive form should be possible, but it should not be possible when the theme is the subject of the active and the location is the surface subject of the passive. Again, we found a selective reluctance to passivize the verbs that the THC deems unpassivizable, though this effect was not as consistently observed as the corresponding effect for actional verbs.

Thus we concluded that children were constraining their productive rule of passivization, at least according to some gradient of passivizability, with agent-subject/patient-object actional verbs most passivizable, patient-subject/agent-object actional verbs least passivizable, and spatial relation and perception verbs in between, with spatial relation verbs being further subdivided into more and less passivizable versions depending on which argument was mapped onto the subject role. And more generally, we can conclude that criteria that distinguish which verbs do and which verbs don't participate in argument structure alternations are active in the minds of children and adults and not just historical residues, though children do not apply them as consistently or as precisely as do adults. (In section 7.3 I discuss constraints on children's lexical rules in greater depth.)

2.5 Problems for the Criteria-Governed Productivity Theory

The criteria-governed productivity hypothesis outlined at length in Pinker (1984) has in its favor three things. First, it is consistent with the linguistic fact that the argument structure alternations studied to date do not apply across the board to all the verbs matching the syntactic conditions of the respective rules, and they do not apply to arbitrary lists of verbs either. Rather, they are all governed by systematic criteria. Second, we have experimental evidence for the psychological potency of the criteria as constraints on productive generalizations. And third, of course, it shows us a way out of Baker's paradox. Unfortunately, it is also faced with three problems.

1. *Do the criteria really work? What happens when they don't?* There are two possible kinds of exceptions to a criterion. Positive exceptions are verbs that should not passivize, dativize, and so on, according to the constraints, but do. Examples are listed in (2.14), (2.15), and (2.16); some of them are taken from Bowerman (1987a, personal communication), Fodor (1985), Gee (1974), Green (1974), Maratsos et al. (1987), and Randall (1987).

(2.14) *Some positive exceptions to the phonological constraint on the dative:*
      Dr. Bear referred me a patient.
      I radioed / telegraphed / netmailed her the news.
      Kathy xeroxed me a copy.
      He bequeathed me his fortune.
      They forwarded me some mail.
      She guaranteed / allocated / reserved him a seat.

(2.15) *Some positive exceptions to the Thematic Hierarchy Condition on the passive:*
      The audience was bored by the movie [audience = goal; cf. The movie was boring TO the audience].
      Russia was invaded by a horde of locusts [Russia = goal].
      The bed was covered by a down comforter [bed = location].
      John was hit by a car [John = goal].
      The mountain was capped by snow [mountain = location].
      The street was lined by trees [street = location].
      The house was surrounded by a moat [house = location].

(2.16) *Some positive exceptions to the directness and stereotypy constraints on the causative:*

Directness:
John's company grows oranges in the Imperial Valley.
Oil Can Boyd walked the batter.
Bond killed Drax by throwing him into the shark-filled pool.

Stereotypy of manner:
John broke the bicycle by riding it over a log / because he was too heavy for its racing wheels / by smashing it with a sledgehammer.
I melted the butter by taping it to the exhaust manifold of my Saab.

The criterion hypothesis is not necessarily refuted by positive exceptions, because they are learnable from positive evidence. Specifically, the theory can tolerate them if (a) they are learned conservatively, that is, on a verb-by-verb basis from positive evidence; and (b) they are few enough in number, compared to the obedient alternating verbs, that the child will not be tempted to discard the criteria altogether as ineffective. It is hard to assess the truth of either of these escape hatches. But where the theory fails more clearly is in the case of negative exceptions: verbs that *should* alternate but do not. Here, conservative learning through positive evidence is not an option; negative evidence is required. In fact, negative exceptions to criteria bring Baker's paradox back in full force. Though fewer exceptional verbs are involved, as the hypothesis stands even a single negative exception requires some novel mechanism to explain its existence, and one would worry about whether such a mechanism could suffice to account for the acquisition of the entire pattern of verb behavior, supplanting the use of criteria altogether.

Some negative exceptions are presented in (2.17)–(2.20). Some are blatantly permitted under the proposed criteria. For others, the situation referred to by the verb could be construed post hoc as failing a given criterion (for example, perhaps *pulling* isn't "really" a way of transferring possession but only a way of changing something's location). But that would defeat the purpose of invoking the criterion, which is to allow the child to know on the basis of the verb form or meaning alone whether the verb can enter into that argument structure.

(2.17) *Negative exceptions to the possessor constraint on the dative:*
   *John pulled Bill the box [cf. John brought Bill the box].
   *Sam shouted John the story [cf. Sam told John the story].
   *Becky credited Bill the money [cf. Becky promised Bill the money].
   *Mary chose Linda a dress [cf. Mary picked Linda out a dress].

(2.18) *Negative exceptions to the directness constraint on the causative:*
   *John went his dog into the room [cf. John slid his dog into the room].
   *The ball fell because Martha fell it [cf. The ball dropped because Martha dropped it].
   *Stephen laughed the baby by tickling it [cf. Stephen burped the baby by patting it].

(2.19) *Negative exceptions to the Thematic Hierarchy Condition on the passive:*
   *The house is had by John [cf. The house is owned by John; John = possessor = location, house = theme].
   *A disk is lacked by that computer [computer = location].
   *Water is contained by the bottle [cf. Water is held by the bottle; bottle = location, water = theme].
   *Water was dripped by the ceiling [cf. Water was emitted by the ceiling; ceiling = source, water = theme].
   *Sap was gushed by the tree [cf. Sap was exuded by the tree; tree = source, sap = theme].

(2.20)   *Negative exceptions to the holism constraint on the locative:*

  *I poured the glass with water [even if the glass is full; cf. I filled the glass with water].

  *I dribbled the floor with paint [even if the floor is completely splattered; cf. I splattered the floor with paint].

  *I vacuumed the rug of lint [even if the floor is completely clean; cf. I stripped the rug of lint].

  *I stole John of his money [even if John is penniless; cf. I robbed John of his money].

  2. *Why does the language have criteria? Why does the child bother to learn them?* These are two sides of the same coin. Compare two rules for productive dativization, one that licenses a pure alternation of argument structures, as in (2.21a), and one that is constrained by a criterion, as in (2.21b); both are taken from Pinker (1984).

(2.21)   (a) verb (SUBJ, OBJ, OBL$_{to}$) —>   verb (SUBJ, OBJ2, OBJ)
         (b) verb (SUBJ, OBJ, OBL$_{to}$) —>   verb (SUBJ, OBJ2, OBJ)
         ONLY IF: [verb is native]
                  [object of OBL$_{to}$ is prospective possessor of OBJ]

Fodor (1985) points out that rule (2.21a) is simpler and that it requires less information to learn. We can add the observation that it confers more expressive power on the speaker. To take an example used earlier, when asked the question "What did John do with the museum that inspired its directors to make him a trustee?" a person possessing the first rule could answer "He donated it that priceless Vermeer he had inherited from his great-grandfather." If the speaker had been saddled with (2.21b) he would be forced to say instead "He donated that priceless Vermeer he had inherited from his great-grandfather to it." The latter is clumsier and less felicitous because its "heavy" noun phrase is in the middle rather than at the end and its "new," focused material, *the painting*, comes earlier in the sentence than its "old," topic material, *the museum* (see Erteschik-Shir, 1979).

  Given all these disadvantages to learning a constrained rule, and the fact that the simple, unconstrained rule is compatible with all the child's linguistic input, why, Fodor asks, does the child do it? Perhaps children are simply built to learn the language of their parents, even if that involves complicating a simple rule in the absence of evidence forcing them to. But why, then, did the parents maintain the constraint in their language (other than the fact that *their* parents had it?). One could answer that there are many arbitrary and difficult patterns that generation after generation learns (e.g., irregular morphology), but most such cases involve the resolution of conflicts between competing subsystems (e.g., rule application and memorization; see Pinker and Prince, 1988), not the adding of arbitrary conditions to simple rules.

3. *Why are certain rules constrained by certain criteria and not by others? How does the child figure out which rule is constrained by which criterion?* Again, these two questions are really one question, to the extent that the structure of the language is caused by the structure of the learner. The criteria listed above involve a motley collection of concepts: number of metrical feet; prospective possession; directness of causation; holism of filling or covering; mapping onto a hierarchy of thematic roles. And these are only for four rules in a single language. The heterogeneity of the list suggests that the universe of criteria from which the child would have to sample might be quite large. In Pinker (1984) I noted that the learning procedures for the criteria-based account require that the list not be open-ended and not be too large: if the list is open-ended, the child might never find the relevant criterion; if it is finite but large, he or she might not find it in a reasonable period of time. Furthermore, as new verbs are learned, hypothesized constraints might have to be given up, so the child might have to search several times for the right constraint before he or she succeeded in acquiring the adult rule. Though I was able to show that many of the components of the criteria, such as choice of thematic roles and gross metrical pattern, did seem to recur across a variety of rules, it is difficult to come up with an explicit list of the possible criteria.

In addition, we still need an explanation as to why certain criteria are paired with certain rules. Could a language have a passive that applied to monosyllabic verbs? A dative rule that required holistic and direct transfer of a substance to a possessor? A causative rule that required the affected entity also to be a source (e.g., "cause-to-send")? It seems unlikely. Some of these possibilities may be ruled out because they would apply to small unnatural classes of verbs or would be too constricting. But as we have seen, the constrained English dative rule is hardly a model of optimal design, so general utility considerations are probably not a big factor.

So how can one resolve, on the one hand, the existence of criteria, their use by adults and children, and the failure of other attempted resolutions of Baker's paradox; and on the other, the problems with the criteria-based account? In the rest of this book I will show that criteria are not units that the child explicitly searches for and appends to rules, but are epiphenomena of more general principles of argument structure assignment. In particular, the criteria are consequences of structures and principles of grammar that provide answers to the following questions:

• What is a possible verb in a language?
• How are verbs associated with their syntactic argument structures?

- When may two verbs share the same root?
- When may a possible verb actually be added to a language?

By deriving the criteria from principles addressed to these questions, we can adopt a new perspective that eliminates the theoretical problems associated with the criteria-based account while preserving its advantages. In addition, we will attain refined criteria that are more likely to be exceptionless.

Chapter 3
Constraints and the Nature of
Argument Structure

In this chapter I pursue the resolution of Baker's paradox that hinges on the child's using semantic criteria to constrain the application of an alternation rule to only those verbs that undergo the alternation in the adult language. What I will try to show is that such constraints are inherently predictable from the nature of lexical rules, if those rules are seen in a different light. After presenting the basic idea, I will examine a range of linguistic phenomena supporting it.

3.1 Overview: Why Lexical Rules Carry Semantic Constraints

Semantic criteria on lexical rules are puzzling because ordinarily one doesn't think of syntactic rules as being constrained by arbitrary semantic conditions. But what if lexical rules were, at least in part, semantic operations? Then their sensitivity to semantic conditions would be natural. In this chapter I will argue that part of what lexical rules do is change the semantic structures of verbs' lexical entries. Syntactic argument structures of verbs are predictable from their semantic structures, via the application of *linking rules.* So when a semantic structure is altered, it is automatically assigned a new argument structure. I will then show that the phenomena I have been characterizing as semantic "criteria" on rule application arise because of the semantic nature of the rules' operations. Because a rule takes a semantic structure as input and alters it in particular ways (adding, suppressing, or redescribing arguments), the changes it tries to effect can interact with the semantic structure that the verb has to begin with. Some semantic changes, when applied to some verb meanings, may produce a new verb meaning that just doesn't hang together. For such verbs the rule is avoided; that is the equivalent of the rule being constrained by a semantic criterion.

The difference between the view offered in the preceding chapter (see also Pinker, 1984) and the refinement of it I will outline in this chapter can be summarized in (3.1) and (3.2). In the old theory (3.1), a lexical rule takes the syntactic argument structure of a verb and transforms it into a different argument structure. The semantic representation itself is basically unchanged; the new and old verb forms are synonymous. Verb-by-verb choosiness arises because the rule is stipulated to apply only if the verb's semantic representation meets certain criteria. In the second view, the lexical rule acts directly on the verb's semantic representation, transforming it into a new one. In other words, the new verb has a different meaning from the old one. Semantic structures are mapped onto syntactic argument structures, thanks to linking rules, so when the verb's meaning changes, its argument structure changes, too, as an automatic consequence. Verb-by-verb semantic choosiness arises because the semantic changes effected by a rule just don't make sense when applied to verbs with certain meanings.

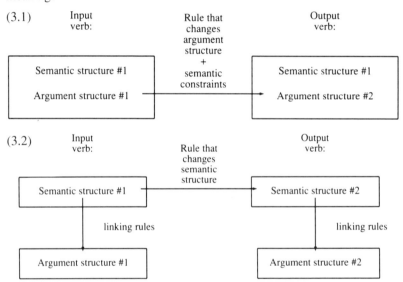

(3.1) Input verb: Rule that changes argument structure + semantic constraints   Output verb:

Semantic structure #1 | Argument structure #1 → Semantic structure #1 | Argument structure #2

(3.2) Input verb: Rule that changes semantic structure   Output verb:

Semantic structure #1 — Semantic structure #2 | linking rules | linking rules | Argument structure #1 | Argument structure #2

What kind of semantic changes would the rules perform? Consider the dative alternation. Dativization, on this view, converts a predicate meaning "to cause X to go to Y" into a second predicate, meaning "to cause Y to have X." There is a linking rule that always maps the argument signifying the causally affected entity onto the grammatical function of object (direct internal argument), so when the predicate is reconstrued as involving an effect on a possessor rather than on a theme, it is the possessor that becomes the syntactic object in argument structure: we have *give John* ... rather than *give a book* ... And because the rule as stated changes a goal ("cause to go to Y") into a possessor ("cause Y to have"), it cannot apply to a verb whose meaning is incompatible with "cause to have." Thus *drive the car to Chicago* cannot be converted into **drive Chicago the car* because driving can't cause anyone to possess anything and Chicago isn't the sort of thing that can possess something else to begin with. Conceiving of the dative rule as a semantic operation converting "cause X to go to Y" into "cause Y to have X" thus unites two phenomena that were formerly arbitrarily glued together: the syntactic change, where the goal argument is promoted to surface object position, and the semantic choosiness, whereby only verbs involving prospective possessors could undergo the change. As we shall see, other aspects of the behavior of the dative fall neatly out of this conception as well.

Moreover, the same kind of analysis works for the other rules. To continue the preview: I will propose that causativization involves converting a predicate meaning "Y changes" into a predicate meaning "to cause Y to change." The causer is mapped onto the subject (external argument) role, the affected thing to the object role (direct internal argument). Verbs with no directly causable change are inherently incompatible with the rule; there is nothing for it to apply to. Locativization involves taking a verb meaning "to cause X to go into or onto Y" and converting it to a verb meaning "to cause Y to change state by means of putting X into or onto it." As in the case of the dative, the entity that is stated to be causally affected (the moving stuff, in the first version; the container or surface, in the second) is mapped onto the surface object position. If a verb has no means of specifying exactly how a container or surface changes state because of the addition of something into or onto it, the semantic change is undefined and cannot apply. Finally, passivization converts a predicate meaning "X acts on Y" to a new predicate meaning "Y is in the circumstance of X acting on it." If there is no "acting on," there is no passivization.

This portrayal of lexical rules leads immediately to a series of questions. Which verbs can be construed as meaning "causing to have"? "causing to change"? "acting upon an entity"? "causing to change state by means of adding stuff"? Without answers, there is no way of explaining which verbs a rule can or cannot apply to. The general answer, it turns out, is complex enough to merit its own chapter, chapter 4. To preview what I will say there: Decisions about which verbs can be construed as capable of undergoing a given semantic change are not made by each speaker for each verb. Rather, the lexicon of a language defines subclasses consisting of verbs whose meanings are variations of a single semantic plan, and it is these subclasses that precisely delineate which verbs a speaker may construe in the two different ways corresponding to the input and output of the lexical rule (e.g., "cause to go" versus "cause to have"). For example, English distinguishes two kinds of verbs of caused motion, those involving the continuous application of force to cause motion, like *pull*, and those involving the instantaneous application of force causing a ballistic motion, like *throw*. Ballistic verbs can be construed as meaning either "cause to go" or "cause to have," and therefore they undergo dativization (*throw the ball to John / throw John the ball*); whereas continuous-force verbs can be construed only as meaning "cause to go," and thus they resist dativization (*pull the box to John / *pull John the box*). The reasons for the difference are partially motivated and partially arbitrary, as we shall see. The principles governing this construability phenomenon define, for a speaker, the difference between rules that predict the *form* of a verb and rules that predict the *existence* of a verb.

This is a description, in a nutshell, of the conclusions that I will end up with in these two chapters. They preserve the idea that Baker's paradox is resolved by systematic criteria applied to the choice of verbs that may undergo an alternation, while motivating the criteria as manifestations of more general principles. Let me now trace the steps that lead to these conclusions.

3.2 Constraints on Lexical Rules as Manifestations of More General Phenomena

3.2.1 Constraints on Argument Structures That Are Independent of Lexical Rules

A first hint that the semantic criteria discussed in the previous chapter are special cases of more general principles comes from examining verbs that *do not alternate* between two argument structures but occur only in a single form, specifically, the form usually seen as the derived version or output of the lexical rule. It turns out that such verbs, even though they could not have been produced by the rule, must conform to the same kinds of criteria as those proposed for the rule.

For example, the double-object datives in (3.3 and 3.4) could not have been derived from prepositional-object forms; the prepositional forms are themselves ungrammatical. But nonetheless they conform to the requirement that the first object be the possessor of the second object (Green, 1974). In the case of (3.3), the first object is a current or possible possessor of the second object who might lose possession of it as a result of the event denoted by the predicate; in (3.4), the first object is a metaphorical possessor of the second object.

(3.3)   Alex bet Leon $600 that the Red Sox would lose.
       *Alex bet $600 to Leon that the Red Sox would lose.

       That remark might cost you your job.
       *That remark might cost your job to you.

       Please spare me your sarcasm.
       *Please spare your sarcasm to / from / of me.

Carolyn envied her her good looks.
*Carolyn envied her good looks to / from /of her.

(3.4)   Lend me your ears!
*Lend your ears to me!

I taught him a good lesson.
*I taught a good lesson to him.

They gave me the flu.
*They gave the flu to me.

Similarly, there are lexical causative verbs that could not have been derived from intransitives, but like derived lexical causatives, they entail that the causation was directly or proximally effected. In (3.5), John could not have been a governor who refused to commute a death sentence, Bill could not have set up a remote control whistle in an empty room, Amy could not have called her daughter and threatened her with punishment if she did not leave, and Bob could not have given an order to a waiter. Such events are, though, compatible with the corresponding periphrastic causative (*make X die / come / go / be cut*).

(3.5)   John killed Mary.
*Mary killed [= died].

Bill brought the dog into the room.
*The dog brought into the room.

Amy took her daughter home.
*Amy's daughter took home.

Bob cut the bread.
*The bread cut.

In the container locatives (i.e., those using *with*) in (3.6), the glass is completely filled, the bed completely covered, and the sponge completely saturated, even though none of the verb structures could be the product of a rule deriving it from a content locative (i.e., one using *into/onto*).

(3.6)   I filled the glass with water.
*I filled water into the glass.

She covered the bed with a sheet.
*She covered a sheet over the bed.

They saturated the sponge with detergent.
*They saturated detergent into the sponge.

What these examples show is that some of the constraints I have been discussing should not be seen as applying to rules generating one argument structure from another. Instead, they seem to apply directly to particular argument structures, regardless of whether they were derived from other argu-

ment structures. This immediately allows us to factor the original problem—
what are the constraints on argument structure alternation rules?—into two,
possibly more tractable problems:

1. What are the constraints on particular kinds of argument structures? That is,
what has to be true of a verb for it to be assigned to a transitive argument structure
or a double-object argument structure or a *with*-locative argument structure?
2. When may two verbs involving different argument structures share the
same root? That is, why is it that in English we can use the same sound to convey
breaking and causing to break but we must use different sounds to convey dying
and causing to die?

3.2.2 Constraints on Grammatical Functions That Are Independent of Particular Argument Structures

Some of the constraints apply to units even smaller than argument structures: the
individual grammatical functions composing them. For example, consider the
holistic requirement on the container version of the locative, whereby the
grammatical object must be completely affected (covered, filled, etc.) by the
action of the verb (see S. Anderson, 1971). This turns out to be a characteristic
of grammatical objects in general, not just of grammatical objects in the
container-locative construction (Hopper and Thompson, 1980; Rappaport and
Levin, 1985), as shown in (3.7).

(3.7) John drank from the glass of beer.
      John drank the glass of beer.

      Beth climbed up the mountain.
      Beth climbed the mountain.

      Bill painted on the door.
      Bill painted the door.

      Betty put butter on the bread.
      Betty buttered the bread.

      Jim removed peel from the apple.
      Jim peeled the apple.

      Gary wrote for many TV shows.
      Gary wrote many TV shows.

In each pair, only the second member, in which the second argument is the object,
implies that the action involved the complete extent or amount of the referent of
the argument (i.e., all the beer was drunk, the entire height of the mountain
scaled, the door completely painted, the bread completely covered, the apple
completely skinned, the entirety of the show written by the author). Thus in the
locative alternation the fact that the wagon is necessarily full when you load a

wagon with hay but not when you load hay onto the wagon is a consequence of the fact that *the wagon* is the grammatical object in the former sentence but not in the latter one.

Similarly, the directness constraint on lexical causatives has something to do with grammatical objects in general, not just the objects of lexical causatives. In (3.8a), only the second member of the pair, in which Mary is the direct object, entails that Sally landed a direct blow as intended (see B. Levin, 1985). Similarly, in (3.8b), the transitive version implies that the action that Squeaky performed succeeded in affecting Ford, whereas the prepositional form is compatible with an absence of any effect at all.

(3.8) (a) Sally slapped / hit / kicked at Mary.
        Sally slapped / hit / kicked Mary.

    (b) Squeaky Fromme shot at Ford.
        Squeaky Fromme shot Ford.

Thus the direct object role is associated with the reading that what the agent did had an immediate impact on the entity that the action was directed at. Perhaps this is what makes lexical causatives, but not periphrastic causatives, entail some notion of direct causation.

Clearly there is something about the difference between being an object and not being an object of a verb that invokes a reading whereby the state signified by the verb is effected directly on the object and effected on all of it. Note that this difference is not contingent on the argument's merely being a surface object. Not only are the direct and holistic readings preserved under passivization (*The wagon was loaded with hay; The window was broken by John*), but the locative alternation itself has a closely related variant with no surface object at all but with the same holistic/nonholistic difference in interpretation (see Salkoff, 1983; Rappaport and Levin, 1985), as shown in (3.9).

(3.9) (a) Bees are swarming in the garden.
        Water dripped from the sponge.
        Vermin were crawling over the cheese.

    (a) The garden swarmed with bees.
        The sponge dripped with water.
        The cheese was crawling with vermin.

In (3.9b) there is an implication that bees were all over the garden, not just in one part, that the water dripped from the entire sponge, not just a corner, and that vermin crawled over the entire cheese. Yet these arguments are surface subjects in all cases, not objects. Whatever generalization forces arguments to support a holistic interpretation when they are not oblique must apply to something more abstract than the surface direct object: an object in some underlying structure (perhaps marked by a trace in surface structure), or else some thematic role that gets mapped either onto surface objects or onto surface subjects if the verb is intransitive (these options will be discussed in more detail later).

3.2.3 Constraints on Verb Choice Are Also Constraints on Interpretation

I have been discussing criteria as if they acted as filters on classes of verbs potentially serving as the input to a rule. In fact the filtering function seems to be a by-product of a more general function of the constraints, namely forcing a certain kind of interpretation on a new argument structure assigned to a verb. Two of the criteria I have discussed, while ruling out the application of lexical rules to certain stems altogether, also alter the meaning of the stems that they do apply to. The directness constraint on the causative, for example, rules out *He laughed the audience*. In (3.10), it allows causativization to apply, resulting in a syntactically well-formed sentence (b), but in doing so it makes the sentence imply that direct contact was involved in the action. Since the adjunct in sentence (b) explicitly contradicts the contact reading, the sentence as a whole is anomalous. Similarly, the holism constraint on the locative rules out *He threw the air with the confetti*. But when it does apply in (3.11) it also affects its interpretation; the the (b) sentence implies that the wall is completely covered.

(3.10) (a) John caused the window to break by startling Bill, who was installing it.

(b) *John broke the window by startling Bill, who was installing it.

(3.11) (a) Irv slathered paint on the wall.

(b) Irv slathered the wall with paint.

The possessor constraint on the dative displays the same dual roles. If a verb is incompatible with a meaning of causing to change possession, it cannot dativize, as in *I drove her the car*. But if the verb does dativize, a successful change of possession is implied in the resulting double-object form. For example, Green (1974) notes that in (3.12a) there is no commitment as to what the students took away, but in (b) there is an implication that the teaching was successful. It is as if the prepositional dative carries no implication about successful possession (in this case, possession of knowledge), but the double-object dative enforces that reading.

(3.12) (a) Mary taught Spanish to the students.

(b) Mary taught the students Spanish.

A related phenomenon can be seen in (3.13), an example from Joan Bresnan:

(3.13) (a) I sent a package to the border.

(b) I sent a package to the boarder.

(c) *I sent the border a package.

(d) I sent the boarder a package.

It seems that *send* in its prepositional form is ambiguous as to whether a goal of location or a goal of possession and location is involved; (a) and (b) involve different senses of *send*, one spatial, one jointly spatial and possessional. Sentence (c) is ungrammatical, presumably because the meaning of the double-object version of *send*, unlike its prepositional counterpart, specifies that the transfer must involve possession.

Finally, it has long been noted that passivization is not semantically neutral. *Beavers build dams* implies something about all beavers and is true; *Dams are built by beavers* implies something about all dams and is false. Roughly, the surface subject of the passive is interpreted as a theme, an entity of which a location or state is predicated (see Anderson, 1977). We can call this the "predication effect": when a verb is passivized, its surface subject must be interpreted as a theme of a predication if the verb has a theme.[1] If the verb's meaning is such that its theme ends up as the *by*-object instead, it cannot be passivized at all (*cost, weigh*, stative *touch*).

What we are seeing here is that verbs must be interpreted in a certain way when they are assigned an argument structure composed of a particular set of grammatical functions. These principles of interpretation act as "criteria" or filters because of an interaction between the mandated interpretation and the *inherent* meanings of verbs that are extended to that argument structure. If the combination of the inherent meaning of the verb and the meaning components forced by the new argument structure is inadmissible (in a sense to be discussed later), the verb cannot undergo the alternation.

3.3   A Theory of Argument Structure

In the preceding section I tried to show that constraints on the application of lexical rules to verbs are epiphenomena of more general principles: those that enforce an interpretation on particular argument structures (regardless of where they come from), those that link grammatical functions with particular kinds of semantic arguments, and those that effect changes on verbs' meanings. In this section I spell out these principles in more detail.

3.3.1   Background Assumptions

Given that no current theory of linguistic representation has provided a solution to Baker's paradox, I will make a number of conservative assumptions about argument structure at the outset so as not to block off avenues in which the solution may be found. I will refer to grammatical roles using GB and LFG terminology fairly interchangeably when possible, avoiding special theory-internal devices and tricks. All I absolutely need is the four-way distinction between subjects, objects, second objects, and prepositional objects, and a way of coindexing them with a verb's arguments. (This has the additional advantage of allowing the current work to touch base both with the LFG-related acquisition theory I developed in Pinker, 1984, out of which this book grew, and with the currently flourishing GB-based work on argument structure.) Furthermore, since notions like "optional argument" and "adjunct" may beg the questions they are designed to solve (see section 1.4.5.2), I will assume that every distinct set of grammatical functions that a verb can appear with is licensed by a different, fully formed argument structure associated with that verb. (Thus there will be two argument structures for *eat*, corresponding to *John ate* and *John ate the apple*, and two for *run*, corresponding to *John ran* and *John ran to the store*.) Third, so as not to saddle myself with unnecessary, possibly harmful assumptions that are implicit in a notation, I will *not* assume that a verb's arguments are differentiated in terms of thematic role labels such as "agent" and "theme" but will simply differentiate them by variables such as X and Y, following Rappaport and Levin (1988) and others. Therefore I will use the term "argument structure" to refer to a strictly syntactic entity, namely the information that specifies how a verb's arguments are encoded in the syntax. With Rappaport and Levin (1988), Burzio (1986), L. Levin (1985), and others, I will assume that this is the *only* lexical structure pertaining to the thematic properties of arguments that the syntax can look at. Thematic information goes into determining a verb's argument structure, but that is the extent of its influence; the rest of the syntax cannot "see" it directly.

To review the basic terminology: A *lexical entry* of a verb specifies an association among (a) morphological information (the morphemes it is composed of, if it is multimorphemic); (b) phonological information (the sound of the morphemes); syntactic information, including (c) its part-of-speech category and (d) its argument structure, the specification of the syntactic properties of those of its arguments that are expressed in the sentence; and (e) its meaning, or *semantic structure*. What I will call semantic structure or lexicosemantic structure is similar to the representation called Lexical Conceptual Structure by Hale and Laughren (1983), Hale and Keyser (1986, 1987), and Rappaport and Levin (1988). I avoid their term because, as we shall see, lexical semantic structures cannot be the same thing as mental representations of concepts for typical actions, events, scripts, or scenarios in which the verb is used. Rather, we will see, they are essentially *constraints* on particular aspects of an event.

As mentioned earlier, I will also assume that the same verb used with two different argument structures actually consists of two distinct lexical entries sharing a morphological root and components of their semantic structures. A *lexical rule*, then, associates one kind of lexical entry with another; it can be seen as taking one lexical entry as input and producing a second as output. There are a number of ways in which sets of words can share a root, involving different kinds of rules and principles. I will be focusing on a certain kind of alternation involving changes of argument structure among verbs. The most straightforward case is the one where the verb stem remains unchanged but the argument structure differs. The causative, the dative, and several variants of the locative alternation in English are the examples I treat in detail, but we will also come across the "conative" alternation (*Bill slapped him / slapped at him*), the "middle" alternation (*John cut the bread / The bread cut easily*), an alternation involving possessors of parts (*John punched Bill's arm / John punched Bill on the arm*), an alternation that has something in common both with both datives and locatives (*I supplied sheets to him / supplied him with sheets*), one that involves the addition of a path argument (*He hit the ball / hit the ball into center field*), and one that deletes an object (*John ate the apple / John ate*). I predict that the very same principles will apply to other alternations that change argument structure, such as "raising-to-object" (*I expect that John will leave / I expect John to leave*) and "resultative complement addition" (*She hammered the box / She hammered the box flat*).

I also lavish attention on the passive, which differs from these alternations in adding an affix to the verb and changing its morphosyntactic category, from a finite verb to a participle. According to Marantz (1984), rules of this sort are formally different from those that leave the stem intact, and should not be subject to semantic constraints. This is a bit too strong: I will present evidence from English and from cross-linguistic surveys showing that similar kinds of semantic principles apply to alternations that are accompanied by affixation and to those that are not. However, there certainly are significant differences between the passive and the nonaffixing alternations, and in sections 4.4.4 and 5.6.4 I modify Marantz's suggestion in an effort to pinpoint the grammatical source of these differences.

One step further we find rules that change a word's syntactic category, such as the rule that derives adjectives from participles or the one that derives nouns from verbs. These alternations appear to be more closely tied to pure syntactic properties of argument structure (such as the number of arguments, which arguments are obligatory, and the external/internal argument distinction) than to the lexicosemantic properties that govern the alternations I focus on, and I will not be concerned with them. See Rappaport and Levin (1988 and in press), Rappaport, Levin, and Laughren, (1987), and Marantz (1984) for discussion.

3.3.2   Semantic Conflation Classes as Thematic Cores of Argument Structures

In section 3.2.1 I showed that argument structures are associated with characteristic semantic properties. Let's say that each argument structure has associated with it one or more *thematic cores*. Informally, a thematic core is a schematization of a type of event or relationship that lies at the core of the meanings of a class of possible verbs. For example, the argument structure types discussed so far could have the thematic cores listed in (3.14).

(3.14) Double-object:
   X causes *Y* to have *Z*.

  Transitive:
   X acts on *Y*.

  Unergative Intransitive:
   X acts.

  Unaccusative intransitive:
   X is in a location or state or goes to a location or state.

  Transitive with oblique containing *to*:
   X causes *Y* to go to *Z*.

  Transitive with oblique containing *with*:
   X causes *Y* to go into a state by causing *Z* to go to *Y*.

  Intransitive with oblique containing *to*:
   X goes to *Y*.

The thematic core of an argument structure is an example of what Talmy (1985) calls a *conflation* of semantic elements, defined in a *semantic field* in which the elements are given a specific interpretation. Each conflation defines a set of possible predicates in a language, or a *conflation class*. For now, imagine that the possible semantic elements consist of variables standing for the participants in the event (the *X*, *Y*, and *Z*) and the elementary semantic functions "act," "cause," "go," "have," "be," and "to." Instead of labeling the participants with thematic roles, one can simply distinguish them by the argument slots they fill in these elementary functions (Rappaport and Levin, 1986; Jackendoff, 1987a). Thus (for now) the thematic role *agent* can be treated as a mnemonic for the first argument of "cause," and *patient* would be the second argument of "cause." Similarly, *theme* is a mnemonic for the first argument of "go" or "be"; *path* corresponds to the second argument of "go," *location* to the second argument of "be," and *goal* to the second argument of "to."

3.3.3   Linking Rules

A thematic core of an argument structure is a specification of a conflation class
defining a kind of possible verb meaning in a language, including a specification
of which arguments are "open arguments" or variables. Open arguments are
those whose referents can be expressed syntactically by a phrase within the same
clause as the predicate. *Linking rules* are regular ways of mapping open
arguments onto grammatical functions or underlying syntactic configurations by
virtue of their thematic roles; they are the mechanisms that create the syntactic
argument structure associated with a given thematic core. Linking rules are
discussed at length in Carter (1976b), Ostler (1980), and Dowty (1987) and play
a prominent role in many theories of grammar, such as the Universal Alignment
Hypothesis in Relational Grammar (Perlmutter and Postal, 1984), the Uniformity of Theta Assignment Hypothesis in GB (Baker, 1985), and the Canonical
Mapping Hypothesis in LFG (Pinker, 1984; L. Levin, 1985).

Let us consider the following linking rules as a first approximation. They
would apply, in unordered fashion, to the open arguments of the semantic
structure of a verb under the constraints that every open argument be linked to
a grammatical function (LFG) or underlying argument position (GB) and that no
grammatical function or argument position be linked to more than one open
argument. These constraints, which rule out such strings as **John put* and **We
drank the beer the bottles of Heineken*, correspond to Function-Argument
Biuniqueness in Bresnan (1982c) and, roughly, to the Theta-Criterion in Chomsky
(1981). (See also Rappaport and Levin, 1988, and Jackendoff, 1987a.)

1. Link the first argument of "cause" (the agent) to: the SUBJ function (LFG)
/ external argument (GB).
2. Link the second argument of "cause" (the patient) to: the OBJ function (LFG)
/ direct internal argument (GB).
3. Link the first argument of "be" or "go" (the theme) to: the SUBJ function if
it is not already linked or to the OBJ function otherwise (LFG) / direct internal
argument (GB).
4. Link the argument of "to" (the goal) to: the OBL function (LFG) / indirect
internal argument (GB).
5. Link the third argument of "cause to have" (Z in "X causes Y to have Z") to:
the OBJ2 function (LFG) / second direct internal argument (GB).

Oblique/indirect arguments are also linked to kinds of locations and paths
other than those expressed by the preposition *to*; accordingly, the proper
formulation of the linking rule for oblique arguments, to be discussed in chapter
5, is more general. The choice of a specific preposition is actually determined
by compatibility between the preposition's own semantic representation and that
of the verb (see Jackendoff, 1983, 1987a). The mechanics of this selection will

be made more precise in chapter 5; the linking rule listed above can be seen as a fusion of a general linking rule for oblique objects and the semantic structure of one version of the preposition *to*. As we shall see, the linking rule for second objects is also more general than the tentative version stated here.

Note that the theme requires a special treatment because it commonly appears in both subject (*The spot disappeared*) and object (*I killed the bug*) positions. In the version of LFG I elaborated in Pinker (1984), the two-part linking rule for themes can be derived from a canonical mapping of thematic roles onto a hierarchy of grammatical functions, so that the theme is assigned to the highest function in the list "SUBJ-OBJ-OBL" that is not already linked to an argument. A slightly more complex possibility within the LFG framework was suggested by L. Levin (1985), namely that the theme first be "classified" as taking a "general [semantically] unrestricted function." Then one of three function assignment rules can apply to this class: one that maps it onto SUBJ, one that maps it onto OBJ, or one that maps it onto OBJ2. When the verb lacks an agent, only the first of these three rules can yield a well-formed argument structure containing a SUBJ, and it is the one that applies. Within Relational Grammar, a theme is assigned as an object in an underlying level of representation, but can be promoted to subject in the surface level by a general rule if the subject role is not already assigned. Within GB, the theme would be assigned as the direct internal argument, but if there is no external argument, the rule "Move α" would apply, moving it into the surface subject position and leaving a trace behind to which it would be associated in an "argument chain." (See the discussion of "Burzio's Generalization" in section 1.4.5.1.) In other words, every theory has some means of accounting for unaccusativity: basically, the existence of intransitive verbs whose subjects are themes.

It is important to note that the account of thematic roles and linking I am using represents a significant departure from the conceptions originally proposed by Gruber (1965) and Fillmore (1968) and adopted more or less intact by LFG (Bresnan, 1982a; Pinker, 1984) and the Extended Standard Theory of transformational grammar (Jackendoff, 1972) including the GB framework (Chomsky, 1981). The Fillmore account and its descendants are based on the following assumptions: (a) Thematic roles are atomic labels drawn from a fixed list. (b) The labels are ordered in a hierarchy (usually agent-theme-location/source/goal) and are linked to the syntactic positions Subject, Object, and Oblique in such a way as to preserve the relative rankings of the two hierarchies (so that an agent is a subject; a theme is an object if there is an agent, a subject otherwise; a location is oblique if there is an agent and theme, an object otherwise). (c) Every argument has exactly one thematic role. (d) Linking rules apply to arguments in terms of the roles they play in motion events (thus Object is linked to the moving or located entity).

Dowty (1987), Jackendoff (1987a), B. Levin (1985), and Rappaport and Levin (1985, 1988) present several arguments against the Fillmore-style theory of thematic roles. First, there are many concepts of the same formal type as "source" and "goal" that do not have traditional labels, such as the role of *the house* in *John passed the house*. Second, arguments often have multiple thematic roles; for instance, *the ball* in *I batted the ball into center field* is the goal of the motion of the bat and the theme of the motion that terminates in center field. Similarly, the subject of *give* is an agent and a source; the subject of *John intentionally rolled down the hill* is an agent and a theme. Third, the change in interpretation that accompanies lexical rules is baffling to a theory of unanalyzed thematic role labels: if *the wagon* has identical role labels in *load hay onto the wagon* and *load the wagon with hay*, why is it interpreted holistically in one but not the other? But if it has different role labels in the two structures, why is it interpreted in both phrases as the destination of the hay?

The alternative view that Jackendoff, Levin, and Rappaport argue for, and that I expand here, substitutes the following assumptions: (a) Thematic roles are positions in a structured semantic representation. (b) Therefore, they do not form a fixed list that can be ordered in a hierarchy; rather, each thematic role triggers a specific linking rule. (c) Arguments can bear several thematic roles simultaneously by virtue of their simultaneous appearance in several semantic substructures (e.g., second argument of "cause" and first argument of "go"). (d) Linking rules can apply to the roles that entities play in any semantic field, not just physical location. For example, a verb can have two arguments playing the role of theme, one corresponding to what moves, the other corresponding to what changes state. The main advantage of this newer formulation of thematic roles in dealing with Baker's paradox, we shall see, is that it removes the arbitrariness of semantic constraints and their pairings with particular lexical rules.

3.3.4 Lexical Rules

Conflation classes built around thematic cores are inherently incapable of allowing new forms to be derived productively. A word is more than a meaning; it needs a sound, too, or people won't know how to pronounce it. Conflation class definitions inherently don't tell you where the sound for a new word is supposed to come from. That function is reserved for lexical rules, which allow a speaker to take the sound paired with a verb in one conflation class and use it with a new, related meaning belonging to another conflation class.

The clearest analysis of lexical rules along the lines I am proposing here comes from Rappaport and Levin's (1985) account of the locative alternation. By discussing it in some detail, I will demonstrate the empirical benefits of the theory, and my application of it to the other three alternations will be straightforward.

3.3.4.1 The Locative Alternation Consider the *into/onto* argument structure by itself, independent of any alternation. It has the thematic core "*X* moves *Y* into/onto *Z*." *X*, the agent, is the subject, following the linking rule mentioned earlier. *Y* is the thing that changes location or theme and is an affected entity or patient, and thus is the object. *Z* defines both the end of the path that *Y* moves along and the location with respect to which *Y* is situated following the motion (i.e., in the interior of, on the top of, or against the surface of). Since *to Z* means "along a path ending at *Z*," *in Z* means "at the interior of *Z*," and *into Z* means "to in *Z*," the choice of preposition must be *into*, or, by similar logic, *onto* (Jackendoff, 1983).[2]

Generally when a verb specifies motion or change, it can also specify the manner of such motion or change and some of the properties of the entity that undergoes the motion or change (Talmy, 1985), so many of the verbs that are built around this thematic core specify the manner of causation of motion of a substance to a medium or container, or the manner of motion of a substance to a medium or container. That is, the verb constrains either how the agent initiates the motion (e.g., by *spilling* versus *injecting* versus *ladling*) or in what manner the object moves (e.g., in a continuous stream, as in *pouring*, or as a mist, as in *spraying*). Note that the verbs do not have to specify how the container or surface changes as the result of putting something into or onto it. For example, if I *pour water into the glass*, the glass can be full, partially full, or even empty (if the glass leaks), but I have to cause the water to move as a cohesive stream; I cannot spray the water into the glass, use the glass to bail water out of a bathtub, let water condense into the glass, or leave the glass on a windowsill during a rainstorm.

In contrast, the argument structure containing an object and a *with*-object has the thematic core "*X* causes *Y* to change its state by means of moving *Z* to *Y*." As before, when a verb specifies a change, it can specify the manner or nature of the change or the properties of what changes. In this case, the entity corresponding to the goal of the physical motion is treated as an entity undergoing a change of state. Specifically, verbs in the conflation class corresponding to the thematic core of this argument structure specify that a surface, container, or medium undergoes a particular change resulting from the addition of material to it. The mere addition of material is not enough, and the manner in which the material moved or was caused to move is irrelevant; all that is captured in the thematic core schematization is that the state of the object is seen to be different as a result of the addition. For example, if I *fill a glass with water*, the glass must have its entire interior occupied by water, but the water could have gotten there because I poured it in, because I used the glass to bail some water out of a bathtub, because I left the glass on a windowsill during a rainstorm, and so on. Likewise, other verbs that have this argument structure, such as *adorn, blanket, impregnate, encrust, infect, riddle,* and *saturate*, specify a particular state of an object subsequent to the addition of something to it.

Once one specifies the semantics of verbs in this conflation class, their common argument structure follows from the linking rules. The causal agent is the subject. The entity that changes state as an effect of what the agent does is a theme—in the field of circumstances or states, not physical locations—so its link with the object function or direct internal argument position preserves the generalization that affected themes or patients are objects, even if it is not the theme of a change of physical location. The mapping between the *with*-object and the thing whose movement to Y changes Y's state is also nonarbitrary: *with* often signifies an instrument, as in *She cracked the egg with a hammer.* Though Rappaport and Levin argue that the *with* function is not strictly speaking an instrument in locative constructions such as *I loaded the wagon with hay*, it is easy to see that the English preposition *with* can embrace either true instruments or more generally the entity that by being moved is the means by which a state change is effected. Rappaport and Levin call it the "displaced theme"; I will informally call it the "state-changer." The label is irrelevant; we can simply assume that there is a linking rule that maps the Z in "X changes Y by means of moving Z to it" onto the oblique function or indirect internal argument, and a corresponding lexical entry for the preposition *with* that makes it and no other preposition compatible with this role.

As mentioned, the holism requirement generally applies to these verbs, whether or not they are related to *into/onto* locatives: the entire object, and not just a part of it, must be completely covered, filled, or saturated with the material. Rappaport and Levin suggest that the holism effect is actually an epiphenomenon of the fact that the verb specifies a change of state. They point out that, taken literally, the effect does not invariably hold: one can say *The vandal sprayed the statue with paint* even if there is only a dab of paint on the statue. The reason is that the status of the statue as an object of beauty changes with even a single blemish on it. Similarly, they point out that you can load a wagon with a single box if a single box is normally considered to be the standard load for the wagon (an observation they attribute to Richard J. Carter). Thus the holism requirement is really just a state-change requirement as it applies to ordinary surfaces or containers: unless they are entirely covered or filled, there is no pragmatic sense in which they can be said to have changed state.

There may be an even deeper reason that affecting something and affecting all of it are so closely tied. Recall that in *throw the paint onto the wall*, paint = theme, wall = location; whereas in *coat the wall with paint*, wall = theme, paint = instrument/state-changer. Talmy (1983) offers an interesting generalization about the intuitive geometric systems in which languages specify the spatial relations that are encoded in their grammars. Most typically, a theme is conceived as a pointlike or dimensionless entity and is located with respect to a place defined by a reference object. The reference object, unlike the theme, is spatially differentiated, and places on it are defined with respect to its dimensionality, orientation, shape, aspect ratio, or endpoints. For example, the English phrases *on the cup*, *under the cup*, and *in the cup* pick out certain aspects of the geometry of the cup as relevant, such as the top or bottom of its vertical dimension or its interior region (and hence a preposition like *in* is incompatible with objects whose geometry lacks the crucial geometric property, e.g., **in the sheet of wood*). However the prepositions are completely nonspecific about the geometric properties of the theme object that is in, on, or under the cup. If the schematization of space and objects underlying spatial relations is carried over to abstract themes and locations, as the Thematic Relations Hypothesis would predict, then the promotion of *wall* to theme of a state change entails that it will be interpreted as a pointlike entity, without differentiation of its internal parts or geometry. The expression *paint the wall* is saying something about the surface conceived of as an undifferentiated whole; if paint is adhering to it, then the unmarked interpretation is that it is adhering to all of it.[3]

Given all these proposals, the locative alternation can now be stated simply: it is a rule that takes a verb containing in its semantic structure the core "X causes Y to move into/onto Z," and converts it into a new verb whose semantic structure contains the core "X causes Z to change state by means of moving Y into/onto it." Basically, it is a gestalt shift: one can interpret *loading* as moving a theme (e.g., hay) to a location (e.g., a wagon), but one can also interpret the same act in terms of changing the state of a theme (the wagon), in this case from empty to full, by means of moving something (the hay) into it. The difference in argument structure follows from the linking rules: in the old verb, the moving thing was the theme and hence was linked to direct object; in the new verb, the location is the theme (of a state change) and hence is linked to object. The argument not linked to object gets linked to an oblique function or position by virtue of other linking rules in combination with lexical entries for specific prepositions. The holism requirement follows from the cognitive content of the notion of "theme" or located entity, which is generally construed as an undifferentiated point. Thus, the two different construals of the same event in this gestalt shift, and the two different argument structures, are closely linked: loading hay into a wagon is something that happens to hay; loading a wagon with hay is something that happens to a wagon. A similar account can be provided for the intransitive variants, such as *Bees swarmed in the garden* versus *The garden swarmed with bees*, where the garden is a theme and hence liable to a holistic interpretation only in the second sentence.

The *constraints* or *criteria* governing the locative alternation stem, to a first approximation, from the ability of a predicate to support this gestalt shift. What is special about an alternating verb is that it specifies the motion of an object or substance (and generally its manner of motion), making it eligible for the *into/onto* construction, and that this kind of motion predictably causes an effect on the surface that receives the substance. For example, when a liquid is *sprayed*, it is sent in a mist or fine droplets. However, as a result of causing such movement, a surface to which it moves predictably has an even coat of deposited liquid adhering to it. This predictability is what is crucial: the *with* form requires a specific change of state, and the meaning of a verb like *spray* allows the speaker to predict exactly what that state change is. More generally, caused motion of a substance in the direction of a particular object and in a particular spatial configuration will result in the substance being deposited in or on the object in a characteristic way, changing its state. This provides part of the explanation for why the alternation does not extend to verbs of pure manner of motion such as *pour*, or to verbs of force exertion (*push, drag, pull, tug, yank*) or verbs of positioning (*lay, place, position, put*): there is no way to predict on the basis of the verb meaning alone what the effect on the goal argument will be. Conversely, this account helps to explain why verbs of pure effect, such as *fill*, which do not specify any specific kind of motion of a theme, cannot take the *into/onto* form.

Rappaport and Levin provide a strong piece of independent evidence for this kind of account. For some speakers it is possible to add the particle *full* to *pour* which introduces a specification how the container is affected: *I poured the glass full*. Interestingly, the addition immediately qualifies *pour* to participate in the locative alternation: *I poured the glass full with water*.

The general idea is summarized in (3.15).

(3.15)

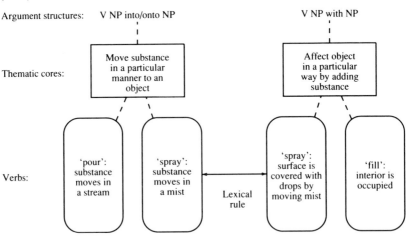

I am not claiming that this view predicts the constraints on the alternation exactly: it would take some semantic gymnastics, for example, to show that *spray* inevitably yields a predictable effect on a surface whereas *dribble* never does. But I do claim that this is the principle behind the fact that criteria exist and take the kinds of forms that they do; the remaining piece of the puzzle, which delineates the alternating and nonalternating verbs more precisely, will be presented in section 4.4.2 and more formally in section 5.6.3.

A closely parallel account can be given of the alternation that involves removing something from something else, as in *I emptied garbage from the bag / I emptied the bag of garbage.* The argument structure that includes an object and a *from*-object has the thematic core "*X* causes *Y* to go away from *Z*," as in *John grabbed the salt shaker from the table,* involving familiar linking rules plus a lexical entry for *from* that specifies a source role (cf. *The boy ran from the dog*). The argument structure incorporating an object and an *of*-object has the thematic core "*X* causes *Y* to change state by means of taking *Z* away from *Y*," as in *John cleared the table of dishes.* The preposition *of* might be used for various kinds of themes by default, serving as the "empty" preposition in English which jumps into action when a preposition is syntactically necessary but when no specialized role is involved. (A familiar example can be seen with argument-taking nouns and adjectives, which are forbidden to have syntactic objects: **Their destruction the city / Their destruction of the city.*) Alternatively, *of* may have a more specialized entry complementary to *with*, indicating state change by subtraction; sometimes this is called the abstrument role (Dowty, 1987).

Verbs that appear in the *from* variant can specify an instrument of removal such as *brush, comb, hose,* or *mop,* a manner of causation of removal such as *rub, rinse, scrub,* or *wipe,* or the effect of physical removal, such as *clean, cleanse, empty, strip, clear,* or *drain.* However, only verbs in the latter class, which specify the effect of removal, can appear in the *of*-object form: *I emptied / *wiped the can of water.* (Unlike the *into/with* version of the alternation, however, the verbs are not restricted from appearing in container-oriented forms altogether; the restriction is only against the container-oriented form that includes the oblique argument. Thus one can still say *I wiped / rubbed / rinsed the can.*) Again, if a particle adds an effect component of meaning to one of the verbs in the nonalternating classes, the verb-particle combination can take the *of* form: *I shoveled the walk clear of snow; They wiped the table clean of dirt.*

In sum, the behavior of locative verbs supports a conception of argument structure alternations as operations that take a verb in one conflation class, serving as the thematic core of one kind of argument structure, and create a new verb, sharing the same root but having an altered semantic representation that places it in a different conflation class serving as the thematic core of a different argument structure. The argument structures themselves are predictable from general linking rules. Rappaport and Levin (1985) summarize the advantages of this kind of theory applied to the locative alternation by pointing out that it provides answers to four questions that at first glance seem independent of one another. First, why does the meaning of a verb change when it assumes a new argument structure in the locative alternation? Because the rule altering the verb directly changes its semantic structure; specifically, it changes which argument serves as the theme. Second, why is the meaning of the verb in one argument structure so closely related to the new meaning of the verb in the other argument structure? Because the first meaning—move Z to Y—is incorporated as part of the second meaning—change Y's state by moving Z to Y. Third, why do the two argument structures contain a grammatical object, linked to different entities in the two forms, and either an *into/onto* or a *with* oblique object, rather than any of the numerous other ways that arguments could link with grammatical roles? Because there is a general linking rule that makes the theme the object, whether it is a theme of a location change or a theme of a state change, and there are other linking rules and lexical entries that assign the other argument to its appropriate preposition. Fourth, why are lexical rules choosy? Because the semantic change effected by the rule requires the specification of information—a specific kind of state change—that can be predicted from the the intrinsic meaning of some verbs but not others.

Now let us see if we can gain these same advantages by applying the theory to the other alternations under consideration.

3.3.4.2   The Dative Alternation   The dative alternation embraces two alternations, one involving the preposition *to*, one involving *for*. The alternation with *to* can be seen as an operation that takes a verb with a semantic structure containing "X causes Y to go to Z" and converts it to a verb containing a structure "X causes Z to have Y." Linking rules, primarily the one that links the theme or patient to the object position, effect the difference in syntactic argument structures. In one case, the entity being caused to move becomes the object; in the other, the entity caused to gain possession becomes the object. In both cases, more specific linking rules take care of the unlinked argument. As mentioned, evidence for the two thematic cores comes from nonalternating verbs: *She carried the letter to the mailbox* shows that "X causes Y to go to Z" is a possible substructure of an English verb and that such a verb is linked to a transitive argument structure incorporating a *to*-object; *They charged him five dollars* shows that "X causes Z to have Y" is a possible substructure of an English verb definition (in this case, causing someone *not* to have something), which is mapped onto the double-object form.

As in the locative alternation, there is often a change of interpretation accompanying the change of argument structure; if both alternations are a result of changes in semantic structure, such changes are to be predicted. Because the possessor in the double-object form is the patient or theme (I distinguish these later) rather than the goal, it should be interpreted as being affected by the transaction rather than simply being its target. This accounts for the contrast between *teaching French to the students*, possibly with no effect, and *teaching the students French*, with success, at least on the most salient reading (Green, 1974). *I threw the ball to John* can mean that John is merely the spatial target (possibly asleep or dead), analogous to *I threw the ball to the target*, but *I threw John the ball* entails that he was meant to receive it and invites the inference that he did. Similarly, it would be odd to say *I told John the news* if he were deaf or dead, whereas *I told the news to John* may be a bit less anomalous in those circumstances. A related effect noted by Green is that the recipient, when it is the object of the double-object form, is entailed to exist. For example, *Juanita told her sorrows to God* would come more easily out of the mouth of an atheist than *Juanita told God her sorrows*.

Richard Oehrle (1977), in a review of Green's book, expresses doubt about some of these judgments. He suggests that the following sentences do not seem to be contradictory: *I read him the figures, but when I looked up, he was gone*, or *When I took him his mail, I found that he had disappeared*. However, most people find these sentences somewhat odd, and in an unpublished paper coauthored with Haj Ross (Oehrle and Ross, n.d.), Oehrle himself marks the sentence *Jim threw the catcher the ball, but a bird got in the way* as being ungrammatical, just as Green predicted. Nonetheless, Oehrle may be right that the intuition of a semantic change can be somewhat weak, especially in sentences like *I gave a book to John / I gave John a book* or *I told a story to my children / I told my children a story*. I suspect that it is because the meanings of those verbs inherently specify change of possession: *give* cannot be used to mean the physical motion of an object (*He *gave / threw a book onto the table*); *tell* can be used only if there is a comprehending listener who can extract the content of the speech (*He *?told/mumbled the lesson to the blackboard*; in this example *told* is natural only on an intentionally ironic reading). In such cases, the dative shift does not *add* the notion of cause-to-change-possession to a verb meaning; it rearranges the verb meaning to make the cause-to-change-possession component apply to the possessor as affected entity. Thus for these verbs the meaning change accompanying dativization is logically vacuous: causing Y to go into the possession of Z is barely different from causing Z to possess Y. It is not psychologically vacuous, however, as it does have discourse consequences, allowing the speaker to focus either on what is done to the possessor or on what is done to the possession (Erteschik-Shir, 1979).

By the way, it should not be surprising that whether or not an argument is playing the role of theme affects its discourse properties. After all, a theme is usually defined as an entity in a location or state or changing its location or state. But *all* objects are in *some* location or state; when an object plays the role of theme, it must be because the speaker is *asserting* or predicating a particular location or state of the object. Such highlighting or focusing, of course, is closely tied to discourse considerations. (See Hopper and Thompson, 1980, for discussion.)

Another piece of evidence showing that the possessor in the double-object construction is represented as a patient or theme is the existence of double-object idioms whose first objects have an identical semantic role to the sole object of nonidiomatic transitive verbs. The role of *John* in *give John a kiss* is the same as his role in *kiss John*; likewise for *give John a punch* / *punch John*, *give John a bath* / *bathe John*, and so on (Green, 1974).

Now that we have characterized the differences between the prepositional and double-object forms, we can see how those differences interact with the verbs in either class that the dative rule might try to reassign to the other. Generally, verbs can alternate only if they signify a transfer of an object that can result in its being possessed. The inadmissibility of **She carried the mailbox a letter* stems from the inability of the action to result in the mailbox possessing anything. Conversely, the inadmissibility of **They spared that punishment to the policeman* stems from the fact that the verb is asserting that the punishment does *not* go to the policeman, contrary to what the *to*-structure would require.

The *for*-dative alternation can be treated similarly. Say that transitive argument structures containing *for*-objects are projected from verbs containing the conflation "*X* acts on *Y* for the benefit of *Z*." Beneficiaries would be linked to oblique objects (indirect internal arguments); the preposition *for* is the only preposition whose semantic structure specifies a benefactive relation. Verbs taking the *for*-dative structure will alternate only if the agent, as a result of affecting the patient in the manner specified by the verb, can cause the beneficiary to possess the patient.[4] Verbs specifying acts of creation (*bake, sew, cook, make*, etc.) dativize because creating something is a means of causing someone to possess it; likewise, verbs of obtaining (*get, buy, find*, etc.) can dativize because one person's obtaining a thing is a means of causing some other person to get it. However, verbs that simply convey acts done for the benefit of a third party, without allowing one to predict the way in which the act can result in that party's coming to possess the affected object, can appear in the *for* prepositional form but not the double-object form (e.g., *I drove his car for him* / **I drove him his car*).

As in the discussion of the locative alternation, these considerations do not give precise sufficient conditions for a verb to dativize. They do give necessary conditions, however, and provide an explanation for the sufficient conditions that I will discuss in section 4.4.1 (also in section 5.6.1).

3.3.4.3 The Causative Alternation The causative (or "anticausative") alternation involves two argument structures: an intransitive and a transitive. Let us assume that the principal thematic core giving rise to the transitive argument structure is "*X* acts on *Y*." Many action verbs, for example, contain this core, such as *hit* in *I hit the wall*. *Y*, the second argument of "act-on," is traditionally referred to as the patient, and I would like to distinguish that role from the role of theme, the first argument of "go" or "be" (see also Jackendoff, 1987a, and Rappaport and Levin, 1988, for arguments that they should be distinguished). A patient is acted or impinged upon or inherently involved in an action performed by an agent but does not necessarily undergo a specified change. Of course, in real life a patient may undergo a change of state or location, but if it does, the verb does not care what that change is (e.g., the wall could shatter, fall over, or tumble down a hill, and the verb *hit* would be equally appropriate). However, the patient must be inherently involved in or affected by the action, playing a role in defining what the action consists of. For example, moving one's hand to within a fraction of an inch of the wall, even if the accompanying wind or static electricity causes the wall to fall over, would not count as *hitting the wall*, because the kind of motion or act denoted by hitting is inherently defined as terminating in contact with some patient. Similarly, the patient has a role in temporally delineating the event referred to by the verb; the hitting is over when the patient is contacted (see Dowty, 1987; Tenny, 1988). A theme, on the other hand, is predicated to be in a location or state or to undergo a change of location or state, whether or not it was caused by an agent. For example, if *a bug dies* (*bug* = theme), it is definitely dead, but it could have become so at the hands of an exterminator or because of old age. Some verbs specify arguments that are both patients and themes: when I *cut* an apple, the apple must have a cut in it, and the cut must have been effected by my acting on it in a certain way (viz., by my moving an object into contact with it; see B. Levin, 1985; Hale and Keyser, 1986, 1987). As we shall see in section 4.2, this purely semantic distinction, involving different entailments, has grammatical consequences.

A verb that specifies an argument that is both a patient and a theme, such as *cut, chip, shatter*, or *kill*, is a causative verb. The agent, by acting on a patient, causes it to change state or location. An elegant way of dealing with the directness condition on causatives is to derive it from the thematic roles assumed by the causee. Assume that the notion of "acting on" that defines the role of patient inherently means "directly act on" (this is independently motivated by the phenomena in example 3.7 in section 3.2.2 and by the larger set of phenomena discussed by Hopper and Thompson, 1980). Then the directness constraint on lexical causatives derives from the fact that in transitive verbs in English, the causee is a patient of the action denoted by the verb as well as a theme; in the periphrastic locution involving an intransitive verb (*cause to die; cause to shatter*), the causee is only a theme. Thus the directness constraint on interpretation would fall out of the inherent definition of the thematic role of patient in the same way as the holistic constraint on the interpretation of locatives falls out of the definition of the thematic role of theme—and the premise that English has a conflation class "*X* acts on *Y* (= patient)" but no conflation class "*X* acts, causing *Y* (= theme) to move or change" which could serve as a thematic core for transitive verbs lacking patients. In other languages, such semantic conflations seem to be possible, as there are rules yielding indirect lexical causatives as well as rules yielding direct lexical causatives, often differentiated by alternative suffixes on the verb (e.g., in Hebrew, Berman, 1982; and in Hindi, Saksena, 1982). However, when languages have both a lexical and a periphrastic or "analytic" causative, the lexical causative is generally the one signifying direct causation (Shibatani, 1976; Comrie, 1985). This suggests that the conflation of an agent and a patient/theme is more natural as a thematic core than the conflation of an agent and a pure theme.

The cognitive content of thematic roles, such as the directness interpretation accompanying the role of patient, must be treated with some subtlety. Viewed with a sufficiently sharp microscope, there is no such thing as direct causation: when I cut an apple, I first decide to do it, then send neural impulses to my arm and hand, which cause the muscles to contract, causing the hand to move, causing the knife to move, causing the knife to contact the surface of the apple, causing the surface to rupture, and so on. Nonetheless, there is a clear sense in which this causation differs from paying a servant to cut an apple. When describing an event, one always chooses a grain size below which events are treated as invisible or irrelevant. For physical actions initiated by a person, muscular events and most intervening physical events are below the grain size, so that you can *break a window* with your fist or by hitting a long fly ball, but the intervention of another agent, such as a jittery window-installer, is seen as interpolating an intermediary of the same grain as the original agent. That is why you can *cause the window to break* by shouting "boo," but you ordinarily wouldn't call that *breaking a window*. However, many verbs can be extended to yield a much more macroscopic perspective, such as in *Man reaches the moon* or *Napoleon invades Russia*. When a verb with a causative component is used at that scale, such as in *Nixon bombed Cambodia* or *John, the president of United Fruit, grows bananas in Guatemala*, the directness condition applies at that scale. These sentences are permissible despite the very long chain of intervening causal links because the links are not comparable in grain size to the decision-making or responsibility-assuming that is predicated of the subject. For that reason it would still be unusual to say that *The National Security Council bombed Cambodia* just because it persuaded Nixon to do so (likewise, *The voters of every state but Massachusetts bombed Cambodia*) or that *Harvard grows bananas* just because the university holds stock in United Fruit.

Let us turn to intransitives. The intransitive argument structure has at least two distinct thematic cores paired with it: one underlying unergative verbs, where X performs some action or activity (e.g., *run, walk, sleep, eat, breathe, cry, dance*), and one underlying unaccusative verbs, where X exists in or undergoes some change of location or state (e.g., *bounce, slide, melt, open*). The definitions of the unergative verbs usually imply that the proximal instigation or causation of the act is due to some internal mechanism, force, or quality; thus, as agentlike entities, they qualify to be subjects. The subjects of unaccusative verbs are generally themes. They are not specified to be in a state or location as the necessary result of any cause; something can open or break or slide all of a sudden and for no apparent reason.

As discussed in sections 1.4.5.1 and 3.3.1, theories of grammar differ as to why both the theme argument of unaccusative verbs and the agent or actor argument of unergative verbs are mapped onto the surface subject position. For unaccusative verbs, GB posits movement from the underlying object position to an empty subject position. L. Levin's version of LFG posits that the theme is first mapped onto a class of functions that is uncommitted to either subject or object, which is then mapped onto subject if that role has not already been assigned. Relational Grammar posits that the theme is mapped onto the object relations in an underlying stratum of grammatical relations and promoted to the subject relation in a superficial one. The attention to unaccusativity within all the major frameworks stems from a recognition that there are widespread grammatical consequences of the unaccusative/unergative distinction, requiring that the distinction be captured in some grammatical representation. One example is the possibility of "impersonal" passivization in Dutch: you can say *Er wordt hier door de jonge lui veel gedanst*, "It is danced here a lot by the young people," but not **Er werd door de kinderen in Amsterdam gebleven*, "It was remained in Amsterdam by the young people." Another is auxiliary selection in Italian: unaccusatives take *essere*, "to be," as in *Giovanni è arrivato*, "Giovanni is arrived," whereas unergatives take *avere*, "to have," as in *Giovanni ha telefonato*, "Giovanni has telephoned." A third example is from English: intransitives can be converted into adjectival passives in English only if they are unaccusative: *wilted lettuce, a fallen leaf, *a run man, *a coughed patient*. If all of these phenomena can be derived as automatic general consequences of an argument's being in direct object position, the GB-style accounts whereby they are initially in direct object position is mandated. If they can be derived directly from an argument's thematic status as theme in a structure lacking an agent, versus agent in a structure lacking a patient, no difference in a purely *syntactic* representation is needed. Grimshaw (1987) points out that not all of the reflexes of the unaccusative/unergative distinction coincide in every language; she suggests that each of the syntactic differences may be caused by different properties of the various verbs (see also Grimshaw, in press; Kiparsky, 1987). This would be consistent with the spirit of the current theory, whereby the criteria that delineate argument structure alternations are stated in lexicosemantic structure, not in argument structure itself.

Among the four alternations I discuss in detail, the causative alternation is the one that is most clearly semantic, as it adds an argument with a specific semantic role, namely that of causal agent. Specifically, the theme argument of an intransitive predicate is assigned the additional role of being the patient of an act, and a new argument, the agent of that act, is added: "*X* goes to a location or state" is converted to "*Y* acts on *X*, causing *X* to go to a location or state." The theme is reconstrued as undergoing a change as the result of being a patient, that is, as the result of being acted on by some agent. The argument structure follows directly from the linking rules that map agent to subject or external argument and patient to object or direct internal argument. The directness interpretation falls out of the additional role assigned to the theme, namely patient. Arguments that were not themes to begin with because they act voluntarily or as a result of causes internal to themselves, rather than passively changing, such as agents of unergative intransitives like *talk*, do not submit to the rule. The presence of an internal cause implies that any external causal entity cannot effect the causation directly; the causation is always mediated by the internal mechanism or force. Arguments that are both themes of motion and agents of unergative intransitives, such as *jog* (where a change of location takes place as well as an action), also do not submit to the rule; again there is no way to act on an agentive potential jogger causing him to jog in the same sense that one can directly act on a window causing it to break.

As I emphasized when discussing the other alternations, this is not meant to be a sufficient condition for the possibility of a verb's alternating, only a necessary one, and one that supplies part of the explanation for the sufficient conditions I will supply in in section 4.4.3 (see also section 5.6.2). There are also some subsidiary alternations that appear to violate the "theme —> patient and theme" rule I have been proposing, including *John drove / I drove John* and *Bill cheered up / I cheered up Bill*; I will also defer discussing these till later.

There are cases that do not conform at all to my depiction of the causative alternation, but one can show that this is because they simply have nothing to do with productive causativization. *Clemens walked the batter*, for example, is surely an isolated verb that is learned by positive evidence; no fan or announcer says *Clemens singled / doubled / tripled / homered / flied out / grounded out / popped out the batter. Similarly, He burped the baby and Dr. Smith bled the patient are freestanding items: *He vomited / ate / slept / cried / cooed the baby; *Dr. Smith coughed / vomited / urinated / spat the patient. These are the kinds of examples that have motivated a putative constraint of stereotypy of causation: one walks a batter only by throwing four balls, one burps a baby by patting it on the back; bleeding a patient was a common locution mainly when causing to bleed was a standard medical procedure (Gergely and Bever, 1986). Therefore it is probably not accurate to say that a stereotypy condition applies to the causative alternation; rather, it applies quite generally to the coining of isolated words. Surely words cannot be created whose meanings are based on knowledge possessed only by a single speaker; no one would understand him (Clark and Clark, 1978). And as we have seen from (2.16), productive causativization does not conform to any obvious stereotypy-of-manner requirement.

3.3.4.4   The Active-Passive Relation   As I mentioned in section 3.3.1, the passive is different in two ways from the other alternations I discuss in detail: it involves a morphological change, and its range of application is far greater. I will discuss the significance of these differences in detail in section 4.4.4, but here I want to show that the theory that argument structures are projections of thematic cores can be applied fruitfully to the passive as well. The basic motivation is the same as for the other cases. Not all transitive verbs passivize (there is "passive resistance," as Robin Lakoff, 1971, put it).   Since the verbs that submit to passivization are delineated by semantic criteria, at least one part of the process producing passives must be an operation on semantic structure (see also L. Levin, 1985, who makes a similar point). That is, the verbwise sensitivity of the passive can be explained by an interaction between the inherent lexical semantics of verbs and a particular semantic change required by the passive rule.

Passivization changes the structure of transitive verbs. This means that there are two ways that one could try to capture the semantic choosiness of the passive. First, one could say that passivization is a purely syntactic operation that applies to any transitive verb, but not all verbs that appear to be transitive really are transitive. Thus the postverbal arguments of unpassivizable verbs like cost and have would not really be direct objects, appearances to the contrary notwithstanding; they might, for example, be the second object of an underlying double-object structure from which the first object has been moved into surface subject position. In that case, the semantic constraints on passivization would really be semantic constraints on what kinds of arguments can be linked to object position. Unpassivizable verbs would be those with an argument that is linked to a bare postverbal NP that is not a genuine direct object or direct internal argument; the passive rule, which requires a genuine direct object, would be blocked. The second possibility is that verbs that look transitive really are transitive, and that passivization is sensitive to verb semantics. It is difficult to tell these hypotheses apart because the traditional test of objecthood in English is passivizability itself. Because there are no generally accepted tests that distinguish "fake" transitive verbs from "real" ones, and to maintain consistency with the other alternations, I treat constraints on passivizable verbs as constraints on the passive rule itself. This is not an iron-clad tenet of the theory, however; if it can be shown on independent grounds that all unpassivizable verbs are not genuinely transitive and vice-versa, the semantic filter I will argue for can be removed from the passive rule and placed in the linking rule that creates the verbs that look transitive but aren't. The nature of the solution to Baker's paradox as it applies to passivization would remain unchanged.

What are the properties of the passive surface structure, independent of the alternation that produces the verb in it? Few or no verbs exist only in the passive. Some putative examples, such as *rumor* in *John is rumored to be a Communist/ *They rumored John to be a Communist*, are probably adjectives, and it is not clear what to make of contrasts where the passive sounds more natural than the active, such as *My mother was twenty when I was born* versus *My mother was twenty when she bore me* (Bolinger, 1977a). In any case we can consider the thematic concomitants of the surface expression of the passive construction's two arguments, the subject of *be* and the object of *by*. Jackendoff (1983) argues that *be* is not a meaningless tense-carrier but a predicate expressing the "location" of a theme, either in physical space (*John is in the room*) or in one of the abstract "spaces" that borrow the vocabulary of physical space, such as identification (*Clark Kent is Superman*), possession (*This is mine*), or circumstance (*John is sick*). This suggests that the subject of the passive participle may be a kind of theme, presumably a theme of circumstance. That is, *John was hit* means John was in the circumstance of someone's having hit him.[5] This would be consistent with the "predication effect" of passivization noted in section 3.2.3. Although I have stated this hypothesis in terms of the underlying object's being directly assigned to the surface subject, it can also be stated in GB terms: the circumstantial theme role can be linked to an internal argument of a predicate that does not have an external argument; the internal argument will generally end up as the surface subject of simple clauses.

The second argument of the passive is prototypically the object of *by*, which signifies an agentlike role in English fairly generally, not just in passives: *This painting is by Monet; No tomfoolery by students will be tolerated; Bribe-taking by politicians will be severely punished; Get your child "Tony the Pony" by Marx!* It is not literally an agent role because it doesn't make much sense to talk about the "agent of a pony" or the "agent of a painting"; the more general notion is of a "responsible entity" or "author." The centrality of this argument role in the verbal passive is underlined by the interpretation of short passives like *John was hit*. Despite the absence of a *by*-phrase, the agent role in short passives is a well-defined "implicit argument" (Keyser and Roeper, 1984). For example, the sentence *The ship was sunk* entails that there was some agent or force that sunk the ship; in the unaccusative counterpart *The ship sank*, no such implication exists. There could have been no apparent reason, or it could have been a long-term consequence of a lack of preventive maintenance. Moreover, purposive adjuncts, which require agentive events to control them, can occur with short passives: *The ship was sunk to collect the insurance* (cf. **The ship sank to collect the insurance*; see also Lasnik, 1984). Thus a crucial difference between the passive and other intransitive argument structures with theme subjects is that the passive forces an interpretation whereby the existence of an agentlike argument or party responsible for the circumstance predicated of the theme is asserted. We can call this the "agency effect." It is now necessary to find a thematic core for passive argument structures out of which should fall the agency effect and the predication effect, just as the directness effect, the holistic effect, and the possessor effect fell out of the thematic cores for the transitive causative, the *with*-locative, and the double-object dative.

Imagine that the following thematic core is created by a passive rule: X is in the circumstance characterized by Y's acting on it (more generally, the circumstance for which Y is responsible; for now let me use the term "agent" to refer to this general sense of causal efficacy and "patient" to refer to the entity that it affects or defines the state of). That is, X is a theme in a semantic field corresponding to being in various states or circumstances; the position in that field that X occupies (in other words, the circumstance that John is now in) corresponds to X's being a patient and Y's being an agent. The rule creating this thematic core would have as its primary operation the suppression or demotion of the agent argument (see Zubizaretta, 1987), from the topmost level of the semantic structure of the verb to an embedded position in the definition of the circumstance predicated of the other argument. With no agent role defined, linking rules would map the theme onto the subject function (LFG), or onto the internal argument position, from which it would be moved to subject position (GB). Assume also that semantic structures can specify arguments that are "implicit," that is, not "open" or linkable to grammatical functions. An implicit argument has no overt syntactic realization but is still defined, ensuring that it is entailed to exist when the sentence is interpreted semantically and that it can play various grammatical roles such as defining the controller of certain adjuncts. Full passives would be the same as short passives except that the agent argument in semantic structure would be marked as being "open"; a phrase containing *by* would be linked to it because the dictionary entry of *by* and of no other preposition defines a quasi-agentive role for it.

As mentioned, if the subject of a passive is being redefined as a kind of theme, then the predication effect or difference in interpretation between *Beavers build dams* and *Dams are built by beavers* would follow. As a consequence, verbs whose objects cannot be interpreted as themes should not passivize. This is compatible with a number of types of nonpassivizability (see, Anderson, 1977, and Bolinger, 1977a, for similar analyses of constraints on the passive). For example, idioms are often cited as an example of the insensitivity of the passive to semantic factors, because the chunks of idioms are taken to be meaningless. But as Gazdar et al. (1985) point out, it is not that the chunks of all idioms are utterly meaningless; it's just that the meaning of a chunk cannot be predicted from the meaning of the same words in isolation or in other phrases. It has been widely noted that the easier it is to conceive of a possible or metaphorical meaning for an idiom chunk, the more passivizable that chunk is (Fiengo, 1977; Gazdar, et al. 1985; Wasow, Sag, and Nunberg, 1983). Thus in *Tabs were kept on subversives* and *The hatchet was finally buried*, *tabs* can be interpreted as "surveillance measures" and *the hatchet* as "a dispute," of which one can predicate various properties or changes. However, in **The bucket was kicked* or **The bullet was bitten*, the idiom chunks lack such themes. Similarly, cognate or "fake" objects are unpassivizable, as in **A hearty laugh was laughed; *A horrible death was died*.

The requirement that the state predicated of the theme be defined in terms of the theme's being a quasi-patient of some agent or agentlike responsible party would, naturally, allow all actional verbs to passivize. This would include the alternating forms of verbs in which the patient can be alternatively construed as the entity caused to undergo a location change (*The book was handed to John; The hay was loaded into the wagon*) and as the entity caused to undergo a possessional or physical state change (*John was handed a book; The wagon was loaded with hay*). With a suitably abstract characterization of agents and patients motivated by an extension of the Thematic Relations Hypothesis (to be discussed in the next chapter), passivization would be compatible with many abstract predicates in which ideas or situations are asserted to cause or be responsible for one another, such as *The horror of the last war justified the new treaty / The new treaty was justified by the horror of the last war*, which is analogous to the obviously agentive counterparts *John justified the new treaty / The new treaty was justified by John*.

Another manifestation of the agency effect can be seen in a phenomenon noted by Perlmutter and Postal (1984): that prepositional passives (e.g., *This bed has been slept in*) are acceptable with unergative verbs, as in (3.16a), but not with unaccusative verbs, as in (3.16b).

(3.16) (a)   The bed was slept in by the Shah.
             The package was stepped on by a camel.

       (b)   *The package was accumulated on by dust.
             *The oven was melted in by an ice cube.

If unergatives involve an actor whereas unaccusatives involve only a theme, the agency effect would be compatible with the former but not the latter. An additional pragmatic factor governing prepositional passives has been noted by Bolinger (1977a) and Davison (1980): they are most acceptable when the prepositional object is seen as being affected in some way by virtue of an agent's having acted upon it, either physically, as in *This bed has been slept in* (it's a mess); *This bridge has been driven on* (its roadway is damaged), or in terms of status or interest value, as in *This bed has been slept in by George Washington* (it's special) and *This bridge has been flown under* (proving how high it is). When the theme/patient analysis is unavailable, as in the examples in (3.17), passivization is impossible.

(3.17) John ran out during the symphony. / *The symphony was run out during by Bob.
       We talked in the park. / ?*The park was talked in by us.
       They drank after the rugby game. / *The rugby game was drunk after.
       We walked to the store. / *The store was walked to by us.

Because the passive argument structure expresses an asymmetrical relation in which the passive subject is in the circumstance characterized by being acted upon by an agent, any verb for which there is no way of construing one entity as an agent and another as a patient should fail to undergo passivization. This would account for the unpassivizability of "symmetrical predicates" like *resemble* (e.g., *Gene is resembled by Tom; *Di was married by Charles; *Four is equaled by two plus two*). Likewise, transitive verbs of pure spatial relations (*contain, lack, fit,* and the static spatial sense of *touch*) and the transitive verb of pure possession *have*, with no possible sense of patienthood that could be predicated of a theme, would be incompatible with the thematic core that the passive argument structure is a projection of. Similarly, for measure verbs, such as in *Five hours were lasted by the party*, there is no way to think of five hours as being in any sort of circumstance or of the party as doing anything to it. Though I will have to give alternative analyses to many of the phenomena that Jackendoff (1972) tried to explain with the Thematic Hierarchy Condition, the general spirit of the THC is that in the passive, the *by*-object should be more agentive (or at least, not less agentive) than the surface subject. This is a powerful constraint on children's passivization of newly learned verbs, and it is closely related to the current proposal, in which the passive is constrained to have its surface subject be a theme in a circumstance characterized by the action of an agent, expressed as a *by*-object (Pinker, Lebeaux, and Frost, 1987).

There is, then, a relationship between the syntactic form of the passive, the change of interpretation that accompanies passivization, and the patterns of verbwise selectivity of the passive. Three questions are still open—what is the exact change effected by the passive rule, why are there semantically similar pairs of verbs that differ in passivizability, and why does the passive appear to apply with fewer restrictions than the other alternations?—and they will be discussed in sections 4.4.4, 4.5, and 5.6.4.

3.4   On Universality

I have tried to show that semantic criteria on argument structure alternations are not odd little conditions tacked onto syntactic rules, but manifestations of general principles of how predicates may be composed out of thematic elements and how arguments are mapped onto thematic roles. If so, we might expect to see the same kinds of constraints operating on the same kinds of rules in other languages. This was not predicted by the earlier view (e.g., Mazurkewich and White, 1984; Pinker, 1984), in which the criteria were simply abstracted from a database of alternating verbs in the language, learned individually. Nor is it an inevitable consequence of the current theory; each language could have its own special linking rules, learned anew by each child, and the lexical rules in the language could display patterns of itemwise selectivity that were systematic and predictable within that language but not replicated in others. However, the theory would obviously be more interesting if it made stronger predictions about other languages and about the innate proclivities of the child.

In many theories, linking rules of some sort are assumed to be universal (see, e.g., Perlmutter and Rosen, 1984), and there is considerable evidence for this position. Keenan (1976) reviews cross-linguistic research showing that agents and causal forces are universally encoded as subjects, at least in each language's "basic sentences." He also shows that an entity of which something is predicated is encoded as subject when there is no agent. Hopper and Thompson (1980) review evidence for a close association across languages between grammatical objects and the argument that is acted upon and caused to undergo a change. Dryer (1986) reviews a diverse sample of languages with ditransitive constructions and notes that the second object is notionally a "patient/theme," generally nonhuman, in the context of a first object that is a "goal/beneficiary," generally human. Thus rules that link agent to subject, theme in a noncausative verb to subject, patient to object, theme of a causative verb to object, and theme of a semantically ditransitive verb with a goal/beneficiary argument to second object seem to be widely applicable across the world's languages.[6] I am not aware of analogous surveys for oblique or indirect arguments, but most of the language-particular properties of prepositions and oblique case markers can be factored out of any linking rule for oblique arguments and localized in the lexical entries for those individual morphemes. Thus it is probably possible to define linking rules for obliqueness itself that are likely to be universal; in chapter 5 I suggest two.

To the extent that the linking rules I have proposed are found in other languages, the argument structures they use should be paired with verbs having similar kinds of thematic cores to those we find in English. Furthermore, lexical rules that map between the same pairs of argument structures should be subject to the same kinds of constraints as those discussed in this chapter. Thus the new theory (augmented by assumptions about the universality of linking rules) makes a very strong prediction that the kinds of constraints I have discussed in this chapter should show tendencies toward universality. Either the criteria should be universal accompaniments of homologous rules (to the extent that they can be identified across languages) or there should at least be a tendency for the particular *kinds* of criteria we see on English lexical rules to be associated with the same kinds of rules in other, historically unrelated languages. Though an original review of cross-linguistic constraints on lexical rules is obviously beyond the scope of this book, we can examine the relatively theory-neutral cross-linguistic surveys done by others, such as those in Shopen (1985a, b).

Causative. Many languages have regular morphological alternations between a predicate X and a predicate cause-to-X. According to Comrie's (1985) review, "The cause, apparently universally, appears as subject of the causative verb" (p. 335). Periphrastic causatives are also widespread; Comrie calls these "analytical" and contrasts them with lexical causatives, which he calls "morphological." He notes: "In general, formation of analytical causatives is completely productive. ... The degrees of productivity of morphological causatives varies immensely from language to language" (p. 332). This variability will be discussed in detail in the next chapter, but the variation is within the limits we would expect: "One often finds that when a language has both analytic and morphological or lexical causatives, the former implies less direct causation than the latter" (p. 333). Nedyalkov and Silnitsky (1973), in their survey of causative constructions in over one hundred languages, state that "If a causative morpheme forms [a causative verb] only from [an intransitive verb], it usually expresses contact causation. In these cases distant causation is usually expressed by combinations with empty causative verbs" (p. 14). Shibatani (1976) offers similar conclusions. Thus the association between adding a subject to a predicate and getting a predicate with a causative reading where the subject plays the role of agent is a widespread phenomenon, as is the association between lexical causatives and the directness constraint.

Passive. Keenan (1985) offers the following generalizations about passive in the world's languages: "If a language has any passives it has ones characterized as basic ... moreover, it may have only basic passives," where "basic passives" are characterized as follows: "(i) no agent phrase (e.g., *by Mary*) is present, (ii) the main verb (in its non-passive form) is transitive, and (iii) the main verb expresses an activity, taking agent subjects and patient objects" (p. 247). Among the corollaries and related generalizations Keenan offers are the following: "If a language has passives of stative verbs (e.g. *lack, have*, etc.) then it has passives of activity verbs. ... Passives are often not formed freely on transitive verbs whose objects are not patients, that is, not portrayed as being affected" (p. 249). Recall that the criteria surrounding passivization in English seem to stem from a predication effect (some state is predicated of the patient) and an agency effect (the state is attributed to the force of some agent). Keenan notes the cross-linguistic prevalence of both: "The subject of a passive VP is never understood to be less affected by the action than when it is presented as the object of a transitive verb" (p. 268); "The distinction between passives and middles or reflexives is made on semantic grounds: the implication or presence of an agent" (p. 254).

Dative. Dryer (1986) presents a "small but diverse" sample of languages that have ditransitive constructions, including Ojibwa and Cree (Algonkian), Huichol, Palauan (Micronesia), Chi-Mwi:ni (Bantu), Khasi (Mon-Khmer, Assam), Lahu (Burmese-Lolo), Kokborok (Bodo-Garo, Assam), Kham (West Tibetan), Nez Perce (Oregon Penutian), and Tzotzil (Mayan). He notes that the semantic roles of the first and second objects are "goal/beneficiary" and "patient/theme," respectively, and all the examples he cites except one (a pure benefactive) contain verbs whose English translations dativize. In other surveys we find other languages unrelated to English that have an alternation similar to the dative pertaining to "recipient" arguments. Foley and Van Valin (1985) mention Nengone (an Austronesian language spoken in New Caledonia) and Acooli and Lango (Nilotic languages spoken in Uganda) as examples; Shona, a Bantu language, and Bahasa, an Indonesian language, both discussed briefly in Dowty (1979a), appear to be similar. Foley and Van Valin also note that in several languages it is only verbs of giving that undergo this alternation, and they imply that this might be true in general when the input form involves the equivalent of the preposition *to*. In addition, many languages add a verb-adjacent object argument, and when they do it generally has the role of recipient, possessor of the theme, or benefactive/malefactive (Foley and Van Valin, 1985), as in the

English *for*-dative (see sections 3.3.4.2, 4.4.1, and 5.6.1). Alternations of this general sort are found in several Mayan languages (Foley and Van Valin, 1985) and in Swahili (Comrie, 1985).

Locative. I am not aware of any cross-linguistic surveys of locative constructions, but it is not hard to find evidence for patterns of association in a variety of languages. Alternations similar to the English locative, often marked with an affix on the verb, are found in Hungarian and Indonesian (Foley and Van Valin, 1985), Russian and German (Comrie, 1985), Berber (Guerssel, 1986), Igbo (a Nigerian language; Nwachukwu, 1987), and Japanese (Fukui, Miyagawa, and Tenny, 1985). Rappaport and Levin (1985) note that "when a language manifests the alternation the verbs that participate in the alternation fall into the same broad semantic class as the English locative alternation verbs" (p. 36). Furthermore, the holistic effect and phenomena related to it are not restricted to English: Foley and Van Valin remark on it in discussing Hungarian, Comrie does so for Russian, and Nwachukwu notes that in Igbo the version of the locative that allows an equivalent of the preposition *with* requires a verb that is compounded with a predicate meaning *full*, for example, "pack-full" = fill by packing. This is obviously reminiscent of the contrast in English between **I poured the glass with water* and *I filled the glass with water* or *I poured the glass full with water.*

Thus the theory of argument structure alternations presented in this chapter, which was intended to explain constraints on alternations as manifestations of the nature of the alternation, has an unanticipated benefit: it is consistent with the fact that the same alternations in other languages are prone to applying to the same kinds of verbs and being constrained by the same kinds of criteria and shifts in interpretation as one finds in English. Of course, languages do differ in the exact sets of verbs that are allowed to undergo each alternation; in the next chapter I try to explain where this variation comes from and how it is defined precisely within a language.

Chapter 4
Possible and Actual Forms

4.1 The Problem of Negative Exceptions

Constraints on lexical rules that furnish criteria for selecting verbs can solve Baker's paradox in principle, but raised two problems in practice. First, why are they there? Second, are there any that work? In chapter 3, I tried to answer the first question. I proposed a theory in which semantic constraints on lexical rules are motivated by the very nature of those rules, and I used it to show why various verbs do not participate in argument structure alternations. Such verbs are clearly ruled out because they are cognitively incompatible with a thematic core associated with the argument structure. You can *sell* but not **drive Mary the car*, because the double-object form expresses causation of a possession change and selling but not driving results in a possession change. You can *spray* but not **put the plant with water*, because the *with*-locative requires a specific state change and *putting* does not specify what it would be. You can *slide* but not **decide the boy*, because the lexical causative requires unmediated causation, which is possible for sliding but not deciding. And *a hatchet* can *be buried* but *a bucket* can't **be kicked*, because the passive predicates something of a theme and the hatchet but not the bucket corresponds to a possible theme.

However, the second problem, ruling out negative exceptions exactly, has not yet been solved. Clearly there are many differences between alternating and nonalternating verbs that cannot be ruled out by such coarse differences in meaning. One cannot simply live with these as unexplained counterexamples. Because they are negative exceptions, Baker's paradox would remain unsolved. Consider how the theory as stated so far would try to explain the differences in (4.1), (4.2), and 4.3).

(4.1)   John took Mary the ball.
        John threw Mary the ball.

*John carried Mary the ball.

John asked Mary a question.
*John shouted Mary a question.

John gave Mary sheets.
*John supplied Mary sheets.

John found Mary a dress.
*John chose Mary a dress.

(4.2) Betty splashed the floor with suds.
*Betty spilled the floor with suds.

Betty wrapped the pole with ribbons.
*Betty coiled the pole with ribbons.

Betty smeared the wall with paint.
*Betty attached the wall with posters.

(4.3) Sam bounced the ball.
*Sam fell the ball.

Sam melted the butter.
*Sam disappeared the butter.

Sam walked Annette home.
*Sam went Annette home.

Amy slid her daughter across the floor.
*Amy sweated her daughter.

One might try to appeal to subtle meaning differences among the verbs. For example, one could say that *taking* and *throwing* can inherently mean "cause X to possess Y by taking/throwing Y to X" but that *carrying* does not mean "cause X to possess Y by carrying Y to X." Similarly, one could say that *asking* inherently implies communication with another party and hence is a way of causing someone to possess a message, whereas *shouting* is merely a kind of behavior, with no necessary causal effect on a listener. Finally, *finding* can mean "finding X as a means of causing Y to have X," whereas *choosing* cannot have the meaning of being a means to such an end.

Similar accounts could be applied to the locative. *Splashing* could be said to effect a predictable state change on the floor (it is covered with liquid over a large part of its surface), whereas *spilling* could be said to constrain only the manner in which the liquid is caused to move, with no necessary effect on the surface where the liquid ends up. Similarly, the argument would go, being wrapped or smeared is a well-defined state, but "having something coiled around oneself" or "having something attached to oneself" is not.

There is clearly something right about all of this, but that something can't solve Baker's paradox. The problem is, what ensures that the child has mastered the crucial difference in meaning? We certainly can't say that a word's meaning changes ever so subtly when it appears in different argument structures and then assert that the admissibility of the verb in the argument structure depends on that aspect of its meaning. For example, strictly speaking, the theory requires one to say that the prepositional form of *give* means "cause an object to go into someone's possession" whereas the double-object form means "cause someone to gain possession of an object"—but it would be useless to say that the only verbs that can appear in the double-object form are those with a meaning of causing someone to possess something. The problem is that acts of causing an object to change possession are also acts of causing a person to gain possession. Thus it is hard to see how a learner could assign a given verb the requisite definition other than by hearing it in the argument structure in question. This is exactly the opposite of what we need for solving the learnability problem! If a verb's syntactic behavior is a function of its complete meaning and its complete meaning is manifest only when it appears in full sentences, we are back to conservatism: the child must hear a verb in a particular argument structure in order to know whether it has the meaning that would license its appearing with that argument structure.

So obviously the "new" meaning components added by an argument structure alternation rule can't have anything to do with the conditions allowing some but not all verbs to be affected by that rule. One does a bit better, but not well enough, by appealing to some notion of "compatibility" between the "old" meaning components possessed by a verb and the "new" ones added to it. Though that criterion can rule out obvious cases like those discussed in the first paragraph of this chapter, it is not clear how much it would really help for examples like those in (4.1) – (4.3). Perhaps *shout*, in encoding a particular manner of the speaker, is less "about" the recipient of the message than *tell*, and hence is less happy about being reinterpreted as an act "done to" the hearer. *Splashing* and *smearing*, which in all their uses involve a particular kind of action on particular kinds of substances, supports a reliable folk-physics deduction about the effect on the target of splashing or smearing, water and gooey substances being what they are, whereas *spilling* encompasses a range of actions (e.g., knocking over with an elbow, bumping into a table) and a variety of substances (coins, sand, etc.) that do not allow such a prediction. Again, this is not good enough. For one thing, the semantic intuitions appealed to are less compelling a priori than the intuitions about the ungrammaticality of the relevant sentences. Furthermore, an appeal to pure semantic compatibility as a way out of Baker's paradox predicts that anyone who knows the meaning of a verb will use it predictably in the argument structures we have been dealing with. This would seem to rule out dialect differences in the syntax of common concrete verbs. But such differences appear to exist: Georgia Green (1974), for example, finds *shout him the answer* and *carry him the box* to be grammatical in her dialect, unlike the one spoken by me. Yet surely Green and I do not differ in our knowledge of what *shout* and *carry* mean—unless the meaning difference is so abstract that it is virtually the same as the difference in syntax that we are trying to explain.

In sum, the criteria that emerge from the nature of the semantic change effected by the lexical rules seem to function as necessary conditions for an alternation, specifying a meaning component that a verb must be capable of including if it is to alternate. But these criteria do not function as sufficient conditions: some verbs seem to be capable of containing the required meaning but still do not alternate. As we shall see, this difference is a consequence of an important dissociation between semantics and cognition.

4.1.1 Why the Negative Exceptions Exist

Consider one of the design problems that language is faced with: providing the means of expressing the arguments of an essentially unbounded set of possible verbs. Predictable linkages between argument structures and verbs' semantic structures help solve the problem: if you know what a verb means, you can guess what syntax it can use without your having to learn its argument structure from the input. But obviously the predictable linkages can't consist of an innate list of all possible verb meanings and their corresponding argument structures; new verbs that natural selection could not have anticipated are constantly being invented (*debug, slam-dunk, out-Reagan*, etc.). Instead, we have been given a much smaller set of semantic elements that recur through thousands of verbs— such thematic subpredicates as "cause," "go," "be," "path," and their arguments "agent," "patient", "theme," "goal," and so on—and linkages to syntactic devices. By looking for such elements in the semantic decompositions of verbs, a speaker can predict the verbs' syntactic privileges, even for brand–new verbs, as long as they contain some of those elements.

But how does a speaker know which semantic elements are in which verbs? Perception and cognition are flexible, and this causes a problem. Most situations can be construed in many different ways involving the crucial thematic elements, especially since thematic relations can apply either literally to spatial location or metaphorically to states and circumstances. When I hit a wall with a stick, is the wall an "affected entity" and the stick the "instrument" with which I affect it, or is the stick the affected entity, because it moves, and the wall the goal of the movement? When I pour water into a glass, am I affecting the water by causing it to move, or am I affecting the glass by causing it to go from not being full to being full? When Sue likes John, is she causing herself to think well of him, or is John causing her to approve of him? If Jim does an impression of Richard Nixon for Bill, is he causing Bill's laughter in the same way that he can cause a spoon to fall, or does Bill have enough free will that "causation" is an inappropriate concept? When Mary shouts across a noisy room to Bob, what is she doing: affecting Bob, creating a message, moving the message across the room, or just moving her muscles in a certain way? Even the choice of the agent and patient of an action event is not irreversibly burned into our minds. "French-kiss my elbow!" shouts the hockey player. In general, these choices can't just be left up to an individual speaker at the moment of the speech act, because they could lead to conflicting applications of thematic-syntactic linking rules—either John or Sue, either Mary or Bob, could be construed as the agent, hence subject, bringing back the ambiguity that the design of language should be trying to minimize.

I suggest that language has chosen a particular solution to the problem it took on when it tried to map flexible cognition onto rigid syntax. Language guards its verbs' grammatically relevant semantic structures vigilantly. In ordinary natural speech, speakers cannot construe the meaning of a verb however they see fit before mapping it onto syntax, even if such a construal is consistent with the referent event. Rather, in cases of potential thematic ambiguity, new meanings can be assigned to old verbs only in fairly precise circumstances. Only certain relatively narrow classes of verb meanings are given the privilege of being reconstruable as having new, related verb meanings.

Here is an example. In the case of the dative, what good is it to know that "verbs can take the double-object argument structure only if they involve causation of a change of possession" if one cannot tell a priori whether a given verb can be construed as meaning "cause a change of possession"? Certain verbs like *give* have that meaning by definition, and other verbs like *sleep* do not mean that under any reasonable construal, but what about verbs in the gray area, such as *throw* or *carry* or *bake*, where changes of possession are possible but not necessary results? I will show that English makes the decision for us. It uses independent, semi-arbitrary configurations of semantic features as criteria about what kinds verbs have meanings that can be construed as ways of causing a change of possession. For example, it turns out that verbs that denote instantaneous imparting of force to an object causing ballistic physical motion—the class that includes *throw, toss, kick, slide, roll*, and *bounce*—can be given a new meaning, roughly to cause someone to possess an object by means of instantaneously imparting force to it. Thus an argument that is ordinarily a goal of a location change can now also be assigned the role of patient of a possession change. When linking rules apply to the new verb form, the rules generating double-object structures from patients of possession change apply, and thus one can say *She threw / tossed / kicked / slid him the puck.* However, this lexical rule, essentially a rule of reconstrual, is so narrowly stated that it does not apply to seemingly similar verbs, such as those whose definitions involve continuous exertion of force resulting in the guided motion of a theme, such as *carry, pull, push, schlep.* Though they are *cognitively* construable as resulting in a change of possession (if the object is pushed over to a person with the intent of giving it to him), they are not *linguistically* construable as such because the licensing linguistic rule is not stated broadly enough to apply to them. As a result, the semantic structure necessary to trigger the double-object linking rules is never paired with these verbs, and they do not dativize as a class: **She pulled / lifted / lowered / dragged me the box.*

In other words, in cases where a verb is cognitively ambiguous, that is, consistent with several possible thematic analyses, the grammar looks at some independent component of the verb's meaning and dictates which analysis or analyses the speaker is permitted to use when linking the verb to an argument structure. The productive use of a lexical rule is thus restricted to a narrow range of verb meanings. This implies that subtle semantic distinctions among subclasses of verbs can result in differences in their syntactic behavior, often giving the appearance of there being arbitrary lexical exceptions to alternations. I will refer to the simple operations on semantic structure introduced in the preceding chapter as *broad-range* lexical rules, and the classes of verbs they apply to as *broad conflation classes.* The more selective versions of these rules that pick out *narrow conflation classes* of verbs (or "conflation subclasses") will be called *narrow-range* rules. Membership in a broad conflation class is only a necessary condition for a verb to alternate; it is membership in one of the narrow conflation classes that is a sufficient condition.[1]

How are these narrow lexical subclasses defined? We will see that they are defined by a distinctive, grammatically relevant subset of the semantic structures that constitute the meaning of a verb (this is the subject of chapter 5) and perhaps by salient morphological divisions in the lexicon of the language. In the rest of this chapter I will do three things. First, I will motivate the addition of narrow conflation classes to the theory by examining a seemingly simple and homogeneous class of verbs—transitive action verbs—whose syntactic behavior illuminates the need to distinguish broad and narrow verb classes. This will serve as an independent motivation for the claim that there are broad- and narrow-range versions of the four rules we have been concentrating on. Then I will apply the claim in detail to the dative, passive, locative, and causative alternations, aiming for a delineation of the relevant classes that will leave no negative exceptions.

Finally, I will clarify the relation between the narrow-range rules that I describe here and the broad-range rules discussed in the chapter 3.

4.2 Transitive Action Verbs as Evidence for Narrow Subclasses

The most prototypical class of verbs is surely transitive action verbs: they are among the first verbs that infants acquire, the first verbs one would come up with if asked to give examples of verbs, and the verbs that appear to be syntactically simplest. However, Beth Levin (1985) shows that this simplicity is an illusion. Action verbs break down into a variety of narrow conflation classes (she calls them "semantically cohesive subclasses") that have predictable differences in their syntactic properties.

Consider the conative alternation, shown in (4.4), in which a transitive verb is allowed to take an oblique object introduced by the preposition *at*, indicating that the subject is trying to affect the oblique object but may or may not be succeeding.

(4.4) Mary cut the bread. / Mary cut at the bread.
　　　Sam chipped the rock. / Sam chipped at the rock.
　　　Bill hit the dog. / Bill hit at the dog.
　　　Irv kicked the wall. / Irv kicked at the wall.

In the present framework, we might say that there is a lexical rule (of broad range) that applies to thematic cores of the form "*X* acts-on *Y*," producing "*X* goes toward *X* acting-on *Y*," where "goes" and "toward" are interpreted in a semantic field where locations are treated as intended states or events. A linking rule for paths and a lexical entry for *at* map the argument of the path-function 'toward' (corresponding to a path that is oriented toward, but does not necessarily extend all the way to, a location) onto an oblique or indirect internal argument containing *at*.[2] This can be seen in a similar use of *at* in *John threw the ball at the tree*, which indicates that the ball traveled in the direction of the tree but did not necessarily get there.

However, (4.5) shows that not all verbs can enter into the construction, even if the combination would make sense on cognitive grounds.

(4.5) *Nancy touched at the cat.
　　　*Jane kissed at the child.
　　　*Jerry broke at the bread.
　　　*Bob split at the wood.

It turns out that the conative alternation, though it always conveys "attempting," applies to much narrower classes of verb than those whose actions can be attempted. Verbs of cutting (*cut, slash, chop, hack, chip*, etc.) and verbs of hitting (*hit, beat, elbow, kick, punch, poke, rap, slap, strike*, etc.) all enter into the alternation. Verbs that fail to enter into it include verbs of touching (*touch, kiss, hug, stroke, contact*, etc.) and verbs of breaking (*break, shatter, crack, split, crumble*, etc.). More precisely, the subclasses of verbs that are eligible to enter into the conative alternation must signify a type of motion resulting in a type of contact.

Laughren, Levin, and Rappaport (1986) discuss another alternation involving action verbs, first studied by Fillmore (1967), which can be called "part-possessor ascension." Examples are shown in (4.6).

(4.6)   Sam cut Brian's arm. / Sam cut Brian on the arm.
        Miriam hit the dog's leg. / Miriam hit the dog on the leg.
        Terry touched Mavis's ear. / Terry touched Mavis on the ear.

Again, the alternation is puzzlingly selective, as (4.7) indicates.

(4.7)   *Jim broke Tom on the leg.
        *Hagler split Leonard on the lip.

There are three narrow semantic subclasses whose verbs behave similarly with respect to the alternation: the verbs of hitting and the verbs of cutting participate, but the verbs of breaking do not. More precisely, the subclasses of verbs that signify physical contact may alternate.

Laughren, Levin, and Rappaport also discuss an alternation resembling the locative, involving physical contact. Examples are presented in (4.8).

(4.8)   I hit the bat against the wall [cf. I hit the wall with the bat].
        She bumped the glass against the table.
        Bill slapped the towel against the sink.

        *I cut the knife against the bread [cf. I cut the bread with the knife].
        *He split the ax against the log.
        *Phil shattered the hammer against the glass.
        *I broke a spoon against the egg.
        *I touched my hand against the cat.
        *I kissed my lips against hers.

(The starred examples are grammatical only on a different reading, where the knife itself gets cut, the ax gets split, and so on.) Here, the verbs of hitting can enter into the alternation, but not the verbs of breaking. More generally, the subclass of verbs of motion followed by contact can enter into it, but the subclass of verbs of motion followed by contact followed by a specific effect (a cut, a break, a split) and the subclass of verbs of contact without a prior change of location (touch, kiss) do not.[3]

Keyser and Roeper (1984) and Hale and Keyser (1987) discuss the middle alternation, which, roughly, specifies the ease with which an action can be performed on a patient. It too is selective above and beyond differences in the degree to which the "ease of performing an action" cognitively coheres with various verb meanings. Specifically, it applies only to verbs that signify an effect, regardless of whether it is the result of motion or contact; no effect, no alternation. Examples are provided in (4.9).

(4.9) I broke the glass. / This glass breaks easily.
I cut the bread. / This bread cuts easily.
She kissed Bill. / *?Bill kisses easily.
He slapped the wall. / *That wall slaps easily.
They touched the wire. / *This wire touches easily.

Finally, consider the causative alternation applying in reverse direction, converting a transitive verb to an intransitive. This transformation, sometimes called the anticausative, is distinct from the middle in that it pertains to an actual event that the theme undergoes, rather than the generic property of the theme corresponding to how easily it undergoes that kind of event. The anticausative alternation, shown in (4.10), applies to verbs specifying a particular effect, either a change of state or a change of position, but only if they signify nothing but an effect, that is, if they are mute as to what kind of event caused the effect.

(4.10) At exactly 3 o'clock, the glass broke.
*At exactly 3 o'clock, the bread cut.
*At exactly 3 o'clock, Mary hit [ungrammatical if taken to mean "Mary was hit"].
*At exactly 3 o'clock, John touched [ungrammatical if taken to mean "John was touched"].

The table in (4.11) summarizes the selective application of the alternations to various subclasses of transitive action verbs.

4.3 The Nature of Narrow Conflation Classes

The analysis of these alternations in B Levin (1985) and Laughren, Levin, and Rappaport (1986) illustrates some crucial properties of argument structure alternations in general:

• The verbs that enter into a construction fall into semantically cohesive subclasses involving a narrower range of meanings than that which is directly associated with the argument structure.

• A common set of elements of meaning, such as contact, motion, and effect, enter into the definitions of the semantically cohesive classes.

(4.11)

Alternation	Subclass	Examples of verbs
Conative	+motion, +contact	hit, cut, *break, *touch
Part-possessor ascension	+contact	hit, cut, *break, touch
Contact Locative	+motion, +contact, –effect	hit, *cut, *break, *touch
Middle	+effect	*hit, cut, break, *touch
Anticausative	+effect, –contact, –motion	*hit, *cut, break, *touch

Verb	Elements in semantic structure defining subclass membership
hit	motion, contact
cut	motion, contact, effect
break	effect
touch	contact

• Whether a verb belongs to a class depends not on the characteristic features of the event in the world that the verb can refer to, but on the aspects of the event that its semantic structure constrains.

The last point, which Levin, Laughren, and Rappaport do not mention explicitly, is crucial to the theory I am presenting. Verb meanings do not correspond to speakers' conceptual categories for kinds of events or states, or to notions like "scripts" or "frames" or "stereotypes," which are popular constructs in cognitive psychology and artificial intelligence. And semantically cohesive subclasses of verbs are not clusters of verbs related by general cognitive similarity (say, according to some continuous metric calculated over the number of shared and distinct features; Tversky, 1977). The problem with these representations is that they capture probable or characteristic features of a kind of event, those that often or typically occur. In contrast, the semantic structure associated with a verb constrains certain aspects of the events or states the verb can refer to and is mute about others, no matter how characteristic, often making surprisingly fine discriminations. Syntactically relevant semantic subclasses depend on exactly which aspects of the event or state the verb's semantic structure imposes conditions on. These conditions are manifested as "semantic intuitions" of what kinds of circumstances a speaker could imagine using a verb in. Other aspects of an event might be well specified in that they are known to the speaker and hearer, inferable from the discourse context, or predictable from conceptual categories or stereotypes of what typically happens in an event, but they are forbidden to enter into the determination of whether a verb can can feed a lexical rule that alters its thematic structure.

In the present examples we see that the conative construction involves verbs of motion-then-contact, such as *hit* and *cut*. Motion is obligatorily involved: if one were to cause a bruise on someone's arm by pressing increasingly firmly against it, that would not be *hitting*, just as causing an incision to appear by hard tugging or by rapid heating followed by freezing is not *cutting*. Furthermore, the role of the motion in causing the effect is specified by the verb: if one were to wave a knife in the air as part of a magic spell, causing the bread to split, that would also not be a clear example of *cutting the bread*. (It's not that magical scenarios alter intuitions about verb use in general; it sounds perfectly natural, given the right supernatural circumstances, to "cut a brick" with a feather, a strand of thread, a shadow, or a breath of air). Contrast this now with *kissing* or *breaking*. Clearly, the typical scenario for kissing someone is to move toward the kissee, then contact him or her, and then initiate the kiss. A typical chain of events in breaking something is to do so by moving one's hand to contact it. But crucially, the typicality of an entire event of a given kind is irrelevant. The semantics of *kiss* do not *require* that the event include prior change of location resulting in contact; two teenagers can start *kissing* hours after their orthodontures have become accidentally entangled. And the definition of *break* does not require that the break be caused by motion followed by contact; John can *break* a bicycle by riding it if he's too heavy for it.

In sum, it's not what possibly or typically goes on in an event that matters; it's what the verb's semantic representation is choosy about in that event that matters. I am stressing this point—let me call it the "autonomy of lexical semantics"—because the criteria that delineate the domain of application of lexical rules do not depend on general cognitive similarity or typicality but on features that are precise enough to guide finely differentiated intuitions of a verb's ability to refer to kinds of situations, and equally fine intuitions about choice of argument structures.

One final point. I suggest that in instances of cognitive ambiguity or vagueness, lexical rules apply productively only to narrow-range, semantically cohesive subclasses. It would be unfortunate if the boundaries of these subclasses were arbitrarily related to the nature of the lexical rule that respected them. That is not the case. Consider why the preposition *at* is used in the conative construction. It is not literally being used in the same way as the spatial preposition *at*, which refers to a path oriented toward a goal but not necessarily arriving there (e.g., *John threw the rock at the tree*). If John *cuts at the bread*, it's not that the knife never arrives at the bread; rather, the bread was not properly cut. (The effect is magnified in *John was cutting away at the bread*: here John could have succeeded in putting one or more cuts in it; the implication is that he is not finished, that he has not yet cut the bread to the extent that he wants to). Even in *Mary slapped at John*, with no effect component, the implication is not that her hand never arrived at John's person, only that the type of contact ordinarily implied by *slap* was not accomplished. But there is a clear parallelism between the "toward" relation in space and an analogous relation in the domain of intentions. This parallelism would seem to play a role in explaining why it is the class of motion-contact verbs, rather than, say, any action verb or only effect verbs, that can undergo the conative alternation. The rationale might be roughly that in motion-contact events such as John hitting Bill, there is a parallel between the physical motion of John's hand, which is spatially aimed at Bill, and the temporal unfolding of the act of hitting, which is "aimed" at the goal of contact. A single notion of "direction toward a destination" embraces both dimensions of the act of hitting. The conative alternation "notices" the temporally coterminous trajectories of spatial motion and of realization of the event in motion-contact events, and it supplies a form that zooms in on the pre-terminal portion of the latter.

I am not claiming that all speakers grasp this rationale—they needn't do so to apply the alternation properly—or that there is a linguistic constraint that preestablishes that conative alternations must apply to motion-contact verbs. For example, it would not be surprising if there were languages or even dialects of English in which one could say *John was breaking at the bread*. Rather, the historical processes that cause lexical rules to be defined over some subclasses but not others seem to favor the addition and retention of verbs whose own meanings exemplify or echo the semantic structure created by the rule. I think that the conditions that characterize the set of narrow classes licensing a lexical rule are an example of what George Lakoff (1987) calls the "motivation" for a category. A motivated class is a family of items whose membership conditions are too varied and unusual to be deduced a priori from universal principles or constraints, but whose members hang together according to a rationale that can be discovered post hoc—so the family is not an unstructured list, either. The full motivation for a subclass may come from the psychology of the first speakers creative enough or liberal enough to extend a linguistic process to a new item, as such speakers are unlikely to make such extensions at random. Thereafter the subclass might be learned by simply memorizing its definition, by grasping its motivation all at once with the aid of a stroke of insight recapitulating that of the original coiners, or by depending on some intermediate degree of appreciation of the rationale to learn its components efficiently, depending on the speaker and the subclass involved.[4]

4.4 Defining and Motivating Subclasses of Verbs Licensing the Four Alternations

If the theory I have outlined—involving thematic cores to motivate constraints on rules, and narrow conflation classes to implement them precisely—is on the right track, then we should be rewarded with criteria that actually work in distinguishing alternating and nonalternating verbs in each alternation; negative exceptions should vanish. These criteria should not be arbitrary but should be motivatable in part in terms of an interaction between the meaning of a verb and the thematic core associated with the argument structure that the alternation yields. I will present hypotheses about the subclasses that do and don't submit to the four alternations we have considered. In the rest of the chapter I will describe the narrow classes and their motivations informally and then draw conclusions about the nature of narrow and broad classes in general. In chapter 5 I will return to each of the alternations one more time and propose explicit representations for the broad- and narrow-range classes in an attempt to characterize them precisely.

4.4.1 Dativizable Verbs
The dative rule obviously applies to verbs of *giving*, where the verb cannot be used in its literal sense unless it denotes a giver having some object and then causing it to enter into the possession of a recipient. Examples are shown in (4.12).

(4.12)   give, pass, hand, sell, pay, trade, lend, loan, serve, feed

This is the prototypical subclass of dativizable verbs; its definitions are compatible—by definition, as they say—with the notion of X causing Y to have Z. A related subclass includes verbs where a transfer of possession is mediated by a separation in time and space, sometimes bridged by a particular means of transfer: *send, ship, mail.*

But among the verbs that can result in a change of possession but do not necessarily do so, some subclasses can be reinterpreted by a narrow lexical rule to denote changes of possession, by means of which they inherit the double-object argument structure, and other cannot. I have already mentioned the subclasses of verbs of instantaneous imparting of force in some manner causing ballistic motion, as shown in (4.13), which allow dativization, and the verbs of continuous imparting of force in some manner causing accompanied motion, as in (4.14), which do not.

(4.13)   Lafleur throws / tosses / flips / slaps / kicks / pokes / flings / blasts him the puck; he shoots, he scores!

(4.14) *I carried / pulled / pushed / schlepped / lifted / lowered / hauled John the box.

It is striking that the verbs *bring* and *take*, which also signify continuous causation of accompanied motion but specify the direction of the motion ("to here" versus "away from "here," respectively) and not its manner, do seem to take the double-object form: *I brought/took him his lunch.* Like the elements "motion," "contact," and "effect" that Levin and her collaborators focus on, the elements "manner" and "direction" turn up again and again in defining conflation subclasses. Lexical rules mind their manners.

Another dativizable class, shown in (4.15), contains verbs where X makes some commitment that Y will have or can have Z in the future, what Green (1974) calls "verbs of future having." The actual acts referred to by the verbs are not changes of possession but proactive commitments of some sort guaranteeing them.

(4.15)   offer, promise, bequeath, leave, refer, forward, allocate, guarantee, allot, assign, advance, award, reserve, grant

We have already seen another subclass of verbs, shown in (4.16), for which X has the potential or desire of causing Y no longer to have Z, the "verbs of future not having" (Green, 1974). (Another possible characterization would be in terms of the first object being a "malefactive" or "adversative" argument of the action or state of the subject, similar to the traditional benefactive case but of opposite affective valence. The object of *on* in *My cat died on me* is sometimes described as having this role.) As mentioned in chapter 2, none of them (except possibly *deny*) can appear in the usual prepositional-dative form (*It cost five dollars to me / of me / from me*). *Ask* is included in its sense of *She asked him the time / the way* (cf. *She asked the time/way to him*), where the information referred to by the second object is given by the addressee, not to him. *Save* is included in the sense of *That saved me the trouble of making a separate trip.*

(4.16)   cost, spare, envy, begrudge, bet, refuse, ask, save, charge, fine, forgive, ?deny

Another nondativizable class of possession-change verbs consists of what B. Levin (1985) calls "verbs of presentation" but which might better be called "verbs of fulfilling." Examples are given in (4.17). These verbs, which do appear in a construction with the prospective possessor as the first object—*She presented the students with certificates; They rewarded him with a promotion*—mark the transferred object with the preposition *with*, not as a second object in a double-object form. The verbs have the following properties: X transfers Z to Y, where (a) Z is not necessarily possessed by X beforehand (X just enables its transfer); (b) Z is something that Y deserves, needs, or is worthy of; (c) Y's relation to Z has certain properties, usually specified by the nominal counterpart of the verb. In (4.17), the nominal counterpart is listed alongside each sentence.[5]

(4.17) ?I presented him the award. [a presentation]
        *I credited his account the amount of the check. [a credit]
        *I credited him the discovery. [credit for the discovery]
        *They rewarded him a promotion. [a reward]
        *Bill entrusted him the sacred chalice. [a trust in him]
        *The commissioner honored them the award. [an honor]
        ?I supplied them a bag of groceries. [some supplies]
        ?*They bestowed him a fortune. [a bestowal]

Among verbs of communication with a direct object signifying the message
and a *to*-object signifying the audience (*Mike told / wrote / shouted / radioed the
story to Mary*), only some can be given a thematic reanalysis whereby the speaker
is treated as an agent of a change of possessional state of the audience, that is, *X*
causes *Y* to know (perceive, apprehend, be aware of) *Z*, in turn enabling the
double-object structure. I will call one of these classes the class of "illocutionary verbs of communication"; the examples are in (4.18). They all involve a
particular kind of communicated content specified by the verb (e.g., a perceptible
object for *show*; a question or problem for *ask, pose*; written language for *write*).
The kind of message is defined with respect to the speaker's intentions concerning how the hearer is to interpret it. For example, the object of *tell* is either factual
information for the hearer to learn or a story to entertain him (the object of *spin*
has a similar property), and the object of *ask* is a question, which by definition
is something calling for an answer.[6] As mentioned in section 3.3.4.2, because the
hearer is a patient and a theme in the double object form, these verbs can entail,
or at least connote, successful apprehension of the idea or stimulus in that form,
most notably for the verb *teach* (Green, 1974).

(4.18) tell, show, ask, teach, pose, write, spin, read, quote, cite

The illocutionary verbs are noncommittal as to the manner in which the
message is communicated: one can *ask* John a question in a scream, a whisper,
and so on. There is a distinct class of verbs with complementary semantic
properties. These "manner-of-speaking" verbs (4.19), though they can be used
to express the idea of successful communication, do not necessarily imply that
it has taken place; what they are choosy about is the manner in which the sender
sends the message.[7] Arnold Zwicky (1971), in an article entitled "In a Manner
of Speaking," shows that these verbs share eleven different syntactic properties
(surprisingly, he omits nondativizability).

(4.19) *John shouted / screamed / murmured / whispered / shrieked / yodeled
        / yelled / bellowed / grunted / barked / Bill the news.

The effect of the illocutionary/manner distinction on dativizability appears to
be confirmed by a recent addition to the language. According to the *OED*, the

transitive verb *to leak* in the sense of "to divulge sensitive information" came into common use in the 1950s (though sporadic examples, usually with scare quotes, appeared in the second half of the nineteenth century and early in the twentieth century). It clearly refers to the nature of the message relative to the intended recipient (i.e., the message is something the recipient is not supposed to know) and imposes no general constraints on the manner. As predicted, it dativizes: I have heard *He's been leaking me bits of information for several months*, and in my judgment it is perfectly natural.

One of the most common verbs of communication (especially among children), *say*, falls into neither of these classes: *She told/*said a story; She shouted/*said.* The object of *say* seems to be individuated by its content rather than either its physical or illocutionary properties. Unlike *tell*, it takes a clausal object (*She said/*told that Elvis died*), a quotation (*She said/*told "Hello!"*), or a quantified NP (*She said/*told nothing / something / a lot / very little*; *told* is acceptable only elliptically). Though it can take a *to*-object, it cannot dativize: *She said nothing to me / *She said me nothing.* Perhaps it belongs to a class of verbs of "transparent" content of communication, where one of the arguments is the actual content of what the communicator means, and the communicator's attitude with respect to the truth of that content may be specified by the verb. *Assert, question, claim, think (aloud about)*, and *doubt*, and others, may fall into this class. For present purposes, it is sufficient to show that *say* clearly belongs to a different class from *tell*.

Finally, for many speakers, a relatively new class of verbs of communication can alternate (see Randall, 1987; Wasow, 1981). These are verbs specifying an instrument of communication, as shown in (4.20); intuitions vary among verbs and speakers. Beth Levin has provided me with an additional example from an article in the *New York Times*—*I'll modem him tomorrow*—and as mentioned, double-object constructions with the new verb *to fax* (to transmit using a facsimile machine) have mushroomed in the late 1980s.

(4.20)   John radioed / satellited / E-mailed / telegraphed / wired / telephoned her
            the news.

Let me turn now to verbs that take the preposition *for*. The prepositional form has the thematic core "*X* acts-on *Y* for the benefit of *Z*." For the moment I will put aside the question of whether the thematic core for the double-object version of these verbs is the same as that for the double-object form of verbs taking *to*, and will first examine the narrow classes of verbs participating in the *for*-dative alternation. One subclass—shown in (4.21)—includes verbs of creation, which in the double-object form express the notion of *X* causing *Y* to come into existence for the benefit of *Z* and then causing *Z* to have *Y*. These verbs can specify means (including specific instruments such as *xerox*, which like all instruments in English are patients in the secondary event that serves as the means of accomplishing the main event), properties of the created object, or, most typically, both.[8]

(4.21) bake, make, build, cook, sew, knit, toss (when a salad results), fix (when dinner results), pour (when a drink results)

Another is the class of verbs of obtaining, where X does not initially possess Y, then comes to possess it for Y's benefit so that X can give it over to Y; examples are given in (4.22)

(4.22) get, buy, find, steal, order, win, earn, grab

In contrast, for most speakers verbs of choosing—see (4.23)—do not accept the double object form, though like other nondativizable subclasses they are conceptually compatible with the possibility of change of possession. Melissa Bowerman (1987a) points out, however, that *I picked her out a dress* is grammatical. This is probably because the particle *out* when combined with *pick* supplies the crucial missing element of meaning, involving obtaining (or, more precisely, obtaining by removal from a location: *I dug / scooped / scraped / pulled out the gold; I got / brought / took out my guitar*). The particle has a similar effect on other nondativizable verbs: **I pried / pulled / yanked her a gemstone* versus *?I pried / pulled / yanked her out a gemstone*. (The particle can have a similar effect when it produces verbs of creation: compare **Juan tapped / banged her a tune on the xylophone* with *Juan tapped / banged her out a tune on the xylophone*.) Thus the effect of the particle is analogous to that of the particles in examples like *I poured the glass full with water* or *I wiped the table clean of crumbs*, discussed in the preceding chapter.[9]

(4.23) **I chose / picked / selected / favored / indicated / preferred / designated her a dress.*

Most often, verbs that simply convey acts done for the benefit of a third party, without that party's coming to possess the affected object, can appear in the *for* prepositional form but not the double-object form (e.g., *I drove his car for him / *drove him his car*). At first this would seem to be a consequence of the fact that the thematic core associated with the double-object form calls specifically for a change of possession. However, we shall see that this is not quite right. The double-object form is not absolutely barred from appearing with benefactive verbs, neither in fact nor in principle. Let me discuss each in turn.

A first suspicion that pure benefactive double-object forms are not invariably and absolutely ungrammatical came from the study of Gropen et al. (1989), in which adult subjects rated the acceptability of novel verbs. Though we found that double-object forms were always rated as sounding better with possession-change scenarios, this effect was significantly weaker for *for*-dative verbs, where the contrast was with benefactive scenarios, than for *to*-dative verbs, where the contrast was with transportation scenarios. This result leads us to ask whether English speakers are capable of showing some degree of tolerance toward double-object benefactives. In certain circumstances this appears to be so.

In standard American English, there are some highly circumscribed subclasses of double-object verbs that seem only to express the benefactive relation, with no actual change of possession (Green, 1974). Examples are shown in (4.24).

(4.24) *Idioms with give and do:*
        She gave him a hand.
        She gave him a kick.
        She gave him a kiss.
        She did him a favor.
        She did him a good deed.

        Artistic performances:
        She danced us a waltz.
        She played us her trombone.

        Symbolic acts of dedication:
        Sam promised to move his lover a mountain.
        Cry me a river!
        God said to Abraham, "Kill me a son."[10]

In addition, there is an American colloquial construction in which a pronoun is used reflexively as the postverbal object to indicate an act or state that benefits the subject. I have heard the examples listed in (4.25), none of them grammatical in my (Canadian) dialect.

(4.25 (a) *From color commentary on basketball games:*
            Vincent had himself ten points in the first half.
            Hinson has himself a good ball game going.
            Robert played himself one heck of a ball game.
            I'll tell you, we've really had ourselves a good ball game.

       (b) Why don't you take yourself a cab and go jump in the lake?

       (c) *From a bluegrass song:*
            I'll pawn you my diamond ring. [The singer, appealing to a sheriff to release her jailed lover, is offering to pawn her ring and give him the proceeds. Note that the referent of the first object would benefit from the pawning of the ring but would not come to possess it.]

       (d) Five more minutes, he'd have got out and chewed himself a hole through the fence. [A truck driver is referring to an an angry businessman whose car was blocked by his truck.]

(e) Barbara Walters: Tell me, Dolly, are they real?
Dolly Parton: Well, Barbara, I'm the kind of gal that, if they weren't,
I'd go out and get me some.

In earlier periods of the language, from Old English until fairly recently, the double-object construction was used more freely with relations such as benefactive, malefactive, or mere "sympathetic interest," as in *They broke him his shoulder*. Visser (1963) cites, for example, *Then cometh the devil and him shorten his days* (word-by-word translation from Old English); *He ate me up half a ham of bacon* (1711); *With great exactitude of purpose he enters me his name in the book* (1820); and *He can knock you off forty Latin verses in an hour* (1835). Aronoff (1980) finds *Who will surgeon me this gash?* in the *OED*, dated 1849.

Furthermore, even when the dative alternation applied to *for* verbs does involve a change of possession, there is an overlay of benefaction conflated with the possession change. Thus, Green (1974) suggests that *She burned John a steak* is well formed if John likes his steaks burned but not if he doesn't. Similarly, *She baked him an arsenic-laced pie* seems to have an ironic tone.

Yet another class of double-object constructions combining possession and benefaction recently came to my attention. Bob Ryan, a sportswriter for the *Boston Globe*, justified a selection on his personal All-Star list by writing, "Meanwhile, Jeff Malone me no Jeff Malones." The Malone in question was a well-reputed basketball player whom Ryan did not care for. I also recall the title of an editorial in *Life* magazine a few years back protesting the standard two-letter abbreviations for American states introduced by the postal service: "UT me no UTs." This semiproductive, self-conscious construction translates as "Don't think you're doing me a favor by offering / saying *X* to me." It is quite stereotyped (cf. **Don't Jeff Malone me any Jeff Malones*) and is probably inspired by a few well-known literary sources. Harrison (1968) notes that it was "a common kind of idiom" in Shakespeare's time. In (4.26), I quote passages cited by Jespersen (1938/1982).

(4.26) "My gracious uncle. —"
"Tut tut, Grace me no Grace, nor Uncle me no Uncle:
I am no traitor's uncle, and that word 'grace'
In an ungracious mouth is but profane."
(Shakespeare, *Richard II*, act II, scene 3)

"What is this?
'Proud' and 'I thank you not,'
And yet 'not proud,' Mistress minion, you,
Thank me no thankings, nor proud me no prouds."
(Shakespeare, *Romeo and Juliet*, act II, scene 5)

"I heartily wish I could, but —"
"Nay, but me no buts—I have set my heart upon it."
(Sir Walter Scott, *The Antiquary*)

"Advance and take thy prize, the diamond; but he answered,
Diamond me no diamonds! For God's love, a little air!
Prize me no prizes, for my prize is death!"
(Tennyson, *Lancelot and Elaine*)

Does this mean we should give up the general claim that the double-object form is inherently tied to change of possession? Probably not. The cognitive content of the notions of "benefactive" and "gaining possession" may be similar. We talk of *having good fortune, having it made, having a good time (a ball, a blast*, etc.), *having it all, having someone* (sexually), and *having someone where you want him*. Green (1974) suggests that in expressions like *Cry me a river*, the beneficiary could be said to "possess" the river of tears as a token or "offering" of his or her lover's dedication. And if someone *does you a favor*, might there be some sense in which you now possess (enjoy, take advantage of) the favor? There is even a form of the verb *have* itself that has a causative-benefactive reading and a distinct malefactive reading (Chomsky, 1965). *I had my leg broken* can mean either "I paid an orthopedist to break my partially-healed leg and re-set it in a cast" (causative-benefactive), or "Some thugs came and broke my leg on me" (malefactive). Green (1974) notes that in Japanese, symbolic benefactive relations can be expressed using the verbs *give* and *receive*, in expressions resembling "St. George gave killed a dragon for Mary" and "Mary received killed by St. George a dragon." These sentences correspond to the English *St. George killed Mary a dragon*, where the dragon is never literally handed over to Mary. Finally, as noted in chapter 3, in other languages constructions similar to the double-object dative can refer to recipients, benefactives, or both.

This pattern of similarity suggests that benefactive relations can be subsumed as cases of metaphorical possession, extending the Thematic Relations Hypothesis. A thematic core embracing possession and a possible extension of it to benefaction/malefaction would underlie all verbs taking the double-object form. Thus nondativizable *for*-datives such as **drive her the car* would be ruled out not by an inherent incompatibility with the thematic core of the double-object form but by the absence from the speaker's dialect of a narrow class including those verbs. (Many ungrammatical *to*-datives, on the other hand, are still ruled out by incompatibility with the thematic core, such as **drive Chicago the car*.)

This account has several advantages over any alternative. If there were only a very general thematic core for all double-object forms meaning "cause to change to a beneficial state," we would be left with no explanation for why all of the *to*-dative narrow classes and most of the standard *for*-dative subclasses do involve change of possession. Even the more general benefactive relations involving *for*-datives (*Vincent has himself ten points; Cry me a river; But me no buts*) are often conflated with states of possession or support metaphoric extensions of possession, and many actually contain the verbs *have* and *get*. Furthermore, if the thematic core were restricted to literal possession, we could not account for the narrow classes involving symbolic acts, reflexive benefactives, "sympathetic interest" in earlier stages of English, and so on. As we shall see, there are also developmental data, discussed in chapter 7, that support a thematic core for the double-object that embraces possession and a metaphorical extension of it to benefactive/malefactive relations.

Motivation for the dativizable classes. Is there a motivation or rationale for which of the conflation subclasses are dativizable? For verbs where change of possession is inherent to the meaning of the verb, such as *give*, the answer is obvious. More generally, if the thematic core of the double-object dative involves an actor acting on a recipient in such a way that causes him to possess something (as opposed to acting on an object in such a way as to cause it to go to someone), then verb subclasses that suggest that the action inherently involves the beneficiary as patient in some direct fashion would be more likely to undergo dativization. Since *throw to X* verbs involve aiming in the direction of the receiver concurrently with causing the motion, whereas the action in *pull to X* verbs can be initiated without having the receiver in mind and can have an ever-changing goal throughout its duration, there is a sense in which the receiver is more involved in defining the action for *throw* and can be more naturally analyzed as a patient. So if we only knew that one of the two classes was dativizable, we could predict it would be the *throw* class. Similarly, when asking a question, what makes it *asking* is how a hypothetical listener is supposed to react to it, but when shouting a question, what makes it *shouting* has nothing to do with a listener and can be defined in terms of the behavior of the speaker alone. Therefore we are not surprised that illocutionary verbs, but not manner-of-speaking verbs, dativize. As I have emphasized, the learnability story does not absolutely hinge on such differences, and I do not insist that the difference be exploited by all speakers or be perfectly predictive across languages and dialects. It does appear, however, that where in the semantic landscape the productive lines are drawn is not completely arbitrary from a cognitive vantage point.

4.4.1.1   The Morphological Constraint on the Dative   In explaining constraints on lexical rules in terms of the theory of thematic cores and conflation subclasses, I have not touched on the morphological constraint on the dative, introduced in chapter 2. How would it enter into the subdivision of verbs into narrow classes? Interestingly, the constraint does not completely cross-classify the semantic subclasses; it conjoins with some of them but not others. For example, the subclass of illocutionary communication verbs demands native stems (*tell/*explain him the story*), but the subclass of verbs of future having (*promise/bequeath her my fortune; offer/refer him a patient*) does not. The fact that morphology and semantics interact, as summarized in (4.27), explains why the morphological constraint is demonstrably psychologically real (Gropen et al., 1989) but apparently so vulnerable to counterexamples that most investigators are skeptical that it could be (e.g., Green, 1974; Randall, 1987; Fodor, 1985). What is going on is that the constraint is real but does not apply to certain subclasses; that's where the apparent counterexamples come from.

(4.27)
Dativizable subclasses sensitive to the morphological constraint:
 1. Giving: give, pass, hand VERSUS *donate, *contribute
 2. Sending: send, ship, mail VERSUS *transport, ?deliver,
     ?*air-freight, ?Federal-Express, ?*courier, ?*messenger
 3. Instantaneous causation of motion: throw, toss VERSUS *propel,
     *release, *alley-oop, *lob-pass
 4. Communication/illocutionary: tell, ask VERSUS *explain, *announce,
     *describe, *admit, *confess, *repeat, *declare, *recount
 5. Creation: build, cook, sew VERSUS *construct, *create, *design, *devise
 6. Obtaining: get, find, buy VERSUS *purchase, *obtain, *collect

Dativizable subclasses insensitive to the morphological constraint:
 7. Future having: bequeath, refer, recommend, guarantee, permit
 8. Malefactive / future not having: envy, begrudge, deny, refuse
 9. Instrument of communication: radio, telegraph, telephone, satellite, netmail

Some nondativizable subclasses that are cognitively compatible with change of possession:
10. Manner of speaking: *shout, *scream
11. Continuous causation of motion in some manner: *pull, *push, *lower
12. Transferring something needed/deserved: *entrust, *credit, *supply
13. Selection/designation: *choose, *pick, *select

This summary given in (4.27) leaves open the question of why any of the subclasses should care about morphology in the first place. Though I cannot answer this question definitively, I will try to render it a bit less mysterious.

First, the morphological or phonological constraint is not ad hoc to the English dative. The native/Latinate distinction or some of its phonological correlates are relevant to a variety of linguistic processes in English:

• The 180 or so English verbs with irregular past-tense forms (*go/went, hit/hit, sing/sang, spend/spent*) are all either monosyllabic or monosyllables with a recognizable native prefix (e.g. *understood, forgot, beset, mistook, withstood, upset*) (Pinker and Prince, 1988).

• The negative prefix *in-* (with phonologically conditioned variants *il-, im-, ir-*) can attach only to Latinate stems: *insatiable, illiterate, irreducible, improbable, *imborn, *illucky, *inhappy, *irrocky*. Adult speakers, when asked to produce or judge negative versions of novel adjectives, are sensitive to this regularity (Baldi, Broderick, and Palermo, 1985).

• The comparative suffixes *-er* and *-est* attach to monosyllabic adjectives (*nice/ nicer/nicest, intelligent/*intelligenter/*intelligentest*) or to polysyllables that are clearly native, with stress on the first syllable (*pretty/prettier/prettiest; simple/simpler/simplest*).

• The suffixes *-ion* and *-ation* attaches only to Latinate verbs: *invert/inversion; chart/*chartion/*chartation*. The semantically similar suffix *-ment* is not choosy (Aronoff, 1976).

• The suffix *-ity* attaches only to the stems of certain Latinate adjectives: *ferocious/ferocity; probable/probability; purple/*purpility; heavy/*heavity*. Adults are sensitive to this regularity in judging nonce words ending in the suffix (Randall, 1980). The semantically similar suffix *-hood* attaches only to native forms: *mother/motherhood; professor/*professorhood*. The suffix *-ness* is indifferent (Aronoff, 1976).

• The phonological rule of velar softening, which, for example, changes *k* to *s* in some environments, applies only to Latinate forms: *electric/electricity; mistake/*mistacen* (Chomsky and Halle, 1968).

• The particle *up*, signifying "to completion," combines with verbs that are monosyllabic or polysyllabic with stress only on the first syllable: *shake it up, jiggle it up, break it up, *vibrate it up, *destroy it up* (Whorf, 1956). In fact the verbs in verb-particle combinations in general are overwhelmingly native (di Sciullo and Williams, 1987): *give up / out / away / in* versus **donate up / out / away / in; make up / out / over* versus **create up / out / over*; and so on.

• Derived nominals from causative verbs can inherit their transitive argument structure only if the verb takes a Latinate nominalizing suffix like *-tion*, not if it takes a native suffix: *corn's growth / *the farmer's growth of corn* versus *the girl's conversion / the priest's conversion of the girl* (Smith, 1972).

Thus a variety of morphological and morphophonological rules in English are sensitive to the native/Latinate distinction. This leads to two questions: why do verbs group themselves into these two classes, and why do the classes govern the application of the dative rule?

As for the first question, we know in general that many languages subdivide their open-class vocabulary and let different kinds of morphological rules apply to these subclasses (e.g., gender classes, Hebrew binyanim; see also Aronoff, 1976). More specifically, McCarthy and Prince (in preparation) propose that every language has a phonological definition of its "basic" or "minimal" words, and many morphological processes are restricted to applying only to these basic words. In English (though not, say, Italian), the minimal word is one metrical foot long. This notion of basicness may also correlate with speakers' intuitions of which words in their language are felt to be natural, neutral, or native, and which are felt to be foreign or learnèd (see Selkirk and Dell, 1978, for a proposal that [+learnèd] is a morphological feature in French). The native/Latinate distinction has some of this connotation for English speakers. It has often been noted that native verbs tend to be high in frequency and to include the common simpler vocabulary of the language. Latinate words are of lower frequency and belong to the learnèd vocabulary, often suggesting a more formal speech register. I remember a cover story on Aretha Franklin in *Time* magazine in the mid-1960s, which described her in performance, "perspiration streaming down her face." An irate reader wrote in: "Aretha does not perspire. Aretha sweats."

There is evidence that English speakers have abstracted the morphological and phonological signatures of the native/Latinate distinction as correlating with the basic versus nonbasic vocabulary distinction. Baldi, Broderick, and Palermo (1985) showed that untutored speakers can judge fairly accurately whether real and nonsense native and Latinate stems were "native" versus "borrowed or foreign." Randall (1980) showed that speakers judged the suffix -*ity* as sounding good not only with Latinate stems but with those whose etymology was Greek. She suggests that a sense of "classicality" was involved.

So the native/Latinate distinction in English is a manifestation of an important cleavage of the vocabulary into two morphological classes, one containing basic, native, natural words and the other containing marked, foreign-sounding, special words. Why does the dative rule care about this distinction? One possibility is the following. In general, lexical rules can effect simultaneous changes in semantics, argument structure syntax, and morphology. The morphological change is seen in English only in the passive (and to a certain extent in the causative in earlier stages of the language, leaving pairs like *rise/raise, fall/fell, sit/set, lie/lay* as a residue).[11] But in several other languages, these alternations involve specific morphological changes. For example, the dative alternation is marked with an affix on the verb in Indonesian (Foley and Van Valin, 1985) and Shona, a Bantu language (Dowty, 1979a). The locative alternation can be marked with a verbal affix in Indonesian, Russian, German, and Hungarian (Foley and Van Valin, 1985). The causative and anticausative are marked by morphological changes in many languages (Comrie, 1985); causative rules that change a verb's membership in inflectional paradigms are subject to similar semantic constraints as causative rules (like that of English) that have no morphological effect (Nedyalkov and Silnitsky, 1973). The sensitivity of the English dative rule to morphological class could then be a consequence of two assumptions:

1. Morphological rules can be selective in their application to different morphological classes.
2. Rules that alter argument structures count as morphological rules, even if they do not effect an overt morphological change.

Thus the English dative rule, though its has no overt morphological operation, is formally a kind of rule that can have morphological operations, and therefore it can be sensitive to salient morphological subclasses in the vocabulary of the language. The dative is the only rule without a morphological change that we have seen be sensitive to the distinction, but in principle others could be.

Interestingly, any child who was prepared for the possibility that a dative rule is conditioned by morphological class would find "evidence" to confirm that suspicion. In Gropen et al. (1989), we combed through the transcripts of Adam, Eve, Sarah, Ross, and Mark in the ChiLDES database (MacWhinney and Snow, 1985), looking at all the prepositional-dative sentences (both *to* and *for*, including benefactives) in the speech of the adults who interacted with the children. Of course, there is no constraint forcing the verbs in these sentences to be native. Nonetheless, the only verb with Latinate phonology from these thousands of examples was *explain*, used once each by the adults playing with Adam and Sarah. (Three other verbs were Latinate but had the native stress-initial prosodic pattern: *measure*, *package*, and *finish*, used once apiece in benefactive prepositional *for*-datives.) So it seems that native verbs just happen to be the ones parents use when talking to their children, presumably because they are more basic and of higher frequency. But this statistical phenomenon has an intriguing consequence: even if English didn't have a morphological constraint on the dative, children would think that it did. This also may have something to do with the fact that the subclasses that don't obey the constraint (the *bequeath* class, the *arpanet* class) are learned later in life when long non-native words are common.

Let me touch briefly on two more aspects of the morphological constraint. First, it is possible that verbs that are transparently derived from nouns, especially nouns perceived to be namelike, lie outside the binary native/Latinate distinction. In many areas of morphology, tacit knowledge that a word's stem is from another category gives it a special status regarding the rules that apply to it. Irregular inflection is a notable case: *The defenseman of the Toronto Maple Leafs/*Leaves high-sticked/*high-stuck the goalie; Mary out-Sally-Rided Sally Ride / *out-Sally-Rode Sally Ride* (see Pinker and Prince, 1988). Many of the salient examples of productive dativization involve names for instruments (*xerox, satellite, microwave, radio, arpanet, E-mail, modem, fax*, etc.), usually with a clear origin as a familiar brand name, neologism, or jargon term. These examples exist even though some are verbs of creation, a subclass that ordinarily respects the native/Latinate distinction. (Such violations cannot be placed in a separate semantic subclass of verbs specifying "instruments of creation," because many of the familiar creation verbs do specify instruments, and none, to my knowledge, is Latinate, e.g., *She hammered me out a disc; he sawed me a piece of wood.*) Thus it seems that verbs derived from common "special" nouns (names, neologisms, etc.) are perceived to be neither native nor Latinate/learnèd, and as a result they escape any restriction of a dativizable subclass to native stems. This would account for the findings of the Gropen et al. (1989) questionnaire study, where we found that people rated double-object sentences with novel monosyllabic possession-change verbs as sounding more natural than novel polysyllabic possession-change verbs only for one of the four verb meanings used. The verb meaning that induced a sensitivity to phonology was the one in which the verb denoted a kind of transfer of possession (a legal means of property transfer). The other three verbs were all denominals involving some instrument whose name contributed the verb stem: causation of motion in a sport by the use of a special piece of equipment, creation by the use of a specific machine, and obtaining by the use of a kind of currency.

A final question that might be raised is whether there is a semantic motivation for the distinction between native and Latinate verbs. I think it's possible, though I would not be prepared to push the point. The argument might go like this. The Latinate verbs appear to be less basic on semantic as well as phonological grounds. Perhaps, because of their abstractness and semantic complexity, they connote less of a sense of directly acting on or affecting the recipient than native words do. For example, in order to *donate* something to someone, as opposed to merely *giving* it, one must have publicly charitable motives, the recipient must be an institution or an individual representing an institution or cause, and the donor need not know the recipient personally. *Explaining*, as opposed to *telling*, involves attention to unpacking the content of the message, not just transferring it to a listener directly; *announcing* is directed to a broad nonspecific audience. If the dativizability of verbs is motivated by the general notion "X causes Y to have Z," a morphological distinction that is correlated with the directness of the interaction between X and Y might be motivated as a condition on dativizability as well.

4.4.2   Locativizable Verbs

In chapter 3, I pointed out that a necessary criterion for a verb to participate in the locative alternation is that it specify or allow one to predict both a type of motion and an end state. This is what prevents the alternation of *fill* (end state only; thus it appears only in the *with* form) and *pour* (motion only; thus it appears only in the *into/onto* form). Conversely, the verbs that do alternate constrain aspects of both: *smear* involves contacting and moving a substance against a surface and adherence of the substance to it in a streaky layer; *load* involves a unit or type of substance appropriate for the containing object that is put in a designated location within the containing object, enabling it to perform some function (e.g., a gun, a camera). However, these constraints are not *sufficient* conditions for the alternation to occur, at least not without begging the question of why some words specify a motion or end state and others do not. For example, it is not convincing to say that the reason that **I dripped water onto the floor* is bad is that no end state is specified—why has the verb *drip* not accumulated a component of meaning specifying that the surface is covered with drops, like *sprinkle*?

Instead, there are finer-grained criteria, independent of end states or motions per se, that antecedently determine whether the verb can retain components of meaning for end states or motions. Rappaport and Levin (1985) have amassed a list of 142 locative verbs that is probably not far from being an exhaustive list for English. According to Levin (personal communication), these include all the locative verbs listed in previous papers on the topic, plus any that either of the authors heard or read over a span of several years while working on the paper. They point out that most verbs taking either of these constructions do not alternate: only 34 of the 142 appear in both forms. They did not mention any precise criteria specific to these alternating verbs. A crucial test for the narrow-class theory is whether such criteria can be found given that the alternation is productive for children but has exceptions for adults. Here I present the results of my own examination of their list. As the theory requires, there are narrow criteria governing the alternation; they are somewhat surprising but, once stated, fairly straightforward. Furthermore, I have found that a handful of verbs that Rappaport and Levin failed to include fall neatly into the subclasses that I derived from their list, and display the syntactic behavior that one would expect from such classification. I take this as support for the current proposals.

I began with the idea that since there are many verbs that take only the *with* form, and many that take only the *into/onto* form, there may be two rules operating in different directions, both of them defined over sets of subclasses. I tentatively subdivided the alternating verbs into those for which the rule seems to take an *into/onto* base form and derives a *with* form, and those where the derivation goes in the opposite direction. Directionality was determined as follows. If the locational theme (the content) is obligatory, it was assumed that the derivation is from *into* to *with*. For example, you can say *He piled the books* but not **He piled the shelf*; this suggests that the verb naturally takes the locational theme as object and that the derivation is from "pile NP-theme" to "pile NP-theme onto NP-goal," which in turn leads to "pile NP-goal with NP-theme." Conversely, if the simple two-argument form of the verb can appear with the locational goal (the container) but not the locational theme, it is assumed that the verb "naturally" takes the goal as direct object and that the form with the theme as object is derived from it; for example, *He stuffed the turkey/ *He stuffed the breadcrumbs*. When both arguments are optional, the derivation could have gone in either direction (followed by deletion of an oblique argument), but often one of the simple transitive forms sounds elliptical and causes the listener to fill in or presuppose the existence of the other argument when hearing it. Thus *He loaded the gun* sounds like a complete thought; *He loaded the bullets* is grammatical but feels like a truncated version of *He loaded the bullets into the gun*. This is somewhat subjective, but I would guess that the direction of the asymmetry is fairly reliable across speakers. Finally, there are only six verbs where both arguments are obligatory, two of them dubiously classified as such, and these are ignored for the purpose of finding the subclasses for each rule and only placed in the relevant subclasses later. I then tried to divide the 142 verbs into semantically cohesive subclasses such that for some of the subclasses, all the member verbs alternate; for others, none of the member verbs do.

The results of my analysis are that verbs for which the *into/onto* form is basic fall into about seven subclasses, of which four allow derivation of the *with* form, and verbs for which the *with* form is basic fall into about seven subclasses, of which two allow derivation of the *into/onto* form. The criteria for the class definitions include the thematic predicates and features used in the previous discussions and also a set of features pertaining to force (see Talmy, 1988), aspects of the dimensional geometry of solids (see Talmy, 1983; Jackendoff, 1987c), and a classification similar to the count/mass distinction in which matter is construed either as a discrete bounded entity or as a boundariless continuum; typically this will result in single objects being designated as countlike, and in liquids, powders, semisolid substances, and aggregates of small indistinguishable objects being designated as masslike.

The exact differentiation of the nonalternating classes from one another is not crucial as long as the criteria distinguishing them from the alternating classes are clear. Similarly, there are several nonalternating classes not listed here at all because their meaning is even more removed from the notion of putting an object into or onto a surface or container, for example, verbs of applying force (*push, shove, force*, etc.).

The content-oriented or *into/onto* verbs fall into the following classes:

1. Alternating. Simultaneous forceful contact and motion of a mass against a surface: *He smeared grease on the axle / He smeared the axle with grease.* Includes *brush, dab, daub, plaster, rub, slather, smear, smudge, spread, streak.* For many of the verbs a resulting shape is specified, usually corresponding to the deverbal noun: *a smear, a smudge*, and so on (Rappaport and Levin, 1985).

2. Alternating. Vertical arrangement on a horizontal surface: *He heaped bricks on the stool / He heaped the stool with bricks.* Includes *heap, pile, stack.*

3. Alternating. Force is imparted to a mass, causing ballistic motion in a specified spatial distribution along a trajectory: *She splashed water on the dog / She splashed the dog with water.* Includes *inject, spatter, splash, splatter, spray, sprinkle,[12] squirt.*

4. Alternating. Mass is caused to move in a widespread or nondirected distribution: *The farmer scattered seeds onto the field / The farmer scattered the field with seeds* (the latter is marginal for some speakers). Includes *bestrew, scatter, sow, strew.*

5. Nonalternating. A mass is enabled to move via the force of gravity: *She dribbled paint onto the floor / *She dribbled the floor with paint.* Includes *dribble, drip, drizzle, dump, ladle, pour, shake, slop, slosh, spill.*

6. Nonalternating. Flexible object extended in one dimension is put around another object (preposition is *around*): *He coiled the chain around the pole / *He coiled the pole with the chain.* Includes *coil, spin, twirl, twist, whirl, wind.*

7. Nonalternating. Mass is expelled from inside an entity: *He spat tobacco juice onto the table / *He spat the table with tobacco juice.* Includes *emit, excrete, expectorate, expel, exude, secrete, spew, vomit.* (In the next section we will see that these verbs also behave as a class with respect to causativization.)

We could also add an eighth, nonalternating class, not included in Rappaport and Levin's list: verbs of attachment, such as *attach, fasten, glue, nail, paste, pin, staple, stick*, and *tape.* They all imply the existence of an intermediate instrument object or substance holding objects together, and usually specify the geometry of the attachment region (e.g., at a point versus sharing a surface).

The container-oriented or *with* verbs fall into the following classes:

1. Alternating. A mass is forced into a container against the limits of its capacity: *They packed oakum into the crack / They packed the crack with oakum.* Includes the wadding sense of *pack*, as well as *cram, crowd, jam, stuff, wad.*

2. Alternating. A mass of a size, shape, or type defined by the intended use of a container (and not purely by its geometry) is put into the container, enabling it to accomplish its function: *Max loaded the gun with bullets / Max loaded*

bullets into the gun. Includes *load, pack* (what one does to suitcases), *stock* (what one does to shelves).

3. Nonalternating. A layer completely covers a surface: *They inundated the field with water* / **They inundated water onto the field.* The layer may be liquid, as in *deluge, douse, flood,* and *inundate,* or solid, as in *bandage, blanket, coat, cover, encrust, face, inlay, pad, pave, plate, shroud, smother, tile. Line* and *edge* are similar, except with one less dimension; *fill* and perhaps *occupy* are also similar, with one more dimension.

4. Nonalternating. Addition of an object or mass to a location causes an esthetic or qualitative, often evaluative, change in the location: *They adorned the gift with ribbons* / **They adorned ribbons onto the gift.* Includes *adorn, burden, clutter, deck, dirty, embellish, emblazon, endow, enrich, festoon, garnish, imbue, infect, litter, ornament, pollute, replenish, season, soil, stain, taint, trim.*

5. Nonalternating. A mass is caused to be coextensive with a solid or layerlike medium: *She soaked the sponge with water* / **She soaked water into the sponge.* The mass may be composed of layers or strings, as in *interlace, interlard, interleave, intersperse, interweave, lard, ripple, vein,* or of liquids, as in *drench, impregnate, infuse, saturate, soak, stain (what one does to wood), suffuse.*

6. Nonalternating. An object or mass impedes the free movement of, from, or through the object in which it is put: *I clogged the sink with a cloth* / **I clogged a cloth into the sink; She bound him with rope* / **She bound rope onto/around him.* Includes verbs pertaining to liquids in containers, as in *block, choke, clog, dam, plug, stop up,* and bound movable objects, as in *bind, chain, entangle, lash, lasso, rope.*

7. Nonalternating. A set of objects is distributed over a surface: *They studded the coat with metal stars* / **They studded metal stars onto the coat.* Includes *bombard, blot, dapple,*[13] *riddle, speckle, splotch, spot, stud.* The type of object is specified by the verb (a splotch, a hole, a stud, etc.).

Finally, there are two alternating verbs that have a unique geometry and hence could be seen as belonging to one-word classes. *String* (as in *They strung lights on the roof* / *They strung the roof with lights*) involves a static arrangement of a linear object along a surface. *Wrap* at first glance seems similar in some ways to *cover* (*with* form only) and in other ways to *wind* or *coil* (*around* form only). Its absolute minimum requirement is that a flexible object conform to part of the shape of an object along two or more orthogonal dimensions. Thus it is not *wrapping* when one installs shelf paper cut to the exact size of the shelf, but it can be called *wrapping* if the paper extends beyond the edges of the shelf and is bent around them.

Motivation for the classes. All the classes are clearly compatible with their respective thematic cores. The *into/onto* classes all specify the kind of force or direction of motion according to which the theme moves or is caused to move: it is forced against something (*smear*), around something (*wrap*), all over the place (*scatter*), thanks to gravity (*dribble*), against gravity (*pile*), or with some imparted force. The verbs in the *with* class all specify a change of state resulting from the addition of material, usually pertaining to the entire object: a qualitative change, usually with esthetic or evaluative connotations (*adorn, pollute*); a decrease in freedom to move (*block, bind*); a definitionally holistic coextensive spatial arrangement either in a solid (*saturate*) or surface (*cover*).[14]

The motivation for which classes alternate comes from two sources. First, as in the case of the dative, the conversion of an *into/onto*-locative into a *with*-locative causes a goal argument to become a patient. Therefore, types of actions that can more easily be construed as something that can happen to the goal are more likely to support the reconstrual of the goal as a patient and more likely, as a class, to undergo locativization. Second, container-oriented (*with*-locative) verbs cannot merely specify that a change of state has occurred by covering or filling but must specify what that state is; otherwise they would all be synonymous with *fill* and *cover* (and we know that languages avoid true synonymity; this "Principle of Contrast," Clark, 1987, will be discussed in more detail in chapter 6). Likewise, content-oriented (*into/onto*-locative) verbs must not merely specify the movement of a substance to a location but must specify some particular manner of causation or motion or some particular kind of substance; otherwise they would all be synonymous with *put*. Therefore the verbs in the alternating content-oriented classes should contain information that allows the speaker to predict a *particular* state change of the goal, not just *that* the goal has changed state, and the alternating container-oriented subclasses should contain information that allows the speaker to predict *what kind* of thing moves or *how* it moves, not just *that* something moves. This kind of interpredictability, in addition to the general ease of cognitively reconstruing a motion as a state change, seems to characterize the choice of which subclasses alternate.

Thus in the *smear* class the location and moved substance simultaneously feel the force of the action, and in the *spray* class the force imparted to the object can aim it in a direction. This is in contrast to the *pour* class, where gravity is a force mediating between the immediate effect on the moving object and the effect on the destination. Furthermore, the kind of pressure, direction, and motion specified in the *smear* verbs allows one to predict with reasonable specificity the distribution of the substance on the surface (a smear, a dab, etc.) that characterizes how the surface has changed. Similarly, in the *spray* class there is a necessary imposition of a shape and distribution of the theme, whose cross-section helps to predict the shape of the adhering layer on the surface at which it arrives. For verbs that alternate in the other direction, we would expect that the specified effect on the container or surface also imposes constraints on the act of moving the contents. Thus for *stuff* verbs, the amount moved is defined as "too much" with respect to the capacity of the container; for *load* verbs the moved objects are of a shape, size, and kind appropriate to the container. Whether motivation-by-interpredictability is psychological or merely historical is an open question, of course; given the strong functional pressure to avoid synonymity in language acquisition (Clark, 1987), it could be psychological.

If the general analysis described in this section is correct, it is also interesting that the conflation subclasses can contain any number of verbs, perhaps even one. That would suggest that subclass-defined generalizations are not licensed by a statistical averaging process triggered by large numbers of similarly behaving verbs, but that each alternating verb defines a generalizable region in semantic space around it, with any verb falling into that region automatically sharing its privilege to alternate. I will explore this phenomenon in greater depth in chapters 5 and 6.

Rappaport and Levin call attention to a number of closely related alternations. As I would predict, all of them apply freely only within well-defined narrow subclasses, not just to any verb in the relevant cognitive domain. For example, among the verbs of "image impression," we have alternators (*He branded his name onto the fence / He branded the fence with his name*) and nonalternators of both kinds (*He wrote his name into the book / *He wrote the book with his name; He illustrated the page with a picture / *He illustrated a picture onto the page*). The *into/onto* nonalternators, roughly, constrain properties of the type of pattern impressed, either by their source (*copy, plot, sketch, trace*), manner of creation (*doodle, scrawl, scribble*), or symbolic type (*draw, letter, write*). The *with* nonalternators entail a specific kind of esthetic, evaluative, or purposive change of the surface (*adorn, decorate, embellish, illustrate*). The alternators, which include *brand, emboss, embroider, engrave, etch, imprint, inscribe, mark, set, stamp*, and *tattoo*, specify a particular manner or means in which the surface was affected and properties of the substance of the image and the medium onto which it is put, all defined in concrete physical terms (e.g., with the use of a brand or thread, made from ink or burned material, underneath skin or on a surface or piercing cloth). What seems to be crucial is that these properties are defined physically and not in terms of either the symbolic properties of image (e.g., drawing versus letters versus numbers) or the esthetic purpose of the inscription (e.g., decoration).

Likewise, the related *empty* alternation consists of three alternating classes and several nonalternating classes. One class of alternators include those that specify a specific kind of void end state regardless of manner (*He cleared dishes from the table / He cleared the table of dishes*; also *clean, cleanse, empty, strip*).

There are also alternators that are a bit less free in that they allow either the *from* form or a form with the source as direct object but lacking an *of*-phrase. These alternators can be neatly characterized as specifying either a particular manner of removal via contact with the source (*She wiped crumbs from the table / She wiped the table (*of crumbs)*; also *scrub, wash, wring, skim*), or a particular instrument of removal (*He vacuumed lint from the carpet / He vacuumed the carpet (*of lint)*; also *comb, filter, hose, mop, sponge*).

Interestingly, Talmy (1985) points out that verbs involving the removal of objects or conditions from people's possession (alienable or inalienable) virtually never alternate: *She robbed him of his money / *She robbed his money from him*; *She stole money from him / *She stole him of his money*. Verbs resembling *steal* include *seize, recover, withhold, grab*; verbs resembling *rob* include *bilk, cheat, cure, fleece, relieve, unburden*. (*Rip off* is the chief exception; one can *rip off Ma Bell* or *Rip off money from Ma Bell*.) This wholesale exclusion of possession-removal verbs is fortunate, because *steal* and *rob* in particular are basically synonyms except for their choice of direct object. If the rest of their semantic field could alternate, they would stand as embarrassing negative exceptions.[15]

4.4.3   Causativizable Verbs

Not all intransitive verbs can be transformed into causative transitives, and not all causative transitives can be transformed in the opposite direction, into "anticausative" intransitives. There are three main classes of intransitives that can be causativized. First, there are verbs of extrinsic change of physical state; examples are listed in (4.28). In the intransitive form the change is not caused by an identifiable external agent; this distinguishes inchoatives such as *The plastic shrank* from passives such as *The plastic was shrunk*.

(4.28)   The box opened / closed / melted / shrank / shattered.
         I opened / closed / melted / shrank / shattered the box.

A second alternating class—see (4.29)—involves contained motion taking place in a particular manner. By "contained" I mean that it is possible for the center of mass of the moving object to remain roughly in one "place" while its parts move, as in *John slid in one spot for an hour*.[16] The motion is of a kind that need not be internally caused; that is, *skidding* can be either voluntary or involuntary, and it belongs to this class; *running* can only be voluntary, and it is excluded.

(4.29)   The log slid / skidded / floated / rolled / bounced.
         Brian slid / skidded / floated / rolled / bounced the log.

A third kind of alternating verb undergoes a semantic change that is not the same as that of the previous classes. One subclass, presented in (4.30a), involves manner of locomotion, and in its transitive version the sense is one of coercing or encouraging the locomotion. The other subclass, shown in (4.30b), signifies an instrument of transportation, and in the transitive form it signifies enabling and accompanying the transportation.

(4.30) (a) The horse walked / galloped / trotted / raced / ran / jumped / past the
             barn.
             I walked / galloped / trotted / raced / ran / jumped / jogged the horse
             past the barn.

       (b) She drove / flew / cycled / ferried / boated / sailed / motored to New
             York.
             Captain Mars drove / flew / cycled / ferried / boated / sailed / motored
             her to New York.

There are several subclasses of verbs that might have been thought to alternate systematically but in fact do not. The most notable is the class of verbs of motion in a lexically specified direction, as shown in (4.31). In contrast to verbs of manner of motion, these verbs treat the theme as a dimensionless point undergoing a translation in space.

(4.31)   My son went to school.
         *I went my son to school.

         His sister came home from the hospital.
         *He came his sister home from the hospital.

         The flag rose.
         *I rose the flag.

         The shoe fell.
         *He fell the shoe. (also ascend, descend, leave, exit, enter, arrive)

Other noncausativizable subclasses include verbs of volitional or internally caused actions, as in (4.32);[17] verbs of coming into or going out of existence, as in (4.33);[18] most verbs of emotional expression, as in (4.34); and verbs of emission including emission of lights, sounds, and substances, as in (4.35).

(4.32)   Sally ate.
         *Bert ate [= fed] Sally. (Also jump, hop, run, drink, sing, etc.)

(4.33)   Bobby died.
         *Catherine died Bobby. (Also expire, decease, perish, croak, pass
             away, kick off, bite the dust, etc.; see Talmy, 1985)

The bird vanished.

*The pin vanished the bubble. (Also appear, disappear, disintegrate, etc.)

(4.34)   The audience smiled.

*Irv smiled his audience. (Also cry, laugh, frown, blink, etc.)[19]

(4.35)   The light glowed.

*Barbara glowed the light. (Also glitter, glisten, shimmer, blaze, etc.)

The saw howled.

*Billy howled the saw. (Also whine, shriek, buzz, chatter, sing)

The sauce bubbled.

*Hazel bubbled the sauce. (Also erupt, smoke, sweat [e.g., as applied to cheese or wood], ooze, puff, leak, bleed, shed.)[20]

Note that the complementary subclasses that express the same kinds of meanings in transitive verbs all resist the reverse process of anticausativization formation: the transitive verbs of causation of directed motion cannot be used intransitively, as shown in (4.36); nor can verbs of killing, creating, or destroying, as shown in (4.37); nor can verbs of inducing behavior, as shown in (4.38).

(4.36)   I took my son to school.

*My son took to school.

I brought my sister home.

*My sister brought home.

I raised the flag.

*The flag raised.

(4.37)   Catherine killed Bobby.

*Bobby killed [= died]. (Also slay, murder, dispatch, liquidate, assassinate, slaughter, exterminate, waste, do in, etc.; see Talmy, 1985)

They created a monster.

*A monster created.

(4.38)   Jack tickled Sally.

*Sally tickled. (Also amuse, nauseate, feed, bribe, convince, etc.)

It is important not to confuse these pure inchoative sentences, which can denote specific events, with middles, which assert a property of the subject. Typically middles appear with adverbials, as in *Bureaucrats bribe easily,* though the adverbial meaning can also be supplied by other elements such as intonation or negation: *This lock won't pick* (it's jammed); *Around here, bureaucrats BRIBE!* (see Keyser and Roeper, 1984, and Hale and Keyser, 1986, 1987).

In addition, as we noted with reference to (4.10), verbs of motion-contact-effect do not anticausativize: *The bread cut / sliced / hacked.* This is true even though causation is inherent to their meaning and visible to other selective alternations such as the middle, which requires it (*The bread cut / broke / *hit easily*), and the contact-locative alternation, which forbids it (*I *cut / *broke / hit the knife against the bread* (= cut / broke / hit the bread with the knife).[21]

Motivation for the causativizable classes. As before, one can discern a motivation for the designation of subclasses that do or do not permit alternations in each direction. Interestingly, the rationales are of two kinds. In some cases, the language simply does not supply any transitive verb allowing one to express the notion that X acts on Y, causing Y to change, act, or move as a result. For example, there are no verbs that mean to cause someone to rejoice, cry, shout, drink, talk, or sleep. It is as if such events are inherently noncausable directly by an external agent, since they involve an inherent internal cause that must mediate any effect of an external agent. In English, most verbs of physical emission assimilate to this pattern, as if the ability to emit a light, sound, or substance inheres in the emitter and can be caused from the outside only indirectly. Conversely, there are cases where there is no way to use an intransitive verb to express the notion that a particular event, usually caused, can occur spontaneously or in the absence of a cause or agent, such as being cut or amused. It is as if such events were conceived as being inherently unoccurrable without some external cause. These are phenomena pertaining to the possible conflations of meaning elements within English verbs, motivated by the cognitive content of the notion "direct causation." (See B. Levin, 1985, and Guerssel, 1986, for discussions of the grammatical consequences of the difference between intrinsic causation, where it is implied that some property inherent to the object itself is responsible for its behaving in a certain way, and extrinsic causation, where the causal antecedent may not be inherent in the object's essence.)

The other kind of motivation is quite different: For some kinds of events, both inchoative intransitive and causative transitive meanings exist, but they are not allowed to share the same verb root, such as *kill* and *die*, *bring* and *come*, or *take* and *go* (this phenomenon is also seen in the possession-depriving verbs in the locative class, such as *steal* and *rob*). This is due not to the existence or nonexistence of possible conflations of meaning but to the existence or nonexistence of narrow-range lexical rules that map between them. (Another way of putting it is that such rules determine whether stems can be shared among verbs in different conflation classes.) Intuitively, the rules governing stem-sharing reflect how much the language lets you bend or enrich a verb's meaning before it has to be treated as a completely different verb. In effect, the lexicon groups some kinds of events together as exemplars of the same kind, to be expressed by a single verb, and differentiates other kinds of events. If John kills Bill, is that just causing him to die, or is there something unique about the act of killing that makes it different from the sum of its parts of causing and dying? English provides one kind of answer to this question.

In their survey of causative alternations in over a hundred languages, Nedyalkov and Silnitsky (1973) offer intriguing partial support for the hypothesis that while the exact verbs that participate in causative alternations differ across languages, there are systematic patterns governing which verbs are most likely to alternate. They found that no language allowed a lexical causative form of *laugh*, or even a suppletive verb meaning "cause to laugh" (though some could express it with a separate causative affix). Causing to laugh is simply not expressible as a simple lexical item. In contrast, *break* was quite likely to participate in a lexical causative alternation (as it does in English). *Boil* and *burn* were somewhere in between; they were also the only verbs among these four that ever appeared in suppletive causative/noncausative pairs. One can speculate that these phenomena are related to those verbs' being associated with notions of going out of existence and/or of emitting substances, which in general are not causativizable in English, presumably because of the greater connotation of important internal causal influences. This all suggests that there is a universal continuum of lexical causativizability, presumably corresponding to the ease of conceiving of a given kind of event as being directly causable from without, running from verbs for human actions to verbs for simple state changes, perhaps with verbs for changes involving emission and disappearance in between.

4.4.4 Passivizable Verbs
In section 3.3.4.4 I proposed that the thematic core of passive participles is "*X* is in the circumstance defined by *Y* acting on it." That is, *X* is a theme in the circumstance field; the position in that field that *X* occupies is defined in terms of *X* being a patient and *Y* being an agent. Thus *Mary was hit by John* means roughly "Mary is in the circumstance characterized by John's hitting her." I tried to show how certain kinds of verbs—symmetrical predicates, prepositional passives and idioms with no possible sense of patienthood associated with the object, and static relations of spatial arrangement, possession, and measurement—are unpassivizable because they are incompatible with this thematic core. The logic was the same as that used in explaining the dative, locative, and causative alternations: the syntactic form of the passive, the change in interpretation that it engenders, and its pattern of selectivity across verbs are all manifestations of a single principle, the principle that argument structures are projections of thematic cores.[22]

The discussions of the dative, causative, and locative alternations in this chapter dealt with the problem that the thematic core theory did not rule out enough verbs: some verbs that were cognitively compatible with the thematic core did not alternate (i.e., they were negative exceptions). This required the additional claim that the thematic cores associated with broad-range rules do not rule out verbs directly but motivate narrow-range rules that license the actual inclusion or exclusion of verbs. For the passive, the story has to be different. The problem isn't that the semantic correlates of passivization fail to exclude some nonpassivizable verbs. On the contrary, all verbs that clearly have agents and patients passivize. There are no agent-patient verbs that puzzle us in the way that *throw* and *shout* did for the dative, *die* and *fall* did for the causative, or *pour* and *coil* did for the locative. Thus there is no need for narrow conflation classes and narrow-range rules that carve up the verbs with agents and patients; the semantics of the broad-range rule are sufficient to include them all.

The passive faces the opposite problem. Many verbs that passivize do not have arguments that we would easily classify as agents and patients. Thus we must explain how the broad-range rule of passivization is *extended* to cover verbs that do not appear to meet its semantic conditions, not how it is *restricted* from applying to verbs that do. The problem is no less hard than those we faced for the other alternations, because the distinctions between verbs lacking patient objects that do and do not passivize appear obscure. First, there are pairs of verbs or verb forms with similar meanings but different thematic roles assigned to their object arguments, and *both* forms passivize. This would appear to vitiate any principle that would restrict passivization to verbs whose objects have particular thematic roles. Examples are the forms related by the dative and locative alternations, and pairs of psychological verbs one of which has an experiencer subject, like *fear*, the other of which has a stimulus subject, like *frighten*. Second, there are passivizable concrete event verbs whose subjects have roles other than agent, such as *receive*, whose subject is a goal, and *open*, whose subject can be an instrument (as in *The door was opened by a brass key*). Third, although certain highly stative or abstract verbs fail to passivize (idiom chunks, measure verbs), many others do, such as *Drastic measures were justified by the dire situation*. Fourth, verbs defining spatial relations sometimes do (e.g., *surround*) and sometimes don't (e.g., *contain*) passivize. Fifth, verbs defining possessional relations sometimes do (e.g. *own*) and sometimes don't (e.g., *have*) passivize. It is these borderline cases that have made the semantic boundaries of passivization so difficult to characterize in the past; I know of no theory that demarcates these boundaries fully.

How can we characterize the very broad range of the English passive? It won't work to say that the passive is a purely syntactic rule that applies to any verb with a syntactic object, because that is false. But if passivizability is due only to the thematic concomitants of the broad-range passive rule, we would expect it to be confined to verbs taking obvious agents and patients, which it is not. A third possibility is that passivization, like the other alternations, is actually licensed by a set of narrow-range rules with subtle semantic conditions and that these numerous mini-passive rules happen to exhaust all of the subclasses of agent-patient verbs in English and embrace some, but not all, of the nonagentive subclasses as well. This is a possibility that I cannot rule out conclusively, but if true it would be surprising that we do not find at least a few pockets of unpassivizable agent-patient verbs, as we do for the other alternations.

The solution that I think is most reasonable takes off from Bolinger (1977a) and S. Anderson (1977), who suggested that passivization seems to apply when the object either is a patient or is capable of being construed as one. More precisely, I will suggest the following. The broad-range rule of passivization applies productively to all and only the transitive verbs that have agents and patients. Thus it supplies a *sufficient* condition for a verb to alternate, and in that regard it is unlike the dative, causative, and locative alternations, whose broad-range rules merely define *necessary* conditions (which then motivate a set of narrow-range rules that are the actual source of the sufficient conditions). However, simple action or change verbs are not the only ones that have agents and patients. English has a number of verbs that are ambiguous between meanings with agent-patient roles and meanings with other roles, and it has a number of rules that convert verbs lacking agent subjects and patient objects into related forms that do have these assignments. It is the versions of these verbs with agents and patients that passivize; similar versions that lack these roles do not. To support this analysis, I will rely on two assumptions that have already pervaded my analyses of other verb subclasses. First, the notion of patient (like other thematic relations) can be used in nonphysical semantic fields, so it does not refer only to entities that are physically acted upon. (The abstract notion of patient that I employ is discussed in more detail in section 5.5.7.) Second, the required agent-patient relations need constitute only one component of the verb's meaning; any number of other sets of semantic relations can also be defined and the passive rule will not be blocked by them.

In the next five subsections, I will use these assumptions to show why passivization does or does not apply to various kinds of verbs, and then I will try to explain why the passive is different from the other alternations.

4.4.4.1 Passivizable Action Verbs Let me start with the most straightforward cases, involving verbs denoting actions. All the subclasses of two-argument verbs discussed so far that have actional patients and themes, including verbs of effect (i.e., lexical causatives) and motion-contact-effect (e.g., *cut*) obviously are compatible with the passive thematic core. There is already a state that the verb predicates of the passive subject, and a patient relation defined for it. Likewise, we have already seen how the verbs undergoing the dative and locative alternations have two related semantic forms, each of which assigns a patient and a theme role to the argument appearing as direct object. In *They loaded hay into the wagon*, the object *hay* is construed as the patient of the action that results in its being the theme of a change of location; in *They loaded the wagon with hay*, the object *the wagon* is construed as the patient of the action that results in its being the theme of a change of state (from empty to full). The *to*-dative alternation is similar. The prepositional form with *to* is construed as having an agent change the location of its object argument; the object is thus the patient of the action performed by the agent and the theme of the resulting location change. Thus it is passivizable, as in *The book was given to John*. The double-object counterpart is construed as having an agent act on a person, causing him to gain possession of something. Thus the person is the patient of the act performed by the agent and the possessor in the possession-change event. This specification of a patient makes the double-object form eligible for passivization: *John was given a book.*[23]

4.4.4.2 The Thematic Relations Hypothesis Extended to Agent-Patient Relations   Now what about nonactional transitive verbs? Earlier I suggested that there is a more general sense of agency and patienthood, having to do with responsibility and abstract causation, that allowed the passive thematic core to be extended to many subclasses of abstract verbs. Can this be stated more explicitly? Lakoff (1977) offers one proposal. He lists a set of properties that characterize a "prototypical" causation event, so that events possessing some but not all of these properties are still construable as involving causation but less prototypically so. Prototypical causation involves a single, willful, human agent who deliberately transfers energy toward a single perceived patient who noticeably changes state as a result in a single local event. Hopper and Thompson (1980) offer a similar definition of the prototypical "transitive" event, and Maratsos et al. (1985) specifically note its relevance to passivizability.

A somewhat more systematic account comes from Talmy (1988). Talmy offers a theory according to which the roles of agent and patient can be generalized in a quasi-metaphorical way to nonactional fields, just as the roles of theme, goal, source, location, and path have been generalized from literal spatial location to fields of circumstance, possession, identity, communication, and so on (Gruber, 1965; Jackendoff, 1972, 1983, 1987a). According to Talmy, there is an intuitive notion of "force dynamics" that pervades lexical semantics, just as there is a notion of topology that underlies the classic thematic relations of themes, locations, and paths (Talmy, 1983). In this force-dynamic model, objects are conceived as bodies with inherent tendencies toward motion or rest.

An *agonist* is a body whose state of motion or rest is being focused on in a sentence. An *antagonist* is a body impinging on an agonist, imposing a counteracting force toward motion or rest, which sums with the inherent tendency of the agonist to determine what happens to it. When the agonist's tendency is toward rest and the antagonist's is toward motion and the latter is stronger, the agonist moves; this is illustrated periphrastically in (4.39a). When the agonist's tendency is toward motion and the antagonist's tendency toward rest is stronger, the agonist stays put; see (4.39b). These are examples of steady-state causation. If the antagonist is not there from the beginning but comes into place and exerts its effect, we have onset causation, as in (4.39c, d). In all four of these examples the result is in opposition to the agonist's intrinsic tendency. If an antagonist is removed, allowing the agonist to move or not move according to its inherent tendency, we have onset permissive or "letting" causation, as in (4.39e, f).

(4.39) (a) The ball kept rolling because of the wind blowing on it.
      (b The log kept lying on the incline because of the ridge there.
      (c) The ball's hitting it made the lamp topple from the table.
      (d) The water's dripping on it made the fire die down.
      (e) The plug's coming loose let the water flow from the tank.
      (f) The stirring rod's breaking let the particles settle.

The force-dynamic analysis offers a common set of elements out of which various related notions associated with agency and causation can be defined, including causation by an event, an agent, or an instrument; causation by onset or within a steady state; permissive or "letting" causation; "inducive" causation of activity by an agent; and causation of change versus absence of change. (In chapter 5 I will outline an explicit theory of how this space of possibilities is mentally represented in semantic structure.) Furthermore, the domain of causation need not be physical motion and rest; Talmy gives examples where the analysis extends to intrapsychic forces, as in the contrast between *He didn't close the door* and *He refrained from closing the door*, and social forces, as in the contrast between *She told him to leave* and *She urged him to leave*. He also suggests that they can be extended to epistemic domains of inference and reasoning, as when one is "forced" to a conclusion.

Of more immediate interest, Talmy argues that the notion of agent can be defined within this system as an antagonist whose intrinsic force tendency is volitional. Thus simple causal sentences such as *John broke the lamp* are not fundamentally different from *The ball's hitting it broke the lamp*. (In agent causation, as in other types of causation, a number of microscopic intervening generic links in the causal chain are usually omitted.) Talmy also formalizes some of the key semantic elements of a variety of definitions of open- and closed-class lexical items, such as *despite, keep, let, because, make, get, stop, try, manage, help, leave,* and the modal auxiliaries.

What this analysis buys us is a set of features that can be used to extend the notions of agent and patient in a way that allows for the possibility that abstract verbs have such roles. In transitive verbs in general, patients correspond to agonists, agents to antagonists; hence the agonist is mapped onto object and antagonist mapped onto subject.[24] We can say that the minimal agent-patient relation is one where two entities are involved in a single asymmetrical relationship defined by one entity's exerting some causal power against the other; the nature of this exertion is specified by the particular verb. Thus many transitive verbs that are not actional can nonetheless be seen as having abstract agent and patient roles, and passivization will apply to them. Let me examine the circumstances in which this can happen.

4.4.4.3   Passivizable Abstract and Stative Verbs   *Instrumental subjects.* Verbs whose subjects play the role of instrument can passivize: *The brass key opened the door / The door was opened by the brass key.* This is often taken as evidence that the English passive can apply regardless of thematic role. However, this assumes that the subject of these sentences truly plays no semantic role other than instrument. This is false. Not just any instrument can become a subject: **A spoon ate the cereal; *The telescope saw the galaxy; *John's graphite racket won the tennis match.* B. Levin (1985) and Rappaport and Levin (in press) point out that only intermediary instruments can become subjects, not just facilitating instruments. An intermediary instrument is basically a participant in the penultimate event of a causal chain, ordinarily unexpressed or backgrounded. In other words, there is a temporally unfolding chain "John acts on key CAUSES key acts on door CAUSES door opens" but no causal chain "John acts on spoon CAUSES spoon acts on cereal CAUSES cereal is eaten," because in the latter case the specified grain size for the events forces inclusion of an additional event of John acting on the cereal in order for it to be eaten. Thus instrumental subjects are also, by grammatical necessity, agentlike proximal antagonists or causes. English appears to have a narrow-range rule that we could call "intermediary instrument promotion," which converts verbs with a multilink causal chain containing an intermediary instrument argument into verbs with a two-link chain in which the instrument argument is the first link, hence a kind of agent, hence subject. That is the version that feeds the passive rule.

Epistemic and deontic verbs. Verbs expressing abstract relations can sometimes be construed as involving generalized agents and patients. Propositions and situations can be seen to possess the analogue of causal or force tendencies that can result in other propositions or situations being true or coming about that otherwise would not, or that by being eliminated no longer prevent them from being true or coming about. In fact, many English verbs—see (4.40)—take either animate or abstract referents as their subjects, which is consistent with the suggestion that agents are simply volitional causes. English seems to have one or more rules that we could call "epistemic agent disembodiment," converting verbs with an animate argument whose actions cause an epistemic or deontic change into verbs with an abstract argument that ensures or engenders such a state by means of the force of its content. If Talmy is correct, these abstract verbs still have a kind of agent argument, and the applicability of passivization to them follows.

(4.40) John justified the new treaty. / The new treaty was justified by John.

The horrors of the last war justified the new treaty. / The new treaty was justified by the horrors of the last war.

The judge nullified the amendment. / The amendment was nullified by the judge.

The principles of the constitution nullify such an amendment. / The amendment is nullified by principles of the constitution.

John proved the theorem. / The theorem was proved by John.

These steps prove the theorem. / The theorem is proved by these steps.

Bob created a golden opportunity for us. / A golden opportunity was created for us by John.

Falling interest rates have created a golden opportunity for us. / A golden opportunity has been created for us by falling interest rates.

"Psych-verbs." Transitive psychological verbs, also lacking agents and patients, are an important topic of current research on argument structure because they come in two complementary forms: those like *please* and *frighten*, where the stimulus is the subject, and those like *like* and *fear*, where the experiencer is the subject. Furthermore, they differ in how various grammatical processes apply to their subjects, such as the binding of anaphoric elements within them (see, e.g., Belletti and Rizzi, 1986; Grimshaw, in press). It is therefore curious that on the face of it, both kinds of verbs passivize: *John was feared/liked by Bill; John was frightened/pleased by Bill.* But how could this be so in a theory in which the links between thematic roles and grammatical functions are critical? There are two possibilities.

One possibility is that only one of these subclasses has a mapping of thematic roles onto argument structure that supports passivization; the other subclass in fact lacks a verbal passive and the passive "participles" we see are actually adjectives. This is clearly the case in Italian where the two kinds of passive forms are morphologically distinct (Belletti and Rizzi, 1986). Grimshaw notes that there is some evidence that this might be true in English as well; if so, it would be consistent with a new version of Jackendoff's Thematic Hierarchy Condition that she has developed. She points out that *frighten* verbs clearly *can* be adjectival passives, because they have uniquely adjectival properties. They can undergo negative *un*-prefixation (*Betty was unperturbed by the situation* / **The situation unperturbed Betty*). They appear as complements to certain adjective-selecting verbs like *seem* (*John seems sick* / *frightened by the situation* / **running* / **hit by Bill*). And they accept a variety of prepositions, not just the verbal passive's *by* (*Berry was frightened by* / *of* / *at* / *about the thought of leaving*). Grimshaw also points out that whereas *frighten* verbs can appear with the progressive in the active (*The situation was depressing Mary*), it cannot do so as felicitously in the passive (*?Mary was being depressed by the situation*). This is exactly what one would expect if the passive was adjectival (cf. *?Mary was being sick*).

The other possibility is that *frighten* verbs in English have both adjectival and verbal passives, because they actually do assign a causal (hence quasi-agentive) role to the stimulus event. Grimshaw notes that the reason that passives of *frighten* verbs are less than fully acceptable in the progressive is that they require the speaker to construe the *by*-object as a kind of agent, which is cognitively difficult when it is something as nonagentive as a situation. However, the sentences are not entirely ungrammatical, especially when the aspectual interactions between the psychological state and the effect of the progressive are weakened, as in *Mary sat around being depressed by the situation*. This suggests that the verbal passive is possible and that it is accompanied by an attribution of responsibility to the stimulus situation, as in Talmy's examples in (4.39). As Dowty (1982) points out, the *frighten*-verbs can all signify an event of causation of a change of state (hence a patient/theme role for the object) as well as extended states (with only an experiencer role): *The thunderclap frightened John* could refer either to John's being startled or to his being concerned. The ability of the stimulus-subject verbs to support a causal reading becomes even more apparent when we consider the fact that virtually all of them can also appear with volitional animate subjects (e.g. *John deliberately tried to frighten* / *worry* / *please* / *arouse* / *excite me*; see Talmy, 1985, for a list of one hundred of them). Thus it is likely that a rule similar to epistemic agent disembodiment (the one discussed in relation to *justify* verbs) relates the two versions of these verbs. If such a rule converts the version of these verbs with an event reading and a causal agent role (perhaps subsuming causation by an event like a thunderclap) into a version with a stative reading in the field of epistemic or psychological causation, the stative version would continue to have an agentlike role, thereby being able to feed passivization.[25]

Thus the passivizability of both *fear* and *frighten* verbs follows from the thematic core of the passive. This can be seen by considering the cognitive ambiguity inherent in the construal of perceptual events. What is the cause in an act of perception? Is it the perceiver, because he or she must be engaged in mental activity (either phasic, such as moving the eyes, head, or an internal mental "spotlight" of attention, or tonic, such as having the right kind of sensorium and being in a conscious state)? This would be consistent with Talmy's (1988) suggestion that the body—and by extension, internal surrogates such as "the mind's eye"—is naturally considered to be inert unless animated by an intrapsychic willful force. Or is the stimulus the cause, because its salient properties call attention to itself or because it puts itself into the perceiver's awareness involuntarily? Again, this option is within the realm of cognitive possibility: Talmy discusses a set of expressions suggesting that the "central" component of mind is generally conceived as having a natural state of repose and requires a stronger force from more peripheral parts of the mind to overcome that tendency. Given that cognition can avail itself of either conceptual gestalt, it should be possible for languages to grammaticize either or both possibilities as conflation classes for transitive perception verbs (see Dowty, 1982, for a similar suggestion). Indeed both stimulus-subject and experiencer-subject verbs are seen in many languages (Talmy, 1985). English has both, and passivizes both.[26]

Verbs of spatial relations. This takes us to verbs of spatial relationships, some of which passivize, others of which do not. Jackendoff (1972) explicitly predicts that a spatial-relation passive is possible only when its surface subject is a theme and its *by*-object or implicit argument is a source, location, or goal. This fails in both directions: **Beer is contained by the bottle* (surface subject = theme; see also the examples in (2.19) in chapter 2) and *The mountain is capped by snow* (surface subject = location). I will propose a simpler solution: verbs of pure spatial events and relations (*contain, gush, drip, lack, fit*) have no patient arguments and thus do not passivize, period. Spatial verbs that do passivize can be shown, by independent tests, to encode more than pure spatial relations. Specifically, they include in their definitions an abstract notion of state-causation or responsibility that motivates the extension of abstract versions of the thematic relations "agent" and "patient" to them.

Passivizable spatial verbs fall into two subclasses. One set, shown in (4.41), was used by Gee (1974) as his primary case of positive exceptions to Jackendoff's Thematic Hierarchy Condition, which should rule out passives whose surface subjects are sources or goals.

(4.41) (a) He was hit by a car.
             The house was struck by lightning.
             The rocks were slapped by the breaking waves.
        (b) Russia was invaded by a horde of locusts.
             St. Sebastian's body was pierced by arrows.
             Her body was infected by a virus.

Examples (4.41a) and (4.41b) are recognizable as belonging to the classes of motion-contact verbs and motion-contact-effect verbs (4.41b), respectively. They do involve goals, to be sure, but they also involve clear-cut patients, entities that are physically involved in defining the action. As long as there is a patient, the thematic core of the passive argument structure doesn't care whether some other set of thematic roles are defined as well.

The second set of examples, called to my attention by Melissa Bowerman, is presented in (4.42).

(4.42) (a) The mountain was capped by snow.
        (b) The street was lined by trees.
        (c) The house was surrounded by a moat.
        (d) The paragraph was headed by a catchy title.
        (e) The canyon was spanned by a bridge.
        (f) The canyon was bridged by a span.
        (g) The side of the house was abutted by a stone fence.
        (h) The crater was filled by a lake.
        (i) The bed was covered by a blanket.

Ignore for now the fact that many of these sentences sound better in their adjectival versions containing *with* instead of *by*; the point is that for most speakers they are grammatical with *by*.) A curious thing about these verbs, but not the unpassivizable spatial verbs like *contain*, *lack*, or *gush*, is that they all also appear in the *with* version of the locative form, shown in (4.43).

(4.43) (a) Hurricane Gloria capped the mountain with snow.
        (b) The planner lined the street with trees.
        (c) The landscapers surrounded the house with a moat.
        (d) I headed the paragraph with a catchy title.
        (e) The engineers spanned the canyon with a bridge.
        (f) The engineers bridged the canyon with a span.
        (g) The architect abutted the house with a stone fence.
        (h) Centuries of rain filled the crater with a lake.
        (i) Sheila covered the bed with a blanket.
        (j) *I contained a ship with the bottle.[27]
        (k) *The architects foolishly lacked the building of a bathroom.

We have already analyzed the thematic roles of sentences like (4.43a)–(4.43i); their objects are themes of a change of state, and their *with*-objects are roughly like instruments; more accurately, they are themes of change of location in a subordinate means event (Rappaport and Levin, 1985), or "state-changers." Thus (4.43a) can be paraphrased as "Hurricane Gloria changed the state of the mountain by adding snow to it, covering its top." Means events are basically penultimate events in causal chains; recall that this is also true for some instruments (those that can become subjects). Let's say that the verbs of (4.42) are derived from those of (4.43) by a rule similar or identical to intermediary instrument promotion. When the beginning of a causal chain is truncated by omitting the first event and promoting the penultimate event (the means) to subject, the theme of the means event now serves as the head of the chain and hence is being construed as the causal agent. Thus passive sentences like those in (4.42) should be analyzed not as having location subjects and theme *by*-objects but as having patient/theme subjects and state-changer *by*-objects. That is, the active version of (4.42a) would be paraphrased as "The presence of snow on top of it causes the mountain to be in a certain state" and the passive version as "The mountain is in the state characterized by snow's being on it." The active subject is a static proximal cause or antagonist, causing the agonist (patient) to be in a state that its natural tendency would not have brought it into. Thus the passive subject is an abstract patient, and the passivizability of the subclass of verbs of state-change-by-addition follows.

Some periphrastic elaborations of these verbs independently support this analysis. The pseudo-cleft construction, which is often said to pick out events, applies to the passivizable but not the unpassivizable spatial verbs: *What the fur does is line the coat; What the trees do is line the street*, and so on; but **What this bottle does is contain the ship* and **What this building does is lack a bathroom*. The pro-verb *do* can be substituted for the state-change-by-addition verbs because the state-changer is construed as having some function in defining the state of the theme. In addition, explicit expressions of the idea of an object existing in one state and changing to another by the addition of an object to it differentiates the two subclasses: *That mountain is much nicer now that snow is capping it; That street is much nicer now that trees are lining it; That paragraph is much nicer now that a catchy title is heading it*; but *?That pint of beer is much nicer now that a glass is containing it*.

One other class of spatial verbs is worth mentioning. Many verbs of pure motion can appear with either volitional or nonvolitional subjects; for example, *John / The ball rolled down the hill*. Though most such verbs specify path arguments and hence take oblique phrases, making passivizability moot, a few, such as *enter* and *approach*, take direct-object phrases. In such cases, it is only the volitional-agent version that passivizes: *The room was entered by a strange man* / **by a balloon*; *Biff was approached by a spy* / **by the train* (Bolinger, 1977a).

Verbs of possession. Transitive verbs of possession can be analyzed in a similar way, though no rules deriving them from more complex forms are involved. When pure possession is involved, passivization is impossible; when possession is conflated with thematic elements involving extended senses of agency, passivization can be extended to the subclass. As has often been pointed out (see, e.g., Miller and Johnson-Laird, 1976), there are several kinds of possession, including inalienable possession (John's nose), possession of property (John's car), relationships (John's father), custody (John's library book), and temporary association (John's lottery number). Many of these distinctions are differentiated in morphology or in multiple translations of *have* in other languages. English uses *have* to refer to the pure concept of possession, ignoring all these distinctions, and *own* and *possess* to refer mainly to property possession (*John owns a car* / **father* / **nose* / **library book* / **lottery number 91854*); *possess* seems to admit of custody as well. What do property ownership and custody entail above and beyond generic possession? Perhaps an alienably possessed object is construable as having an inherent tendency to move away from the owner, but the owner exerts a stronger opposing force keeping it with him and allowing him to do with it what he pleases. If so, the owner would have a quasi-agentive or antagonist role with respect to the possession/agonist. Thus property possession (*own*, *possess*) might be seen as an exemplification of generalized agent-patient relations, whereas pure possession (*have*, *lack*) specifies a static spatial/possessional relation and nothing else. This is why only the property possession verbs passivize.[28]

4.4.4.4 Other Passivizable Verbs Lacking Concrete Agents and Patients
Verbs of enabling. One of the toughest cases for any theory of passivization appealing to thematic roles is *receive*. The verb is puzzling because it seems to violate the linking regularity that when an event involves an agent and a goal (e.g., *send*), it is the agent that is the subject; for *receive*, the recipient or goal is the subject. Indeed, *receive* is exceptional in a number of ways. Dowty (1987) notes that verbs with goal or patient subjects (*undergo* and *succumb* are two other examples) are few in number, low in frequency, acquired late, and more common in elevated than in casual speech. Higginbotham (1988) suggests that the semantics of these verbs is fundamentally different from that of most other verbs. Whereas the meanings of most verbs correspond to a kind of event or state, and their arguments encode the thematic roles of various participants in the event or state, the meaning of *receive* (and verbs like it) directly expresses the thematic

role of one of the participants in an event or state whose nature is otherwise unspecified. Thus *receive* means "to play the role of recipient/goal." Higginbotham suggests that "light verbs" such as *do, have, be,* and *go* (discussed in chapter 5) have similar kinds of meanings; they directly assert that their subjects play a particular thematic role.

Regardless of how *receive* receives its subject, we must account for why it passivizes given that the subject is not agentlike. To begin with, one should note that the subject cannot be a mere goal but must be a possessor: one cannot talk of a tree receiving an arrow or a mailbox receiving a package. But in addition, *receive* appears to be consistent with two slightly different meanings, one where a person merely comes to possess something, another where a person *enables* something to come into his possession. An enabling cause can be construed as an abstract "agent" by Talmyan force-dynamic analysis: the enabler removes or weakens the antagonistic force that opposes the tendency of the theme to arrive into his possession. The voluntary enabling sense can be seen in sentences like *John refused to receive any more packages from the Fruit-of-the-Month Club* or *Bill received the packages to placate the mailman.* Although in many cases the two meanings overlap, there are also cases where they do not. When someone receives *a snowball in the eye* or *a blow to the head,* clearly no enabling is going on. Conversely, when someone *receives a guest* (or when a person is "well received" or an institution sets up a "Receiving" department), the receiver is doing something or at least allowing something to happen. The passive clearly distinguishes these extreme cases, applying only in the second, where a sense of enabling is involved: **A blow to the head / *A snowball in the eye was received by John,* versus *The guests were received by the debutante / The package was received by the clerk.* I suggest that even in the intermediate cases, the passive forces the enabling sense of *receive* to dominate. For example, it seems acceptable to say *For months after his death, John received packages,* but quite odd to say *Packages were received by John for months after his death.*

Raising-to-object verbs. The most recalcitrant class of verbs for an analysis of passive that invokes operations on semantic structure is the class of "exceptional case-marking" or "raising-to-object" verbs such as *expect, consider, regard, view.* These verbs passivize (*John is considered to be a fool by his friends*), but their objects do not even appear to be arguments of the verb, let alone arguments playing a particular thematic role. What allows this class to passivize? Oehrle and Ross (n.d.) and Lakoff and Johnson (1980) note that the raised object is not utterly devoid of a semantic role with respect to the matrix verb: in *Ed found the chair to be comfortable,* it is implied that Ed directly experienced the chair by sitting in it; in *Ed found that the chair was comfortable,* no contact is necessary. Thus the phrase may play the role of a stimulus entertained by the referent of the subject, in addition to whatever role it is assigned by the embedded predicate. Interestingly, this test may provide insight into the biggest challenge of all to thematic constraints on the passive: passivizable raised dummy elements, such as *Sue found it to be a drag to itemize deductions* / *It was found by Sue to be a drag to itemize deductions*; or *Sir Edmund found there to be rampant discontent in the colonies* / *There was found to be rampant discontent in the colonies by Sir Edmund.* (Note, though, that not all speakers accept these sentences with *by*-phrases.) Compare these sentences to *Sue found that it was a drag to itemize deductions* or *Sir Edmund found that there was rampant discontent in the colonies.* In the former (raising) sentences, there is an implication that Sue actually filled out her own tax forms and that Sir Edmund visited or directly studied the colonies; in the latter (tensed sentential complement) sentences, Sue could merely be a tax commissioner reading human factors studies and Sir Edmund a reader of historical novels. This suggests that in these examples *it* and *there* verge toward being pronouns roughly referring to "the action" or "the situation there," which are stimulus arguments of *find.* The fact that most of these verbs also appear as simple transitives with stimulus direct objects (*John expected an earthquake; I considered her offer; They viewed the painting,* etc.) hints that some aspect of this analysis might be correct. Di Sciullo and Williams (1987) explicitly analyze these constructions as assigning a thematic role to the raised object: they propose that *Bill expects John to win* involves the complex predicate "expect-to-win" and the arguments "Bill" and "John." Thus this class of verbs could be treated as having a thematic analysis similar to that of the stimulus-object psychological verbs.

4.4.4.5   What Makes the Passive Different from Other Alternations?   As we have seen, the passive is strikingly different from the dative, the locative, and the causative. The passive broad-range rule supplies sufficient conditions for it to be applied productively, and narrow subclasses of verbs play no role (except possibly as conditions for other rules, such as instrument promotion, that feed the passive with forms that meet those conditions). For the other three alternations, the conditions of the broad-range rule are necessary but not sufficient, and narrow-range rules intervene. Why is the passive different, and how do children know the difference?

An obvious difference between the passive and the other alternations is that the passive rule alters a verb's argument structure, adds an affix to its stem, and changes its morphosyntactic status from finite verb to participle, whereas the other rules only alter argument structure. Marantz (1984) suggests that in general, alternations that involve the addition of an affix are fundamentally different from alternations in which the stem survives intact. Levin and Rappaport (1986; and Rappaport and Levin, in press) make a similar suggestion with regard to alternations that involve a change of syntactic category. Roughly, when an affix is added, the change in argument structure is associated directly with that operation, and the content of the verb is ignored. Thus such alternations should be entirely insensitive to the verb's meaning. When the identical verb form appears in two argument structures, however, the two instances are treated as distinct verbs sharing a stem. According to Marantz, to the extent that speakers can generalize such an alternation to other verbs, it is a simple analogy based on the cognitive similarity of the new verb to one of the members of the alternating pair, and here verb meaning will play a role. This account is consistent with the conventional wisdom of many linguists that the English verbal passive is a textbook case of a purely syntactic operation; in fact, some linguists call it "the syntactic passive."

This is too strong. Not all transitive verbs passivize, and those that do not passivize can be characterized semantically. Baker's logic is inexorable: if children learn a productive passive rule that tolerates some unpassivizable transitive verbs without the benefit of negative evidence, they must be wired to build the rule in a form that respects the semantic differences between the passivizable and nonpassivizable verbs. There is a problem on the other side of Marantz's dichotomy as well: as we have seen, generalizations of the dative, causative, and locative alternations are governed not by overall cognitive similarity of verb meaning but by well-specified components of their semantic structure.

However, a weaker version of the correlation between affixation and semantic insensitivity may be defensible. Perhaps rules that add affixes (and/or change category) have broad-range semantic operations, and the input conditions for that operation are both necessary and sufficient conditions for a verb to alternate. For rules that leave the stem unchanged, the broad-range operations impose necessary but not sufficient conditions; a set of narrow-range operations applying to narrow conflation classes must be acquired to license generalizations. The child would notice whether an alternation involved the addition of an affix (or a change of category) and would constrain the rule to narrow subclasses if it did not. This is consistent with the key tenet of the current theory that argument structures are projections of semantic structures and hence that argument structure changes must be accompanied by semantic structure changes, changes that could interact with verbs' inherent meanings. However, it preserves two of the intuitions behind Marantz's proposal. First, since a broad-range rule accompanied by affixation usually gets its way in effecting the specified argument structure change, one could conceive of it as a rule that directly acts on syntactic argument structure, yielding a change in semantic structure via linking rules acting "in reverse" (and then blocked only if the inherent meaning of the verb made this difficult or impossible). In other words, for affixation rules one can think of the syntactic operation as doing the pulling and the semantic change as being the passenger, whereas for nonaffixation rules the semantic change, with its highly detailed sensitivity to verb semantics, would do the pulling and the syntactic change would follow. Second, it preserves the intuition that when a rule creates a verb with a transparent "stem + affix" structure, the learner attributes the argument structure change and the semantic change to the telltale affix and largely ignores the verb, whereas when the verb appears unchanged in form, the learner perceives the alternation more as a case of polysemy and analyzes the verb's semantics in detail in order to understand the chemistry between the semantic change and the parts of the verb's inherent meaning that remain unchanged.

It seems reasonable to suggest, then, that the presence of affixation (and possibly also any change in morphological category, such as finite form versus participle) is the cue children use to recognize which argument structure changing rules are productive as broad-range semantic operations that can be applied to any verb within the broad conflation class defined by the rule. The English passive is an example; others include morphological causative affixes, which often apply quite freely and permit indirect causation readings (Nedyalkov and Silnitsky, 1973; Comrie, 1985), and "applicative" affixes, which are similar to the English benefactive *for*-dative alternation but less restrictive.

Clearly, the notion of "affixation" must be made precise; the child cannot merely look for any verbs that change in form or have stuff added onto them. To take the simplest problem, English irregular verbs like *hit* and *cut* have no overt affixes in the passive. In the other direction, some languages have phonologically related verb pairs that are not truly derived by an affixation operation (the English vestigial causative pairs *rise/raise* and *sit/set* are examples that are close to home). Somehow the child must analyze the morphological system of the language to distinguish genuine affixation operations from mere similarity of forms. I cannot treat this problem here but instead refer the reader to Pinker and Prince (1988), where it is discussed in detail.

Affixation may distinguish the English passive from alternations like the dative and the causative, but what causes the differences in breadth of the passives of different languages? It is unlikely that there is a single parameter of breadth of application. Some of the differences among passive rules might be traceable to differences in their forms. One possible factor is that any passive that is not marked by a general affixation rule should be productive only for narrow-range subclasses. Another is that some productive passives may have slightly different broad-range conditions because they are not tenseless participles appearing with *be* but rather are finite forms or complements of more specialized verbs (e.g., *receive* or even *eat*; see Keenan, 1985). But the main factor I have relied on in the discussion of passivizable verbs in English is the large inventory of mechanisms that English uses to create verb forms with patient objects in nonlocational and nonactional semantic fields. It may be that the English passive itself is not that much broader in range than that of other languages, but that many other rules in the language feed it with eligible semantic forms containing patient objects. This is simply a lexicosemantic version of the more traditional syntactic accounts, in which the passive is fed by rules that reanalyze certain kinds of surface phrases as objects of the verb. (For example, [$_V$take] [$_{NP}$advantage] [$_{PP}$of John] is said to be reanalyzed as [$_V$take-advantage-of] [$_{NP}$John], which then allows *John was taken advantage of*; see Bresnan, 1982b, for discussion of a variety of such rules.) In the current account, the crucial antecedent of passivization in most cases is not the creation of surface objects (if it were, *contain* and *have* and *weigh* would passivize), but the creation of surface objects that are patients.

Nonetheless, the prevalence of patient-object verbs in English, and the rules creating them, could have arisen in response to the need for a very general passive operation. In English, the passive serves several functions that are accomplished in other languages by other means. First, it serves to focus what is usually the object argument, an important function given that the language lacks constituent order freedom, deletable subjects, and grammatical marking of the sentence topic. Furthermore, the passive can be used to avoid mentioning a specific subject. Crain, Thornton, and Murasugi (1987) present a nice example of this "evasive passive": Ronald Reagan, describing the Iran-contra scandal besetting his administration, admitted only that "mistakes were made." Third, the English passive also serves to move the object argument to the front of the sentence, which can reduce the processing load on the listener in constructions like relative clauses by minimizing the duration of the resource-hungry process of remembering the head noun until the gap appears (see Wanner and Maratsos, 1978); compare *She tickled the monkey that the giraffe kicked* with *She tickled the monkey that was kicked by the giraffe*. In contrast, the freer constituent orders in other languages allow speakers to reorder the elements of an embedded clause without having to resort to the passive voice (see, e.g., Hakuta, 1981). Thus it would not be surprising if mechanisms allowing the English passive to be very broad in range evolved under pressure for the passive to fulfill these functions for which no other grammatical device is available. (We know that in even more extreme cases, this pressure seems to have an effect. In some languages—many Bantu languages, for instance—one cannot question the subject position, so passivization is the only means of questioning agent arguments—*Who hit me?* is ungrammatical; one has to say *Who was I hit by?* Such languages have a passive rule that is even less restrictive than the English passive; see Keenan, 1985; Foley and Van Valin, 1985.)

The suggestion that the English passive diachronically increased its range in part for functional reasons is not new. Historians of English such as Curme (1935/1983) and Visser (1963) have speculated that the passive spread in English because of the lack of an indefinite pronoun analogous to the French *on* or the German *man*. They note that the equivalent pronoun was lost in English by the fourteenth century, at which time an expansion in the range of passivization in English, such as to prepositional objects, began. In fact, historical accounts of the passive commonly note that it is not a unitary phenomenon but appears to be tied to a gradual tendency to reanalyze verbs as taking object arguments (arguments that are objects because they are patients, in my account) following the leveling of the accusative/dative case distinction in the Middle English period. While Old English contained passives of transitive verbs, more extended classes seem to have flourished only later, and probably not all starting at the same time. According to Lieber (1979) and Lightfoot (1981), passives of double-object forms were very rare in Old English and increased in the Middle English period from the thirteenth century on. Prepositional passives began to appear in numbers in the fourteenth and fifteenth centuries; passives of predicative verbs (e.g. *consider*) increased in the fifteenth century; passives of complex verbs (e.g., *advantage was taken of John*) first appeared in the fourteenth century but experienced their biggest growth spurt in the eighteenth and nineteenth centuries. (Of course, vagaries in sampling make the picture a complicated one.) Closer to home, Dowty (1979a) quotes Marchand (1951) as characterizing passives of double-object *for*-datives as a mid-twentieth-century development: "In World War II it was so often repeated how necessary it was to 'find the returning soldiers a job' that it required [*sic*] the character of a phrase. This paves the way for 'the men would be found a job' (*Spectator*, May 18, 1945, 441)."

In sum, the passive differs from the other alternations I have discussed in applying to any verb meeting its broad-range conditions (viz., having a patient object) rather than merely motivating a large set of specific narrow-range rules. Presumably this is related to the fact that it adds an affix and changes the verb's category; the resulting participle is perceived as being composed of a meaning contributed by the original stem and a meaning change localized to the affix, rather than as a new lexical item with its own complex meaning. The reason that the English passive extends not only to all transitive action verbs but to many nonagentive and stative verbs as well is that these passivizable verbs actually do have patients, according to the Thematic Relations Hypothesis.

4.5   The Relation Between Narrow-Range and Broad-Range Rules

Let me summarize the theory. In chapter 3 I characterized argument structure alternation rules as involving very general operations on lexical semantic structure. I showed that this proposal had the right consequences for their concomitant changes in interpretation, for the choice of grammatical functions associated with them, and for necessary conditions defining broad patterns of selectivity in the kinds of verbs that can undergo the alternations. In this chapter I examined in detail the sufficient conditions. For the dative, the locative, and the causative, the fine patterns of selectivity can be explained by the rules' being restricted to very narrow conflation classes, where the choice of the subclasses was motivated by the thematic core of the broad rule but the choice of individual verbs was determined locally by the verb's membership in the narrow subclass. For example, *She drove Chicago the car* is ruled out because it does not conform to the broad-range dative rule, which makes possession change a necessary condition for dativization. *She pulled John the suitcase*, though it does meet the necessary condition, is ruled out because it does not conform to any of the narrow-range dative rules, each of which imposes a set of sufficient conditions (such as ballistic motion). For the passive, on the other hand, narrow-range rules play no role; the broad-range rule defines necessary *and* sufficient conditions for passivization.

This raises the question of the relation between broad-range and narrow-range rules for the alternations that have both. Could the broad-range rule be eliminated entirely from an account of the psychology of language, replaced by the list of narrow-range rules that actually determine how speakers generalize? Recall what the arguments for broad-range rules are. First, the broad-range rules determine what all the narrow-range rules have in common. All the mini-dative rules, for example, involve the double-object construction with the possessor as first object, not a family of different constructions with various combinations of prepositions or various assignments of roles to surface functions. Second, the motivation for why certain subclasses alternate and others don't is provided by the broad-range rule. For example, the dativizability of the *tell* class as compared to the *shout* class is probably related to the fact that what makes a speech act an example of "telling" presupposes something about the interaction between the speaker and the target of the transfer of information whereas what makes a speech act an example of "shouting" does not, and the fact that the thematic core of the double-object form specifies acting on the recipient. However, neither of these facts strictly requires that all speakers mentally represent broad-range rules; each of the narrow classes could be acquired individually.

There is evidence, though, for the on-line operation of broad-range rules in people's speech and writing. Bowerman (1982a) noted that adults occasionally use causative forms that are obviously productive (they sound quite unusual), but clearly recognizable as the causative of some intransitive predicate (see also Stemberger, 1982). In other words, such forms are consistent with the broad-range causativization rule, but not licensed by any of the narrow-range rules. The examples derived from verbs are reproduced in (4.44).

(4.44) (a) UL-approved outdoor lighting sets are weatherproofed so that water will not deteriorate the sockets.

(b) He said that the Agnew and Watergate affairs have tended to deteriorate confidence in the American system.

(c) The relatively steep nose-up attitude after take-off climbs the airplane quickly to decrease noise on the ground.

(d) Sparkle your table with Cape Cod classic glass-ware.

(e) Zia conforms Pakistan law with Islam.

(f) Mr. Castellito simply disappeared permanently in 1961, but the jury apparently believed the testimony of other figures who said Mr. Provenzano had arranged to disappear him.

(g) At the end of the week "Here little doggie, here is your bone, now last it until next week."

(h) We're gonna splash and we're gonna spin ya. We're gonna scream and we're gonna grin ya. [In promotional brochure for an amusement center]

(i) The aspirations have been risen again.

(j) They've grown it to where it's a large company.

(k) The experience grew me up in a hurry.

(l) What's fussing her? [A Grandpa wondering why baby is crying]

(m) He just popped it up out of the clear blue sky. [Wife telling how husband thought of name for their baby]

(n) They break her out. [Mother telling how disposable diapers give her child a rash]

Let me refer to these kinds of utterances as "Haigspeak," after the presidential Chief of Staff who appalled the nation with creative usages such as *Let me caveat that* and *That statement needs to be nuanced.* (A MacNelly cartoon had him announcing his resignation: "I decisioned the necessifaction of the resignatory action/option due to the dangerosity of the trendflowing of foreign policy away from our originatious careful coursing towards consistensivity, purposity, stead-fastnitude, and above all, clarity.") The phenomenon is intriguing because it illuminates the psychological role of broad-range rules in adults and, as we shall see in chapter 8, children. In the next section I show how pervasive the phenomenon is and discuss some of its salient properties. Then I will discuss its implications for the respective roles of broad-range and narrow-range lexical rules

4.5.1 Ungrammatical Uses of Lexical Rules in Adult Language

Productive uses of argument structures in adult speech and writing are not hard to find. Examples I have heard or read in a 6-month period are discussed in this section. (I am afraid they show that my free time is not exactly spent at the opera and the ballet.) For some of the examples, I cannot make a crisp judgment as to their naturalness; I have prefixed them with a question mark.

Causatives. The examples in (4.45) replicate Bowerman's observations.

(4.45) (a) But if my client is a man, and we get Shirley, I know we're croaked. [A lawyer referring to a judge]

   (b) You should hang yourself up. [To a computer user on a dial-up line] Can you hang yourself up?! [Shouted to a person on another phone in the same house]

   (c) Well, that decided me.

   (d) I don't know who I'm going to pitch the first ballgame. [A baseball manager speaking]
They haven't found the time to play him a whole lot of minutes (= let him play for a substantial portion of the basketball game).

   (e) Stream on the flavor! [TV ad for melted-butter dispenser]

   (f) If she subscribes us up, she'll get a bonus [= gives our name to a cable TV company, resulting in our subscribing].

   (h) It started in 1976 when the Parti Québecois began to deteriorate the health care system.

   (i) Small company's new golf ball flies *too* far; could obsolete many golf courses. [Headline of a fictitious news item in a magazine ad]

   (j) A lot of teams collapsed zones on him [= used a defensive strategy where basketball players distributed in "zones" converge on an opposing offensive player].

   (k) In early Modern English, the vowel of the singular was conformed to that of the plural.

   (l) He corresponded the stages to the training sets.

   (n) Sunbeam whips out the holes where staling air can hide. [Advertisement for bread]

   (m) Is the universe including man evolved by atomic force? [Sermon title, found by Beth Levin]

Bowerman said she did not notice examples of productive intransitivization, but as Lord (1979) and Maratsos et al. (1987) point out in regard to children's speech, such errors are generally not as salient to an observer unless they are specifically attended to. In (4.46), (4.47), and (4.48), respectively, I reproduce examples I have heard of anticausatives, middles, and an unusual example that is neither.

(4.46) (a) The bacteria live off the dissolved minerals that exude from the vent.
   (b) [From basketball play-by-play descriptions] The ball slaps around.
       The rebound tips to the hands of Sichting. [From transitive *tip* = "touch with the fingertips," not intransitive "tip over"]
       That causes Robert to release downfloor. [From transitive *release* = "allow a player to break out of a pack," not "relinquish the ball"]
       The ball kicks around and ends up near midcourt in the hands of Cavs guard Ron Harper.
       It kicks out of bounds off the Bullets.
       The ball hits into the right field stands.
   (c) Mary presented as an attractive, neatly dressed woman.
   (d) Can germs harbor in these things?
   (e) When I slow down at a corner and take my foot off the gas the car wants to kill ["die" or stall].
   (f) If she whips into shape, then I'll see her.

(4.47) (a) Its batteries can store up to ten years. [Advertisement for a flashlight]
   (b) The soup that eats like a meal. [Advertisement]
       It eats like steak but costs like ordinary dry. [Advertisement for dog food]
       Steaks that look the same may not eat the same. [Meat industry executive]
   (c) This game isn't playing very well. [A sloppy basketball match]

(4.48) The aftereffects [of the operation] don't seem to be telling at all right now. (Said by a basketball player; = "one can't tell that the operation had aftereffects; I don't feel the aftereffects of the operation.")[29]

Datives. I have also heard a variety of violations of the narrow constraints on the dative alternation. Morphological violations are not uncommon, as shown in (4.49).

(4.49) (a) Sun donated them a bunch of computers.
       What does he want me to do—donate them blood?
   (b) I returned her the books.
   (c) I explained him the problem.
       Can you explain me language breakdown?
   (d) An intriguing down side to the three-hour ceremonies ... was the snub extended Michael Jackson.

(f) ?I just want to schedule you some appointments.

(g) I'll suggest her that she come over.

(h) ?If the fee schedule is adjusted so that you would have paid a lower amount than the one you signed up for, Information Systems will reimburse you the difference.

There are also semantic violations involving verbs that are grammatical with *to* or *for*, shown in (4.50). Some of them(e.g.,(j) and (k)) are rendered ungrammatical (at least to me) because of the presence of a particle that changes the meaning subtly.

(4.50) (a) Can you reach me that book?
            Will you reach me my socks for me? Reach me my socks.

        (b) It [a letter of support] will add the grant a little legitimacy.

        (c) Even if he dribbles me in one subject a year ...

        (d) Mr. [ ] was made no bones about the fact that ...

        (e) When you go I'm going to preach you a great funeral.

        (f) I put you out a big piece [of pie].

        (g) Fix me up [build] a handle.

        (h) She didn't have to snap me about it.

        (i) ?K. C. tried a new strategy and he lost them the game.

        (j) She gave me out a form to fill in.
            I don't want to give you out his private number.

        (k) I'll send him out the proposal.

Interestingly, some examples could not be generated even by a broad-range rule for the dative alternation as it is conventionally stated, since the prepositional form uses neither the preposition *to* nor *for*. In (4.51a–b), the preposition would have to be *at* because English construes visual perception as involving the "motion" of one's gaze toward, not all the way to, the target (see Gruber, 1965). In (c), the preposition would be *from*.

(4.51) (a) ?He shot me a look like you wouldn't believe.
            ?She doesn't shoot me any looks. [Said by the same person]

        (b) The next time you make eyes at someone, make them eyes they'll find unforgettable. [magazine advertisement for colored contact lenses][30]

        (c) He stripped him the ball. [basketball play-by-play]

A number of violations, shown in (4.52), are based on the *present* class (verbs of fulfilling, deserving, or presenting). Semantically these verbs involve the notion of giving but syntactically they behave like locative verbs and thus alternate with the prepositional form containing *with* rather than the double-object form. (Some of these forms are marginally acceptable to me, and I suspect that the distinction for these verbs is eroding.)

(4.52) (a) ?I am proud to present you this trophy.
?The president was presented a policy that wasn't arms for hostages.
?They are presented these cards under three conditions.
   (b) We have been served papers by the District Court.
   (c) ?... the tubing that we would persuade [the company] to provide him.
   (d) ?Can you furnish me an address for George Augusta?
   (e) The most precious gift a father could bestow a son. [TV advertisement for a car]
   (f) The bank credited my account $100.
   (g) If you'll indulge me just two in-jokes. [Note: only acceptable using preposition *with* or *in*]
   (h) If you're not satisfied, return the record with your receipt within 2 weeks and we'll credit you back the full purchase price toward any merchandise in the store.

The odd double-object forms shown in (4.53) also do not have the usual source but would ordinarily require use of the preposition *in*. The sentences, which seem to be based on an analogy with the verb *teach*, are from graduate school application materials written by computer experts.

(4.53) (a) She demonstrated fine teaching abilities in training other students the complex procedures and complex equipment we use in our lab.
   (b) The uses of such a program are myriad and include use as a compositional device and as a method for individually tutoring students musical improvisation.

Locatives. Examples of both argument structures participating in the locative alternation containing verbs that make them marginal to ungrammatical in my dialect are listed in (4.54) and (4.55).

(4.54) (a) He's trying to fob me off with that guy.
Now I'll just fob her off with some colored pencils.
   (b) They filed him with charges.
   (c) They and a lot of other public figures were bestowed yesterday with the 1987 Bozo awards.
   (d) ?He was pumped with a liter and a half of glucose solution.
   (e) He squeezed them [fish fillets] with lemon juice.
   (f) Drizzle them [apple slices] with fresh lemon juice. [From a cookbook]
   (g) [from recipes in a magazine article] This version is dribbled with a lively Worcestershire-spiked mayonnaise. ...serve at once with toasted French bread rounds dribbled with olive oil. ...slices of

uncooked beef drizzled with a Worcestershire mayonnaise.
Arrange the meat on a platter and dribble it all over with the mayonnaise....serve at once with crusty Italian bread or toasted bread
slices dribbled with olive oil.

(4.55) (a) I said I was sorry to serve a manuscript on him. [A publisher referring
to a person he had asked to review a manuscript; cf. "serve him
with a subpoena"]

(b) Take a little of the mixture at a time and fill it into the zucchini.
[Quoted by Rappaport and Levin, 1985; from a cookbook]

(c) I'm just going to rinse some water now. [A periodontist speaking]

(d) Sometimes before they do brain surgery, they probe in electrodes.

(e) ... by inoculating living R cells into mice ...

(f) She pierced needles under her fingernails.

(g) It's not just all that water filling up ... [in the basement; describing
why someone is upset]

(h) He jumped both knees on it. [A goalie in hockey trapping a puck; cf.
"He jumped on it with both knees"]

(i) She said we just dug up some trash someone littered.

(j) I'll just touch this to your ear.

(k) If they endow $400,000 to MIT ...

(l) Isn't that just another way to bilk money from the ignorant?

(m) Endurance training at less than 70–80% of a cyclist's peak performance depletes glycogen from the slow-twitch muscle fibers.

(n) As an actor, it has the odd effect of zapping him—for lack of a better
term—of a soul ["it" = the fact that the actor's mind is a "spinning
gyroscope"].

(o) I had to rob the front wheels off some support bikes to have enough
for changes.

(p) They're working on a plan to rob your resources.

(q) We're going to make this a better community, and we're going to rid
the negative element.

Just as we saw in the case of the unusual productive datives, some of the
locative-like constructions are not the product of what we ordinarily think of as
the locative alternation. Although they involve roughly the same kinds of
meanings, the closest related form does not take the expected prepositions. In
fact, (4.56c) is the inverse of the unusual dative forms listed in (4.52).

(4.56) (a) Norman and Frances Lear were divorced last year after he settled
approximately $125 million on her.

(b) She had to pinpoint it onto someone [blame someone for it].

(c) We have charged your Visa account with $300 for the required deposit.

Other argument structures. Aside from the alternations I have focused on, there are other argument structures that are occasionally extended to verbs outside the narrow classes that ordinarily allow them. These include the uses of prepositional phrases and clausal complements listed in (4.57).

(4.57) (a) I looked the ball into my hands [= "I looked at the ball all the way until it reached my hands"; from Landau and Gleitman, 1985].

(b) They are excellent at creating missed shots into fast-break opportunities at the other end.

(c) For purposes of counterbalancing against the possibility that any effects are due to a particular set of stimuli...

(d) ... reinforcing subjects that version is irrelevant ... should remove the need to discriminate between versions of a character [= "In our instructions to the subjects in our experiment, we reinforced the fact that which version of a character they saw on the screen was irrelevant to the discrimination task they were asked to perform"]. K.C. always reinforces him to shoot.

(e) Bounce pass to Bird who touches it back to McHale.

(f) Ainge saves it nicely to Acres.

(g) I'll include the paper back to him.

(h) I tried to hint this to her.

(i) She tried to convince me out of it.

(j) I expressed that it would be difficult for one person to manage both the Suns and the Microvaxes.

(k) I'm proud of her to get some of that [credit].

(l) The best way to solve many of the problems with taking too much time in both loading the image from memory and storing it to the EGA is to use smaller images.

(m) I don't think it can be done by a hacker from the outside. It is a potential that could occur by a disaffected employee [computer sabotage].

Passives. According to the proposal in section 4.4.4, passivization is accomplished directly by a broad-range rule, so blatantly ungrammatical passives in spontaneous speech and writing should be quite rare. I have encountered only two possible examples. The one shown in (4.58a) involves a pure spatial verb, though it is possible that we have an adjectival passive here. The other, in (4.58b), at first glance seems to involve a pure temporal relationship, but there is also an implication of inter-event causation that might allow the passivization.

(4.58) (a) Break out your favorite bicycle grease, but keep it contained until you're finished splashing solvent around.

   (b) That was led up to by what happened at the last party.

The only other odd passives I have heard, listed in (4.59), are the result of speakers aiming for a breezy, jocular, or emphatic effect by passivizing idioms or other specialized forms.

(4.59) (a) Well, the soot was blown. [Richard Pryor commenting on his reckless driving in a new sports car, in response to "They say you have to blow the soot out of them once in a while."]

   (b) Sometimes you get a pooch that can't be screwed [The idiom *to screw the pooch* = "to commit a grievous error." From the movie *The Right Stuff*; comment on the lack of negative publicity following an astronaut's mistakes during the popular Mercury program.]

   (c) The public is having the hell scared out of it.

   (d) They were wiped the floor with [= soundly defeated].

   (e) [from a television script]
   Him: What are you doing?
   Her: I'm making out my will.
   Him: Make sure you leave me something.
   Her: Consider yourself left. [She leaves.]

4.5.2 Property-Predicting Versus Existence-Predicting Rules

What is the psycholinguistic status of Haigspeak utterances? They are certainly not a reason to abandon constraints on lexical rules, because they are undoubtedly deviant to my ears and to those of most people I have shown them to. Though a few may come from dialects or idiolects in which they are well-formed sentences, most do not: When I was able to confront the speakers of some of the sentences in (4.45)–(4.57) with their utterances (mixed with distractor sentences they had never used), their reactions ranged from mild cringing to outright incredulity at the suggestion that they themselves had uttered them. On the other hand, they are not obviously speech errors of the standard sort (Spoonerisms, perseverative or anticipatory substitutions, etc.). Many are from written sources; they do not sound like quasi-random distortions, were never self-corrected, and cannot all be systematically derived from some intended target by the effects of internal noise, decay, or interference in some output buffer. Finally, they are not obviously ungrammatical, at least not in the same sense as *Furiously sleep ideas green colorless* or *Walks the boys*. Chomsky (1965, 1987) has stressed that linguistic judgments should not be treated as all-or-none placements of asterisks or even as scalar confidence ratings. Rather, grammars assign multidimensional structural descriptions to strings, and some levels of description can be well formed at the same time that others are ill formed. The in-between status of Haigspeak is due to its violating the narrow-range rules while obeying a broad-range rule or at least being consistent with one of the broad conflation classes related by such rules. This shows that the broad-range rule is indeed part of adults' competence.

But then, why should both kinds of rules exist, and what are their respective functions? I suggest that the difference coincides with the distinction between what Janet D. Fodor (1985) calls "property-predicting rules" and what she calls "existence-predicting rules." Property-predicting rules dictate what grammatical properties a form would have to have were it to exist. However, they do not actually license the addition of a new form to the language. Existence-predicting rules allow a speaker who possesses one form to add a related form to his or her grammar automatically. Specifically, I suggest that nonaffixing broad-range rules are psychologically real but are merely property-predicting; only their narrow-range rules are existence-predicting. The utterances in section 4.5.1, then, unlike productive usages licensed by narrow-range rules, are perceived as sentences that *could be* English but *don't happen to be* English. They are possible or likely ways to extend English by a minimal amount and are perceived by most speakers and listeners as innovations.

Making this distinction allows us to understand the role of another kind of structure that I have discussed frequently, conflation classes (both broad and narrow). Recall that a conflation class definition states that a given combination of semantic elements can be the basis of a possible word meaning in a language. Clearly, conflation class definitions by themselves can only be property-predicting, not existence-predicting. A word is more than a meaning; it needs a sound, too, or people won't know how to pronounce it. Lexical rules map entries from one conflation class into another, and crucially, they provide a sound for the new entry: the stem associated with the old entry. Conflation class definitions by themselves, on the other hand, don't tell you where the sound for a new word is supposed to come from. At best, one could pick some other word that is roughly associated with one aspect of the event the new verb is expressing. And in fact, that is exactly what speakers seem to be doing when they innovate a new form that cannot be the product of a broad-range lexical rule, as in *He settled $125 million on her* or *She trained other students the complex procedures.* Some of the functional limitations of such linguistically-unpredictable stem borrowing can be seen in Clark and Clark's (1979) study of the way people use noun stems to label new verbs, often resulting in forms that out-Haig Haig (e.g., *He enfant* *terrible'd gracefully; I've been Rolling Stoned and Beatled till I'm blind; I wanted to Rosemary Woods out that conversation).* According to Clark and Clark, the meaning of each of these forms—in particular, which of several possible semantic roles the referent of the source noun plays in the event denoted by the new verb—is not predictable by any rule of grammar. Instead, the meaning must be created by the speaker on the basis of his or her beliefs about what the hearer can infer on that occasion based on their mutual knowledge. Since language is most useful when it can communicate meaning to any listener in any situation, we might expect there to be mechanisms to limit such extreme situation-sensitivity. Lexical rules do just that; they make interpretation less a matter of shared knowledge and guesswork on the part of the hearer because they dictate *why* a particular sound was chosen to convey a new word. Of course, I am taking this argument one step farther—not just any stem-sharing lexical rule can be used to predict the existence of forms, only a narrow-range one.

4.5.3   Why Are Only Narrow-Range Rules Existence-Predicting?

The distinction between property-predicting rules and existence-predicting rules lead to an obvious question: Why can't the broad-range rules (other than the ones that add affixes) be used to predict the existence of forms? If I am right, it appears that languages have a deep-seated conservatism built into their lexicons. Regardless of how pervasive a generalization across existing pairs of lexical entries may be, the default condition is not to allow new entries to be added freely by individual speakers. The default is abandoned only for words that are in some sense minimally different from ones that already exhibit the generalization—new words that are of the same morphological type and whose meanings are "similar" (in a sense to be made precise in the next chapter) to those of existing words. Thus although I rejected *itemwise* conservatism in chapter 1, I am forced to a *classwise* conservatism by the discussion in this chapter. The extension of full existence-predicting productivity to narrow-range rules, resulting in classwise rather than itemwise conservatism, may be a minor relaxation of a basically conservative policy: languages tie speakers not to the exact verbs they have heard, but to the small family of verbs that are similar to the ones heard. In fact, in the next two chapters I will consider the radical but simple possibility that in some sense the linguistic faculty has no choice—it simply lacks the means to "see" the differences among the verbs that display full productivity, and blocks the extension of syntactic privileges to any verb that it *can* see as being different from the ones that have been heard in the input.

Is there a good reason for this minimally relaxed conservatism? Perhaps there is. Consider the analogy of a monetary system. Currency, like language, is a system of social exchange based on conventionalized symbols. Users can treat the symbols as having a fixed value because they are grounded in tacitly shared, arbitrary pairings: the gold standard or its equivalent for currency, and the sound-meaning relation for words. The mechanisms for introducing new tokens into the system must be very sharply circumscribed, not left up to the desires of individual players on individual occasions, or else the system will collapse in inflationary chaos.

Lest this seem too far-fetched in the case of language, consider two of the possible effects of rules affecting argument structures if they were totally unconstrained by semantic considerations. First, there is the possibility of rampant ambiguity. Atkins, Kegl, and Levin (1986) note that English has at least six distinct alternations between transitive and intransitive forms (Beth Levin has suggested to me that there may a dozen or more in all). Several involve disappearing objects (e.g., unspecified object deletion, as in *John eats food / John eats*). Several others involve disappearing subjects (e.g., anticausativization, as in *John broke the cup / The cup broke*). If the rules could be applied productively, bidirectionally, and without regard to semantics, any transitive verb could lead to the derivation of another transitive verb with the opposite meaning: X eats Y —> X eats (after object deletion) —> Y eats X (after causativization). Similarly, intransitives with transitive counterparts would be totally ambiguous: X eats Y —> X eats (after object deletion); X eats Y —> Y eats (after anticausativization). It's not that languages have utterly avoided such ambiguities, as (4.60) shows.

(4.60) Groucho: Call me a taxi.

Chico: You're a taxi.

Waitress to Dick Gregory, Mississippi, 1960: We don't serve colored people here.

Dick Gregory: That's OK, I don't eat colored people. I'd like a piece of chicken.[31]

However, argument structure ambiguities are fairly rare, at least in English, relative to the numerous hypothetical possibilities for creating them with broad-range rules. This functional consideration is consistent with Marantz's (1984) suggestion that rules that add an affix to the verb are broader in range than rules that leave the stem unchanged. When there is a telltale affix, it can be seen as carrying a specific kind of meaning change, and one can look up the lexical entry of the affix to determine what it is. If there is no affix, the verb itself must have acquired a new meaning, and the listener should be equipped with an alternative route to determining what that meaning change is; given narrow-range rules, the verb's semantics can allow one to retrace the alternations that could have created it.

The second possibly harmful effect of existence-predicting rules that are too broad is indeterminacy of semantic composition. If the semantic operation of a rule is very general, how it combines with the original meaning of a verb is often very hard to determine. Consider causativization. It's utterly clear that *John broke the cup* means that John acted on the cup, causing it to break. Similarly, *Bill bicycled Susan to Concord* must mean that Bill carried or accompanied Susan to Concord by bicycle. It may even be easily deducible that *That event decided me* means that that event made me come to a decision, or that *What's fussing her?* means "What's causing her to fuss?" But what exactly would *Sam came Bill out in favor of Nixon* or *Sheila ran Susan a mile in four minutes* or *Eric danced Francis* mean? The semantic change accomplished by a broad-range lexical rule may be too vague to yield output words with predictable meanings. In the case of the locative alternation, the problem is even more severe: the derived *with* form defines a specific state or property that is simply absent from the meaning of the *into/onto* form, and the speaker and listener must have some way of predicting what that state is. One advantage of restricting the existence-predicting powers of lexical rules to semantically cohesive subclasses is that any vagueness in composing an input verb's inherent meaning with the new meaning contributed by the rule can be eliminated by a single scheme of interpretation that applies across the entire subclass, deriving a meaning for the new form in a determinate way from seeds of information residing in the old one.

Each basic word in a language involves an irreducible, arbitrary pairing between sound and meaning. Thus using words presupposes independent but identical prior episodes of brute-force associative learning on the part of each person who speaks the language. It would not be surprising if the language faculty used the means available to it to restrict the automatic, natural usages of words to highly circumscribed extensions of existing forms.

Chapter 5
Representation

5.1 The Need for a Theory of Lexicosemantic Representation

The reason that Baker's paradox can be resolved, at least in principle, by appealing to semantically defined classes of verbs is that children have to learn the meanings of verbs anyway. They have to learn the difference between *pouring* and *splashing* or between *throwing* and *pulling* to use them in the right situations, regardless of syntax, and it is a nonobvious discovery that certain aspects of those distinctions correlate with certain of their syntactic privileges. This of course raises the important question of how children represent and learn verb meanings. Unlike some of the other hypotheses I considered in chapter 1, the conflation class hypothesis cannot point to any simple and obvious formal feature as the crucial distinction that children must respect. That is, there is no elementary feature like [±obligatory] or [±attested-in-input] associated with a verb that the learner could look at in deciding how to use it. The learner must instead decide whether a "verb's meaning" is "compatible" with a "conflation class," a much more obscure notion.

There are two possibilities as to what that might mean. First, verb meanings could be cognitive categories for certain types of events or relations, and conflation classes could be broader categories of the same type, and the decision about whether a verb belongs to a class could be a case of ordinary cognitive categorization. Deciding whether *cutting* is a causative relation would be analogous to deciding whether a dog is an animal and would depend on the individual's real-world knowledge of causation and of what events typically happen in scenarios involving cutting. If so, the constraints on productive alternations would ultimately be a part of the cognitive psychology of the categorization of events and states, and would simply correspond to the ways that a given culture finds it useful to carve up the universe of possible happenings. "Similarities" among families of verbs could be captured in a variety of ways, such as conceiving of their underlying concepts as nearby points in a multidimensional semantic space, as sets of partially overlapping features (Tversky, 1977), or as nonorthogonal vectors composed of large numbers of values of "microfeatures" (e.g., McClelland and Kawamoto, 1986). In principle, any culturally salient distinction could be used as a dimension or feature helping to define similarity, and the syntax could reflect those similarity clusterings. This is another way of saying that from the point of view of grammar, verb meanings are not constrained at all. Let me call this the "Unrestricted Conceptual Representation" hypothesis about lexical semantics.

The second possibility would be far more interesting. Perhaps there is a set of semantic elements and relations that is much smaller than the set of cognitively available and culturally salient distinctions, and verb meanings are organized around them. Linguistic processes, including the productive lexical rules that extend verbs to new argument structures, would be sensitive only to parts of semantic representations whose elements are members of this set. The set would consist of symbols that have cognitive content, such as "causation" and "location," but not all cognitively meaningful concepts are members of this privileged semantic machinery. Thus a verb like *to butter* would specify information about butter and information about causation, but only the causation part could trigger or block the application of lexical rules or other linguistic processes. Let me call this the "Grammatically Relevant Subsystem" hypothesis.

The particular resolution of Baker's paradox that I have been pursuing is compatible with either hypothesis about lexical semantics, but it would obviously be more satisfying if the Grammatically Relevant Subsystem hypothesis was true. A characterization of a culture's common-sense categorization of events and states is closer to cognitive anthropology than to psycholinguistics, and the psychological mechanisms responsible for their acquisition and representation are going to be those responsible for knowledge in general, something that we are far from being able to characterize precisely. But without such a characterization, the meaning differences crucial to syntactic differences are going to be vague and ad hoc, and how they are learned will remain obscure. On the other hand, if there is a relatively small and precisely characterizable set of grammatically relevant meaning distinctions, the characterization of linguistic criteria could be suitably constrained. Furthermore, if the special subsystem involved decomposition into structured representations with a well-defined syntax and vocabulary, we could point to the critical meaning components that differentiate otherwise similar verbs and try to *explain* why particular semantic differences have predictable syntactic consequences. Finally, if we could thoroughly characterize the semantic subsystem that syntax cares about, the theory of learning would be far more explicit. Despite all its complex guises, learning can always be analyzed as a set of "hypotheses" the organism is capable of entertaining and of a "confirmation function" by which the environmental input tells the organism which one to keep (Fodor, 1975; Osherson, Stob, and Weinstein, 1985; Wexler and Culicover, 1980). Characterizing the learner's possible hypotheses is the first step to characterizing its learning mechanisms (a task I will take up in the next chapter), and the more constrained the set of hypotheses, the better the explanation of how the learning succeeds.

The world is a messy enough place that a compromise outcome is also envisionable. Perhaps most syntactically relevant meaning distinctions within and across languages hinge on a small number of recurring privileged elements, while a few hinge on idiosyncratic bits of cultural knowledge. However, in this chapter I will push the Grammatically Relevant Subsystem hypothesis as far as possible. I will do so by proposing a theory of semantic structures, motivated by cross-linguistic generalizations and aspects of grammar other than those under consideration, in which most or all of the subclasses I have appealed to so far can be characterized mechanically. The theory of representation will have many tentative and imperfectly motivated assumptions, and I will not pretend to be laying out the unique best theory. Rather, the primary goal is to flesh out the proposed resolution of Baker's paradox with a fairly explicit and precise theory of the crucial distinctions it appeals to rather than waving the hand; in doing so I also hope to show that the Subsystem hypothesis is viable and quite probably true in some form.

5.2   Is a Theory of Lexical Semantics Feasible?

5.2.1   Skepticism About Decompositional Theories of Word Meaning
The suggestion that there might be a theory of verb meaning involving a small set of recurring elements might be cause for alarm. Some linguists and psycholinguists doubt that there can be one. Previous attempts at explicating word meanings by definitions or decomposition into smaller meaning elements (e.g., Katz and Fodor, 1963; Ross, 1972; Schank, 1973; Miller and Johnson-Laird, 1976) have been criticized on a number of grounds (e.g., Fodor, 1970; Fodor, Fodor, and Garrett, 1975; Dresher and Hornstein, 1977; Fodor, Garrett, Walker, and Parkes, 1980; Fodor, 1981; Armstrong, Gleitman, and Gleitman, 1983). There is skepticism both about the idea that verb meanings are autonomous structures built out of a constrained set of elements and about the idea that they are structured entities at all.

First, there are arguments against decomposing verb meanings into configurations of more basic meaning elements, mainly put forward by Jerry Fodor (e.g., Fodor, Fodor, and Garrett, 1975; Fodor, et al., 1980). Fodor points out, for example, that when putative decompositions of verb meanings into smaller elements are translated back into English, they lead to paraphrases that are rarely, perhaps never, synonymous with the original word. *Chase* is not the same as *try to catch*, for example, and *kill* is not the same as *cause to die*. Furthermore, often there is no principled reason to stop the decomposition at any given level of detail. Should *run* be defined as "locomote rapidly by moving the legs" or "locomote rapidly by flexing the hip, bending the knee, shifting one's weight, ...," or at an even more microscopic level? There is also no reason to prefer one decomposition at a given level of detail over another: should *to paint* mean "to put paint on something" or "to cover something using paint"? Finally, evidence from psychological experiments such as sentence verification response times or ratings of relatedness often fail to provide corroborating evidence for putative decompositions of verb meanings (though see Jackendoff, 1983; Gergely and Bever, 1986; and Gonsalves, 1988, for contrary arguments).

Second, some have argued that there is no clear demarcation between "linguistic" knowledge pertaining to what a word means and "real-world" knowledge pertaining to what entities tend to interact predictably in the world; between the mental dictionary and the mental encyclopedia. For example, the verb *devein* is a word that one naturally uses only in reference to shrimp; *assassinate* is done only to politically prominent people; *diagonalize* is done only to matrices (McCawley, 1968). Since no one would propose linguistic features like [±shrimp], [±politically-prominent], or [±matrix], it means that arbitrary facts about Western cooking practices, politics, or mathematics can enter into whatever aspects of so-called word definitions enforce their selection restrictions.

Given the present goals, these objections are beside the point. I will not try to come up with a small set of primitives and relations out of which one can compose definitions capturing the totality of a verb's meaning. Rather, the verb definitions sought will be hybrid structures, consisting of a scaffolding of universal, recurring, grammatically relevant meaning elements plus slots for bits of conceptual information about things like shrimp, butter, fame, and so on. The rich and idiosyncratic nuances of verbs' meanings will derive from three factors: (a) the information in the grammatically irrelevant conceptual slots; (b) the cognitive content of the various grammatically relevant elements and configurations, for example, the directness constraint on the interpretation of patients or the holism constraint on the interpretation of themes, discussed in chapter 3; and (c) general principles of lexicalization (such as conventionality, genericness, and stereotypy) that dictate that when a semantic structure is lexicalized into a single word, this in and of itself can lead to emergent semantic properties. Thus a semantic structure translated into a paraphrase need not be exactly synonymous with the single word it is designed to represent.

Furthermore, since the purpose of positing articulated semantic representations is to capture grammatically relevant distinctions, there are two converging
empirical constraints on what grain size and what arrangements of elements are
mandated. The first and most obvious constraint is that the elements must be
"meaningful" in the following sense: they cannot simply be arbitrary diacritics
(otherwise Baker's paradox would be "solved" vacuously) but must have
translations into conceptual terms that can enter into defining the range of
situations in which a speaker could truthfully and naturally use a verb. (For
example, the notion of an "effect" is what allows us to decide that rubbing a knife
against a steel pipe with no change in the latter is not an example of *cutting*.) The
other constraint is that the elements and configurations must do some work in
capturing grammatical generalizations and distinctions—ideally not only the
argument structure alternations that define Baker's paradox but other kinds of
grammatical distinctions as well.

These kinds of empirical considerations make the Grammatically Relevant
Subsystem hypothesis quite bold: for it to be true, there would have to be a single
set of elements that is at once conceptually interpretable, much smaller than the
set of possible verbs, used across all languages, used by children to formulate and
generalize verb meanings, used in specifically grammatical ways (for example,
being lexicalized into closed-class morphemes), and used to differentiate the
narrow classes that are subject to different sets of lexical rules. Let me review
some evidence that this is indeed the case.

5.3   Evidence for a Semantic Subsystem Underlying Verb Meanings

*Nonequivalence between cognitively and linguistically motivated semantic
classes.* Throughout chapter 4 I stressed that the subclasses delineating existence-predicting lexical rules were defined by subtle semantic criteria. By
"subtle" I meant that they would not correspond to the kinds of distinctions that
would occur to someone who was simply classifying verbs into cognitively
similar kinds of events. To take the most obvious example, even linguists and
psycholinguists, people who presumably are quite reflective about cognitive
distinctions relevant to language, are apt to talk about "action verbs" as if that
were a linguistically natural class. But we saw that verbs as cognitively similar
as *cut*, *break*, *hit*, *touch*, and *raise* belong to five very different subclasses. The
reason for the disparity is that cognitive similarity tends to be defined by typical
chains of events as defined by mental schemas, scripts, or stereotypes, whereas
linguistic semantic similarity is defined by constraints on a smaller set of
necessary components of events (see section 4.2 for extensive discussion; I
return to this point in the final chapter). Similar disparities between cognitively

available and linguistically significant features arise in the discussion of all four lexical alternations; indeed it is this disparity, I suggest, that led linguists and psycholinguists to the premature conclusion that productive alternations apply to arbitrary lists of idiosyncratic lexical items.

Recurring semantic distinctions. Levin (1985) and Laughren, Levin, and Rappaport (1986) showed that certain semantic elements like motion, causation, and contact recurred in different combinations in delineating the range of different argument structure alternations. More generally, there are strong universal tendencies for large sets of verbs within and across languages to make the same kinds of semantic distinctions (i.e., to be choosy about the situations that they apply to in the same kinds of ways) and for grammatical processes to attend to those distinctions. Conversely, there are other semantic distinctions that verbs rarely make in any language (Carter, 1976a; Bybee, 1985; Talmy, 1985). I will summarize these distinctions in the next section.

Interchangeability with closed-class morphemes. Many of the recurring semantic elements that define certain verb meanings can appear in the definitions of closed-class morphemes and affixes in the same language or in other languages (Bybee, 1985; Talmy, 1985). For example, some languages have productive causative affixes that turn an inchoative stem into a causative transitive. Since closed-class morphemes draw their meanings from a restricted set of possible elements (by definition, in a given language), and since productively inflected and derived forms are semantically complex, with a meaning composed of the meaning of the stem modified by the meaning of the affix, a similar analysis strongly suggests itself for synonymous verbs elsewhere in the language or in other languages that happen not to be morphologically complex. Note that closed-class elements have distinctive nonsemantic properties, such as typically being bound, unstressed, and in special syntactic positions, so this claim is in no danger of being circular.

An extreme example can be found in certain languages like Lisu (see Li and Thompson, 1976) that do not signal grammatical relations either with affixation or with stable word order. Ambiguity about grammatical relations in these languages is not as bad as an English-speaker would predict because its individual verbs can encode properties of their arguments, selecting features that in other languages can be specified in the case and agreement systems. In such a language one says, roughly, *As for John, Bill bit* or *As for Bill, John bit* and they both can mean either that John bit Bill or that Bill bit John. But for many other verbs, the ambiguity does not exist. For example, transitive *burn* can apply only to an inanimate patient; *As for John, the stick burn* and *As for the stick, John burn* can only mean that John burned the stick, and *As for John, Bill burn* and *As for Bill, John burn* are ungrammatical (a causative construction similar to *As for John, he caused Bill to be burned* would have to be used). Another example is the equivalent of the verb *kill*, which, unlike English, does not require an animate patient argument, but instead requires a noun phrase meaning "an end," so one says the equivalent of *As for John, end kill* ("John killed and an end resulted") and it could only be John who did the killing.

Variability of verb meanings across languages. Though languages tend to make the same kinds of distinctions in defining verbs, they show considerable variability in the exact meanings of individual vocabulary items. One language may have a verb meaning to walk in a particular manner; another may have only a verb for walking itself, which must combine with one adverb or another to express that kind of walking. Some languages have a single verb for *making* and *doing*; others distinguish them. See Talmy (1985), Gentner (1981, 1982), and of course Whorf (1956) for discussion. Since extreme linguistic determinism is false, verbs probably do not label unanalyzed concepts, but varying amalgams of elements.

Statistical similarities to closed-class morphemes. When we look at words' frequency of occurrence in English, we find that verbs display a statistical profile that differentiates them from nouns and reveals certain resemblances to closed-class morphemes (Gentner, 1981). Closed-class morphemes predominate in the high-frequency quantiles, but their numbers drop to zero in the middle and low frequencies. Nouns show the opposite pattern: the lower the frequency, the greater the proportion of words that are nouns and the larger the absolute number of nouns. Verbs are somewhere in between: rarest in the high-frequency quantiles, peaking in the high-to-medium frequencies, and dropping off steadily in the medium and low frequencies. This pattern is consistent with the possibility that verbs are most naturally attached to meanings that are neither wildly idiosyncratic nor rigidly tied to specific linguistic functions (e.g., tense), but something in between.

In fact, there is a set of verbs that acts something like a transitional case: the "light verbs" such as *come, go, make, be, bring, take, get,* and *give*. Syntactically they are full-fledged verbs, but semantically they are less filling, resembling closed-class elements. Their meanings are fairly nonspecific and may correspond to simple semantic configurations that are encoded into affixes in other languages (e.g., the use of *make* in the periphrastic causative). They often function as little more than tense-carriers or verb-slot-fillers in idioms whose objects carry most of the meaning of the predicate (e.g., *make love; take a bath; go crazy;* and most uses of *be*). Some have auxiliary-like semantic and syntactic properties (e.g., *We're going to eat; How goes it?; Have you any wool?; Are you hungry?*) or are homophonous with auxiliaries (possessional *have* and the copula *be*).

Adult psycholinguistic evidence. In the psychology of language, verbs do not function as cohesive, indivisible gestalts. Compared to nouns, verbs are not remembered well verbatim, do not survive intact in double translations (where one bilingual speaker translates a passage and another translates it back), and frequently do not survive intact in paraphrases of sentences (see Gentner, 1981, for a review). All of this suggests that verbs are stored and processed in terms of assemblies that can lose existing elements or accumulate new ones (see also Gergely and Bever, 1986).

Developmental psycholinguistic evidence. Children acquire verbs later than nouns in general (Gentner, 1982) and are prone to making errors in using verbs with their correct meanings, errors that are in many cases attributable to incomplete or mislabeled semantic structures. Since this is an important topic in the present study, I will discuss this evidence in detail in chapter 8.

Neurolinguistic evidence. Intriguingly, verb meanings may be represented in the same parts of the brain as information about grammar (Gentner, 1988). Damage to certain regions of the left cerebral hemisphere can lead to agrammatism, a syndrome characterized by dysfluency, reduced phrase length, a restriction of the range of syntactic constructions used, and frequent omission of closed-class morphemes. Agrammatic aphasics often have particular difficulty with verbs. They make errors in inflecting them, have difficulty producing them, and often omit them entirely (Gleason, Goodglass, Obler, Green, Hyde, and Weintraub, 1980; Marin, Saffran, and Schwartz, 1976; Miceli, Mazzuchi, Menn, and Goodglass, 1983; Miceli, Silveri, Villa, and Caramazza, 1984). Since these deficits involve the use of verbs in sentences, they could reflect the difficulties in coordinating syntactic constraints with verbs' representations, rather than difficulties in representing or processing the verbs themselves. But Miceli et al. (1984) showed that verbs themselves suffer in agrammatism. They simply asked agrammatics to name objects and actions depicted in drawings; no sentence processing was required. Agrammatics had more difficulty naming actions than objects. This was not due to the intrinsic difficulty of the task; anomics—brain-injured patients with general difficulties in naming—showed the opposite pattern, and intact control subjects showed no difference. As Gentner notes, these findings suggest that verb meanings and syntactic rules share some of their neurological machinery.

5.4   A Cross-linguistic Inventory of Components of Verb Meaning

If there are recurring elements of verb meaning, what are they? An answer will provide the first bits of evidence for what the crucial meaning features organizing verbs' semantic structures are. Carter (1976a, b) offered some suggestion based on English with a few comparisons to other languages, but the most extensive cross-linguistic survey of verb meanings comes from the work of Talmy (1985) on what he calls "lexicalization patterns." Talmy is not completely explicit about what a lexicalization pattern is; in particular, he does not distinguish between semantic distinctions made by large numbers of verbs, roughly independent of the syntactic frame that the verb appears in (for example, distinctions governing the situations in which one could point to some event and truthfully say "This is blicking"), and semantic distinctions that have widespread grammatical consequences. His examples suggest that these two senses of "lexicalization pattern" very often coincide. In fact, in the theory I am presenting, we should expect such a correlation. If all verbs must be organized around a set of grammatically relevant structures that can have slots for idiosyncratic cognitive elements, but not vice versa, this will lead to a sheer frequency difference in which semantic distinctions are prevalent across languages. An analogy: if one were to do a word token frequency count of a pile of college application forms, there would be a large difference in the frequency of the words like *name* and *address* compared to words like *John*, *Smith*, and *Main*, even if the latter are non-negligibly frequent.

The universe of conceptual features that, logically speaking, could be co-opted into verb representations is virtually limitless. McClelland and Kawamoto (1986), for example, assume (without evidence) that one of the dimensions of similarity among verbs that has consequences for argument assignment is a 4-way distinction concerning the nature of the change that the patient undergoes: "into pieces," "into shreds," "chemical," or "none." However, most conceptual elements are rarely or never systematically encoded in the predicates of a language. Talmy claims that languages rarely encode into verb meanings the mood, attitude, degree of hedging, or state of mind of the speaker; the rate of a moving or changing object; the symmetry, color, person, or gender of the participants of an event; the relation of the event to comparable events; the physical properties of the setting of the event (temperature, indoors versus outdoors, land versus air versus sea); tense; and many other aspects of the event that are possibly or even typically entertainable on the part of a speaker. Of course, individual verbs can encode any of these notions, such as *to redden, swelter, doubt, symmetrize, swim*, and so on, but the distinctions do not apply across large numbers of verbs, do not differentiate verbs into syntactically relevant subclasses, and do not receive encoding by closed-class morphemes.

Below I list the set of semantic elements that according to Talmy are employed by large numbers of verbs in many languages. I also give examples of closed-class morphemes that express similar meanings.

"The main event" : a state or motion. The "main event" is a position, state, or change of position or state predicated of a theme, for example, the fact that John moved in *John ran.* Presumably it would apply also to an act committed by an agent or actor in cases where there is no theme. The main event is the backbone of a verb's meaning and so has no equivalent in the closed-class system; rather, it defines the event or relation whose temporal location is fixed by the tense markers on the verb, whose temporal distribution is specified by aspect markers, whose truth value is modified by the auxiliary, and so on.

Path, direction, and location. A verb can specify a particular path of motion of a theme with respect to an object (e.g., *enter*), with respect to the speaker (e.g., *come*), or with respect to a specific kind of object (e.g., *the ship berthed*; other languages have much richer possibilities of this sort). Verbs can also obligatorily specify the existence of motion along a path, with the path itself specified in the verb's arguments (*The bird darted into the house*). In such cases the exact kind of path is specified by closed-class morphemes such as prepositions, postpositions, case markers, or particles. The intuitive geometric system in which paths are defined has special properties discussed at length in Talmy (1983).

Causation. Verbs can specify whether an event has been caused or just occurs (e.g., *kill* versus *die*), what kind of causation is involved (e.g., by an agent, an instrument, or an event), and in some cases what the cause is (e.g., the wind in *The pencil blew off the table*). Following Talmy's later work (1988), this is extendible to the various kinds of causation that can be analyzed in terms of force-dynamic interactions, such as enabling, preventing, failing to prevent, and so on. These correspond to various closed-class morphemes that encode causativity itself, such as verb affixes in certain languages, or prepositions, complementizers, and case markers for various causal arguments or subordinate clauses such as agents (e.g., *by*), instruments (*with*), causing events (*from eating too much*), and so on.

Manner. This refers to how an actor acts or a theme changes, or to something the actor or theme is doing concurrently with the change. For example, it is the difference between *punch* and *slap* (manners of action) or between *bounce* and *roll* (manners of motion). Manner elements can also be expressed grammatically in adverbial adjuncts, such as *Sally came home skipping* or in adverbs, often marked with the suffix *-ly*.

Properties of a theme or actor. Verbs can specify that their arguments have certain specific properties. These include material and shape properties of the theme or patient, such as the English verbs *to rain* or *to drink* where the theme must be liquid. (In certain northern Californian Indian languages, there are many verb roots expressing the fact that particular types of objects or substances are moving.) Other allowable generic distinctions include singular versus plural and human versus nonhuman (as in the German *essen* versus *fressen*, verbs meaning to *eat* but differing as to whether it is a human or an animal that is doing the eating), though many others, such as person, gender, or color, are never found. In the closed-class system, determiners, pronouns, agreement and concord markers on verbs and adjectives, and other kinds of "classifiers" are sensitive to these distinctions (Allan, 1977; Denny, 1976).

Temporal distribution (aspect and phase). Talmy notes that verbs can describe situations as pointlike events (*hit*) or as boundariless processes (*run*); they can describe iterated events (*beat*); entering a state (*sit down* as opposed to *sit*); pointlike events that terminate a process (*arrive*); events consisting of an on-off cycle (*flash*); and so on. Perhaps the best-known taxonomy of verbs in terms of their temporal distribution was suggested by Vendler (1957). In this classification, verbs first divide into "states" and "processes," where a state is temporally homogeneous and static, such as *knowing the answer* or *being in Michigan*, and a process specifies something that changes over time. Processes in turn divide into three varieties: "activities" such as *running*, which are extended in time but have no clearly demarcated endpoints, "accomplishments" such as *drawing a circle*, which are extended over time but are defined by the fact that they terminate in the attainment of some state, and "achievements" such as *winning a race*, which are construed as referring to the instant at which a state is attained. The intrinsic temporal distribution of a verb interacts in complex ways with the aspectual notions specified in verb affixes.

Purpose. Verbs can encode activity in pursuit of a goal, such as *chase, hunt,* or *wash.* Similar notions can be expressed in adjuncts marked with certain prepositions or complementizers, such as *I threw the rock to knock the apple off the tree* or *I bought a book for Mary to read.*

Coreferentiality ("personation"). In some languages, the verb *to comb* ordinarily means to comb someone else's hair; in others, it means to comb one's own hair. (An English analogue might be the distinction between *to dress*, which can be used intransitively to refer to something one does to oneself, versus *to clothe*, which cannot be used intransitively; Jackendoff, 1987a). Related notions are expressed by anaphors such as *himself* in English and reflexive clitics in Romance languages.

Truth value (polarity and factivity). Verbs can express the assumptions of the speaker or of some participant concerning the truth of a proposition: a person's attitude toward a proposition versus its negation (*think* versus *doubt*), whether the speaker believes a proposition to be true or only apparent (*be* versus *seem*), whether the speaker assumes a proposition to be true or only asserts that someone else assumes it (*John knows/thinks that it will snow today*); and whether the speaker's assertion was witnessed or learned through hearsay. These distinctions figure prominently in the definitions of many auxiliaries (Steele, 1981).

Talmy lists a handful of other notions that occasionally are expressed in verbs, and some, like valence and voice, that are more syntactic than semantic.

5.5   A Theory of the Representation of Grammatically Relevant Semantic Structures

In the rest of this chapter I will present a sketch of a theory of verb semantics adequate to support the syntactic distinctions I have been using to get the English speaker out of Baker's paradox. The sketch is close to the theories of Jackendoff (1975, 1978, 1983, 1987a, b) and Carter (1976a, b), though it borrows heavily as well from the work of Talmy (1983, 1985, 1988) and is similar in a variety of ways to other proposals such as those of Green (1974), Hale and Laughren (1983), Miller and Johnson-Laird (1976), Pustejovsky (1987, in press), Rappaport and Levin (1985, 1988; Laughren, Levin, and Rappaport, 1986), and other decompositional theories (see B. Levin, 1985, for a review). I am forced to be eclectic because no existing theory of semantic structure is aimed squarely at the current problem. Theories from the Generative Semantics movement (e.g., G. Lakoff, 1971; McCawley, 1971; Ross, 1972), though contributing many insights to later approaches, were motivated in part by theoretical considerations that are not relevant to the current goals, most notably the assumption that structures representing words' meanings are subject to syntactic transformations. Most theories coming out of psychology and computer science (e.g., Schank, 1973) are not aimed at explaining linguistic data at all but at explaining how people make certain kinds of inferences. Talmy's and Rappaport and Levin's characterizations themselves are too informal to support the learning theory I need, and Jackendoff's theory does not distinguish broad, property-predicting regularities from narrow, existence-predicting regularities. As a result, his theory is too impoverished in some places, too powerful in others, relative to the current goals. I will try to adapt his theory to make the kinds of distinctions needed in the resolution of Baker's paradox. But given the demanding nature of linguistically motivated psycholexicology, it should come as no surprise that the framework I present has some rough edges here and there.

5.5.1   Conceptual Constituents and Functions for Motion Events
Jackendoff proposes that there is a set of basic conceptual or ontological categories: Thing, Event, State, Action, Place, Path, Property, and Amount (see also Keil, 1979). There is also a set of conceptual formation rules that combine them into more complex concepts. For example, an event can consist of a thing moving along a path. The function relating them is called GO. The first argument of GO, the moving entity, is what is traditionally called the theme, but the label

itself need be nothing more than a mnemonic for "the first argument of GO." The conceptual formation rule stating that an event can consist of an entity moving along a path is shown in (5.1).

(5.1) EVENT —> [$_{event}$ GO (THING, PATH)]

Because Jackendoff's linear notation calls for unreadable strings of brackets when the concepts become complex, I will use a tree-structure notation, shown in (5.2), to display the same information. It can be interpreted roughly like a phrase marker for an English X': the mother node indicates the type of constituent; the leftmost daughter stands for the predicate; the other daughters stand for its arguments. (Note that functions, arguments, and modifiers are distinguished in this notation only by their labels and positions, not by some visual device.)

(5.2)

The PATH category can be further expanded as indicated in (5.3).

(5.3)

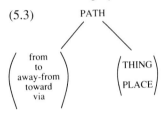

This structure defines a path by naming a reference object (a PLACE or THING) and a path-function specifying some path or direction with respect to it. The most common path-functions define paths that terminate at a reference object ('to' or 'from', depending on the direction of travel along the path), that point in its direction but do not necessarily reach it ('toward' or 'away-from'), or that coincide with it at some intermediate point ('via'). 'Up' and 'down' could be treated as monadic paths. A PLACE is a region defined with respect to an object, such as the interior of the object, its surroundings, or one of its surfaces. As shown in (5.4), it is defined by specifying an object and a "place-function" (e.g., 'on', 'under', 'near', 'around'). I use English prepositions as mnemonics for different path- and place-functions, but the correspondence is highly inexact. There are many place- and path-functions that English has no names for, and instances where one preposition stands for several distinct place- or path-functions. (Accordingly, I use single quotation marks to distinguish lower-case mnemonics for semantic elements from actual English words.) The cognitive content of path structures corresponds to a certain schematization of motion whereby a moving object is idealized as a point traversing some trajectory (see Talmy, 1983).

Occasionally the moving object is called a "locatum" and a reference object that helps define its place or path a "location."

(5.4)

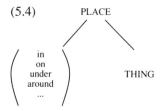

5.5.2 Interfacing Semantic Structures with Syntax

To get from a generic conceptual structure to a semantic structure suitable for the lexical entry of an argument-taking verb, it is necessary to indicate which of the conceptual constituents can serve as an "open argument," linked to a syntactic role in a verb's argument structure. Jackendoff (1983) proposes a constraint called the Lexical Variable Principle: arguments must always be complete conceptual constituents. For example, "to place [something] [somewhere]" is a possible verb, where the open arguments are a THING and a PLACE; whereas "to place something [in some spatial relation to] an inanimate object," where the open argument is a bare place-function, and "to try to [move in some direction] an animal," where the open argument consists of a combination of a GO function and a path, are not possible verbs. We can thus indicate open arguments in semantic structures by appending open brackets ("[ ]") to a conceptual constituent. For example, the semantic structures for the verb *go* and the preposition *into* (which Jackendoff points out really means "to in") are shown in (5.5).[1] "Suppressed" arguments that are entailed to exist but not expressed in the syntax, such as the agents of short passives or the understood patient in *John ate*, are listed in semantic structure but lack the brackets designating them as being open to syntax.

(5.5)

The argument structures for these words are then created by the application of linking rules. Linking rules map open arguments in a semantic structure onto syntactically distinguishable argument types, based on their position in semantic structure. Three linking rules—one mapping themes onto direct internal arguments, one mapping goals (and other constituents of paths) onto indirect internal arguments, and a third mapping locations (and other places) onto indirect internal arguments—might look something like (5.6). Similar rules could be formulated for LFG.

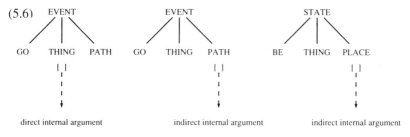

(5.6)

direct internal argument   indirect internal argument   indirect internal argument

There are also rules that Jackendoff calls categorial correspondence rules. Major syntactic phrasal categories such as NP, VP, AP, PP, and S must correspond to complete conceptual categories. There are probably universal contingencies governing which conceptual categories may be expressed by which major phrasal categories (see Pinker, 1982, 1984, for a theory of how these correspondences help the child acquire his or her first phrase structure rules), and some language-particular variability as well. In particular, NPs can express any conceptual category, though in the unmarked case they correspond to things. PPs express places and paths (and in English sometimes properties, as in *Bob is in the dumps*). S and VP express events and states. These correspondence rules specify how phrases can stand for semantic constituents; together with phrase structure rules or their equivalent, and the argument structures of predicates, they dictate how the semantic structure for a sentence as a whole is built out of the semantic structures of the individual words composing it. For example, the sentence *John went into the room* is represented semantically as in (5.7). (The parentheses around the names for the content of the arguments indicate that they came from elsewhere in the sentence, not from the verb's lexical entry.)

(5.7)

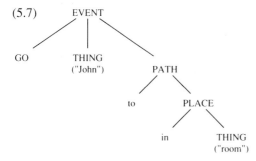

Sentence structures are well formed only if they contain phrases corresponding to the conceptual categories selected by the verb (e.g. THING versus PLACE versus PATH), in configurations (GB) or with grammatical functions (LFG) consistent with the verb's argument structure. For example, the fact that the verb *enter*, which incorporates a direction of motion, takes a direct object, not a prepositional phrase, is enforced by its semantic structure containing an open argument corresponding to a thing, not a path, as (5.8) shows. At the same time it shows how the verb can internally specify the kind of path and place ordinarily expressed by the preposition *into*. A new linking rule, not shown, would associate the argument of place-functions and path-functions with the object role; it would also apply within locative prepositional phrases, serving to link the syntactic objects of prepositions with the corresponding argument positions within the prepositions' semantic structures.

(5.8)   enter:

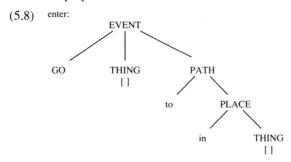

Verbs that select for certain types of directional or locational argument can be represented in similar ways. For example, *put*, which requires a preposition incorporating the direction "to" and a place (*She put the pencil into / onto / under the desk; *She put the pencil toward / from the desk*; Jackendoff, 1987), has an open argument corresponding to a path stipulated to contain the path-function 'to', as indicated in (5.9). As we saw in (5.5), the prepositions *into* and *onto* specify the path 'to' leading to the place 'in X' or 'on X'. Less transparently, many English prepositions such as *under* and *around* are ambiguous, serving either as place-designators or as a 'to' path leading to the designated kind of place (Jackendoff, 1983). Any of these prepositions can thus be *fused* (see Jackendoff, 1987a) with the semantic structure for *put*. In contrast, any preposition incorporating an incompatible path-function or no place-function will lead to an inconsistent, unfusable pair of semantic structures. (In (5.9) I omit the part of the semantic structure specifying the causative component.)[2]

(5.9)   put:

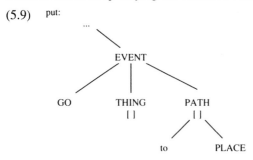

This treatment of the selection of oblique objects has the advantage that a verb that selects generic arguments for locations or directions does not have to specify a list of all the prepositions it can appear with, a list that would in any case be redundant with the lexical entries for the individual prepositions. (The reason for this redundancy is that prepositions need their own free-standing definitions so they can be used in nonargument positions, as in *In the park, John met Mary.*) As we shall see, more abstract prepositional arguments such as instruments and benefactives submit to the same treatment. Another advantage of this treatment is that it is consistent with developmental evidence showing that children are prone to confusing prepositions in passives and adjuncts, where they often mark the agent phrase using *from* or *with* instead of *by* (e.g. *The doll is scrunched from somebody ... but not from me*; Bowerman, 1983b; Maratsos and Abramovitch, 1975; Clark and Carpenter, in press). I know of no cases where children leave the agent phrase unmarked (*The doll is scrunched somebody*), or where they use a random preposition unrelated to notions of causation, agency, or sources (e.g., *The doll is scrunched to somebody*). Children also confuse semantically related prepositions in locative and temporal expressions, such as *They went to stay at the puppy*; *He's pointing his finger to it*; and *He took me at the circus* (Menyuk, 1969). These phenomena suggest that children appreciate that verbs take oblique arguments of a general semantic type at a level removed from specific knowledge of which preposition it must be.

At first glance selection of prepositions by lexicosemantic structure may seem incompatible with the common observation that verbs can "idiosyncratically" select their prepositions or case markers, as in *John relied on Mary* or *You shouldn't put up with that*. However, this fact could be captured in word-specific semantic representations as easily as in word-specific syntactic representations. Prepositions could have multiple entries with different specialized semantic structures, and verbs could select for those representations. (It is important to bear in mind that semantic structures are partly conventionalized linguistic representations, not conceptual category representations, a point I return to in chapter 8.) The advantage of this kind of account over direct listing of prepositions in argument structures is that it lacks the harmful and unnecessary descriptive power of literal listing, it naturally represents verbs that select families of semantically similar prepositions instead of specific prepositions, and it is consistent with the widespread systematicity of how prepositions are paired with kinds of verbs.[3]

It is important to note that this treatment of the representation of open arguments as pointers to syntax and the instantiation of them by fusion is a strong theoretical claim, not mere notation. I discuss the importance of this claim in section 8.2.

5.5.3 Manner of Motion

Manner of motion, if the verb specifies it, is listed as another daughter node of the EVENT, as in the semantic structures for the two entries in (5.10) corresponding to *The ball rolled* and *The ball rolled down the hill*. Note that distinct entries are needed: in Spanish, for example, only the first exists; in English, a lexical rule creates the second from the first (a good example of why direction phrases, often treated as "adjuncts," cannot be treated as being independent of argument structure).

(5.10)

There are several important features of the cognitive content of these structures. First, the symbol "rolling" is shorthand for a description of the physical topography of rolling, specifying the particular manner encoded by the verb. Its internal structure is irrelevant for our purposes because *particular* manners (as opposed to the *existence* of a specified manner) play no role in the mapping of verb semantics onto argument structure. (For a hypothesis about the mental representation of particular postures and manners of motion, see Marr and Vaina, 1982, and for its interface with conceptual structure, see Jackendoff, 1987d.) This is an example of the hybrid nature of semantic structure that I appealed to at the beginning of the chapter. The idiosyncratic information about the topography of rolling is a black box as far as grammar is concerned, and we need not be concerned about decomposing it, whereas the information that there is a manner specified, or a manner and a path, is something that grammar cares about. The distinction is indicated in this notation by quotation marks around the opaque-to-grammar material.

The cognitive content of the MANNER constituent, whatever it is, interacts with the content of the GO and PATH constituents in specific ways. For GO events with no PATHs, the MANNER information specifies the motion of the theme or parts of the theme relative to its own internal frame of reference (i.e., its prominent axes or center of mass), or with respect to its local environment, with no implication that there is any translation of the object as a whole with respect to the environment. An object should be able to display a manner of motion while remaining in one "place": it is not contradictory to say *The penguin rolled / skidded / bounced / slid / spun in one place on the ice for a solid minute*. A GO event, on the other hand, implies translation of the object as a whole with respect to the environment, independent of its internal or local motions. Although nothing can **go in one place on the ice*, a dimensionless point can *go from A to B*. When an event has both a GO and a MANNER, a composite motion is synthesized out of the global translation and the set of local motions (rotations, oscillations, and so on). The motions are synthesized by uniting the local reference frame defining the within-object motion with part of the global reference frame defining its translation: *The bottle floated into the cave* must mean that the cave is situated on a body of water; it cannot refer to an event in which someone carries into a cave a tub of water with a bottle floating in it. These schematizations are crucial in delineating certain syntactically relevant distinctions involving the causative and the dative, among others.

5.5.4 States

The other major conceptual category that verbs express are STATEs. An example of a state is a thing being situated at a place, which uses the predicate BE. The verb *be* is the prototypical example; the lexical entry of one of its versions is shown in (5.11).

(5.11) be:

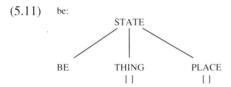

GO is canonically an EVENT, and BE is canonically a STATE. However, the two contrasts are not totally redundant. It is also possible for GO to be an example of a state, when the trajectory of a motion event is frozen in time and conceived of as a static path: *This road goes from Toledo to Columbus* is an example (Jackendoff annotates the function GO with a special symbol to indicate this (GO$_{ext}$), but this is not necessary if it is listed as a STATE). Conversely, Jackendoff suggests that a nonmotional situation can be an example of an event: the function STAY indicates that a thing continues to be situated at a place, for example in *John stayed in the room* or *Mary kept John in the room*. Again, the new function name is not strictly necessary; we could express the relation by simply allowing BE to be a kind of EVENT.

5.5.5 Properties

Verbs can select more than just broad ontological categories such as THING versus PLACE as open arguments. They can also specify a particular kind of object, for example, in verbs like those in *The ship berthed; She boxed/bagged the apples; She boned the fish, She milked the cow*, and *She buttered the bread*; see Clark and Clark (1978). Other languages, such as the native Californian language Atsugewi described by Talmy (1985), have much more systematic possibilities of this type. They have verb particles that can specify the motion of a type of object (e.g., spherical and shiny, slimy and runny) or motion of an entity into an object of a certain kind (e.g., fire, the ground). The semantic structure for *berth* is shown in (5.12). Jackendoff suggests that the machinery necessary to handle these "incorporated arguments" also gives rise to the set of phenomena known as "selection restrictions" when the specific information is associated with an open argument instead of a closed one. For example, the verb *splash*, also shown in (5.12), specifies that its argument be liquid: sand can move in roughly the same manner as water, but it seems odd to say *The sand splashed*. The difference in interpretation of the specific quoted terms in *berth* and *splash* is that in the latter the information is associated with an open argument and is fused with the information gathered from another sentence constituent (just like in the semantic representation of *put* when it is fused with its arguments). If there is a conflict of conceptual category type or other conceptual information, the sentence is interpreted as being semantically anomalous. This rules out sentences like *John elapsed* and *The sand splashed*.

(5.12) berth: splash:

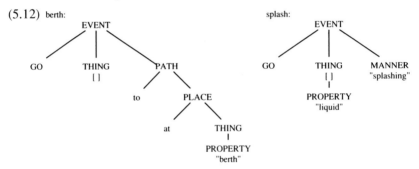

   The fact that specific terms are introduced as "properties" of arguments in the notation reflects an interesting constraint on the incorporation of these terms into verbs' semantic structures. Verbs never specify a true constant, in the sense of an individual or even a very specific kind of object or substance. It is not contradictory to say *She buttered the bread with imitation margarine*, for example (Rappaport and Levin, 1985). Somehow when a putative "constant" is incorporated into a verb, it becomes a generic specification. This may be a special case of a more general principle proposed by di Sciullo and Williams (1987) that word meanings are "generic" or "nonreferential" (Aronoff, 1980, makes a similar point). According to this principle, specific reference to things, times, or truth values is a phrase-level and sentence-level, not a word-level, assignment process. Di Sciullo and Williams note three phenomena in support of this principle. *John is a bank robber* (where *bank robber* is a compound noun) does not mean that John is currently robbing a bank; it indicates only the kind of person he is (in fact, he may never have robbed a bank). In contrast, the phrase *a robber of banks* implies that the person has actually done so (see Rappaport and Levin, in press). Second, one cannot say *John is a that-robber*, pointing to a bank, or *John is an it-robber*, referring to an antecedent in discourse, though one can of course say *John robbed that / it*. Finally, there is a strong contrast in acceptability between saying *John is a Nixon-admirer in every sense except that he does not admire Nixon* and saying *John admires Nixon in every sense except that he does not admire Nixon*. This genericness constraint would be implemented as the interpretive convention that the cognitive content of a constant X in verb definitions is a (presumably pragmatic) interpretation of an argument as being similar to X.[4]

The Grammatically Relevant Subsystem hypothesis, of course, requires that the contents of specific (quoted) terms be opaque to lexical rules. A rule can be sensitive to whether a verb specifies that a location argument have some property, any property (as opposed to being completely free in its properties), but it cannot interpret material in quotes so as to apply selectively to arbitrary cognitively represented properties. For example, no rule should be able to tell the difference between, say, verbs involving "butter" and "jam" on the one hand and verbs involving "oil" and "grease" on the other, or between verbs of "splashing" and "spraying" and verbs of "splattering" and "spattering"; they are all just atomic symbols. However, rules in many languages, including English, as we shall see, can apply selectively to items containing *certain kinds* of specific information (Talmy, 1985). I will suggest a version of the Subsystem hypothesis that allows for some transparency of specific terms without going all the way toward the Unrestricted Conceptual Representation hypothesis that the full meanings of specific terms are accessible to linguistic rules. I will do so by proposing a small set of object properties that will be represented by specific features that lexical rules can be sensitive to, rather than as quoted opaque terms that merely point to conceptual categories. A plausible first approximation to these features is that they are the ones that tend to turn up in classifier and agreement systems (excluding deictic features like person and morphological features like gender and declensional class); we know that these are a small subset of the specific object categories that languages can have names for (see Denny, 1976; Allan, 1977). Specifically, something like the following set of features seems to express most of the recurring grammatically relevant distinctions we find in English and other languages:[5]

- Animacy: animate versus inanimate.
- Humanness: human versus nonhuman
- Shape (extendedness or dimensionality). Grammar does not pick out Euclidean shapes such as "square" or "circular," local geometry such as "pointy" or "containing a hole," or metric properties such as equilaterality. However, it often

uses a categorization in terms of how many dimensions an object is extended in. Objects can be extended in one dimension (e.g., sticks, ropes), two dimensions (e.g., sheets, leaves), or three dimensions (e.g., boulders, apples). Shapes can also be specified more finely, especially in the semantics of prepositions and of several subclasses of verbs relevant to the locative alternation. Jackendoff (1987c) suggests that objects are schematized in terms of "major" and "minor" dimensionalities (see also Talmy, 1983). The major dimensionality of an object is the number of dimensions the object has in its sparsest recognizable caricature or schematization. The major dimensionality can be further constrained to be bounded or not so constrained. The "minor" dimensionality is the "less important" dimension, always bounded, projected over the entire axis of a major dimension. Hence, a road, river, or ribbon is 1D X 1D (major dimension is 1D, either bounded or not; minor dimension is 1D). A spot is 0D x 2D. A layer or slab is 2D X 1D. A tube or beam is 1D X 2D. A Sphere is 3D. Naturally, the dimensionalities of the major and minor axes have to add up to 3 or less. In addition, a fixed dimensionality can apply to an object as a whole, or to the boundary of an object; for example a "crust" is the 2D x 1D surface of a 3D object, and an "endpoint" is the 0D boundary of a 1D line.

• Count/mass. Things are often subcategorized in terms of whether they are construed as bounded, formed, objects capable of being individuated, or as unbounded, formless substances or media. I will use the mnemonics "count" and "mass" to refer to this distinction.[6]

• Rigidity. Objects may be classified in terms of whether they are rigid or flexible.

• Substance/aggregate. Masses may be either homogeneous substances, which can be further subclassified as liquid or semisolid, or aggregates of parts. The parts themselves can be classified in terms of some of the properties used to classify objects as a whole, such as substance type or dimensionality.

This set of object properties is summarized in the schema shown in (5.13), which is also tries to capture the major dependencies among the properties to a first approximation. For example, only inanimate objects can be categorized in terms of their dimensionality; only masses can consist of aggregates. Sets of features within parentheses are optional and mutually exclusive alternatives. The AGGREGATE feature can further be elaborated in terms of the PROPERTY that each of its parts must possess. Because of the way the diagram captures dependencies among features, each of the rightmost labels in a line implies the entire horizontal chain of labels extending to its left. Thus a semantic representation for a verb can impose selection restrictions on its arguments by listing exactly one label from any of the parenthesized sets in (5.13). Note that since the dimensionality values and count/mass values are not contained within a set of their own parentheses, they both may be specified simultaneously. Some examples, appropriate perhaps for arguments of *splash*, *fressen*, and *coil*, are shown in the first three structures in (5.14). The latter two could be used to specify the 2D boundary of a 3D object (e.g., a container, for *fill*) or an aggregate consisting of drops of liquid (e.g., for *sprinkle*).

(5.13)

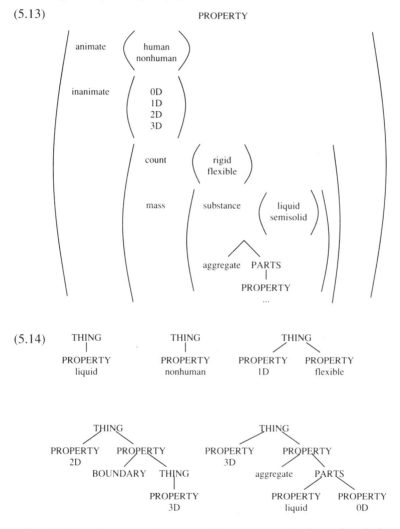

In addition, there may be a need for two mechanisms for designating properties of things compositionally. Jackendoff (1987b) suggests that complex properties may be defined from states, especially in the semantic representation of adjective phrases. For example, the meaning of *covered with snow* may be something like "such that [snow covers *X*]," where "covers" is a kind of state. He suggests the symbol 'such' as an operator that effects this conversion. Another possible complex object property may have to be specified for objects that are defined in terms of their purpose. For example, the argument of the verb *pack* corresponding to suitcases and lunchboxes might have to be specified as a container designed for the purpose of containing objects (cf. *?John packed his hand with candies*, which can have only the "stuff/wad" sense of *pack*, not the "load/put" sense). I will call the operator that converts a state into the property of having that state as its intended use or function 'for/to'. These operators, whose representation is summarized in (5.15), are probably too powerful as stated, as they can lead to unnatural embeddings of clauses in verb meanings. One reasonable constraint is that they cannot be recursively embedded within themselves or each other: no property is defined in terms of its participation in some event or state involving other objects whose properties involve particular events or states. This at least prevents these operators from defining infinite sets of arbitrarily large semantic structures. I assume there are other constraints on these operators as well.

(5.15)

5.5.6 Extension to Nonlocational Semantic Fields

Several things must be defined to extend the machinery for spatial events and states to nonlocational fields in accord with the Thematic Relations Hypothesis. According to Jackendoff (1983), each kind of extension must specify (a) the type of conceptual constituent that can serve as a theme, and the type of constituent that can serve as a reference object; (b) an interpretation scheme that maps the notion of "a theme being at a location" onto whatever relational notion is central to that field. For example, in the possessional field, themes and reference objects both must be THINGs; the notion of "X being at location Y" is interpreted cognitively as Y possessing X. I will express this in the notation by appending the name of the field to the maximal conceptual constituent; this name will symbolize how the basic concept of "location" is extended in the particular field under consideration, and thus it will affect the interpretation of all the functions it immediately dominates. That is, GO, 'to', and other elements will all receive the appropriate interpretation analogous to their spatial meanings.[7] Subsidiary classifications of semantic fields, such as different kinds of possession, can be expressed by additional symbols appended to the field name.

The possessional field. Thus the definition of *belong* might be as in (5.16). (I am assuming that the central meaning of the English preposition *at* selects nonanimate spatial locations, and that there is a version of *to* that can indicate possessional 'at'.)

(5.16)   belong:

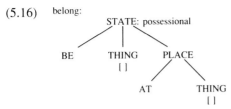

Despite the appeal of the Thematic Relations Hypothesis for the possessional field, in Jackendoff's formulation it leaves us with an embarrassing fact: the verb *have* itself. Presumably it too would be represented as in (5.16). But if it is, why should it take a possessor subject and a possession object? The possessor, as a location, should be linked to an oblique object, and the possession, as a theme, should be linked to the intransitive subject. One could posit a highly marked pair of linking rules or an idiosyncratic argument assignment directly associated with the verb *have* that preempted the usual ones, but his leads to two problems. First, as Hust and Brame (1976) and Pinker, Lebeaux, and Frost (1987) point out, this assignment renders the verb *have* in full accord with Jackendoff's Thematic Hierarchy Condition (the location argument is mapped to subject and is lower on the thematic hierarchy than the theme, which is mapped onto object). Therefore *have* should passivize—but it doesn't. Second, any theory that would depict *have* as a highly marked exception going strongly against the thematic grain would leave it a mystery that *have* is such a high-frequency, ubiquitous verb, and one that children acquire early and without any reversals of subject and object or intrusions of spatial prepositions (Bowerman, in press).

I suggest an alternative. Possession can be conceptualized in two ways: as a relation between a metaphorical theme and location, or, as involving a new primitive state type that I will call HAVE. The first argument of HAVE, the possessor, is linked to SUBJ (LFG) or to the external argument (GB; alternatively, to an internal object in a structure lacking an external argument, hence one that would be moved into subject position to satisfy the Case Filter and Extended Projection Principle). The second argument would be linked to OBJ (LFG) or to an internal argument that somehow receives case (GB). The verb *have*, whose representation is shown in (5.17), would express nothing but this relation. Cognitively, the HAVE state is simply the inverse of the BE state, treating the location, rather than the locatum, as the "logical subject." How would the cognitive relation between HAVE and BE be captured? According to Jackendoff (1978, 1983), there are "inference rules," defined over semantic structure by virtue of their cognitive content, that capture logical redundancies among distinct semantic configurations and support certain kinds of reasoning. For example, Jackendoff proposes the inference rule "If *X* GO to *Y*, then at some time

X BE at *Y*." We could add the inference rule "If *X* HAVE *Y*, then *Y* BE (place-function) *X*," capturing their logical equivalence while maintaining the linguistic distinctiveness that reflects this gestalt shift.

(5.17)   have:

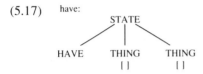

There are four advantages to introducing HAVE as a primitive in semantic representation. Two have already been mentioned: it explains the existence and unmarkedness of the verb *have*, and it explains the unpassivizability of *have* and a number of related verbs, to be discussed later. The third is that it meshes well with an analysis of the representation of double-object verbs that I will discuss in the next section. Finally, it explains the puzzling construction *This box has apples in / on / under / around it* (Gruber, 1965). Jackendoff (1987a) points out that this construction appears to violate any condition that would prohibit a single thematic role from being assigned to two distinct noun phrases, in this case *this box* and *it*. (He uses it to confront Chomsky's (1981) Theta-Criterion, but it would apply to Bresnan's (1982c) Biuniqueness Condition as well. Indeed, virtually any grammatical theory would seem to need some version of this condition, to rule out countless strings such as **Bill ate supper every pizza*.) However, if HAVE and BE are distinct semantic predicates, the problem disappears. Just as BE is ordinarily defined in the locational field but can be extended to the possessional field, HAVE is ordinarily defined in the posses-sional field but can be extended to the locational field. However, its structure defines no slot for a place-function, so *This sheet has a stain* (on it), *That gift has a ribbon* (around it), *That pot has decaffeinated coffee* (in it), and *My house has a garage* (near it) are all possible sentences, and *This box has some books* is vague. This vagueness is eliminated by the prepositional phrase, however, so in *This box has books in it, this box* plays the role of possessor (in the locational field) and *it* plays the role of location. Thus the sentence is neither grammatically ill formed nor cognitively redundant.

Other Semantic Fields Based on Location. The other main fields that, according to the Thematic Relations Hypothesis, submit to a spatial analysis are the temporal, the identificational, the existential, and the epistemic. In the temporal field, EVENTs or STATEs function as themes, TIMEs as reference objects, and *X* being at location *Y* is interpreted as event/state *X* occurring at time *Y*. Thus the definition of *last* in *The meeting lasted from 2:00 till 4:00* would be highly similar, except for the field name, to the definition of *go* in *The road went from Chicago to Decatur*.

In the identificational field, a THING can be located at a PROPERTY and is interpreted as having that property. Some verbs, such as *be, turn into, keep,* or *become,* as in *John became a doctor,* express the property or type as an open argument. Others, such as the intransitive change-of-state verbs, specify the property or type as a constant within the verb definition, as in *The glass broke.*

However, this analysis raises a question. Many properties are all-or-none; it does not make much sense to extend the notion of a continuous "path" from not being broken to being broken. Jackendoff, in his 1983 book, suggests that in certain fields paths simply degenerate into their end states. However, in his 1987b paper he introduced a new function, INCH (inchoative), that maps a state onto the event of that state's coming into existence. Combined with the 'such' operator that maps states onto properties, we have a possibly redundant way of expressing objects' coming to take on new properties: "*X* goes to property *Y*," or "The state of *X* being at *Y* comes into being." I will assume that this is not a spurious redundancy but corresponds to the difference between conceptualizing change via intermediate states (as in *John went from being sick to being well*) and conceptualizing instantaneous change (as in *John got well*). Instead of adding the function INCH to the current inventory, I will extend the existing notation in a minimal way by allowing GO to take a PROPERTY (rather than a PATH) as a second argument when it is part of a nonlocational event, yielding the interpretation that the event consists of a theme's instantaneously coming to assume a property. Verbs that do express continuous changes in a property will specify a PATH as an argument of GO, but the embedded path-functions will take PROPERTYs as arguments in this field as well even though so far they have only been allowed to take PLACEs or THINGs. This is because it makes little sense to have to define a PLACE by means of a place-function in these cases. Nonlocational *go,* inchoative *get* (as in *get sick*), and *break* are represented in (5.18).

(5.18)

In the existential field, a THING or a STATE can be in or out of a single location corresponding to that thing or state existing, in verbs such as *exist, make, create, destroy, bake, knit,* and so on. A definition for *exist* is shown in (5.19). Evidence that existence is treated as a location in English comes from expressions such as *come into existence, come into being, go out of existence, stay in existence,* and so on.

(5.19) exist:

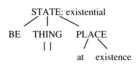

STATE: existential

BE   THING   PLACE
[ ]   / \
         at   existence

Jackendoff also suggests that there is a "circumstantial" semantic field in which events or states function as locations, and a theme going into, being in, or leaving those locations is interpreted as that entity starting to participate in that event, being in the process of participating in that event, or stopping participation in the event. This allows one to capture certain generalizations involving choices of prepositions or complementizers by certain verbs (e.g., *John allowed Susan to go; John prevented Susan from going*) and relations among the meanings of certain polysemous verbs (e.g., *John kept the book on the shelf / John kept his dog running in circles*; see Jackendoff, 1978, 1983). In the representation we could prune the unnecessary 'at' place-function and allow circumstantial states and paths to be represented directly as "BE THING EVENT/STATE" and "[path-function] EVENT/STATE," respectively. Recall, too, that I have been treating the surface subjects of passives as playing the role of theme in the circumstantial field; explicit representations of passives will be discussed in section 5.6.4.

Jackendoff does not discuss the epistemic field, but based on the verbs discussed earlier it would appear that THINGs or EVENTs or STATEs can be interpreted as ideas, and that the locations—or, more specifically, possessors—of these ideas can be interpreted as sentient minds containing the ideas. Thus a part of the semantic representation of the version of *know* that takes NP complements might be roughly captured in (5.20).[8]

(5.20) know:

STATE: epistemic

HAVE   THING   THING
        [ ]   [ ]

5.5.7 Actions, Agents, and Patients

Oddly, theories of thematic relations have tended to deal with one of two disjoint realms. The Gruber/Jackendoff approach has concentrated on expressions for spatial relationships and their analogues, focusing on themes, locations, sources, and goals. The "agent" role is also mentioned, but it does not really function as an alternative to the other roles, which are mutually exclusive (that is, no verb has an argument functioning both as source and as location, but many verbs, such as *give*, have a subject argument that is both an agent and a source). Approaches associated with Fillmore (1968), while largely relegating the complexities of spatial relations to the "location" case role, have a richer set of roles concerning agency, such as agent, benefactive, manner, experiencer, and instrument. Rappaport and Levin (1988), Culicover and Wilkins (1986), and Jackendoff (1987a) suggest that the two approaches may simply be dealing with different subsystems, one concerning agency, one concerning location, both of which can be defined in the semantic representation of a verb. I will adopt this assumption, which helps to capture a number of crucial phenomena. Unfortunately no one has outlined an explicit theory of how these two systems are related; I will propose a first approximation here.

Let's consider a new kind of event and function involving actions. Actional events involve the function ACT, which takes one argument, an actor, or two arguments, an agent and a patient. (The two-argument function could be called "ACT-ON" but the difference between the monadic and dyadic versions provides the necessary disambiguation.) In the dyadic version, the second argument, the patient, can be equated with Talmy's "agonist"; the first argument, the agent, can be equated with Talmy's "antagonist." These events may also specify a number of other subordinate roles. The simplest actional event has a single argument and can be found in unergative intransitive verbs, most of which also specify a manner. The example *yawn* is shown in (5.21).

(5.21)   yawn:

Kiss, shown in (5.22), is an example of a dyadic ACT event. The second argument is the entity that is "affected," but only in the sense that it is involved in the act and its participation helps to define what kind of act it is; it does not necessarily change state or location.

(5.22)   kiss:

Manner of acting on for agent-patient relations, like manner of motion for theme-path relations, is specified in a quoted grammatically opaque symbol, serving as a pointer to some cognitive representation of the physical and geometric properties of the manner. And like manner of motion in dyadic GO events, manner of acting on (i.e., MANNER in a dyadic ACT) is inherently defined as an interaction, in this case between the agent and the patient; it is not just a specification of the motions of the agent. For example, in "kissing" the manner specifies the nature of the contact between the lips of the agent and the body of the patient that makes an event an example of kissing.

It is important to characterize the abstract essence of the dyadic ACT relation with its agent and patient arguments because my analysis of the passive depends on it (see sections 4.4.4 and 5.6.4). First, an ACT defines a relation between two entities that is direct or unmediated, underlying the directness effect discussed in relation to the causative. There is experimental evidence that the subjective "closeness" of two arguments is determined mostly by whether they stand in an agent-patient relation: Fodor et al. (1980) found that people rated the subject and the object as being no more closely related in *John killed Mary*, where *Mary* is a patient and a theme, than in *John bit Mary*, where Mary is only a patient. The dyadic ACT also defines a relation that is asymmetric in that the first argument is causally responsible for the relationship; it is also the assumed cause of any changes explicitly represented as consequences of the agent-patient interaction, with the patient linked to the theme of the change. Furthermore, an ACT event also serves as a locus for a MANNER specification that defines the exact nature of the relationship between agent and patient, making inherent reference to the role of the patient. Finally, Dowty (1987) and Tenny (1988) note that the patient plays a role in the temporal interpretation of the event: the event referred to by the verb is delimited or "measured out" in terms of the time course of what happens to the patient. For example, an act of *hitting* has taken place only when the patient has received the blow. I will return to this point when I examine temporal/aspectual information in semantic structures.

Actors, agents, and patients are linked to their associated positions in argument structure by the linking rules in (5.23). In LFG, "SUBJ," "SUBJ," and "OBJ," respectively, would replace the position labels listed.

(5.23)

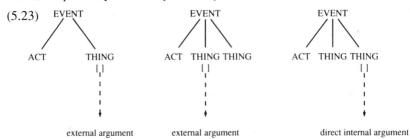

<table>
<tr><td>external argument</td><td>external argument</td><td>direct internal argument</td></tr>
</table>

5.5.8 A Possible Featural Representation for Basic Predicates

In the unmarked case, ACT, like GO, will be an EVENT, though as we shall see it can be extended to STATEs as well. Another unmarked conflation will be that the first argument of ACT has the property 'animate' or 'human'. Since this is also an unmarked convention for HAVE, we have an intuitive basis for a feature set for the four kinds of predicates expanding conceptual constituents, allowing natural subsets to be expressed by specifying the value of one of the features. Say one feature picks out whether the unmarked kind of constituent type in which the predicate is found is an EVENT or a STATE; the feature could be <±dynamic>. Say the other feature picks out whether in the unmarked case the first argument of the predicate is human and in control of the event/state; the feature could be <±control>. GO and ACT are canonically EVENTs, HAVE and BE are canonically STATEs. The first argument of ACT and HAVE canonically are humans that control the action or possession; the first arguments of GO and BE are canonically dimensionless, will-less points. The featural representation is summarized in (5.24), together with its predictions about which pairs of predicates a semantic representation could treat as interchangeable. Except when a rule is actually noncommittal between the members of one of these natural classes, I will use the mnemonic label for the predicate itself rather than its feature decomposition.

5.5.9   Inter–event Relations: Effects, Means, and Coreference

How are acts related to other events, such as resulting changes of location? Jackendoff (1987a) suggests that the two systems exist as separate "tiers" in semantic representations, analogous to the independent but cross-linked representations for stress, tone, consonants, vowels, and so on in modern phonological theory (see also Culicover and Wilkins, 1986). However, tiers are probably not the right kind of representation for verb meanings. First of all, there are often combinations of several acts and several changes of location in a verb structure; one tier for actions and one tier for locations cannot represent them all. Second, the different events specified by a verb always stand in some quasi-causal

(5.24)	Features	
	Dynamic	Control
Predicates		
GO	+	–
BE	–	–
HAVE	–	+
ACT	+	+
Possible natural classes		
GO and BE		–
GO and ACT	+	
ACT and HAVE		+
BE and HAVE	–	
Impossible natural classes		
GO and HAVE		
ACT and BE		

relation to one another; for example, one causes another, is the means for attaining the other, or is the purpose of another. There are no verbs that mean "Simultaneously, John yawned and the cat fell off the roof." (Carter, 1976a, makes a similar point.)

This is not just due to a pragmatic principle ruling out verbs for low-frequency or uninteresting conjunctions of events. There are many different kinds of inter-event relations that verbs just don't like to encode. For example, there is no English verb meaning "to do A for a specified duration, then B, then repeat the process, until one realizes one should do C"; or "to do A repeatedly, increasing the likelihood of B"; or "to do A and fail to achieve B, requiring one to do C"; or "to do A, then do B, hoping that C"; or "to do A, change your mind, then do B"; or "to do A repeatedly in order for B to happen, where A cannot cause B"; or "to do A and experience B." To prove that these nonoccurring relations are not just logicians' esoteric fantasies, we need only examine some "sniglets" (Hall, 1984). A sniglet, according to their creator, is "any word that doesn't appear in the dictionary, but should"; I suggest they are examples of culturally shared, cognitively salient, but linguistically impossible lexical meanings. Here is a sniglet for each of the kinds of inter-event relations listed above:

wattbobble   To remove a hot light bulb by turning it several seconds, letting your fingers cool, then repeating the process. This is generally followed by the glorious revelation of using your shirttail.

toastate   To impatiently pop toast up and down in the toaster, thus increasing the likelihood of burning it.

tolloaf   Act of missing a toll basket and having to climb out of your car to retrieve the coin.

subnougate   To eat the bottom caramels in a candy box and carefully replace the top level, hoping no one will notice.

purpitation   To take something off the grocery shelf, decide you don't want it, and then put it in another section.

phosflink   To flick a bulb on and off when it burns out (as if, somehow, that will bring it back to life)

escalasticize   To lean against the rail of a moving escalator and have the sensation of being pulled in opposite directions.

I will capture constraints on inter-event relations by using a small set of "subordinating relations" (actually, each subordinator will have a feature structure defined by a system of possible causal relationships) that allow one event to be embedded in another event in which it plays an identifiable causal role. Thus it is a formal constraint on lexicosemantic representations in the current theory that they are single-rooted, connected graphs, and a substantive constraint that whenever a verb specifies multiple events, they stand in some causal relation to one another (where "causal relation" refers to causation as conceived by the language user, of course, not necessarily literal physical causation).

The most obvious subordinating relation is a successful sequence of cause and effect: an action results in some event that is its effect. I will represent this by subordinating to the ACT function an EVENT that can be interpreted as its result or effect. One can consider this subordinating relation as another type of argument, the "effect" or "result" argument, or one could consider it to be an adjunct; it makes little difference. In either case it is helpful to annotate this link with a mnemonic label, which I will call 'effect'.

Another notational device is needed to express the coreference between entities involved in an action and in an ensuing effect; I will use indexes X, Y, Z. Although an argument can have thematic roles specified for it in several places in a verb's semantic structure, only one of these places can serve as a trigger for a linking rule. This primary position is the one symbolized by the presence of square brackets; other positions coindexed with the primary one are merely annotated with the index. The coindexing of arguments in semantic structure can also be used to represent relations of control (see Culicover and Wilkins, 1986; Jackendoff, 1987a) and what Talmy calls "personation." Let us consider semantic structures for the motion verb *run*, the pure causative verb *break*, and the motion-contact-effect verb *cut*.

Run, in its English version conflating a manner of motion with translation along a path, as in *John ran into the room*, would represent the motion along the path as a result of the running action. For *run*, as with many other verbs, it is not clear on conceptual grounds whether we should represent the event as "to run, with the effect of motion along a path" or "to move along a path, by means of a running action" (Talmy, 1985). The former can be justified on linguistic grounds, however, as it helps to differentiate verbs of voluntary motion (typically unergative) from verbs of physical motion (typically unaccusative). It also yields the distinction necessary to capture the ambiguity of *John rolled down the hill*, which can imply voluntarily initiated movement (= "John acted to roll down the hill") or pure motion identical to what an inanimate object might undergo (= "John moved down the hill, rolling"), with no embedding ACT. The semantic structure for *run* is shown in (5.25).

(5.25)   run:

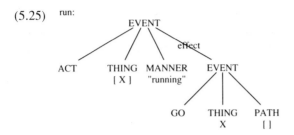

The pure causative verb *break*, shown in (5.26), involves an unspecified type of direct interaction between agent and patient (hence there is an ACT function with no MANNER) and a specified effect on the patient (hence there is an effect argument, an identificational event, in which the patient assumes an additional role as the theme). The periphrastic *cause to break*, formed out of entries for *cause* and intransitive *break*—see (5.18)—would not have the breaking entity listed as a patient in the actional event; this is a simple way of representing the directness effect. A similar representation could be used for languages that have verbs denoting indirect causation by means of specialized causative verb affixes.

(5.26)   break:

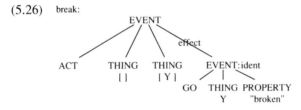

Not only does the verb *cut* specify a causative meaning (the patient must end up with a cut in it), but, as mentioned in chapter 4, the causation must have been brought about in a certain way, by moving an instrument into contact with and through the patient (Hale and Laughren, 1983). There is again some intuitive uncertainty about which events are subordinate to which other ones, but the most parsimonious theory is one where the semantic representation predicts its syntactic form. Since the patient (not the instrument) is the direct object of *cut* in English, there is no motivation for defining it as "to move an instrument to *X*, causing a cut in *X*"; instead, it should be "to effect a cut in *X* BY MEANS OF moving an instrument against it." This introduces a new causal subordinating relation, 'means'. Cognitively, the means by which an event happens is the penultimate event in a causal chain resulting in that event (Talmy, 1988); in addition, there is usually an implication that the final event in the chain is a goal of the agent's action. Thus "*X* causes *Y* by means of *Z*" is similar to "*X* causes *Z* which causes *Y*" (where *Y* is the goal of the action). These are two ways of describing a multilink causal chain, involving different construals of an event (one coarse-grained, one slightly finer-grained), and they can be expressed differently in language. To capture the fact that an event containing a means is being

construed at a different grain size than an event embracing only the first cause and the last effect, I will label 'means' as a distinct type of event subordinated to an action. Thus the verb *cut* might be represented as something like (5.27). To make the representation a bit more readable, I use real names for actors and patients instead of indexes. They are in parentheses, a reminder that their actual content is not specified by the verb but (for open arguments) by constituents in the rest of the sentence. The representation can be paraphrased as "Bob acts on a pear, causing the pear to become cut, by means of acting on a knife, causing the knife to go against and through the pear."
(5.27)

cut:

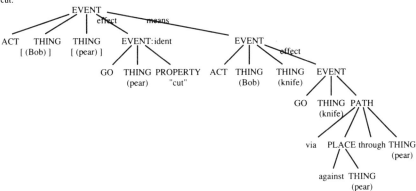

5.5.10 Linking Oblique Arguments

If the patient argument of the 'means' clause in the representation for *cut* had been annotated with the square-bracket open argument designator, we would have the lexical entry underlying the version of *cut* that allows an instrumental *with*-phrase. A similar representation would underlie the version of *hit* that appears in *John hit Bill with a stick*, but it would lack the 'effect' branch predicating a change of the patient of the hitting (Bill).

The preposition *with* would be selected in these entries by a combination of two structures enforcing linking regularities: a linking rule for oblique arguments in general, and a lexical entry for the specific preposition. The diagrams in (5.6) showed that arguments of GO or BE are oblique when they are paths or places. Now that we have a feature set for basic predicates, we can unite these two linking rules; they would pertain to the second argument of <–control> predicates. A different linking rule would apply to arguments of HAVE or ACT (predicates in the class <+control>): they are linked to oblique phrases when the structure they are in is not the root event/state, but embedded in a substructure of the root event. The two linking rules for oblique/indirect arguments, which are listed in (5.28), must be implemented in slightly different ways (at least in languages with free prepositions, like English). For the first rule, pertaining to locative arguments of GO/BE predicates, the entire prepositional phrase expresses the open argument; for the second rule, applying to ACT/HAVE predicates, only the object of the prepositional phrase expresses the open argument. The difference between the two linking rules corresponds roughly to the difference between the two kinds of roles that prepositions and morphological case markers are traditionally thought to play: as semantically contentful locative functions whose meanings are composed with those of other constituents of the sentence to build the sentence interpretation, and as grammatical markers that identify their objects as bearing some semantic role with respect to the verb (see, e.g., Kaplan and Bresnan, 1982; Bresnan, 1982d).

(5.28)

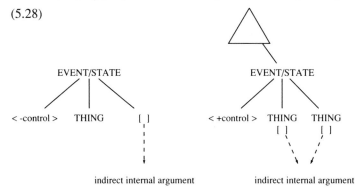

The lexical entry for the instrumental preposition *with* would call for an open argument corresponding to the patient within a 'means' substructure; it is depicted in (5.29).

(5.29)   with:

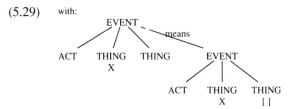

5.5.11 A Family of Causal Relations

Given these independent mechanisms for denoting acting upon and effecting, Talmy's (1985, 1988) types of causal interactions can be captured explicitly. Steady-state or extended causation (e.g., *The ball kept rolling because of the wind acting upon it*), in contrast to the "onset causation" we have discussed so far, can be represented by having the ACT event be a STATE, not an EVENT. Such stative ACTs would be involved in the definitions of verbs like *support, keep, suspend, occupy,* and so on, where not just a spatial relationship is encoded, but the notion that some force continuously exerted by an antagonist object on an agonist is responsible for the state of the agonist. (Recall that this plays a role in the fact that some verbs of spatial relationships are passivizable but others are not; see section 4.4.4.) The semantic representation in (5.30) is an example; the meaning of the new subordinating causal relation 'prevent' is just what its mnemonic suggests.

(5.30)   support:

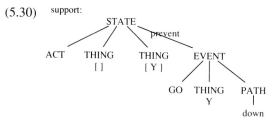

Two other distinctions are naturally represented in terms of different kinds of subordinating relations. One is whether it is the result of an agent's action or the action itself that is focused on as the main event. The 'effect' link is used for verbs that focus on the causing action, adding information that some other event ensues. Reversing the perspective defines a complementary link called 'cause' that can be used when the focus is on the effect, and information is added that the event was caused by some antecedent agent-patient relation. The subordinating relation 'cause', like the other semantic primitives I have invoked, can be encoded elsewhere in language using closed-class morphemes. For example, in English it is encoded in the conjunction *because* and in the prepositions *for* (in *I rewarded / condemned John for his actions*) and *from* (in *She became sick from too much dancing*), and perhaps verb-internally in predicates such as *concede*, *acquiesce*, or *relent*.

The other kind of subordinating relations are defined by whether the agent/ antagonist is stronger than the patient/agonist, resulting in a change. If we take the 'cause' relation but assert that the agent/antagonist of the antecedent subordinated event failed to affect the inherent tendency of the patient/agonist, we get a new subordinating relation that we can refer to using the mnemonic 'despite'. It will be found in the definition of the English conjunction of the same name, or verb-internally, in the definition of verbs like *resist* or *withstand*.

The fourth possible combination defined by these contrasts—reversing the perspective of 'despite'—would consist of an agent-patient main event and a subordinate event in which a resulting effect on the patient/agonist is asserted *not* to have occurred. This might correspond to verbs such as *try* or *fail* and perhaps conative constructions such as *John cut at the bread*. 'But' seems like an apt mnemonic for this subordinating relation; it and 'despite' are sometimes called concessive relations.

Enabling or letting, and preventing or stopping, are two other prominent types of subordinating causal links. Letting corresponds to the cessation or nonoccurrence of an agent-patient event or state, with an effect involving a moving or

changing theme. Conversely, preventing corresponds to an agent-patient relation whose effect is the cessation or failure of occurrence of a moving or changing
theme. A feature set such as 'focus' (on the cause or on the effect), 'potency'
(antagonist succeeds in exerting its usual effect on the agonist by virtue of its
greater strength, or fails), and 'occurrence' (the cause event occurs or fails to
occur, and the effect event occurs or fails to occur) could capture these causal
links, as shown in (5.31).

There are several reasons to believe that causal links are mentally decomposed
in something like this fashion. Some languages have single devices that are
indeterminate between causing and letting. Some novel causatives produced by
English speakers have meanings that correspond more to letting than causing;
see the examples in (4.45d). And as we shall see in chapter 7, children learning
English often confuse the two (Bowerman, 1978). For notational and mnemonic
simplicity, however, I will simply use the six shorthand labels in the first column
of (5.31). See Miller and Johnson-Laird (1976), Talmy (1985, 1988), and
Jackendoff (1983) for discussion of the advantages and disadvantages of atomic
and decomposed representations for causal relations.

Another subordinating relation is intent, goal, or purpose. It is needed to
capture part of the distinction between *kill* and *murder*, *follow* and *chase*, and
pour and *spill*, and may be useful in characterizing the meanings of verbs of
directed action such as *tell* in *tell him to go*, *persuade*, *order*, *command*, and so
on. This can be represented by spelling out the goal state and subordinating it to
an actional event. Since a purpose or intent event is the goal that an event is
expected to cause, and a 'means' is an event that causes a goal to come about, they
might be taken to refer to the same causal link between an event and the goal that
it brings about, differing in whether the cause or effect is being foregrounded.
Thus they could be distinguished using opposing values of the feature <cause-
focus / effect-focus> in the feature system used for causal links in (5.31), in
conjunction with a new feature called <purposive> that signifies that the final
effect in the causal chain is the goal of the agent. For mnemonic purposes,

(5.31)   Features

	Focus	Potency	Cause occurrence	Effect occurrence
'effect'	cause	success	yes	yes
'cause'	effect	success	yes	yes
'despite'	effect	failure	yes	no
'but'	cause	failure	yes	no
'let'	cause	success	no	yes
'prevent'	cause	success	yes	no

though, I will continue to call the effect-focus subordinator for goals 'means'; I will use a mnemonic for the cause-focus subordinator for goals spelled 'for/to' since in English these subordinates can be grammaticized periphrastically in purpose clauses using the complementizers *for* and *to* (e.g., *Richard built the house for his daughter to live in it*). A possible semantic structure for *chase*, a notoriously complex verb that incorporates a purpose, is shown in (5.32), with real nouns serving as mnemonic indexes. Roughly, it can be glossed as "The cat acts and goes toward the mouse (which is going away from it) in order to be at the mouse."

(5.32) chase:

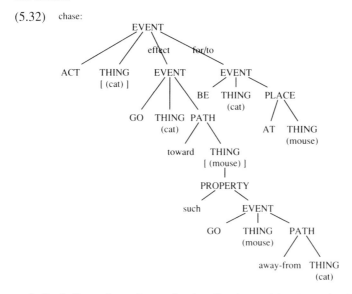

A final dimension of causal subordination, which is typically encoded in deontic auxiliaries like *should* or *ought* but may turn up in the definitions of main verbs, is obligation. Sometimes a verb might specify that an event causes there to be an obligation for one of the parties to do something in the future, as in *buy* or *sell*. Conversely, some verbs specify acts that are done to fulfill an obligation, such as *reward* or *repay*. Again, the difference is in cause-focus versus effect-focus, so we can again borrow the corresponding feature introduced in (5.31) and add the feature <deontic> to the set, yielding the ability for verbs to specify that an event incurs an obligation or that it fulfills one. I will use the mnemonics 'obligates' and 'fulfills' so that the depictions of the relevant subordinating linkages will be more compact and transparent.

Parsimonious formalists will note that the feature system for causal subordinators has allowed for a reduction in the representational machinery from ten primitive causal subordinators to six primitive causal subordination features.

This also predicts that verbs in the world's languages are capable of expressing $2^6 = 64$ possible subordinating relations if no further constraints are specified. Surely there are constraints on combinations (for example, goals and obligations do not seem to cross-classify in English, nor do obligations and potency), but verbs do seem able to express fairly complex relations pertaining to the attainment of means and ends (e.g., *manage to*, *fail to*, *succeed at*). Thus the features system's gain in parsimony for primitive symbols and its concomitant increase in the number of complex causal relations that are expressible seems to be a good tradeoff.

One more formal point is worth making. If ACTs could be embedded inside one another without limit, an infinite number of syntactically distinguishable kinds of verbs would be possible. In fact, I have found that the following two constraints hold for all the English verbs I have examined, some quite complex: (a) no more than a single kind of subordinated event is possible for any level of semantic structure (i.e., an ACT has at most one 'effect', one 'means', and so on); (b) embedding is not recursive but "Degree-1" (see Wexler and Culicover, 1980)—there can be only one level of subordination within an event that is itself subordinated (i.e., not at the root). I suspect that these generalizations are justifiable as general constraints; Carter (1976a) was led to suggest similar ones. If so, causal subordination does not result in an infinite number of arbitrarily complex verb meanings. For example, no verb can specify an argument that is the means of a goal of an effect of a prevented action. This is not necessarily a conceptual constraint on the maximum length of a causal chain that can be encoded as the meaning of a verb, but it is a constraint on the length of the causal chain that linking rules and lexical rules ever need to look at.

5.5.12   Nonphysical Semantic Fields for Acts

According to the extension of the Thematic Relations Hypothesis outlined in chapter 4 in connection with passivizability (section 4.4.4), the antagonist-agonist or agent-patient relation in ACTs can be analogized from the semantic field of physical force to nonphysical semantic domains in the same way as the theme-path or theme-location relation in physical space can be analogized to nonspatial fields like possession. The choice of field can be expressed in the current notation by appending the field name to the EVENT or STATE node, just as for fields based on location. Talmy hints at a social field, in which force is extended to social pressure in verbs like *urge* and *persuade*, an intrapsychic field in which different parts of the mind are pitted against one another (e.g., *refrain*), and an inferential field, in which some ideas have implications for the truth or plausibility of others (e.g., *imply*). Another field, which we can call responsibility, expresses relations among states that are asymmetrically responsible for the existence of other states. Finally, we can consider a psychological field, involving direct and asymmetrical relations between minds and ideas. When the first argument is a 'represented' entity and the second an 'animate' entity, the interpretation is of a perceived object, event, or idea impinging on the perceiver, possibly causing some subordinated event such as the perceiver changing state (e.g., *The news calmed John*) or the percept entering the perceiver's store of knowledge. When the first argument is 'animate' and the second 'represented', some mental activity or state of the perceiver is responsible for the idea standing in some relation to the mind of the perceiver. These of course are the two kinds of psych-verbs discussed in section 4.4.4. Simplified entries for one of each kind of verb, *learn* and *remind of*, are shown in (5.33) and (5.34).

(5.33) learn:

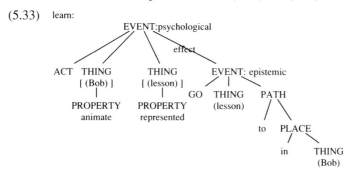

(5.34) remind:

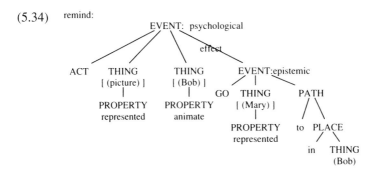

5.5.13 Temporal Information

One more kind of information must be specified: time. For example, the distinctions between processes and punctate events (*run* versus *sneeze*) and between achievements and accomplishments have not yet been given an explicit representation. Furthermore, the temporal relations among certain within-verb subevents need to be expressed, such as the difference between *give* and *send*; as we shall see, these differences have syntactic implications.

Many linguists and logicians have suggested a modified time-line for the representation of tense and of verbs that encode time explicitly, such as *last*.

Events and states are located as parts of the line, and aspectual distinctions correspond to how those parts are delineated. States or processes are regions of the line with no distinct boundaries; instantaneous events such as *hitting* are points; accomplishments such as *drawing a circle* are regions bounded at their ends by a point; achievements such as *winning a race* are points bounding the end of a region. More complex temporal relations, such as those effected by the addition of aspectual affixes, can also be defined in terms of the time-line representation by "zooming" in to a point or a nondelimited subregion within a delimited region, by aggregating sets of points into regions, and so on (see, e.g., Talmy, 1985; Langacker, 1987). I will adopt Jackendoff's (1987a) suggestion that such a time-line representation serve as a separate tier in the representations of a verb's semantic structure, mapping each EVENT and STATE onto some part of it (see also Pustejovsky, 1987, in press). A simple example is shown in (5.35) for the verbs *eat* (as in *eat the apple*) and *break* (as in *break the stick*), which are accomplishment and achievement verbs, respectively. Large open dots signify points in time (boundaries or punctate events), thick line segments signify regions, and dashed line segments signify unbounded ends of regions.

(5.35)

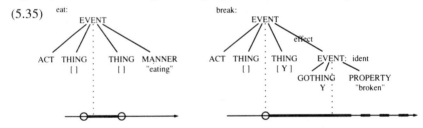

5.5.14   A Remark on Redundancy, Constraints, and Decomposition   For better or worse, the time line introduces considerable redundancy in semantic representations. Events must precede or be simultaneous with their 'effect' and 'but' subordinate events; they must follow their 'cause', and 'despite' subordinate events. Purposive ('for/to') substructures are interpreted as goals that precede the events they are subordinated to, themselves defined in terms of an event that would have to follow the main one if it took place. EVENTs presumably refer to parts of the time-line designated with boundaries, STATEs to unbounded regions. Furthermore, events bounded at their ends are intimately linked with the notion of patient and theme: Vendler's (1957) examples of activity verbs were usually intransitive, his examples of achievement and accomplishment verbs usually transitive. (See also Pustejovsky, 1987 and in press, for discussion of some of the connections between aspectual and thematic relations.) Tenny (1988) proposes that the internal argument of a verb can be defined as that which temporally delimits or measures out the event; she actually reverses the current

perspective by proposing that the temporal/aspectual representation is the interface between lexical semantics and argument structure, with the rest of semantic representations being essentially epiphenomenal. The extent to which one can eliminate components of causal/spatial semantic structure by predicting them from temporal/aspectual representations, or vice versa, is beyond the scope of this discussion. As far as I can see, we need both. For example, there are no obvious aspectual differences between *roll* and *bleed*, *own* and *have*, *choose* and *win*, or *load with* and *fill with*, though they contrast in their willingness to undergo alternations. Therefore I will use both, leaving open whether possible redundancies should be eliminated, and if so, how.

The need for partly redundant lexicosemantic structures may be quite general. Consider, for example, the verboseness of the semantic structure of *cut* in (5.27). On the one hand, there must be an explicit representation of the motion of the instrument, the effect on the object, and the contact of the instrument against the object so that various syntactic generalizations distinguishing different subclasses of action verbs, discussed in section 4.2, can apply properly. For example, the grammaticality of *She cut at it* requires that a rule "see" the motion and contact components of *cut*'s semantic structure, and the ungrammaticality of **She cut the knife against the bread* requires that a rule see the effect component. That's why it wouldn't suffice to adopt a more compact representation in which "cut" was a primitive unanalyzed term implicitly incorporating the motion, contact, and caus ation. (This strikes me as a telling argument against the view of Fodor et al., 1980, that verb meanings are not mentally decomposed.) On the other hand, a structure composed out of that many independent parts would seem to license too many verbs that probably do not exist, such as acting on *A* to cause a change in *B* by means of acting on *C* to cause *D* to move against *E*. Thus we face conflicting demands: certain rules must see the componential structure of a verb, but not every arrangement of these components can serve as a possible verb.[9]

These conflicting demands suggest that we must dissociate *primitiveness* from *constrainedness*—a theory of possible verb meanings cannot simply fall out of the set of semantic primitives and the elementary syntax of their combinations. This dissociation is familiar in phonology: phonological theory specifies an inventory of distinctive features, but not every subset of feature values is a possible segment (for example, no segment can be [+vocalic] and [−sonorant]). This underscores the importance of rules defining broad conflation classes (some universal, some language-specific) that license only certain subsets of the combinatorially possible configurations of semantic elements. They may do so, for example, by providing a set of intermediate-level clusters of elements whose internal structure is transparent to lexical rules but that serve as the smallest allowable building blocks of semantic structures. For example, to explain the fact that (at least in English) it is the patient that is the theme of the change when an agent physically acts on a patient and produces an effect, there could be a prefabricated conflation chunk in which the subordinated effect clause has its theme role linked with the patient of the superordinate. Similarly, a pre-packaged conflation chunk would ensure that when an agent acts on a patient by means of using an instrument, it is the agent that acts on the instrument, and if the instrument moves, it is toward the patient.

5.5.15 Summary of Semantic Machinery   In (5.36) I list the semantic elements that I will assume lexical rules can be sensitive to. Though the inventory is more complex than the list of a half-dozen or so thematic roles that previous treatments of verb semantics have appealed to, it is nonetheless quite constrained. First, in sheer numbers it is very small relative to the thousands of semantic distinctions that the verbs in a given language can make. Second, all of the elements have reflexes in particular closed-class morphemes in many languages, and most can be found in the closed-class vocabulary of English. Third, the elements define simple semantic structures that, unadorned with idiosyncratic ("quoted") information, could serve as the meanings of "light" verbs like *make*, *be*, or *give*. Fourth, virtually all of them correspond in a straightforward way to the meaning elements that Talmy lists as recurring across languages. Further constraints on which combinations of them are well-formed could be captured in universal and language-specific conflation rules. The question I will ask in the next section is whether the list can delineate the fifty-odd classes that I have suggested are the units of generalization in Baker's paradox.

(5.36)

Conceptual Constituents:
EVENT
STATE
THING
PATH
PLACE
PROPERTY
MANNER

Functions expanding conceptual constituents:
±dynamic, ±control (features yielding the predicates ACT, GO, BE, HAVE)
place-functions (at, on, in, under, ...)
path-functions (to, into, toward, ...)

Features of subordinating relations:
cause-focus versus effect-focus
success versus failure
occurrence versus nonoccurrence
purposive
deontic
Properties:
animate/inanimate
human/nonhuman
0D/1D/2D/3D extendedness
count/mass
rigid/flexible
substance/aggregate
liquid/semisolid

Temporal objects:
time-line
point
region

Other mechanisms:
open arguments
coindexing
semantic field annotation
quoted constants (manners, properties)

5.6 Explicit Representations of Lexical Rules and Lexicosemantic Structures

Now that we have an explicit system for representing verb meanings, we can try to characterize broad- and narrow-range lexical rules more precisely. To do that, we will first need to examine the semantic representations of the sets of words inside and outside the various conflation subclasses to see what kind of information must be stated in a rule to pick out the class properly. Once we know the relationship between semantic structures for words and semantic structures for the classes of words that rules apply to, we will be able to turn, in the next chapter, to the question of how the child learns the rules.

In this section I will represent lexical rules by simply listing the entire input structure and the entire output structure related by the rule. This cannot be taken as the actual operation of the rule; if a lexical rule really consisted of a fully specified input structure and a fully specified output structure, we would have no explanation for why much of the input structure is carried over verbatim in the output. Formally, the rule could just as easily pair two arbitrary, unrelated structures. A standard kind of explanation in linguistics (see, e.g., Pinker and Prince, 1988) is that rules consist of individual operations that transform parts of representations; the parts that are not specifically operated upon come through untouched. Since the input and the output do overlap in lexical rules, they must be composed of more elementary operations on parts of lexicosemantic structures.

It might be possible to characterize a set of semantic operations that underlie the syntactic alternations in grammatical relations that are prevalent cross-linguistically (see, e.g., Perlmutter and Postal, 1984; Marantz, 1984; Foley and Van Valin, 1985). When one looks at a variety of alternations in English and other languages, one finds that they most commonly involve operations such as the following:

• Add or delete a cause argument.
• Make a patient argument a theme of a predication.
• Embed an act as the means of accomplishing some effect.
• Add or delete path, purpose, benefactive, or instrument arguments.
• Assign the patient role to an embedded argument such as a source, goal, beneficiary, possessor, or instrument.
• Suppress nonspecific or characteristic arguments.

Each of these (and perhaps a small number of others) could be made into an elementary operation on semantic structure, and lexical rules could be constrained to consist of small sets of operations of these kinds. Presumably these elementary operations might be motivated by considerations of the most likely possibilities for cognitive "reconstruals" or "gestalt shifts": what types of events or states are seen as similar enough that a single lexical root can be used for both. Synthesizing the cross-linguistic research in a way that would lay out a precise set of operations, and explicitly decomposing lexical rules into sets of them, are beyond the scope of the present investigation. Thus my listing of the input and output structures for each rule should be seen as an expedient shortcut.

In the next four sections I lay out explicit representations for the broad- and narrow-range versions of the four alternations. They are intended to show that a theory of verb meaning like the one outlined in section 5.5 is adequate to represent the syntactically relevant differences among narrow subclasses. A warning: these sections are heavy going and can be skipped by readers who are not interested in seeing such a claim fleshed out.

5.6.1   Representations for the Dative

The representation in (5.37) is a first approximation of a broad-range, property-predicting lexical rule for the *to*-dative alternation in English. (The *for*-dative will be discussed shortly.) The thematic core of the prepositional-object form is on top, the thematic core for the double-object form is on the bottom. Real referent names are listed to make the diagram more readable.

(5.37)

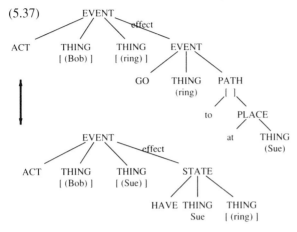

The relevant linking rules for the prepositional form and for the first two open arguments of the double-object form have already been discussed. A possible linking rule for second objects is shown in (5.38); it would apply to a possession argument embedded in an act as a possible effect of that act. The causal subordination feature <cause-focus> indicates that the embedded event is an effect, not a cause, but it does not specify whether the event is actually effected or even whether it occurs. Thus it embraces both actual 'effects' and 'for/to' intentions, as we will require, and is an explicit representation of the notion "prospective" in "prospective possession" (see, e.g., Oehrle, 1976; Mazurkewich and White, 1984).

(5.38)

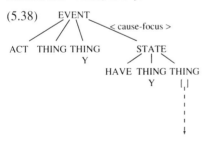

second direct internal argument

There are two main differences between the prepositional and the double-object representations. First, in the prepositional form, the transferred object is the patient; in the double-object form the recipient is the patient. Though seemingly a minor change, this is the representational distinction that underlies the differences discussed in sections 3.3.4.2 and 4.4.1. It causes the pragmatic differences in which argument is construed as "affected" or "acted on" in the double-object form (hence *What John did to Bill was give him a book* / *?give a book to him*) and the entailment differences in terms of the extent to which the recipient is affected (as in the difference between *teaching Hebrew to the students* and *teaching the students Hebrew*), and it provides a motivation for why certain subclasses are more likely to have been deemed dativizable in the language than others (e.g., the difference between the *throw* class and the *pull* class).

The other difference is that in the double-object form the change of possession is expressed not as an analogue of a motion of the object going to (GO 'to') the recipient, but as the direct causation of a state whereby the possessor has (HAVE) the object. This has several desirable consequences. First, we have seen that the double-object form is incompatible with any expression of pure physical motion. Although this fact could be stipulated by saying that the double-object form is linked to GO:possessional and not just GO, if the double-object form is simply projected from HAVE, the possessional field is the unmarked one. In addition, Green (1974) points out that *give*—a verb whose representations are virtually identical to the double-object thematic core shown in (5.37)—has a number of idiomatic uses that exist only in the double-object form. Crucially, when they do, the sense is always compatible with the notion "cause to have" and often incompatible with the notion "cause to go to." For example, (a) and (b) of (5.39) imply that Jack's daughter had a bath and had an inferiority complex, but it is nonsense to talk about transferring a bath and an inferiority complex from Jack to his daughter; Jack needn't have ever had them himself. The contrast is even clearer in (5.39c–f). The double-object form is compatible with John's being caused to have an idea, whether it is because someone else (Janice) who originally had the idea transferred it to him or because it was caused to come into being through an episode of inspiration. However, the prepositional-object form is natural only when used to denote transfer by communication. This difference is captured nicely by the distinction between the GO and HAVE substructures in (5.37).

(5.39) (a) Jack gave his daughter a bath.

  (b) Jack gave his daughter an inferiority complex.

  (c) Janice gave John an idea.

  (d) Janice gave an idea to John.

  (e) Janice's behavior gave John an idea.

  (f) *Janice's behavior gave an idea to John.

Yet another piece of evidence that the double-object form is mentally represented as cause-to-HAVE rather than cause-to-GO-to comes from examining the semantics of verbs of creation that enter into the *for*-dative alternation. The following actual usage illustrates the crucial contrast. A television character stumbles into a room with his head in a pumpkin and shouts *Will someone carve me some eyes?* Obviously the predicate could be paraphrased not as "make some eyes and transfer the eyes to me" but as "make some eyes, causing me to have the eyes."

Now let us consider narrow-range rules. Each such rule will specify an input structure, defining the verbs it can apply to, which should contain a version of the input structure of the broad-range rule in (5.37), and that portion of the input structure will be changed in the manner of (5.37). (The remainder of the input structure will function like a context term in a context-sensitive rule.) Since the nature of the change is predictable—that is why I called the broad-range rules "property-predicting"—we can focus on the input structures themselves and how they filter out nondativizable verbs. We currently have neither a format for the input structure of a rule nor a matching function by which a semantic structure for a word would be deemed to match or not to match a rule; by examining the range of structures of verbs in a semantically cohesive class that undergoes a given alternation, we can see how to state the rule and matching function so that they can include verbs that we observe to behave similarly while excluding those that behave differently. In the case of the dative, I am interested only in the process that converts from the prepositional form to the double-object form. In many cases the prepositional form itself will have been created by a prior lexical rule (e.g., *throw X —> throw X to an inanimate target —> throw X to an animate possessor —> throw an animate possessor an X*). I will usually show only the immediate input to the dativization rule, though to keep matters simple I will occasionally omit certain minor bits of information that would have been provided by intervening rules.

Verbs of giving. Let's consider the semantic representations of the prepositional forms of the verbs that inherently involve possession transfer, and the differences among them that the narrow-range rule would have to ignore to encompass them all. *Give* would have a representation virtually identical to that in the input of rule (5.37), though with the semantic field specified as "possessional." *Pass* would specify the semantic field more precisely, as "possessional:physical-custody" rather than generic possession (one can *give*, but not *pass*, a car to someone by signing a title transfer agreement; one can *pass*, but perhaps not *give*, an object one doesn't own).[10] *Hand* would be similar to *pass* with the addition of a MANNER branch specifying the use of the hands. The small subclass that embraces *send, mail,* and *ship* would be represented similarly, except in the time-line component of the representation, which would show the ACT event and the GO:possessional event as being linked to distinct event times rather than the single one used in the simple verbs of giving. (Though I will often omit the time

line in the depictions of narrow semantic representations in this chapter, I assume
it is always specified in the representation.)

 Sell, trade, and *pay* would have a subordinate countertransfer event to which
the agent is committed, as in (5.40) (underlying *Bob sold a ring to Sue for $100*
= "act on the ring, causing it to go to Sue, obligating Sue to act on $100, causing
it to go to Bob"). The actual participants (in parentheses) are not really specified
in the verb's meaning, of course, but the "money" property is. For *pay*, the
"money" property would be attached to the upstairs theme rather than the
downstairs one; for *trade*, it would be absent. The patient/theme of the
countertransfer ($100, in this case) would be linked to the oblique argument role
because of its being embedded under ACT, and it would be expressed with the
preposition *for* in particular, thanks to a lexical entry for *for* specific to such
countertransferred objects. As the theory predicts, the lexical entry for this
closed-class morpheme cares about the semantic representational topology that
defines a countertransfer but is oblivious to idiosyncratic information about
"money" and thus applies freely to *trade*. Possibly, *lend* and *loan* would have
representations similar to (5.40) as well.

(5.40)   sell:

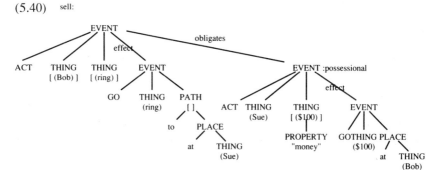

Finally, *serve* and *feed* would be similar to *give* except that they would append
an idiosyncratic "consumable" property to the theme, and perhaps a 'for/to' (i.e.,
purpose) or 'let' subordinate structure in which the goal argument would be
specified as "eating" or "consuming" the theme.

 Verbs of communication. According to the Thematic Relations Hypothesis,
these verbs involve a subfield of possession involving the communication of
ideas. In addition, verbs like *tell, ask*, and *write* differ by virtue of specifying
messages with different illocutionary force, differentiated with respect to an
intended effect on a hearer. That is, the message is such that a hearer is supposed
to come to know it (*tell*), learn it (*teach*), answer it (*ask, pose*), read it (*write*), see
it (*show*), or hear and comprehend it (*read*). That would result in a semantic
structure like that in (5.41) for *tell*, in which the tellable argument is constrained
by the 'for/to' property substructure to be something that a listener is supposed

to be able to know (obviously this is an approximation). The other verbs would differ with regard to the embedded 'for/to' property, and some would also have a 'from' substructure listed as part of the PATH (for verbs like *read*, *cite*, and *quote*).

(5.41) tell:

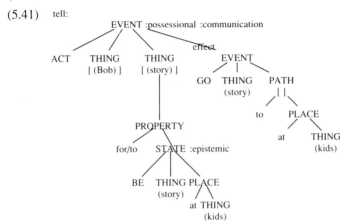

One can easily represent verbs of instrument of communication (*radio, telegraph*, etc.) using a variation of (5.41). The PROPERTY specification for the theme would be omitted, and a 'means' substructure would be added in which the agent would ACT on a THING specified as a quoted constant (e.g., a "radio").

Verbs of manner of speaking. This, of course, is a nondativizable class. A plausible semantic structure for the version of *shout* appropriate to *shout the news to John* is shown in (5.42). Presumably it is an elaboration created by a prior rule from simpler structures used in the two-argument transitive version of the verb, itself perhaps derived from the intransitive version. The field of the root event must be "physical," because that is the field in which the MANNER must be interpreted and the verb specifies a manner. The theme is specified to be a sound so as to rule out **Bob shouted some spit to John.* Other verbs in the class would have identical representations except for the quoted manner specification, which would be "muttering," "mumbling," "shrieking," "yelling," and so on.

(5.42) shout:

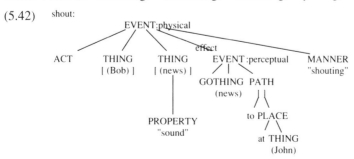

Verbs of future having. These verbs differs from verbs of having in two ways. Grammatically, they are insensitive to the morphological constraint prohibiting Latinate verbs. Semantically, the main event is not an act of giving but an act of commitment, with the possession transfer an "effect" of the commitment bound to a different event on the time-line. The act of commitment can be contractual (*bequeath, guarantee, reserve, assign, allot, leave*) or verbal (*refer, recommend, offer*), but in all cases the act by its nature involves a designated future possessor. I tentatively suggest that these verb-specific pieces of information are subordinated as means substructures, capturing the intuition that the main event is the act of commitment that has as its effect a future possession transfer. Offering, assigning, recommending, bequeathing, and so on, differ primarily in having different means of bringing about that future event (through persuasion of the beneficiary, conveying of information, legal acts, etc.). In (5.43), a representation of the "bequeath" meaning of *leave*, this information would be embedded in the position indicated by a triangle.

(5.43)

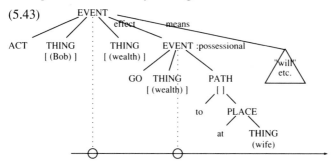

Verbs of fulfilling/deserving. These difficult-to-characterize verbs (*present, reward, honor, entrust, credit, supply, furnish*) generally do not dativize but encode the transferred theme as a *with*-object in the alternative form. Recall that the semantic thread they have in common is the notion that the recipient deserves, needs, or is worthy of the theme before the transfer, and that the form of the verb itself is related to a noun standing for the relationship between the theme and who it is destined for (*an honor, a present, a reward, a credit, some supplies, some furnishings*).

Do these verbs have any grammatical properties that give us hints as to how they are mentally represented? Note that verbs in the *to*-form shown in (5.45) are probably derived from the corresponding *with*-forms, not vice versa, and share certain properties with locative verbs such as *load* and *decorate*. *Honor* and *reward* are not even grammatical with a *to*-object (**They rewarded/honored five hundred dollars to the man*), presumably because the person bestowing the honor or reward is not necessarily transferring something that that person currently owns—cf. (5.39). *Reward, credit, furnish,* and *supply* exist as nonelliptical transitives with the recipient as grammatical object but with no overt theme, suggesting that some change of state of the recipient is being asserted, independently of any transfer of an object, as can be seen in (5.44).

(5.44) I rewarded Fido (by tickling his neck).
       They honored John last night (by naming a scholarship after him).
       He didn't credit her properly.
       His company supplied the army.
       They furnished him adequately.

Note also that the verb *entrust* gives a clue to its representation in the prefix *en*, suggesting that it means "to put into a state of trust" (cf. *enslave, encode, enrage*). All of this suggests that the alternation involving *present* verbs involves representations that share features both with the dative verbs (the change of possession, leading to the use of the preposition *to* rather than *into* and *onto*) and the locative verbs (the change of state and the existence of the *with* form, linked to the entity whose transfer effects the state change).

These facts motivate a representation of the *present* verbs similar to the one depicted in (5.45), in which I have used mnemonic indexes corresponding to a sentence like *Bob presented the medal to Sue*. The transferred object has the property "for the recipient to possess it" because of some deontic cause (= 'fulfills') specified idiosyncratically (in the triangle) by the individual verbs. The structure can be glossed as "Bob acted on the medal (which is supposed to be Sue's because of something that involved Sue), causing it to go into Sue's possession."

(5.45)

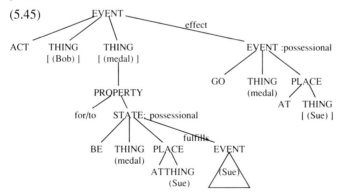

The question now arises as to why the dative rule doesn't create a double-object form from the *to*-object versions of *supply*, *entrust*, *credit*, and *furnish*, standing side by side with the original *with*-object versions. One possibility is that the dative rule does apply, yielding a structure in which the goal is correctly linked to the direct object, but that the semantic representation of *with* fused with the linking rule for oblique arguments of ACTs blocks or preempts the second object linking rule because it is more specific than the one for the second object. A slightly different possibility is that the prior existence of the independent *with* form blocks the semantic structure that the dative rule would create because of their near-synonymity. A possible problem for both these accounts is the existence of the verbs *present, furnish*, and *provide* which for many speakers admit both the double-object and the *with*-object forms; see, e.g., (4.52). Therefore I will go with a third, simpler possibility, that the precise configuration and subfield of the *furnish* verbs, with their complex, deontically caused property affixed to the theme, renders them so dissimilar to the conditions for the various narrow-range dative rules that none of these rules can apply.

Verbs of causation of motion: throw *versus* pull *versus* take. Here we wish to see differences in representations among verbs like *throw* and verbs like *pull*, because despite their cognitive similarities the former dativize and the latter do not. The crucial difference is an interaction between aspectual and force-dynamic components of the event: for *throw* verbs, the causing act is an instantaneous event preceding the motion of the object; for *pull* verbs, it is a continuous process that is temporally coextensive with the motion of the object. Although *pull* verbs typically have the agent accompanying the moving object (as in *carry*), this is not a necessary feature, since one can *lift* or *lower* a box to someone using a winch or rope and the verbs still do not dativize. The structures in (5.46) and (5.47), appropriate for the argument structures in *Bob threw / pulled the box to Bill*, display this difference.

(5.46)   throw:

(5.47)   pull:

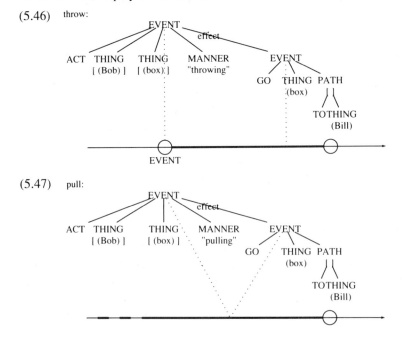

In contrast, a third subtype comprising *bring* and *take*, which do dativize, differs from the *pull* verbs in not specifying a manner, in specifying deictic information concerning the path, and also in implying that the agent moves—one can *pull* a box either while staying in one place (using a rope) or by moving with the object, but one can't *take* or *bring* a box anywhere while seated on a rock. The structure in (5.48) shows one way to represent the meanings of these verbs when they appear with *to*-objects; it corresponds to the version of *bring* that would appear in *Bob brought the rose to Sue*. The deictic variable HERE symbolizes the location of the speaker or addressee or of a perspective point that the speaker has set up in the discourse. The representation for *take* would be similar except for using the deictic variable THERE, corresponding to "not HERE." The same symbols would be used for the verbs *come*, *go*, and perhaps *send* (see Miller and Johnson-Laird, 1976). The path-function 'with' is used for objects whose path of motion is defined as being whatever path some other object happens to go along; it would also be used for verbs like *carry* and *accompany* and for the comitative sense of the preposition *with*. As I have represented it, the motion of the agent is implicit in the motion of the patient/theme along a path and the fact that the patient/theme moves 'with' the agent. This has two theoretical advantages. It captures the intuition that the motion of the agent is in some sense entailed rather than asserted (for example, *John didn't take the package to Chicago* does not necessarily mean that John didn't go to Chicago). It also spares me from having to enrich the representational apparatus (by, say, allowing an ACT to have two 'effects'—the motion of the agent and the motion of the patient/ theme—or by allowing for conjunctions of two THINGs). The time-line links specify these as accomplishment verbs.

(5.48)   bring:

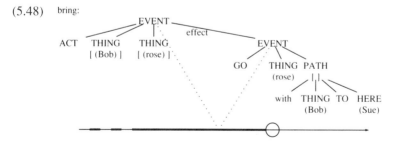

For-datives: a broad-range rule. One version of a broad-range rule for *for*-datives is shown in (5.49). As with many of the other representations, I have depicted it with mnemonic labels (in parentheses) to improve readability, but recall that the rule itself simply specifies abstract indexes for the arguments. Its input (top half) specifies the kind of argument structure we see in a sentence like *Bob baked a cake for Sue*, involving an agent performing some act on an object with the intent of allowing a third party to have it. Roughly, the representation could be paraphrased as "Bob acted on a cake in order for Sue to have the cake." Unlike the broad-range rule for the *to*-dative, no causation is specified; if I bake a cake for someone, I want them to have it but they may not actually have it at the time of the baking. No 'possessional' field is specified anywhere, so the rule would encompass pure benefactives like *Miriam drove the car for Sam*, as the arguments in section 4.4.1 mandate (recall that benefactive double-object forms in standard modern English are ruled out by narrow-range, not broad-range rules). Following Green's (1974) suggestion, we could represent benefactive relations as a form of having distinct from literal possession, where the beneficiary metaphorically possesses the acted-upon object (perhaps in an altered state or location). This could be represented in a semantic field for nonliteral possession such as 'benefactive', where "possessing" something is interpreted as being able to enjoy its advantages. Possibly the benefactive field also has a subfield for the kind of symbolic benefactive expressions involving acts of dedication discussed by Green (1974). The linking rule for oblique arguments of HAVE and ACT applies to the possessor/beneficiary embedded in the 'for/to' substructure, and fuses only with the preposition *for*, one of whose entries spells out an open argument in that semantic configuration.

(5.49)

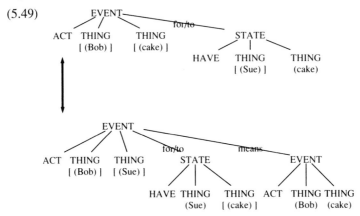

The output of the rule, the bottom half of (5.49), essentially demotes the main act to the role of the means of fulfilling an intention with regard to the beneficiary. The beneficiary, now an argument of ACT at the root level, is thereby linked to the first object. The representation could be paraphrased approximately as "Bob acted on Sue, in order for Sue to have a cake, by means of acting on the cake." The possession is linked to the second object by rule (5.38), which recognizes the 'for/to' link as being an example of a "prospective" effect by virtue of its feature decomposition.

Putting the beneficiary as, in effect, a patient of the main predicate may seem like an ad hoc expedient to get it linked to the first object. However, it is independently defensible. Green notes that the relation between the agent and the beneficiary is somewhat different in the double-object form than in the prepositional form, as shown in (5.50). In the double-object form, the agent and the beneficiary must exist at the same time, and the agent must know that the beneficiary exists.

(5.50)   I leave my poker chips and all my debts to my children, however many they may be.
          *I leave any children my wife may bear me my poker chips and all my debts.

          The American ambassador baked a cake for James I.
          *The American ambassador baked James I a cake.

          I bought a ring for my wife in case I should decide to marry.
          *I bought my wife a ring in case I should decide to marry.

          She's going to sing a song for her late lover.
          *She's going to sing her late lover a song.

Green proposes that the meaning of these double-object forms involves a component "X intends Y to have Z," and that the predicate "intend," unlike, say, "wish," "want," or "hope," has a presupposition that X believes Y and Z to exist. We could say that X must have Y in mind when entertaining his intention, and in fact that the X-Y relation is part of the definition of what X's intention is. That would be the interpretation of the representation "X ACTs on Y for Y to HAVE Z" in the lower half of (5.49) and would motivate the difference between it and the prepositional form. The actual action would be a means to realizing this intention, though the intention itself needn't actually be realized. (See also Dowty, 1979a, 1987, for related discussion.)

Admittedly, this is a *very* abstract definition of a patient, and one might wonder if speakers invariably analyze double-object *for*-datives in this way. In fact, there is evidence that they do not. As we have seen, passivization is linked to patienthood, and while some double-object *for*-datives have passives that are marginally acceptable, for others the passive is completely out, as shown in (5.51).

(5.51)   (a)   ?Bob was found a job by Sam.
                *Bob was stolen a watch by Sam.
                ?Bob was bought a present by Sam.
                *Bob was gotten a watch by Sam.

          (b)   ??Bob was cut a slice of pie by Sam.
                ?Bob was baked a cake by Sam.
                ?*Bob was knit a sweater by Sam.
                *?Bob was built a house by Sam.

          (c)   *Bob was earned a promotion by his hard work.
                *Bob was gained a friend by his warmth and generosity.

(d) *?Bob was played the trombone by Sam.

(e) *?Julie was cried a river by Sam.

The combination of the piecemeal passivizability of double-object *for*-datives with the abstractness of the patienthood analysis of their surface objects suggests that they can be represented in either of two ways, depending on the verb and other factors. The representation in the lower part of (5.49) would underlie the passivizable double-object forms and the ones where the conceptual link between the beneficiary and the agent's intentions is strongest (by hypothesis, these forms should be the same). Unpassivizable forms would be identical except that the beneficiary would not be represented as the second argument of the matrix ACT. It would have to be mapped onto the surface object role by some linking rule that I had not needed to use beforehand, perhaps one that would also embrace "causee" themes that are not patients in languages with indirect morphological causatives.

Though the semantic field for HAVE is left unspecified in the broad-range rule so as to embrace benefactives, the default semantic field for HAVE states would be literal possession, and we would expect that it would be stated in most of the narrow-range rules. The two main narrow-range *for*-dative rules perform the broad-range transformation on the representations of verbs of obtaining and verbs of creation, respectively. The verb *get* in its prepositional form might be represented as in (5.52); with suitable fillers for the argument slots it is paraphrasable as "Bob acted on a ring, causing the ring to go to Bob, in order for Sue to have the ring." The representation for *get* is the basis for other verbs of obtaining, in which a variety of ancillary substructures may be specified. *Buy* specifies a caused obligation of a countertransfer of an object with "money" properties to a third party; *grab* specifies a physical manner; *win, earn, order* involve means; *find* and *steal* specify properties of the obtained object, probably using the 'such' operator. The verb *make* might be represented as in (5.53), which when filled with real-world arguments can be glossed as "Bob acted on a hat, causing it to come into existence, in order for Sue to have the hat." Other verbs of creating would have essentially similar representations, but with slots for means, properties of the created object, or both.

(5.52) get:

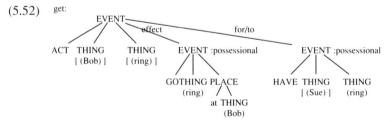

(5.53)   make:

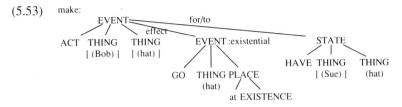

It is easy to see that verbs of choosing, even if compatible with a goal of transferring the chosen object to another party, would not match either of these narrow-range representations. According to Lakoff (1987), verbs of choosing are mentally represented like verbs of touching (which would involve a completely different semantic structure from verbs of obtaining). He notes that expressions involving touching can be metaphorically extended to signify choosing, such as *He was tapped for service, The boss handpicked his successor*, and *Sam was passed over for promotion* (where the relevant spatial sense of *over* entails noncontact).[11]

Benefactive structures that exist in standard English only as adjuncts freely attached at V″ (*She drove the car to Chicago for Ben*) would most likely not even have the third argument represented in the semantic structure of the verb and so would not come close to matching (5.52) or (5.53).

5.6.2   Representations for the Causative

A broad-range lexical rule for the causative and anticausative alternations appears in (5.54). It allows a verb that specifies an event involving a thing to be embedded as an effect of an agent acting on that thing. The predicate of the effect event can be either GO or ACT, so it is specified by the feature <+dynamic>, which embraces the two predicates by virtue of their both canonically being kinds of EVENTs. This captures the intuition that the concept of causation inherently involves an event (see also Carter, 1976a), and it embraces the subclasses that we actually find to be causativizable: no verbs with BE or HAVE causativize.

(5.54)

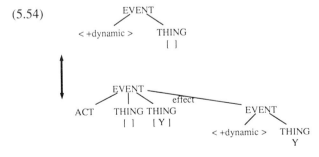

Change-of-state verbs. The largest subclasses to which causativization actually applies as narrow-range rules are the verbs of changes of state and the verbs of manner of motion. The representation of a typical inchoative or change-of-state verb, *break*, was shown in (5.18), and the transitive causative version, created from it by rule (5.54), was shown in (5.26). Most causativizable verbs of change of state can be treated this way, with different quoted constants in the specification of what the state is. A few, however, will require more complex representations. *Melt*, for example, specifies that the thing not only go 'to' a liquid state but come 'from' a solid state; condensation of a gas is not an example of melting (Jackendoff, 1987a). Manner is probably not specified in any of these verbs' structures, because even when those changes of state have typical manners, the verb can be used perfectly naturally when some unusual manner characterizes the change. For example, one can say *the paper burned* whether it flashed or smoldered and whether it was due to fire, the sun, or spontaneous combustion.

Manner-of-motion verbs. The structure of verbs of manner of motion was illustrated in (5.10). (Incidentally, I am using the term "manner" here to refer to how someone or something GOes, such as rolling; elsewhere I use the term to refer to how someone ACTs, such as walking. This does not lead to ambiguity.) Both the simple one-argument version and the version that admits an open path complement can causativize. The causative version has the motion event embedded with an 'effect' link within an ACT structure, as in the change-of-state verbs. Note that though both change-of-state verbs and manner-of-motion verbs have a GO function, they signify different kinds of processes: inception of a state, and ongoing motion, respectively. This correctly captures the fact that the causativized manner-of-motion verbs are not inchoative. If John rolls a ball, he needn't have started the ball rolling; he could have continued its motion after it had rolled to him.

Inherently directed motion verbs. A crucial distinction we must capture is that between manner-of-motion verbs and the verbs of inherently directed motion, which are noncausativizable. There seem to be two distinctive properties of this inherent-direction class. First, they specify a direction using a specified transitive or intransitive path-function, or a combination of a path-function and a place constant: 'up' for *ascend, rise*; 'down' for *descend, fall*; 'to PLACE' for *arrive*; 'from PLACE' for *leave*; 'from in THING' for *exit*; 'to in THING' for *enter*; 'to HERE' for *come*; 'to THERE' for *go*. Second, manner is totally irrelevant: none of these verbs is constrained to a manner of motion, and no manner should be specified in their semantic representations. The representation of *enter* that we saw in (5.8) displays these features.[12] Verbs that specify directions of motion of parts of an object relative to the whole or relative to a local frame of reference, as opposed to some direction of translation of the center of the object with respect to the environment (e.g., *topple*, *tilt*), would do so in quoted material inside the MANNER slot and so would fail to fit the rule both by having a manner and by lacking a PATH containing a constant path-function or place.[13]

Change-of-existence verbs. Verbs of coming out of or going into existence, all noncausativizable, would have distinct representations by virtue of the 'existential' field specifier appended to their EVENT nodes, and by a constant path 'to' or 'from' the constant metaphorical place 'existence'. (Since there are only two possible "places," no change-of-existence verb needs to specify both a 'to' and a 'from', unlike the analogous *melt*.)

Action verbs. Verbs for human actions, such as *jog* or *laugh*, would be represented with ACT events at their top level and so would quite clearly be distinct from intransitive verbs of manner of motion or change of state, each of which involves GO. This is the broad semantic basis behind the unergative/ unaccusative distinction; across languages one tends to find that verbs of voluntary action, manner of speaking, and some involuntary bodily processes are unergative, and verbs of being in states, changing state, and changing existence are unaccusative (Perlmutter, 1978). However, there are some differences in the classification of particular verbs in particular languages, especially for verbs that are cognitively ambiguous between internal and external causation, such as *sweat* or *die* (Rosen, 1984). This is exactly what we would expect given the cognitive ambiguity of thematic relations and the ability of grammars to define narrow conflation classes that reduce that ambiguity in semiarbitrary ways; in some languages the specific meaning of sweating (and meanings similar to it) may be expressed as a kind of ACT, in others as a kind of GO or BE. Moreover, the syntactic consequences of the unergative/unaccusative distinction may be a result of a set of independent narrow-range rules that subdivide the class of ACT verbs and the class of GO and BE verbs in slightly different ways in different languages and perhaps even in a single language. This would account for why the different syntactic concomitants of unaccusativity do not invariably hang together (see Grimshaw, 1987, for a review). A good example is causativization in English; as we saw in section 1.4.5.5, not all unaccusative verbs with GO causativize (though many do) and not all unergative verbs resist causativization (though most do).

The only causativizable unergative verbs in English are in two rather specialized subclasses involving locomotion. The first involves verbs like *trot*, *race*, and *gallop*, where there is voluntary motion in some manner, differing from verb to verb. A representation for intransitive *trot* (as in *Dobbin trotted down the path*) is shown in (5.55). Many of the felicitous usages of the transitive form involve locomotion by nonhumans (usually horses, for that matter), and the few admissible usages with humans (*He marched the soldiers across the field; She walked her baby across the room*) either involve the next class I will discuss or involve cases that connote something less than freely willed humanness on the part of the actor (such as soldiers or babies).

(5.55)   trot:

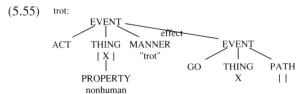

The second quasi-causativizable class with actors involves accompanied motion, usually via some 'means' (*walk* is an exception, involving a MANNER instead). The structure of these verbs, in both their intransitive and transitive forms, is shown in (5.56), a representation of the two forms of the verb *drive*. The representation of the intransitive version in the top half of the diagram, as in *Sue drove to Chicago*, when fleshed out with real referents could be roughly paraphrased as "Sue acted, causing her to go to Chicago, by means of acting on a car." The representation of the transitive version in the lower half, as in *Bob drove Sue to Chicago*, could be paraphrased as "Bob acted on Sue, causing her to go to Chicago with him, by means of Bob acting on a car." These verbs, such as *sail*, *drive*, and *fly*, are formally different from most cases of causativization because the intransitive form is not embedded intact as an effect structure in the transitive version. When Bob drives Sue to Chicago, he is not causing Sue to drive—Sue may not even know how to drive—though he is causing her to go to Chicago and necessarily with him. The transitive form inherits the GO substructure of the intransitive but "raises" the MANNER or 'means' structure up into the embedding ACT-THING-THING-effect structure. This also automatically changes the interpretation of the 'means' structure. When Sid flies to Memphis, he is going to Memphis by means of merely getting into an airplane, but when Sally flies Sid to Memphis, she is causing Sid to go to Memphis by means of flying the plane. In other words, the 'means' structure receives different interpretations depending on whether it is a means of going or a means of causing someone to go.

(5.56) drive:

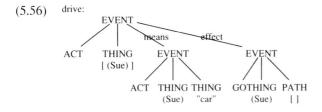

drive:

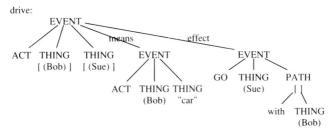

Interestingly, for most of the verbs in these subclasses the pathless version of the verb is marginal in the causative when used nonelliptically: *I walked her home* / *?I walked her; He bicycled her home* / *?He bicycled her; He trotted the horse around the track* / *??He trotted the horse.* This suggests that narrow-range rules can be sensitive to the presence of the full set of arguments accompanying a verb, including optional path constituents. If so, there would have to be separate narrow-range rules for verbs with and without such arguments; *She rolled the ball into the box* would be created by a different rule than the one creating *She rolled the ball.* Though this seems uneconomical, the overall generalization embracing the two is still captured by the broad-range rule, and I suspect that there are other cases in which the presence or absence of an extra constituent affects the susceptibility of a verb to an alternation. Another possible example comes from Wasow (1977): *Mary showed John's inexperience* / *John's inexperience showed* versus *Mary showed John's inexperience to be a problem* / *John's inexperience showed to be a problem.*

Verbs of emission. Another subclass of intransitive verbs with inanimate subjects may also be noncausativizable on account of being ACTs instead of simple changes or motions. These include verbs of internally caused change of state (see section 4.4.3). As noted, these classes seem to involve emission of energy or substances (sound, light, liquid, etc.) by and from within an object; aside from being noncausativizable in English, such verbs tend to bear the hallmarks of unergativity across languages (Perlmutter, 1978). Since emission of any sort appears to rule out narrow-range causativization, I am spared having to define classes by referring to ad hoc properties of things such as sounds or lights. Though all of these verbs involve some kind of change of state, they also involve internally instigated causation, hence possibly an ACT event as their root structure, effecting the motion of material (of some sort specified idiosyncratically by the verb) in a specified path ('from in' the object). Since any of these meaning components would be necessary for understanding the verbs and they are easily stated in terms of existing machinery, these verbs would not be represented in the same way as simple change-of-state verbs and hence would not match the narrow-range causativization rule applying to those verbs.

5.6.3   Representations for the Locative

The broad-range rule for locativization is shown in (5.57), with mnemonic argument labels appropriate to Bob's spraying paint on walls. The input is a verb of causation of motion to a location, as in *Bob sprayed paint onto the wall*, whose representation can be made clearer by paraphrasing it as "Bob acted on the paint, causing it to go onto the wall." The output is a verb of causation of change of state by means of causation of motion of some entity, as in *Bob sprayed the wall with paint*, whose representation can be glossed as "Bob acted on the wall, causing the wall to become sprayed, by means of Bob acting on the paint, causing it to go onto the wall." The patient of the means clause in the *with* form is linked to the oblique or indirect internal argument role by virtue of its place in an embedded ACT and the lexical entry for *with*, which has an open argument for the patient and theme of a 'to'-path within a 'means' structure. (As discussed in chapter 3, this is similar but not identical to the entry for *with* that marks instrumental phrases.)

(5.57)

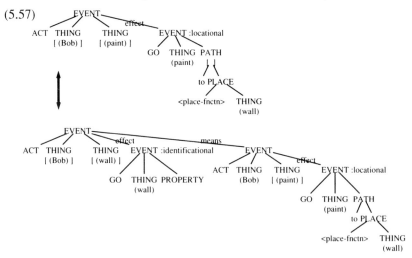

Note an important difference between the locative, on the one hand, and the causative and the *to*-dative, on the other. The causative simply embeds a one-argument structure within an ACT structure intact, and the dative performs a similarly mechanical transformation of a structure (BE) to another structure

(HAVE) related to it by a simple inferential rule (the two functions are basically inverses of each other). But for the locative a PROPERTY appears in the *with* form that has no direct counterpart in the *into/onto* form. If a speaker productively derives the *with* form from the *into/onto* form using a narrow-range lexical rule, therefore, the rule must tell the speaker how to fill in the slot for that property. Each narrow-range rule does so in a slightly different way.

Let us consider the representation of some of the classes that do and do not undergo the alternation in each direction.

The smear *class and the* spray *class.* Structure (5.58) shows the representation of verbs such as *smear*, *dab*, and *streak* that appear to be transformable from the *onto* form to the *with* form. The top representation underlies the verb entry in *Bob smeared jam onto the bread* and is shown with the corresponding mnemonic indexes; it can be glossed as "Bob acted on a semisolid substance, namely jam, causing it to go against and along some bread in a smearing manner." The place-function 'against' refers to the space immediately adjacent to and including the surface of an object; the path-function 'along' refers to a path confined to some surface. The manner constant "smear" refers to the idiosyncratic spatiotemporal distribution a substance assumes as it is being smeared (in terms of the relevant change in thickness or patchiness); it would also underlie the meaning of the related noun *a smear*. The bottom diagram shows the representation of the verb form in *Bob smeared the bread with jam*; its rough gloss is "Bob acted on the bread, causing it to attain the property of having jam smeared against/along it, by means of acting on jam, causing jam to go against and along it in a smearing manner."

(5.58) smear:

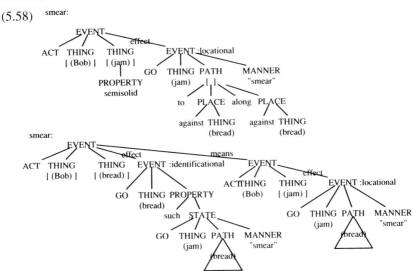

A crucial aspect of this representation is that the property predicated of the surface argument in the *with* form is systematically related to the motion of the substance argument in the *onto* form. The most straightforward way of representing this dependency between the act of smearing and the state of being smeared with something is to use the stative version of GO (Jackendoff's GO_{ext}), ordinarily employed in expressing static configurations such as *This road goes to Chicago*. That is, the property of being smeared is simply the frozen trace of the act of smearing.[14] Other verbs in the class would specify different manner constants for the motion of the substance itself ("snudge," "spread," "streak," etc.); some could also specify various manner or means specifications for the act of causing the motion ("dab," "daub," "brush"). The presence of the additional manner or means link in the ACT structure correlates negatively with the ability of the verb to appear without an agentive subject: *When she looked up, her face was a mess: makeup streaked/*daubed her cheeks from top to bottom*. This is probably just the anticausativization rule discussed in the previous chapter, which is blocked when a manner or means of acting is specified: *The lamp doesn't work because a wire broke/*cut*.

Verbs in the *splash* class have representations in the *onto* form that are similar to those of the *smear* class but with several systematic differences. The moved substance generally has the property 'liquid' instead of 'semisolid';[15] the path lacks the 'along against THING' component. Perhaps most important, the temporal representation of the *smear* verbs would link the ACT event and the GO event to the same interval on the time-line. Assuming that complex paths have separate links to the time-line for each of their parts, the 'against' and 'along' parts would be co-linked with the ACT, representing the fact that the agent continues to act on the substance as it moves along the surface. In contrast, the representations of the *splash* verbs would have an ACT event linked to a point (for *splash* or *squirt*) or an interval (for *spray* or *inject*), and the GO event would be linked to a distinct point or interval later on the time-line; this corresponds to the fact that the agent is not necessarily acting on the liquid at the moment it arrives at the target surface.[16] (This is the same distinction that split the *throw* verbs and the *pull* verbs with regard to dativization.)

As before, the verb representation specifies a manner of motion (e.g., the distribution of liquid that defines *spray*) and for some verbs a manner or means of acting (e.g., for *inject*). As expected, mannerfulness or meansfulness blocks the anticausativization of these verbs (e.g., *Water splashed against the sand castle / *Water injected into the sand castle*). The *with* versions of the *splash* verbs would also be similar to those of the *smear* verbs, with the attainment by the surface of a property that is defined by a stative, extensional GO containing the same manner as the dynamic version. This sharing of machinery may seem problematic, because when an object is splashed, splattered, sprayed, and so on, it is not the frozen trajectory of the substance through space that defines a state, but the frozen results of the moment of impact (basically, a cross-section of the shape of the moving liquid). However, since there already is an aspectual difference between the motions of smearing (interval) and of splashing (point), a suitably explicit theory of the effects of staticizing motion events into states would presumably lead to this consequence automatically. Thus the narrow-range rules for the locativization of *smear* verbs and *splash* verbs are similar and perhaps could be collapsed; I tentatively keep them separate because of the possibility that any collapsed superordinate category might also embrace some nonlocativizable verbs.

Push *verbs and* pour *verbs.* Now we can look at some seemingly closely related but nonlocativizable classes. Verbs of force exertion such as *push* or *shove*, even when they take *into* phrases, have no specification of any property of their patients (i.e., they need not be semisolid or liquid); they always specify a manner within the ACT structure; they never specify a manner of motion of the patient/theme within the GO structure; and they never specify particular path- or place-functions within the path structure (i.e., you can push Momma out the door, into the car, from the train, around the room, etc.).

For verbs in the *pour* class, involving enabled motion of a mass via gravity, the representation would look something like (5.59). The representation, appropriate to the entry for *pour* that appears in *Sue poured water onto the floor,* can be glossed as "Sue acted on a mass, in this case water, letting it go from inside something down to on the floor, in a pouring manner." Though the representation is similar to that of *spray* verbs, there are several crucial differences. The motion of the substance is caused by gravity and merely enabled by the agent's releasing it from some container, rather than being caused by the imparting of force from the agent (hence the subordinating link is annotated by the cluster of force-dynamic features that I abbreviate as 'let'). And, possibly as a consequence, the path substructure specifies a motion downward and onto an object. If we set aside *drip* and *drizzle*, which sound somewhat unusual with agentive subjects anyway, an additional semantic substructure the verbs in this class share is that the moving substance comes from inside some container, unlike, say, *splashing*, which one can do with one's hands while chest-deep in the ocean. (Interestingly, the path 'out-of' or 'from in' seems to differentiate narrow classes, inhibiting productivity, in several other cases: in the *spew* verbs, which resist locativization, and verbs of emission of light, sound, or matter, which resist causativization.) As a result of the presence of this specification of a source, these verbs can be assigned open arguments allowing them to take overt *from* or *out of* phrases as well. Although it is crucial that the verbs specify that the substance is enabled ('let') rather than forced to move, it is less clear that the downward direction is an essential part of the specification of the subclass. That would depend on whether people have a clear sense that sentences like the following are grammatically anomalous: *Astronaut Sally Ride poured some Tang up onto the ceiling of Spacelab.*

(5.59)   pour:

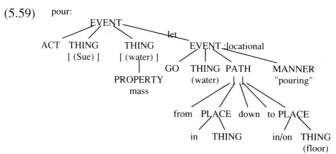

Other kinds of content-locative verbs. Several other classes of verbs specify particular spatial arrangements and paths, and kinds of moved objects. Verbs of circular arrangement (*coil, spin, twirl, twist, whirl, wind*) do not alternate; semantically, they specify a flexible object whose major axis is one-dimensional, which is moved along a path 'to' the place 'around' the goal object. Two other subclasses consist, as far as I know, of three verbs apiece. Verbs of vertical arrangement, which do alternate, require mass (*heap*) or aggregate (*pile, stack*) themes and a path 'to' a place defined by the place-function 'on'. In addition, there must be some specification that the parts of the moved assemblage are arranged vertically with respect to one another. No set of path-functions or place-functions will suffice to specify this arrangement, because the "GO THING path-function (place-function THING)" representation inherently idealizes the theme as a dimensionless point that is simply located at a place on the target object (Talmy, 1983), and we have to specify the arrangement of parts of the theme relative to each other. Here we see clearly that the representational format I have adopted can be surprisingly restrictive—there is no easy way to state the obvious "procedure" for piling, namely putting one part of the aggregate theme 'on' the surface, a second part 'on' the first part, a third 'on' the second, and so on. Nor have I availed myself of a mechanism for specifying two distinct effects of an action, in this case, putting the theme 'on' the table and arranging the theme so that it defines a vertical stack. The only option using the machinery I have introduced so far is to specify that the theme must already have the property of being in a pile. The geometry of the pile can be enforced by constraining the object to be an aggregate whose shape has a one-dimensional extension; its necessarily vertical orientation can be specified using Jackendoff's GO_{ext} (my

stative GO) formalism with the intransitive direction 'up'. The representation in
(5.60) shows one way this could be done. It results in a prediction: the sentence
Irma piled books on the table should be available as a way to describe an event
in which Irma picks up prearranged piles of books and places each pile on a table.
This prediction seems to be correct. It is difficult to pinpoint a state definition for
the surface in the *with* form other than that piles are on it; I will simply assume
that such a state is defined using 'such' and the relevant portion of (5.60).

(5.60)   pile:

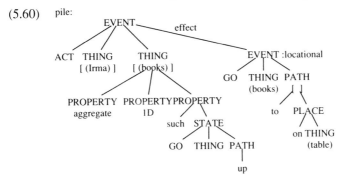

Verbs of dispersal (*scatter, sow, strew, bestrew*) alternate for some speakers;
semantically, they require patient/themes with the property 'aggregate' and a
path eventuating in a place defined by a place-function roughly similar in
meaning to the English particles *about, around,* and *all over.*

   Container locatives: verbs of covering. Now let us consider classes of verbs
that are used exclusively or primarily in the *with* form ("container locative").
Several classes that do not alternate specify some target spatial distribution of a
moved object onto a location object, which I will represent as a change of state
of the location effected by means of an agent acting on the moved object. The
representation of *cover* in (5.61) is paradigmatic for the class that includes
bandage, coat, face, pave, and other verbs. The representation can be glossed as
"Bob acted on the bed, causing it to attain the property of having a 2D object,
namely a sheet, on it, by means of acting on the sheet."

(5.61)   cover:

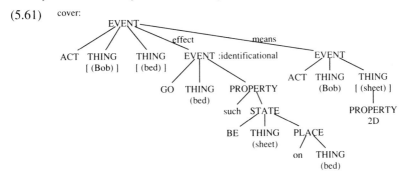

Several aspects of the interpretation of these symbols are important. Despite the English mnemonic, the place-function 'on' used here is different from the 'on' used to specify the top of an object; it would correspond to coextensiveness of surfaces. The 2D property specification requires only that the object can be construed as being extended in two dimensions; it need not literally be two-dimensional. Because the location object is asserted to change state, the holistic interpretation applies. In the representational subsystem, multiple properties can be listed, and it is conceivable that some more elementary idiosyncratic property similar to "obscured" or "invisible" or "unexposed" is listed as well. There is a 'means' substructure, so as to provide the trigger for the linking rule that provides the *with*-phrase. However, it need not be the case that the agent causes the cover to GO 'to' the location; one can *cover a bed* by arranging disheveled sheets already strewn on top of it. Thus no specific path or specific manner of motion, or even the existence of a translation of the object as a whole, is mandated by the verb, differentiating them from all the classes of alternating verbs we have discussed so far.

Other verbs in the class would differ in terms of the properties asserted of the patient in the *with*-phrase that helps to define the state change, such as liquid (*flood, douse*); an aggregate of rigid 2D parts (*tile*); or more specific idiosyncratic properties (*bandage, pave*).

The fill *class and other nonalternating verbs.* By using different combinations of dimensionalities and properties of the content (state-defining) and container (state-assuming) objects, together with various place-functions, one could arrive at representations for verbs specifying complete alignment or coextensivity of selected dimensions of objects. For example, for *line*, the container is a 1D boundary of a 2D object or a 2D boundary of a 3D object, the content is 1D or 2D, respectively, and the place-function is 'on' (a similar set of specifications would be used for *edge*). For *fill*, the content is mass, the container is a 2D surface of a 3D object, and the place-function is 'in'. For verbs in the *saturate* class, the container is a 3D object and the content is a 3D liquid (*drench*) or an aggregate of 0D or 1D or 2D parts (*intersperse, vein, interleave*); the place-function is 'in'. For verbs in the *riddle* class, the container is a 2D object or a 2D boundary of a 3D object, the content is an aggregate of 0D parts, and the place-function is 'on'. Within each of these classes, the verbs would be differentiated from one another by more idiosyncratic object properties (e.g., for *stud* or *stain*).

Alternating container-oriented verbs: load, pack, stock. The only two classes of container-oriented or *with* verbs that can trigger the formation of corresponding content-oriented or *into/onto* forms involve the notion of a container's intended capacity. *Load, stock,* and *pack* are surprisingly complex verbs, each of which pertain to the filling of a container designed for a certain kind of item with items of that kind: if one puts bullets into a storage receptacle hidden in the handle of a gun, that is not an example of *loading the gun.* In addition, the location object changes state as a result of the action; that state is defined by some action or capability of the location object with respect to the goals of the agent. For *load*, it can be firing bullets, recording on a tape, taking pictures, or transporting hay; for *pack*, it can be transporting something; for *stock*, it can be temporarily holding some commodity. Note, for example, that a drug dealer slipping cocaine into the suitcase of an unsuspecting passenger is not *packing a suitcase.* This purposive component of the state definition (i.e., when a wagon is "loaded," it is ready to do something) and of the specification of the receptacle (i.e., the place in the wagon where the hay goes is designed for holding stuff) can be captured using the 'for/to' property operator. This is shown in (5.62), a representation of the verb entry for *load* in an argument structure like that in *Bob loaded the wagon with hay.* It can be glossed as "Bob acted on the wagon, causing the wagon to go into the state of being able to act as it was designed to act, by means of Bob acting on the hay, causing it to go to a place in the wagon intended for hay to be in it." ("As designed" is the opaque idiosyncratic representation of what a tape player, gun, wagon, printer, camera, and so on, are intended to do when they are loaded.)[17]

(5.62)   load:

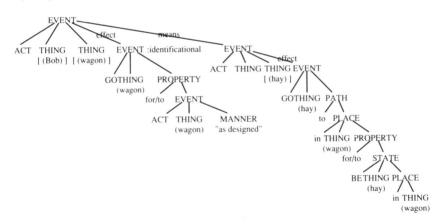

When the locativization rule applies in what we think of as the reverse direction, deriving the *into* form from the *with* form (see section 4.4.2), the change of state is no longer asserted to be an effect of the action; otherwise the holistic effect would apply to it (for example, we do not want to rule out the possibility that Bob *loaded hay into the wagon* but stopped before the wagon was loaded). *Pack* and *stock* would have similar representations to *load*, except for differences in the composition of the EVENT substructure that for *load* contains the "as designed" manner.

Verbs of stuffing. The other alternating class contains *cram, crowd, jam, stuff, wad*, and the sense of *pack* that one would use to refer to fiberglass insulation in cracks rather than to clothes in suitcases. It is not clear how to characterize this class formally, and its requirement reveals a nonobvious constraint of the model of space implicit in the representational system. The verbs in the *with* form all entail that the container is in some sense "overfull." But how should this state be represented? Conceptually, it is not a "place": there is no place associated with a room such that people are in that place when the room is crowded. Nor is there some path to a room such that when people traverse it the room becomes crowded. Morphology corroborates these intuitions: there is no preposition in English (nor, I would guess, in most other languages) corresponding to the notion "overfull." Rather, the closest English closed-class morpheme, namely the prefix *over-* (modifying the meaning of verbs and adjectives to create prefixed forms such as *overfill, overload, overstock*, and *overstuffed*), clearly modifies a relation between a substance and a container—the action or state referred to is such that there is "too much" substance for the capacity of the container. As in the representations of *pile, heap*, and *stack*, we seem confronted with a case where the usual linguistic model of space, in which the theme is idealized as a point, is too impoverished to allow the necessary specification of the subclass at hand. In particular, the quantity of the theme in this case must be part of the definition of the relationship "overfull" underlying the *stuff* verbs. Jackendoff (1983, 1987a) presents no formalism to handle spatial relationships where both the geometry of the theme and of the reference object are relevant (thus he could not easily represent the meaning of certain complex prepositions either, such as *across*; see Talmy, 1983, for discussion).

A natural extension to the existing machinery would be to allow a STATE to be defined as [BE THING CONFIGURATION], where CONFIGURATION would be defined as [config-function THING]. The CONFIGURATION constituent of BE states would be analogous to the PATH constituent of GO events. (In fact, we could maximize economy at the expense of readability by using a single symbol to be interpreted as PATH when accompanied by GO and as CONFIGURATION when accompanied by BE.) Let us assume that a small number of configuration functions are available. 'Perpendicular-to' and 'parallel-to' would presumably be included in the set to help represent the meaning of prepositions like *along* and *across*; for our present purposes, 'over-' would be needed, signifying that the theme exceeds the capacity of the place at which it is located.

The *into/onto* form of the *stuff* verbs need not imply the accomplishment of such a configuration—Bob can *cram pencils into his briefcase* through a narrow opening, even though the briefcase is largely empty—but it does specify some condition of forcing something into some container against some resisting force exerted by the container. This is nicely captured by the cluster of force-dynamic link features abbreviated as 'despite' (see the table shown in (5.31)), and the static exertion of force, which I have represented as STATEs consisting of ACTs (for example, in the representation of verbs like *support* shown in (5.30)). The representation of verbs of this class, then, would be as in (5.63). The top diagram, representing the verb entry in *Bob stuffed breadcrumbs into the turkey* and fleshed out with corresponding mnemonic labels, can be glossed as "Bob acted on breadcrumbs, causing them to go into the turkey, despite the turkey's resisting the breadcrumbs." The bottom diagram depicts the entry in *Bob stuffed the turkey with breadcrumbs*, and can be glossed as "Bob acted on the turkey, causing the turkey to be overfull with breadcrumbs, by means of acting on the breadcrumbs, causing the breadcrumbs to go into the turkey."

(5.63)

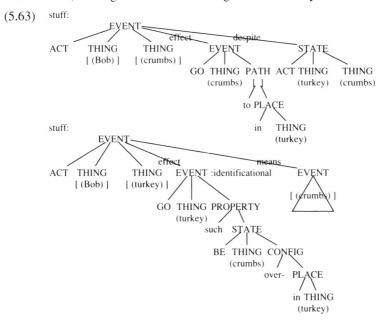

The triangle in the *with* form is an abbreviation of the act-cause-motion structure in the *into* form, presumably minus the 'despite' substructure. If so, the derivation of the 'despite' structure would have to be inferred conceptually from the 'over-' configuration (or vice versa when the rule is applied in the reverse derivation), rather than being created by a mechanical rearrangement of semantic structure. (Alternatively, the representations of the 'despite' clause and the 'over-' configuration might overlap in some finer-grained decomposition than I have presented here.) The other verbs within the class would differ from one another in their specification of the necessary properties of the moved substance (mass for *stuff*, aggregate and possibly human for *crowd*, 2D for *wad*, and so on) and in specifying particular manners of acting on for the verbs *cram, jam*, and *wad*.

Nongeometric state-change verbs. Verbs conveying the change of an object to a state characterized nongeometrically (often with esthetic or evaluative connotations) by means of putting something in or on that object will be represented as in (5.64), a representation of the verb *adorn* as it appears in *Sue adorned the car with decals.* The gloss is "Sue acted on the car, causing it to become adorned, by means of Sue acting on decals, causing them to go onto the car."

(5.64)   adorn:

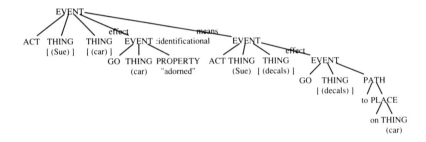

Others in the class include *embellish, enrich, ornament, clutter, infect*, and *taint*. It is not clear whether the evaluative/esthetic meaning itself must be specified or whether the listing of an idiosyncratic property not cashed out in geometric or purposive terms would suffice in distinguishing the class. (A possible way of characterizing a common evaluative component would be to introduce a new grammatically relevant property, 'eval', that would define this subclass and perhaps also the possessed objects in benefactive and malefactive structures that do not involve literal possession change. However, it is not clear whether such a property is necessary.) The verbs in the class would differ in terms of the idiosyncratic state specified and in terms of other properties, both idiosyncratic and classificational, asserted of the participating objects (e.g., mass and color for *stain*, weight for *burden*, and so on).

Binding and clogging. Finally, verbs expressing the change of state of an object to one whereby some other substance or object is not free to leave it can be represented as in (5.65), a representation of the entry of *clog* appearing in *Sue clogged the sink with a rag.* The only novel symbol is the subordinating causal link whose features are abbreviated as 'prevent'. The representation can be glossed as "Sue acts on the sink, causing it to change to a state such that a rag statically acts on a liquid, preventing that liquid from going out of the sink, by means of Sue acting on the rag, causing the rag to go into the sink."

(5.65) clog:

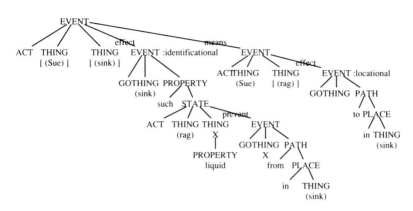

This subclass contains a number of verbs like *clog* pertaining to impeded motion (*block, choke, clog, dam, plug, stop up*), which would differ from one another in imposing different property specifications on their arguments. Similar structures would capture the meanings of verbs denoting some kind of bondage, such as *bind, chain, entangle, lash, lasso, rope*, and *tie*, except that the moved object would be specified as 1D and flexible and the impeded object as being prevented from moving 'from at' rather than 'from in' the location object. Individual verbs are free to specify idiosyncratic properties of the moved object (e.g., chains, lassos, or ropes), and additional idiosyncratic information about the manner in which the moved object acts on the bound object (e.g., lashed versus entangled versus tied.)

5.6.4 Representations for the Passive

The broad-range rule of passivization is shown in (5.66). The passive is represented here as a circumstantial state, in which the "place" or circumstance predicated of the theme is an event or state corresponding to the one expressed by the active form (thus an ACT event is listed in the slot corresponding to PLACE in the circumstantial state structure, omitting the redundant place-function 'at').

(5.66)

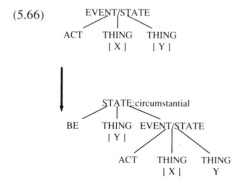

Though this representation at first glance might appear to collapse the meanings of verbal and adjectival passives, the adjectival passive form is represented differently: the semantic field is 'identificational', and the theme is predicated as being at a PROPERTY, specifically, the property 'such' that the agent ACTs on it.

The second open argument in (5.66) would be expressed overtly as a *by* phrase thanks to the linking rule shown in (5.28) that associates arguments embedded in ACT/HAVE structures with oblique phrases, and the lexical entry for *by* containing an open agent argument that is part of a circumstantial "place." Short or "agentless" passives (e.g., *John was hit*) are based on a structure identical to that of (5.66) but with the "suppressed" agent argument lacking the square brackets that allow it to be "open" to syntactic expression. Its presence, however, causes the verb form to be interpreted as entailing the existence of an agent or author and can allow the event to control adverbials such as *deliberately* when appropriate (see Keyser and Roeper, 1984; Lasnik, 1988).

For the passive, showing the representations underlying alternating verbs does not require enumerating a set of narrow-range rules. Recall that the broad-range rule of passivization, presumably because it adds an affix, applies to any verb with a compatible semantic structure. Now we can say what that "compatible semantic structure" is. The verb must have a dyadic ACT, because that is the substructure that gets embedded in the part of the passive representation that defines the circumstance predicated of the theme in which the theme is a patient. Any verb that is built around a dyadic ACT, then, is passivizable. Obviously this includes all action verbs, including both versions of the dative and of the locative, as discussed in section 4.4.4. Now I will flesh out and justify the claim that representations for nonactional verbs that passivize do include a dyadic ACT, whereas those that do not passivize lack one.

The representational theory provides two loci associated with dyadic ACT structures that can embrace nonactional verbs. First, there is the EVENT/ STATE distinction. We have already seen—see (5.30)—that ACTs that are STATEs can be used to represent verbs of static exertion of force, such as *support*. Second, events or states defined by ACTs can be differentiated in terms of the semantic fields in which an ACT is defined. Verbs whose ACT events are defined in the psychological field were shown in (5.33) for experiencer-subject verbs and in (5.34) for stimulus-subject verbs. Similar representations dominated by STATE instead of EVENT (and with different kinds of 'effect' substructures) would characterize psych-verbs such as *like* and the static sense of *frighten*. Likewise, field specifiers such as 'deontic' or 'epistemic' (some of which allow STATEs, EVENTs, or 'represented' THINGs to function in roles ordinarily taken by physical THINGs; see Jackendoff, 1983) would define the scaffolding for abstract transitive verbs like *justify* or *refute*, where ideas and situations abstractly "act on" one another. Another semantic field in which ACTs can be defined might be called "efficacy" (or perhaps "potency"), and would be appropriate to define situations in which some quality of one object with respect to a second allows the first to affect the second. This field might be used to define the role of instrumental subjects and the "state-changer" subjects of verbs of spatial relations, where the first argument of ACT is not the usual animate agent but an inanimate object serving as a proximal cause. The representation in (5.67) corresponds to *The knife cut the bread* (which can yield *The bread was cut by the knife*); its rough gloss is "The knife effectively acted on the bread, causing the bread to become cut, by means of someone acting on the knife, causing the knife to go against and through the bread."

(5.67)   cut:

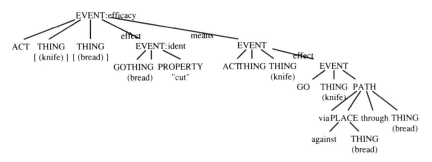

The representation in (5.68) corresponds to *Snow covered the ground* (which can yield *The ground was covered by snow*); its gloss is "The snow statically affected the ground, causing the ground to be in the state of having snow on it."[18]

(5.68)   cover:

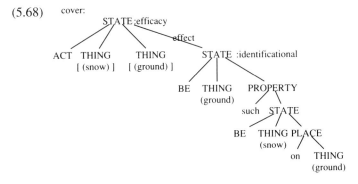

What about the unpassivizable classes? One part of the problem is, in a sense, easy. Verbs with more than one argument that do not have an ACT structure must be built around some other structure, such as BE and GO. But BE structures involve places or paths defined by place-functions and path-functions. These constituents, unlike the second argument of ACT, which is mapped onto the object by a linking rule, will be mapped onto an oblique phrase by the linking rules. Thus they should not passivize and indeed do not, to no one's surprise (e.g., *The tree was walked toward by Sy*). The exception, of course, occurs in constructions like *This chair has been sat in*; the usual hypothesis is that such verbs are reanalyzed as having their goal or location argument assume an alternative primary role as a kind of patient (see Bolinger, 1977a; Davison, 1980; Bresnan, 1982b; and section 3.3.4.4.)

The more challenging cases are ones where the verb does take an adjacent noun phrase but does not passivize. How do these verbs get objects in the first place, if objects come from a linking rule that applies to patients or to themes of verbs with agents? We must provide plausible representations for verbs that lack ACT structures (rendering them unpassivizable, according to theory) but have structures that trigger linking rules that give them transitive argument structures to begin with (or, argument structures that only appear to be transitive, for the alternative account of passivization mentioned in section 4.4.4 in which the passive would be a purely syntactic rule applying to any genuine transitive structure).

Unpassivizable possession verbs. One such representation is the HAVE structure, whose first argument generally ends up in surface subject position and whose second argument ends up in surface object position. Thus for any verb built around a HAVE state we have a NP-V-NP structure to which the broad-range passive rule cannot apply. The unpassivizable verb *have*, of course, shown in (5.17), is a prime example. As I argued, verbs of alienable property possession such as *own* would be built around STATE consisting of an ACT (corresponding to Talmy's notion of the static exertion of force). This is shown in (5.69); the 'efficacy' semantic field used previously for verbs taking instrumental subjects might be used again to express the relevant kind of dependency. *Lack* would be represented similarly to *have*, except for additional information specifying its negative polarity, plus its quasi-deontic components (i.e., that the nonpossessed object is in some sense "needed" or "normally possessed"). The sense of *possess* used for inalienable possession would be represented in a similar way to *have*, and as we would expect, it does not easily passivize: *?A keen moral sense is possessed by Abe.*

(5.69)   own:

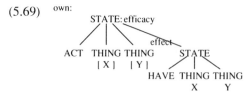

Unpassivizable spatial verbs. A good case can be made that nonpassivizable transitive spatial verbs are also built around the HAVE function, which would accept a 'locational' semantic field instead of its unmarked 'possessional' one. (This would complete the symmetry of BE and HAVE I discussed when the HAVE function was introduced.) For one thing, the verbs *have* and *lack* can themselves be used in a physical sense: *This car has/lacks a radio.* More striking is the verb *contain*, always problematic because it is one of the few transitive spatial verbs that do not passivize, conformity to Jackendoff's Thematic Hierarchy Condition notwithstanding. As discussed in section 4.4.4, *contain* does not lend itself to overt locutions involving changes of state, presumably because it lacks an ACT structure. But if it is simply a BE-THING-PLACE verb, why is the location (the container) in subject position and the theme (the contents) in object position? It would be undesirable to invent a one-word, ad hoc linking rule that would supersede the one mapping locations onto prepositional objects, especially since the translations of *contain* in other languages including French, German and Swedish also have the container as subject and also fail to passivize (Carter, 1976b). The solution is that *contain* is represented just like spatial *have* but with the place-function 'in' incorporated into it (it is not important for now which subordinator would embed the structure with the 'in' function under the HAVE structure). Thus *The box contains books* would be near-synonymous with *The box has books in it*; indeed, *The box contains books in it* sounds redundant. The nonpassivizability of *contain* would thus be caused by the same representational structure that makes *lack* and *have* nonpassivizable.[19]

Why does English not have any other verbs conflating spatial *have* with a specific place-function, such as hypothetical verbs meaning "have under it," "have on it," and so on? Carter (1976b) points out an interesting generalization: in two-argument verbs of spatial relations, the argument that by definition must be as large or larger than the other one is the argument that appears in the subject role. For example, if *X covers Y*, *X* must cover an area at least as large as the relevant surface of *Y*. Similarly, he notes, when *X contains Y*, *X* must define a volume at least as large as the volume of *Y*. The generalization is consistent with a broader principle that Carter defends, that the "more important" argument in any relation is linked to the subject role: the agent, if there is one; the possessor, if there is one. This meta-linking rule is easily stated in the current formulation: we could collapse the linking rules for HAVE and ACT by having a single rule refer to the first argument of the predicate-type defined by the feature <+control>; see (5.24). Thus any spatial relation with an argument that by definition is at least as big as its other argument could be expressed with the larger argument as subject, through one of two means: with the larger argument imposing a state via stative ACT, or with the larger argument being the first argument of HAVE.

This turns the question into the following one: Why is only *contain* built around HAVE?

The answer seems to be that only *contain* incorporates a common place-function that entails the notion of "at least as large as" as part of its definition: the place-function 'in'. Generally, a place need not be as large as the theme situated at it. Either an elephant or a mouse can be *at* a phone booth, *against* a phone booth, *on* a phone booth, *near* a phone booth, *under* a (suspended) phone booth, and so on. The notion "at least as large as," if it is to be expressed at all in connection with one of these spatial relations, must be specified by other means, specifically, by coindexing the larger argument with the stative-agent role in a container-oriented locative verb such as *cover*, *fill*, *surround*, *block*, and so on, where it can be interpreted as being responsible for a holistic state predicated of the other (smaller) argument, spelled out in a manner specific to the verb. The one exception among the common place-functions is 'in': the mouse, but not the elephant, can stand *in* the phone booth, because it is part of the very notion of an object's being in the interior of a container that the container be large enough for the object to fit inside. Thus the unadorned and unelaborated meaning of the place-function 'in'—but not of any of the other common place-functions—assigns one of its arguments the role of being "at least as large as" or "more important." This allows the second argument of 'in' to be coindexed with the first argument of HAVE, with nothing more said, and allows it to be mapped onto the subject position of a transitive verb. However, that route to subjecthood is not the one that allows it to passivize, since the ACT structure has been completely bypassed. Another way of putting it is that for no common spatial relation other than 'in' is the location argument compatible with the cognitive content of the first argument of HAVE, namely an abstract "possessor."

Measure verbs. Recall that Jackendoff and Gruber showed that the concepts underlying measure verbs like *cost* and *weigh* can involve a spatial schema in which measurements or amounts function as locations on an abstract scale. It is not completely clear, then, why these verbs are transitive. The Thematic Relations Hypothesis would lead us to expect English to mandate **Moses weighs at 240 pounds* and **Broccoli costs at $1.75 a pound* (which would have made their nonpassivizability unsurprising). For the present purposes, it suffices to note that no ACT structure is mandated for any reason. I will assume for now that there is a conflationary rule in English that allows measure verbs to associate an open argument slot (square brackets) directly with their AMOUNT constituents rather than with the PLACE constituents that serve as their arguments in semantic structure. The representation in (5.70) shows a semantic structure for *weigh*.

(5.70)   weigh:

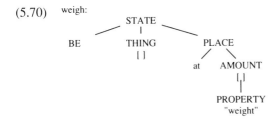

The role of the open argument of measure verbs would thus be formally similar to that of the verb *enter* in the analysis of Jackendoff (1983, 1987a), which has an open argument associated directly with a THING, not with the PLACE that the THING helps define, and that open argument would have to be matched by the linking rule mentioned in connection with (5.8), which links arguments of place- and path-functions with the object role. This predicts *enter* should not passivize when it is used purely spatially, with no component of voluntary locomotion. As discussed in section 4.4.4, this seems to be the case: *The room was entered by a balloon*. Other highly specialized transitive predicative verbs probably submit to a similar analysis, such as *"Cat" is spelled by C, A, T*.

Symmetrical verbs. Supposedly symmetrical verbs seem to subdivide into two classes. Reciprocal verbs, such as *marry* and *meet* (which passivizes only in the sense of "wait for at an airport"), can appear with plural intransitive subjects (*John and Marsha met; John and Marsha married*), and probably call for a special kind of compound structure, also used for sentences with reciprocal anaphors such as *each other*, in which each argument is simultaneously assigned two roles. I will not explore the mechanics of this representation, but it is clear that whatever its form, it will be formally distinct from that assigned to ordinary agent-patient verbs. Verbs like *resemble*, *equal*, and *last* are probably not symmetrical at all, certainly not psychologically (Tversky, 1977; though see also Landau and Gleitman, 1985) and perhaps not linguistically either in the sense of calling for reciprocal structures. Rather, they probably involve BE-THING-PLACE structures, like those of the measure verbs, in an identificational semantic field, with open arguments associated with the THING within an 'at THING' place, for *equal*, or within a 'near THING' place, for *resemble*. (*Last* probably calls for a stative GO-THING-PATH.) In all cases the surface object role is not assigned by the linking role for patients of ACT, because there is no ACT, and thus passivization does not apply.

5.7 Summary

Some of the semantic analyses of verb classes presented in this chapter may have seemed complex and picayune, so it is important to summarize what I hope to have accomplished. I have presented or described explicit representations for about fifty verb subclasses, embracing many hundreds of verbs, using a semantic vocabulary that was independently motivated by syntactic and morphological criteria and fairly constrained given the job that was demanded of it. The vocabulary basically included six kinds of conceptual constituents (EVENT, STATE, THING, PLACE, PATH/CONFIGURATION, MANNER), two binary features defining predicates for kinds of events/states (the <dynamic> and <control> features that define GO, BE, ACT, HAVE), six binary force-dynamic features defining causal subordinating relations (focus, potency, cause-occurrence, effect-occurrence, purposive, and deontic), temporal entities (points and regions), about a half-dozen place-functions (at, in, on, around, over, under, near) and path-functions (to, from, toward, away-from), a dozen or so object properties (human, 2D, flexible, semisolid, and so on) plus a couple of devices—'for/to' and 'such'—for creating properties from states. By defining a variety of semantic fields, this machinery could be applied to widely different domains. Virtually every element of this semantic vocabulary entered into the definition of several subclasses, was motivated by Talmy's cross-cultural survey, and was shown to be be grammaticized into closed-class morphemes or light verbs in English or other languages. And of course every one has cognitive content that plays an essential role in delineating the situations that the individual verbs could be applied in and that support inferences based on the verb's meaning; none of the elements was a formal diacritic snuck in to make an ad hoc syntactic distinction. Furthermore, in most cases it was possible to motivate one representation for a verb or subclass in preference to a number of logically equivalent alternatives (e.g., "BE at" versus "HAVE") using semantic and syntactic judgments as data. I think that the system could be extended to other lexical domains with relatively few increases in the number of representational devices.

Needless to say, the system has many indeterminacies, arbitrary decisions, and areas of vagueness, and I do not claim that it is anything like a formal theory. But working out a semantic system in some detail and applying it to a variety of syntactic constructions was necessary in pursuit of two goals. First, it shows the viability of the hypothesis that a restricted, grammatically relevant subsystem of conceptual representation is sufficient to delineate the boundaries of productivity for the kinds of argument structure alternations that produce Baker's paradox. In particular, the modicum of success attained should defuse any pessimism that no such system could ever be constrained or motivated by evidence. Second, the representations presented in this chapter have brought us to the point where we can discuss learning mechanisms for verbs and lexical rules with a degree of precision than was not possible before. That is the topic of the next chapter.

Chapter 6
Learning

If the account I have presented is true, one aspect of the learnability problem for verbs' argument structures has been solved. Speakers in possession of correct verb definitions, narrow-range lexical rules, and linking rules can generalize beyond the argument structures they have heard in the input and productively extend verbs to new argument structures—"learning" them, in a sense. For speakers at this point in development, there is no longer any paradox. However, there is an aspect of the problem that has not been solved: how do children get to the point at which they possess the right structures for verbs and rules? That is, how do children learn to do the right kind of learning? Without an answer to this question, we do not know whether our resolution of the first paradox has created a second one.

There are several kinds of structures the child must possess: linking rules, conflation class definitions (broad and narrow), broad-range lexical rules, narrow-range lexical rules, and verbs' semantic structures. Of these, the two crucial ones are the lexicosemantic structures and narrow-range lexical rules. If the theory is correct, the subtleties of which verbs are permitted to take which argument structures in a given language, giving rise to Baker's paradox, are localized in these structures, so it is especially important that plausible learning accounts be provided for them.

In learning these structures, the child can arrange them into the hierarchy shown in (6.1) so that acquisition of one structure constrains the acquisition of the ones above and below it.

(6.1) Linking rules

Broad-range conflation classes and rules

Narrow-range conflation classes and rules

Semantic structures for individual verbs

Conceptual structures for particular kinds of events and states

Narrow conflation classes, for example, are generalizations of information from individual verbs. A narrow-range rule maps one narrow conflation class onto another, and each such rule is a specific cases of a broad-range rule. Broad-range rules can be seen as generalizations of sets of narrow-range rules (or of sets of alternating lexical entries) and also can be motivated by running linking rules backward from input sentences. Within this hierarchy of mutually constraining structures, the top and bottom levels have an obvious special status in that they can get the learning started. Linking rules, I will suggest, are essentially innate and don't have to be learned at all. Conceptual structures are formed by the perception of the situations in which verbs are used, providing a set of constraints outside of the linguistic system altogether. Once we understand how these two kinds of structures are established, we can see how they might be used to guide the learning of the remaining structures, including the crucial narrow-range lexical rules.

6.1   Linking Rules

Linking rules probably present us with the easiest case, because, as mentioned in chapter 3, they seem to be near-universal in their essential aspects and therefore may not be learned at all. This is not an attempt to sweep difficult problems under the rug. Linking rules can be universal and innate in the current theory largely because what they do is very simple and circumscribed. Their simplicity is the result of the claim of the theory (indeed, of much of current linguistic theory) that what appear to be complex rules can often be factored into interactions among a set of fairly simple principles in combination with complex lexical entries (e.g., Chomsky, 1981). A linking rule links syntax and semantics. At the syntactic end, the actual spelling out of grammatical functions or argument types into surface syntactic devices is accomplished by lexical entries for prepositions and morphological case markers, and rules or principles pertaining to phrase structure, government, and case assignment. That is, symbols like "SUBJECT" and "external argument" are pointers to information inside these other modules of grammar. At the semantic end of the link, most of the variation among entries as to how they map thematic roles onto syntactic arguments is localized in differences in their semantic structures. For example, the variants in the locative alternation employ the same linking rule for surface objects, but differ in terms of which entity is represented as the patient and theme. The simplicity and generality of linking rules, of course, place a corresponding burden on the learning theory for phrase structure and inflection (see Pinker, 1984, for explicit proposals as to how these are learned) and on the learning theory for semantic structures (discussed in this chapter). But given how this tradeoff offers an elegant way out of Baker's paradox, I think it is the correct tradeoff.

6.1.1 Problems with Using Innate Linking Rules

There are two problems that I must address, however. First, since linking rules are not a bedrock upon which future learning can proceed but a consistency-enforcing link between two kinds of structures each of which must be learned, there is a possibility of vicious circles arising during acquisition. Second, if linking rules are not 100% universal, how do we explain the acquisition of languages that violate them?

6.1.1.1 Can Linking Rules Form Vicious Circles in Acquisition? Linking rules constrain the relation between syntax and semantics, so they could be used to acquire bits of syntax given reliable information about bits of semantics, or could be used to acquire bits of semantics given reliable information about bits of syntax. An example of using linking rules and information about semantics to learn syntax can be found in Pinker (1982, 1984), where I proposed a learning theory for phrase structures and inflections in which the child identifies the subject and object positions in his language by assigning them in such a way that the universal linking rules are rendered true. That is, the child assumes that the subject of an action verb is its agent, and so he or she looks for the phrase that expresses the agent argument of the verb and builds a syntactic structure appropriate to its being the subject. This presupposes, of course, that the child has analyzed the semantic structure of the verb accurately as having an open agent argument. But what if we also need to use linking rules plus correct assumptions about syntax to learn semantics? If variation among argument structures of near-synonymous lexical entries is captured by differences in their semantic structures (e.g., in the forms related by the locative alternation, whether the moving object or the location is assigned as the "patient" and "theme"), the child might have to know the morphosyntactic cues for grammatical functions in the input in order to assign the verb entries their correct semantic structures. For example, the child might have to learn that the location argument of *load the wagon with hay* is the theme and patient by virtue of the fact that it is a surface object (a process I discuss in more detail below). This pair of processes could form a circle: phrase structure and inflections are acquired by applying linking rules from lexical entries, but some lexical entries are supposed to be acquired by applying linking rules backward from independently identified phrase structures or inflections. The worry is not that the child would be perpetually lost in thought because of this circularity, but that he or she might build incorrect but

mutually compatible structures in the syntactic and lexicosemantic components. A stable but incorrect configuration like that is not harmless; it could ruin the complex chains of inference that lead the child to countless subtle details of grammar that we hope to explain (see Grimshaw, 1981, and Pinker, 1984, 1987, for discussion).

Many difficult issues are involved in these interdependencies, but I do not plan to discuss them here (see Bowerman, 1987a; Elliott and Wexler, in press; Grimshaw, 1981; Landau and Gleitman, 1985; Lasnik, in press; Maratsos, 1988b; Morgan, 1986; Pinker, 1982, 1984, 1987). Rather, I just want to show that there need be no vicious circularity in the use of these complementary learning mechanisms. If I can make this basic point, we can concentrate on the problems that are directly involved in the acquisition of argument structures and the full resolution of Baker's paradox.

Logically, the circle can be broken in two ways. Let us first consider the case where the linking rules are valid for at least part of the language. The child could begin his learning in a state at which the circularity does no harm. Let's say parents of very young children restrict themselves to using verbs that can be handled correctly by universal linking rules and lexical semantic structures that are replicas of the child's cognitive representation of the underlying event. For example, the adult would use, among other things, a transitive action verb that the child construes—correctly, as far as the language is concerned—as involving an agent and a patient, and the verb maps them onto subject and direct object, in accord with universal linking rules. Then the child can with impunity assign a syntactic structure to the sentence in which the agent *is* the subject. (A similar situation arises if parents use more problematic constructions, but the child can filter them out by virtue of special intonation, a preponderance of unfamiliar morphemes, special discourse contexts, or other nonsyntactic cues.) If the resulting phrase structures are consolidated into the grammar in phrase structure rules or parameter settings, then later in development, subsequent encounters with new verbs with noncanonical semantics can be handled by restructuring them so as to be consistent with the phrase structure assignments learned in the first phase. See Pinker (1982, 1984) for an extensive discussion of how this would work, and Hochberg and Pinker (1989) for a defense of some of its empirical assumptions.

The second way to break the circle, requiring less stringent assumptions about sequencing in the input or the child's nonsyntactic filters, is to have the child combine a variety of sources of partially predictive evidence in deciding how to structure phrases, of which the satisfaction of universal linking rules would be one. This requires that the child give some weight to a variety of properties of, say, subject phrases that are correlated across languages. For example, subjects tend to precede objects in linear order, tend to occur high in phrase structure trees, tend to have their features encoded into agreement markers on verbs, are coreferential with understood arguments in embedded and conjoined clauses, and may have characteristic prosodic correlates. Though each of these cues is unreliable in isolation, especially in early stages of acquisition when they may be imperfectly analyzed, they may act in a conspiracy that correctly points the child to the subject configuration in input sentences, even in sentences requiring unorthodox verb semantic structures or even nonuniversal versions of linking rules (discussed in more detail in the next section). See Pinker (1987) for a discussion of this possibility and suggestions as to how it might be implemented as a constraint-satisfaction problem in a symbol-passing networklike architecture.

Regardless of which of these proposals is correct in which form, all I need to assume is that *some* mechanism that reliably identifies grammatical functions is in place before the learning of non-cognitively-given verb semantic structures begins. This digression was included simply to make that assumption plausible in the face of the worry that learning mechanisms for syntax and inflectional morphology interacted perniciously with the learning mechanism for argument structure that I outline here.

6.1.1.2 Syntactic Ergativity Another problem arises when we note that linking rules themselves are not completely universal. The most blatant counterexample is the phenomenon of syntactic ergativity (Comrie, 1978; Dixon, 1972; Marantz, 1984; Pye, in press), where patients, not agents, are linked to the subject role, and transitive agents, not patients, are linked to the object role. These languages are rare (not more than 5% of the world's languages, according to Haider, 1987; see also Comrie, 1978; Marantz, 1984), but they do exist, and there may be variation in other linking rules as well. A child could identify cases of syntactic ergativity or other variations in linking rules if he could independently acquire phrase structure and morphology, on the one hand, and lexicosemantic structures, on the other, which the preceding subsection suggests might be possible in enough cases to break any vicious circles. But if linking rules are an unmarked universal, why do syntactically ergative languages exist to begin with? Obviously I will not solve this challenging problem here (as far as I know there are no successful proposals; see Pinker, 1984, and Pye, in press, for discussion) but will offer some remarks that may make the phenomenon something other than a total mystery given the centrality of linking rules within the present framework.

Syntactically ergative languages are also morphologically ergative: objects of transitive verbs and subjects of intransitive verbs get one morphological case marker, the absolutive, and subjects of transitive verbs get another, the ergative. This is in contrast to morphologically accusative languages like English, in which the subjects of transitive and intransitive sentences get one case marker, the nominative, and the objects of transitive sentences get another, the accusative. For example, English uses the same nominative pronoun, *he*, in *He ate apples* and *He ran* and uses an accusative pronoun, *him*, in *Mary saw him*. If English were morphologically ergative, one would say *He ate apples*, *Him ran*, and *Mary saw him*. Many morphologically ergative languages are split, with ergative marking in some parts of the language (persons, tenses, clause types) and accusative marking in others. While all syntactically ergative languages are at least in part morphologically ergative, the converse is not true: many languages use ergative case marking but associate transitive agents with the syntactic properties of subjects and patients with those of objects, as English does.

Intuitively, we can understand the phenomenon of morphological and syntactic ergativity by noticing a basic mapping problem faced by all languages: the four-way thematic distinction among actors, agents, patients, and themes must be reduced to a two-way case distinction between surface subjects and surface objects. In solving this problem, languages seem to be trying to satisfy two constraints on morphological case marking. First, they always give different case markers to transitive agents (first argument of dyadic ACT) and transitive patient/themes (second argument of dyadic ACT, and often coindexed with the first argument of a subordinated effect structure). Since these are the argument types that can simultaneously appear in a single clause and that a listener thus must be able to distinguish, the universality of this case distinction is not surprising. Second, languages usually insist that all intransitive subjects receive the same case marker, whether they are actors, as in unergative intransitives, or themes, as in unaccusative intransitives. (See Comrie, 1978, for cross-linguistic evidence for these two generalizations.) However, languages act as if they have weaker convictions about how to fit the intransitive subjects into the binary contrast used for transitive agents and patients. (They can afford to, because by definition intransitive subjects never have to be discriminated from either transitive subjects or transitive objects within a given clause.) Accusative case-marking systems are impressed by the similarity between intransitive actors (sole argument of monadic ACT in unergatives) and transitive agents, and so they use the same case marker for agents and all intransitives, whereas ergative case-marking systems are impressed by the similarity between intransitive themes (first argument of GO or BE in unaccusatives) and transitive patient/themes, and so they use the same case marker for patients and all intransitives. This is one way of understanding the morphological ergative parameter.

What about the syntactic ergative parameter? Let's say that the child is subject to two biases: a bias to retain the linking rule that maps the first argument of ACT onto subjects, and a bias to keep the case-marking system maximally consistent with the linking rules in terms of how subjects are distinguished from nonsubjects. All children face a conflict between semantics and syntax/morphology for intransitive subjects because they are thematically heterogeneous, comprising themes and actors. The previous paragraph showed how this conflict is resolved in syntactically accusative languages: they retain the unmarked linking rules and bend the case system for intransitive subjects in one or the other direction, toward the transitive subject (for morphologically accusative languages) or the transitive object (for morphologically ergative languages). For syntactically ergative languages, it is the linking rules that are bent. To keep the grammatical functions consistent with the morphological case-marking system, which distinguishes agents from actors, agents cannot also be linked to subjects. So actors and agents are distinguished. Agents are linked to objects, while patients, morphologically identical to intransitive actors and themes, are made to mimic them by also being linked to subjects. (The difference between morphologically and syntactically ergative languages could be signaled to learners at the surface by the nonthematic properties of subjects listed in the preceding subsection, such as controlling understood arguments in embedded and conjoined clauses.) In other words, the child learning a syntactically ergative language does not throw out the unmarked linking rules and adopt a completely incompatible system. The linking rules mapping intransitive actors and themes to surface subjects are retained; the linking rules for the other two kinds of thematic roles, however, are bent to be consistent with the ergative morphology.

Nothing hinges on the details of this rough sketch for the vast majority of languages, which are not syntactically ergative. It is simply one way of showing that for the minority of languages that do not obey the putatively universal linking rules, those rules are partially modified under the influence of an external factor, the morphological case system, not utterly discarded. It would be helpful to the current theory if something like this was true. Linking rules are central to the theory; it would be odd to have to build a mechanism into the child that gave him or her the option of jettisoning them at the outset.

6.2 Lexical Semantic Structures

6.2.1 Event-Category Labeling The simplest possible assumption about how verbs are learned is that verb meanings correspond to concepts given by the child's perceptual and cognitive mechanisms, and that to acquire them, the child simply has to map a sound uttered in the presence of an exemplar of a concept

onto the mental representation of that concept. For some verbs, this is probably correct. Children must carve the flux of unique situations into recurring event types, and it is not unreasonable to expect that among them are ones that can be defined by chunks of semantic structure corresponding to the definitions of some common verbs. Possessing an object, hitting an object, moving, acting on an object causing it to move, acting on an object causing it to go into someone's possession, and so on, are surely concatenations of conceptual elements that the child naturally forms in interacting with the world and generalizing across situations. And presumably parents use verbs like *have, hit, move, put* and *give*, or their equivalents in other languages, in talking to their children. I will assume that the child can link verbs to these conceptual structures upon hearing the verb used in a situation exemplifying that structure. This is a common proposal in developmental psycholinguistics, based on the reasonable assumption that children think about many events in roughly the same way adults do, and in the next chapter I discuss some of the evidence for it. Let me call this process *Event-Category Labeling*.

6.2.2   Semantic Structure Hypothesis Testing

There are, of course, severe limits on how much of the verb lexicon the child can learn by Event-Category Labeling. Different languages conflate sets of semantic elements into verb meanings in different ways, and a single language often has words that cross-classify events, such as *pour* and *fill* in English.

The ambiguity of what a verb means in a single situation, however, is eliminated by the behavior of the verb *across* situations. Though a given instance of filling a cup may be ambiguous between pouring and filling, *pour* but not *fill* will eventually be used when water is put in a glass up to the halfway mark, and *fill* but not *pour* will eventually be used when a glass is left on a windowsill in a rainstorm long enough to make it full. Thus for a learner with the right kind of memory across situations, there exists information in the nonlinguistic input relevant to distinguishing verb meanings.

How could such learning work? In the previous chapter I noted that the grammatically relevant parts of verb meanings bear a close resemblance to the semantic feature structure of closed-class morphemes. Clearly, Event-Category Labeling will not allow a child to learn the meaning of *-ing* or *-en*, and in Pinker (1982, 1984) I presented a theory of how such meanings are acquired. The basic logic of that learning mechanism can be extended to the acquisition of verb meanings, as I suggested in Pinker (1984, p. 180). The mechanism is a version of simple hypothesis testing. Consider the target in the learning of an inflection, namely, a list of features (e.g., [−singular] [+definite]). The features are drawn from a finite universal set of possible grammaticizable features. Each one has a conceptual or perceptual correlate: the child can determine, for example, whether the referent of a noun in a particular context is singular or plural, human or nonhuman. When attempting to learn a given inflection from its use in a given utterance, the child samples a subset of features with their currently true values from the universal pool. If a previously hypothesized feature value for that inflection is contradicted by the current situation, that feature value is permanently stricken from the list of hypotheses for that morpheme. For example, if the child heard the morpheme used with a human referent in a sentence and so falsely added [+human] to the morpheme's entry, that feature would be expunged the first time the inflection is used in reference to a nonhuman. As the child continues to work on that morpheme over a large set of sentences, all incorrect hypotheses will be discarded at some point or another, any correct hypothesis will be hypothesized sooner or later (assuming every feature in the universal finite set has a nonzero probability of being hypothesized), and only the correct ones will survive in the limit.[1]

This mechanism can easily be extended to the acquisition of verb meanings that do not correspond exactly to the child's preexisting event categories. What we need to show is that the child is capable of entertaining as a hypothesis any possible verb meaning, and that he or she is capable of eliminating any incorrect hypotheses as a result of observing how the verb is used across situations. Here we begin to reap the benefits of the system for verb meanings outlined in chapter 5. First, the representational scheme is constrained, as any source of hypotheses in a learning system must be. Place-functions can be encoded explicitly, for example, but the speaker's mood, the ambient temperature, or the rate of motion cannot be. Causal relations between an act and a motion can be coded explicitly, but the relation whereby one event reminds the speaker of another cannot be. Furthermore, if the tentative constraints I proposed in chapter 5 on the embedding of subordinate causal events and property-defining operators are true, then the semantic formalism defines a finite class of grammatically distinguishable verb representations. Thus the child need not encode arbitrarily long causal chains in a verb's grammatically visible semantic representation; in fact, he or she need not entertain more than a single effect of a given kind nor causal chains longer than three links. Of course, verbs are open-class morphemes, so for most of them parts of their semantic structures are not tightly constrained and are drawn from an essentially unlimited pool, such as "butterlike" in the verb to *butter*. But even these bits of information are allowed only as the values for certain allowable slots, like MANNER or PROPERTY, introduced as dependents of other structures that play determinate roles such as acts, themes, or locations (Clark and Clark, 1978).[2] As for eliminating the parts of hypothesized structures that are incorrect, one need only note that the structures all have conceptual content, and it is possible to test whether a specific structure is currently instantiated in a concrete context in which the verb is used.

Let's say the child can mentally represent, on one occasion or across various occasions, a variety of the semantic relations typically associated with the usage of a verb, using structures of the form presented in the preceding chapter. Most of these structures will be irrelevant to the meaning of the particular verb, but some subset will be the correct verb meaning. For example, for the transitive verb *fill*, the child could encode a semantic structure representing the presence of an agent-patient relation, the manner in which the agent causes the liquid to move, the fact that the moving thing is a liquid, the manner in which the liquid moves, the shape of the container, the end state of the container (full), the goal of the agent (e.g., to move the full container), and so on. Basically, these hypotheses are parts of the child's maximal possible conceptual representation of a given instance of an event involving filling. If the child retains this representation over a number of instances in which transitive *fill* is used, adding structures to it as he notices various new potentially grammatically relevant details and permanently erasing structures that are contradicted by the current situation (e.g., the shape of the container, the manner of causation of motion, the liquidity of the substance), eventually an accurate representation will survive. Let me call these processes *Semantic Structure Hypothesis Testing.*

This process, though it is capable, given the right assumptions, of accounting for the acquisition of verb meaning in a brute-force way, is plausible only to the extent that the child can converge on the correct configuration of semantic structures reasonably quickly. The child must not spend decades refuting silly hypotheses about a verb meaning (such as that *see* selects a semisolid object, or that *splash* selects a goal thing that is meant to be taken away) while waiting for his mental dice to fall in such a way as to cause him to posit the correct structures. There are several sources of "practical constraints" on the child's hypotheses. I call them "practical" constraints since they act to reduce the size of configurations of semantic structure and to increase the likelihood of their being correct, as opposed to the "representational" constraints discussed in chapter 5, which dictate the form and content of possible semantic structures.

First, there may be helpful aspects of the simple event-labeling process just discussed. Surely children assemble combinations of semantic-conceptual structures not at random but rather in such a way as to define cohesive scenarios or types of events over which cognitive generalizations can be made. Although I have been emphasizing that we cannot count on children homing in on just the categories that are lexically encoded in their target language, it is also true that the various assemblies of elements that constitute their event categories are unlikely to be bizarrely off the mark. Any degree of overlap, of course, is useful in reducing learning time. Let me refer to these tendencies as the child's *semantic biases*; I will discuss them at length in the chapter on development.

Second, discourse contexts, especially contrastive ones, can often narrow the options. For example, any situation in which an adult insists that a glass be full by using the verb *fill* could give the child the idea that the state of being full is a component of the definition of *fill*. We know that such factors can be relevant in the learning of adjectives. Carey and Bartlett (1978), for example, showed that a casual contrastive request to a child—"Give me the chromium one, not the red one"—inspired many children not only to retain the word, but to know that it was a color word in particular. Third, there is an important principle that Clark (1987) calls the Principle of Contrast: virtually no two words have the same meaning. Clark shows, moreover, that there is good evidence that the child adheres to such a principle in establishing the meanings of existing verbs and in coining new ones. The child therefore should not consider a hypothesis for a verb meaning that is identical to the semantic structure of some other verb. Since the basic structures formed out of the simple combinations of semantic elements will be used up quickly by light verbs such as *be, have, go, do, make, put, give, take,* and *get*, the child will be forced to hypothesize additional semantic elements (manners, means, object properties, and so on) for other verbs.

6.2.3   Syntactic Cueing of Semantic Structures

There is another source of constraints on the child's hypotheses that cannot be exploited in full at the very outset of language acquisition, unlike the processes discussed so far, but can kick in once some grammatical structure is in place. Because of the possibilities for circularity, though, it is important to distinguish the various kinds of inferences that could be made, and evaluate them separately.

When a child hears a verb used in a sentence, the child is receiving direct evidence about the verb's argument structure. The clause will contain overt phrases in argument positions in a sentence (i.e., in positions other than those used for topics, appositives, modifiers, complementizers, and so on). If such phrase positions can be recognized (see section 6.1), the child can record a syntactic argument structure for the verb directly from the input. This is simply itemwise conservative learning, and it was the primary learning procedure for argument structures in the theory of Pinker (1984), where it was called "L1: Direct Learning from Positive Evidence." However, it cannot be adopted intact in the current version of the theory, because argument structures are projections of verbs' semantic structures. If an argument structure is picked up from the input directly and accurately, the verb's semantic structure must either already be consistent with it or be altered to make it consistent via the application of linking rules in a backward direction.

It would be circular to say in this section that the child learned verb meanings from argument structures while in the rest of the book I have been claiming that argument structures are projected from verb meanings, but this circularity is only apparent. Strictly speaking, it arises only if the child is using semantic structures to deduce argument structures and vice versa *for the same verb entry.* Since the entire lexicon is not acquired in one step, syntactic information can be used in varying degrees of specificity at various interim stages of the learning process.

Using the presence of arguments. The most basic strategy is for the child to note which of the semantic arguments of a predicate were reflected in the conservatively learned argument structure and to define open argument slots in the semantic structures of the relevant predicates. This would be necessary to avoid violating general principles such as the Theta-Criterion or Bresnan's Coherence principle and would be subject to other important constraints. Given Jackendoff's (1983) Lexical Variable Principle (see section 5.5.2), the child will know that each of these open arguments must correspond to a complete conceptual constituent like a THING or a PATH, not an arbitrary subassembly of semantic structure. Furthermore, the basic architecture of the representational system for lexical semantics and syntax assumed here and in most of linguistics rules out a variety of logically possible influences of arguments on the rest of verbs' semantic structures; some of these will be discussed in section 8.2.

Using linking rules and the grammatical functions of arguments. More specifically, the child could apply universal linking rules in a backward direction. For example, a semantically indeterminate NP in object position of a transitive phrase would suggest an open "patient" argument slot (second argument of ACT) in the predicate's semantic structure. Some form of this learning seems to be mandated by my treatment of verbs undergoing certain alternations (e.g., the passive and locative), as it is doubtful that the child would inevitably assign the NP in object position to a patient role on the basis of the cognitive content of "patient" alone. Once made, this kind of assignment is not merely notational, however. For one thing, interpretive effects (such as directness) automatically apply. Furthermore, since ACT-THING-THING structures are the host for two-way MANNERs, 'means', and 'effect' specifications that pertain to the dyadic interaction between the agent and the argument treated as patient, which otherwise would have no structure to attach themselves to, the recognition of a transitive argument structure could trigger the hypothesizing of candidate values for these potential slots, especially if the verb would otherwise be synonymous with an existing verb. In addition, the child would list some specification of a semantic field in which an antagonist-agonist relation could be given cognitive content. For example, upon hearing a sentence such as *She covered the bed with a blanket,* a child who recognized that *the bed* was in direct-object position would have to create an open argument slot for it in the entry for *cover* as a second argument of ACT. If the child knew (through Event-Category Labeling or Hypothesis Testing) that a state change of the bed was part of the structure, its place in semantic structure would have to be as an embedded 'effect' substructure of this ACT. Similarly, if the child had done a sufficiently complete syntactic analysis to know that *a blanket* was an oblique object, he or she would have to make room for it in the semantic structure, in some position other than patient or theme. The conceptually driven procedures could tell the child that a 'means' substructure is one possible place. Prepositional phrases whose prepositions are semantically transparent because of their use in other contexts (e.g., *the ball on the table*) could inspire more specific substructures in the form of places, paths, or other configurations encoded by prepositions. This would be how verbs with semi-idiosyncratic selections of prepositions would receive the right semantic structures.

Using conflation classes. All of this can take place close to the beginning of language learning, in principle. However, since the effects of linking rules in a given language are mediated by the conflations of semantic elements found in its semantic structures, it would be better if this reverse linking procedure was done in two steps. First, linking rules are used in the reverse direction to help acquire conflation classes (a process I will describe in some detail in the next section). Second, the conflation classes, once acquired, are used more directly to drive the learning of semantic structures for particular lexical entries. Recall that conflation classes are incomplete semantic structures that define a class of possible verb meanings in a language. A child in possession of a conflation class that (through linking rules) defines an argument structure corresponding to the one that a current verb is used in could then hypothesize structures that are included in the conflation class but lacking in the current verb. For example, a child with the English conflation class for GO-THING-PATH-MANNER verbs could hear a verb in a sentence like *The ball glipped into the room* and guess that the current manner of motion of the ball is encoded into the meaning of *glip*. Although there may be more than one conflation class that matches the syntactic argument structure of a given unknown verb (for example, ACT-THING-PATH-MANNER for verbs like *run* and *walk*, GO-THING-PATH for *move*, GO-THING-PROPERTY for *turn*, *change*, and *shrink*), semantic structure hypothesis testing and conformity to the Principle of Contrast will rule out spurious applications of existing conflation classes.

Here we are beginning to flirt with circularity, because imposing conformity to conflation classes, unlike running linking rules backward or adding slots for arguments in argument phrase positions, depends on prior learning which itself presupposes the acquisition of correct semantic structures. This circularity need not be vicious: the child could learn some verbs' semantic structures via Hypothesis Testing or Event-Category Labeling, peel conflation class definitions off them, and use those classes to guide the learning of the meanings of future verbs sharing their argument structures. The potential viciousness is in the child's hypothesizing an incorrect semantic structure for a given verb, deriving a conflation class from it, and using the conflation class to hypothesize incorrect verb meanings for a host of syntactically similar verbs, propagating the damage through the lexicon. For example, a Spanish child who thought that *entrar* (to enter) meant "to float along some path," because he first heard it in reference to a balloon floating into a room, could create the incorrect conflation class GO-THING-PATH-MANNER and apply it to *subir* (to go up), *bajar* (to go down), and so on, tacking on whatever manner of motion was fortuitously demonstrated by the theme on the occasion of its use. However, the presence of the semantic structure hypothesis-testing mechanism to inactivate incorrect guesses imposes a strong brake on the potential runaway circularity, as the example suggests. Surely no child in his right mind would continue to think that *bajar* meant "to skip" after hearing it used in connection with a variety of events, all of them involving something going down, and most of them not involving skipping!

Hypothesis testing must, for this reason, be the final arbiter in the acquisition of verb meaning; an inspector that would prune out any branch of a semantic structure that did not stand up to a confrontation with the conceptual world. Syntax-guided learning, especially as it exploits conflation classes or other learned structures, would play a different role: as a guide to the formation of likely hypothesis structures, and as a strong influence on the form of these hypotheses, preselecting semantic structures that are structurally consistent with the syntax from among the various candidates that are roughly equivalent in conceptual content.

Using sets of argument structures associated with a stem. An even more specific form of syntax-guided learning of verb meaning has been suggested by Barbara Landau and Lila Gleitman (1985). They point out that the acquisition of verb meanings is surprisingly robust. Their congenitally blind subject learned the meanings of nonphysical verbs like *see* and *look* with surprising ease, despite many areas of possible indeterminacy in (what I call) Event-Category Labeling and Hypothesis-Testing. They also note that sighted children's access to evidence about word meaning is different in degree but not in kind. Therefore they suggest that children rely on a particularly rich form of syntactic cueing of verb meaning. This kind of inference, which they later call "Syntactic Bootstrapping," has the child examining an *entire set* of verb entries sharing the same stem, and using them to narrow down the meaning components that are shared by all of them. They write (pp. 138–139):

In essence our position will be that the *set* of syntactic formats for a verb provides crucial cues to the verb meanings just because these formats are abstract surface relexes of the meanings. ... there is very little information in any single syntactic format that is attested for some verb, for that format serves many distinct uses. However ... the *set* of subcategorization frames associated with a verb is highly informative about the meaning it conveys. In fact, since the surface forms are the carriers of critical semantic information, the construal of verbs is partly indeterminant without the subcategorization information. Hence, in the end, a successful learning procedure for verb meaning must recruit information from inspection of the many grammatical formats in which each verb participates.

They give an example of how a child might learn the meaning of *see* using nothing but linguistic input. The stem *see*, unlike *touch*, takes sentential complements, suggesting that it is a cognitive/perceptual verb. It takes directional phrases (e.g., *to see from the room*), suggesting that it has an abstract motion component. But in comparison with *look*, it does not appear in the imperative, showing that it is stative. Nor does it appear in the pseudo-cleft *What John did was see Bill* or with purposive *to* adjuncts, which shows that it is nonagentive. Taken together, these inferences strongly constrain what the verb *see* could mean.

This is an interesting hypothesis. Within the present framework, it would correspond to the child's use of lexical rules and linking rules not only in their linguistic functions of predicting the existence or form of verb argument structures, or as simple cues in semantic learning helping to mold, prune, and select from among conceptually driven semantic structures for a given verb entry. Rather, lexical rules and linking rules would be used with sets of related verb entries as a major source of semantic structures.

Syntactic bootstrapping does not necessarily form a circle with the use of lexical rules and linking rules in grammatical productivity. Lexical rules are used productively to create new, nonwitnessed argument structures for a verb. Syntactic bootstrapping is used exactly when grammatical productivity is unnecessary: when the child has already heard a verb form in all of the basic argument structures that the language allows it to appear in.

Though Landau and Gleitman and I agree that the learning of verb meanings uses both syntactic and contextual information, we differ somewhat in perspective, as they strongly emphasize the role of syntactic cues, and I will argue that its role is highly circumscribed and that it works in a somewhat different way from the way they describe it. I will give reasons to doubt that it can play a foundational role in the acquisition of verb meanings, as their label "Syntactic Bootstrapping" would suggest; rather, it is parasitic on the prior acquisition of verb meaning by the kinds of mechanisms I have proposed. Second, I will show that the mechanism does not really involve the use of a linguistic mapping run backward, but rather a form of nonlinguistic cognitive inference. Thus it uses some of the same cognitive faculties as Event-Category Labeling and Semantic Structure Hypothesis Testing, and cannot be assumed to be more reliable by virtue of exploiting formal linguistic rules.

Landau and Gleitman assume that their mechanism exploits grammatically reliable syntax-semantics correlations of the sort that I have been discussing throughout this book, running them backward to go from argument structure to lexical semantics: "much of the [semantic] information can be read off from the subcategorization frames themselves by a general scheme for interpreting these semantically" (p. 142). The kind of verb meaning they are interested in is the common component of meaning shared by a given morphological stem across all of its related argument structures; they explicitly note that a single verb argument structure does not provide enough information to identify the meaning of that verb. (That is because there is an enormous reduction of information in going from a verb's semantic structure to the argument structure it shares with related verbs in the same subclass—any information that differentiates the verb from semantically related ones is lost—and an even further reduction when one goes to the syntactic argument structure type in and of itself, because several different subclasses can be mapped onto the same argument structure.) However, strictly speaking, these two assumptions—inferring meaning from argument structures through reverse linking, and simultaneously examining an entire set of argument structures sharing a stem—are mutually incompatible.

A central finding of the research I presented in chapters 3 and 4 is that when a given stem is used in two argument structures, we are seeing two distinct semantic structures (as, for example, the locative alternation makes especially clear). Certain semantic components will be shared across the two versions of the verb, and some will differ. Crucially, the components of meaning that are reliably predictable from a given argument structure are the components that are *not* shared across the different forms of a given verb, but the ones that are shared by many *different* verbs appearing in that argument structure. For example, the appearance of an *into* phrase in *The ball floated into the cave* must *not* be used as evidence that *float* has something to do with moving into or even with moving; a ball can float without moving anywhere. The form of *float* that co-occurs with *into* indeed does imply movement into (just as it implies that for *roll into*, *bounce into*, and so on), but that is predictable from the meaning of *into* itself; it does not tell the child what the stem *float* itself means across its different argument structures. This is why Landau and Gleitman eschew inferences based on single argument structures. But the problem of running linking regularities backward to derive semantic structures does not disappear as one examines more and more argument structures; it only gets worse. Each additional argument structure simply adds its own characteristic semantic component that is not necessarily shared by that verb in any of its other argument structures. For example, *She sewed me a shirt* reliably indicates an intended transfer of possession; *She sewed a shirt out of the remnants* suggests that an act of creation has taken place; *She sewed a pocket onto the shirt* suggests an accomplishment of attachment; *She sewed the shirt* indicates mere affecting; *She sewed* shows mere activity (see B. Levin, 1985). Though in each case we learn something about the meaning that a verb assumes in a particular argument structure, we learn nothing directly *from the language* about what it is that all of these structures share that makes them all examples of *sewing*. In general, the more argument structures for a given verb one simultaneously examines, the fewer grammatically predictable meaning components are going to remain across the set. Rather, in the limit one is left with exactly the component of meaning that is *not at all* predictable from argument structure information—the nugget of idiosyncratic meaning that is associated with a sound in the brute-force, arbitrary listing in the lexicon that every meaningful morpheme must submit to somewhere or other.

Nonetheless, there is usable information in the set, of two kinds. First, the kernel of meaning arbitrarily associated with a morpheme across all its argument structures has some cognitive content, and that content is *inferentially* related to the different meaning components of the argument structures that the verb appears in. Thus the child could do a kind of cognitive problem solving, using as premises the different semantic components that are reliably predicted by working backward from the different argument structures a verb appears in. Imagine solving the following riddle: "What activity performed on an object, potentially attaching it to something, can result in the creation of a new object, possibly for the purpose of giving it to some beneficiary?" (Answer: sewing.) Or: "What state, involving a kind of nonagentive, inalienable motion in a direction, can result in the apprehension of some proposition?" (Answer: seeing.) It would certainly be fascinating if children engage in this kind of riddle-solving, and I have no particular reason to believe that they do or don't. (Note, though, that this procedure would be useful only for verbs that appear in a variety of argument structures, hence provide many clues in the riddle; for verbs like *die* or *devour*, which basically appear in a single structure, it is hard to see how significant semantic deductions could be made from syntactic premises.) But the crucial point is that it *is* a variety of cognitive problem solving; it cannot be accomplished by using existing linguistic contingencies and directly following the arrows backward.

There is another, more specifically linguistic kind of information that is that the child could use as well. I have been emphasizing the fact that the truly productive, narrow-range lexical rules are highly constrained by complexes of semantic information defining narrow classes of verbs. For example, in English, motion verbs that alternate between intransitive and causative transitive forms cannot specify a constant direction but may specify a manner of motion; verbs of communication appearing in both versions of the dative alternation cannot pertain to a manner of speaking but can pertain to the kind of illocutionary force of the message. Once these narrow-range rules have been mastered, the child could use them in a backward direction to predict the range-delineating meaning components for verbs that have been witnessed in the two relevant argument structures. (For reasons discussed above, though, this process cannot in general be carried backward through successive pairs of argument structures: *sew* dativizes because it signifies creation in the transitive form that feeds the narrow-range dative rule, but it is only that transitive form that involves creation, not *sew* in general.) However, as Landau and Gleitman point out, these kinds of conflations of semantic information are highly specific to a given class of verbs in a given language (unlike linking rules and broad-range lexical rules, which apply across the language and are versions of universal regularities). Mastery of these narrow-range rules to learn these meaning components presupposes that the highly detailed structures of the rules have themselves been correctly learned. But it is impossible to show how they were learned without assuming that the precise meanings of at least some of the verbs undergoing the narrow-range alternation have been learned independently—where else would the language-particular, somewhat eccentric class definitions for the narrow-range rules come from? The precise meanings for at least *some* of those verbs must have been acquired without the use of the narrow-range rules (or else we would be courting a truly vicious circularity). Thus syntactic information of this sort cannot be a "major evidentiary source for the discovery of verb meaning" (p. 136) or something that is "required for verb learning" (p. 154), because it *presupposes* that precise verb meanings can be acquired by a completely different mechanism. It is that *other* mechanism that is *required*.

Neither of these reservations is meant to eliminate a role for semantic inferences based on sets of independently learned argument structures, which Landau and Gleitman (1985) defend in a rich and insightful discussion (in which they also point out the need for learning based on situational information). I am only suggesting that if their mechanism is used at all, it is used either as a sophisticated form of cognitive problem solving rather than a general interpretive linguistic scheme, or that it is used as an adjunct to some other learning mechanism for verb meaning that it must presuppose.

6.3 Broad Conflation Classes (Thematic Cores) and Broad-Range Lexical Rules

A thematic core is a semantic structure that is part of the meanings of an entire set of semantically related words (a broad conflation class) that are mapped onto a given argument structure by a given set of linking rules. A broad-range lexical rule defines a possible way of sharing a morpheme between two of these thematic cores whose open arguments can be put into a rough conceptual correspondence; formally it consists of a set of semantic operations mapping an input thematic core onto an output thematic core and a set of morphological operations mapping the stem of the input onto the stem of the output (which would be null for most broad-range rules in English). From the learner's point of view, then, thematic cores and broad-range rules are constrained from two directions. Since they involve a set of arguments that are expressed in syntactic argument structures, they must be consistent with linking rules or else one of the thematic cores involved in the rule would have no way of expressing its arguments in syntax. In fact, a broad-range class or rule by definition is not cluttered by details such as complex paths or properties of things; its semantic structure is composed of nothing but those pieces that are immediately linked to the grammatical functions in the argument structure. Second, they must be consistent with the semantic structures of the set of words taking the relevant argument structure.

Constraining broad conflation classes using syntactic information. Imagine the following kind of procedure for deriving a broad-range conflation class definition, say, for the dative. The child identifies a syntactic argument structure and then applies any applicable linking rules backward from the listed grammatical functions. For the prepositional form, this would give the child an ACT structure with open agent and patient slots, and if the preposition *to* had been identified (through its participation in a variety of structures), a 'to' path. According to the formalism for lexicosemantic structures presented in chapter 5, paths require GO structures, so such a structure would also be created; since semantic structures in the present formulation are single-rooted and connected graphs, it would have to be integrated with the ACT structure. GO structures can be embedded in ACT structures but not vice versa, given the available machinery, so the embedding would be effected, using an underspecified causal link.

For the double-object structure, an analogous sequence of operations would be performed, resulting in a distinct skeletal thematic core for it. An ACT structure would be created for the first two arguments. According to the linking rule for second objects, the second object must be the first argument of an embedded HAVE, linked to the second argument of the matrix ACT, and that is the structure the child will build. Let me call this procedure *Conflation Class Skeleton-Building Through Reverse Linking.*[3]

Multiple candidate skeletons will usually have to be built, because several kinds of semantic structure can be linked to a given set of grammatical functions. For example, a transitive surface structure could correspond to an ACT, a HAVE, a GO (e.g., *enter*), or a BE (e.g., *weigh*). Furthermore, some pieces of information that are needed to flesh each skeleton out into a cohesive and complete semantic structure are left unspecified at this stage. In the current example involving the dative, this includes the semantic field and the features labeling the causal subordinating link between the ACT and the embedded GO.

Completing broad conflation classes by abstracting over lexical entries. These degrees of freedom can now be eliminated by examining the words that the language actually contains. Imagine that the argument structure for the thematic core being built indexes all the lexical entries of verbs associated with tokens of that argument structure. Information resolving the ambiguities left open by reverse linking—semantic field specifications, EVENT/STATE constituent labels, GO/BE/ACT/HAVE predicate labels in some cases, labels for subordinating links or place- or path-functions when an independently acquired preposition does not specify them, and enough coreferencing links to yield the right number of open arguments—is examined in these entries. Any piece of information of this sort left unspecified in the skeleton that is shared by all the verbs in the lexicon that are built around that kind of skeleton is extracted from those verbs and added to the skeleton. If each of two incompatible candidate skeletons corresponds to a set of verbs, both are filled in and retained; if a candidate skeleton has no verbs corresponding to it, it is discarded. For the prepositional-dative thematic core, an examination of the prepositional-dative lexical entries would basically add the information that the GO structure would be embedded via an 'effect' link, and a coreference link joining the patient of the ACT and the theme of the GO. Any other putative piece of information in the candidate skeleton, such as a semantic field specific to location or possession, would be canceled out, as not all verbs built around the ACT-GO structure would share it (for example, *give* as in *give the house to Mary* is possessional, not locational, whereas *lower* in *lower the box to the floor* is locational, not possessional). Information that might be fortuitously shared by many of the entries in an immature lexicon but not necessary for fleshing out a complete semantic structure around the skeleton, such as, perhaps, all themes being inanimate, would not be placed in the thematic core. Call this procedure *Conflation Class Completion Through Lexical Abstraction.*

Jill Gaulding (1988) and Marc Light (1988) have pointed out to me that there are computational advantages to examining the arguments in a particular order in applying the Skeleton Building procedure, and in intertwining the application of Skeleton Building and Lexical Abstraction rather than running one completely and then running the other. Since there are dependencies among types of structure, resolving a local ambiguity in one part of the structure can prune the possibilities for what the rest of the structure could be. Thus if the lexicon was checked every time there is an indeterminacy in a node label, that could spare one from having to build a variety of possible expansions of the structure that would later prove useless. For example, checking the lexical entries with prepositional dative forms would show that there is a GO event embedded as an 'effect' under the ACT. That means that the oblique argument can be linked to a PATH; the possibility that it might be a PLACE instead need not be kept alive. In fact, the use of top-down linking information and bottom-up lexical information may be so closely intertwined that putting them in separate computational algorithms is probably a convenient fiction; they are better viewed as providing sets of constraints that must be simultaneously satisfied.

Why is Reverse Linking even needed, given the potential power of Lexical Abstraction alone? If all we had to account for was the acquisition of a single language by a single generation of learners, the need would be less evident. Since broad-range classes and lexical rules are form-predicting, not existence-predicting, rules, speakers could get by on a day-to-day basis with the narrow-range class definitions and rules. What Reverse Linking does is make it difficult to learn a language in which the class of verbs possessing a given argument structure or undergoing a given alternation is "too narrow" or "too broad." On the one hand, they militate against a language that might possess, say, only a single narrow class corresponding to an argument structure. The highly specific bits of information associated with individual verbs would not be directly attached to the pieces of semantic skeleton that the linking rules mention and that Reverse Linking could establish. Therefore a speaker forming classes with the aid of Reverse Linking would be required to keep such classes broad and would be disposed to creating—and as we shall see, easily learning—verbs in a *variety* of narrow-range classes all of which fall within the broad-range class. On the other hand, Reverse Linking also militates against a language that has a totally heterogeneous set of verbs with a given argument structure or undergoing a given alternation, licensing free generalizations from alternating pairs to any verb with the same number and kind of surface arguments. That language would be ruled out because no semantic structure could embrace all of the verbs. In sum, Reverse Linking is the learning-theoretic instantiation—in one sense, the explanation—of the generalization that the individual narrow-range classes and rules of a language that share an argument structure also share a thematic core and are defined not by arbitrary conditions but by conditions motivated by that thematic core. That is, languages do not contain, presumably because learners do not like to learn, an argument structure restricted to a single idiosyncratic narrow class of verbs, or an argument structure paired with a totally heterogeneous and arbitrary set of narrow classes.

In the actual course of language acquisition, Reverse Linking would be useful in helping the child avoid overly narrow or vacuously broad classes, because temptations to form such classes surely arise. Sets of lexical entries in a learner's lexicon at any given time are liable to have a variety of accidental incorrect substructures (such as 'for/to' and object properties) that are orthogonal to the possibilities for extending the argument structure in the language and should not stand in the way of future generalizations of these argument structures. Similarly, we shall see in the next section that they help in establishing the boundaries of the narrow-range classes and rules. Furthermore, Reverse Linking is necessary to help the child cope with "syntactic syncretisms" in which a given set of surface arguments embraces two large classes each of which is semantically cohesive but which have little or nothing in common with one another. The unergative and unaccusative intransitives in English, if the child cannot distinguish them by purely syntactic analyses, are an example. The Lexical Abstraction procedure has no way of recognizing such a major split to posit two thematic cores, rather than positing a single degenerate one comprising the null intersection of the spuriously collapsed superclass. However, Reverse Linking would begin the process by formulating two candidates for thematic cores, because two different sets of linking rules could be applied in reverse to an intransitive surface structure: "actor —> subject," and "theme —> subject." (In GB, the latter linking rule would be "theme —> direct internal argument"; we would have to assume that the child always sought to undo the possible effects of "move α" before applying linking rules backward.) The fact that two linking rules could be run backward from the argument structure would inspire distinct candidate skeletons consisting of one-argument ACT and GO structures, respectively. Any lexicon that contained distinct unergative and unaccusative verbs would supply ample evidence that both such cores should be retained.

Broad-range lexical rules. Formation of a lexical rule would be triggered by the existence of a set of independently acquired verbs sharing the same root but differing in argument structures, each of which is associated with some thematic core. Entries with a given root don't necessarily come in pairs but in sets (e.g., *sew, sew the shirt, the shirt was sewed, sew the pocket onto the shirt, sew him a shirt*, etc.). Presumably the child does not coin all possible $[n(n-1)]/2$ pairwise rules but sorts the set into the pairs that are likely to related by individual rules. The members of each pair would be matched up because their semantic structures were minimally different, in that one could be turned into the other by the fewest number of component operations on semantic structure. For example, the criterion of minimal semantic change would juxtapose, for example, *sew* with *sew a shirt* as needing a rule, and *sew a shirt* with *sew him a shirt*, but not *sew* with *sew him a shirt*. In addition, for rules involving morphological alterations, input and output forms could be paired up on the basis of their stems being minimally different, in that one could be turned into the other with the fewest number of possible morphological operations.

A broad-range rule would be coined in the following way. When stems differ, a morphological operation deriving one stem from the other would be posited. (I will not consider the mechanism that accomplishes this, nor the one that recognizes the morphological relatedness between the sets of word pairs to begin with. See Pinker, 1984, chap. 5, and Pinker and Prince, 1988, for discussion.) A set of operations capable of deriving one thematic core from another (the addition, suppression, embedding, and reassigning component operations on semantic structure discussed in section 5.6) would be set up as the semantic operation of the rule. Let me call the procedure *Broad-Range Lexical Rule Formation*. It is analogous to the procedure in Pinker (1984) that coins lexical rules, L3, but very different in its product and mechanism, because the old procedure coined operations altering argument structures directly, raising Baker's paradox and requiring the puzzling subprocedure that appended semantic criteria onto the coined rule. Thus there is a sense in which the general nature of the Broad-Range Lexical Rule Formation procedure is the key insight in the current theory regarding Baker's paradox.

6.4   Narrow Conflation Classes and Narrow–Range Lexical Rules

Narrow conflation classes define very specific kinds of possible words in a language, based on a structural analogy to existing words. Narrow-range lexical rules map one narrow conflation class onto another, allowing a verb in the second to be created on the basis of the existence of a verb in the first. Recall that narrow-range lexical rules are the only existence-predicting rules for nonaffixing alternations. Narrow conflation classes by themselves cannot be existence-predicting, because they leave the speaker without the means to pronounce a word he has created in such a way that his addressees could understand him. Broad-range rules lacking an affix in fact are not existence-predicting, perhaps because the semantic operation they consist of is too broad to guarantee that the resulting semantic structure for the new verb is conceptually coherent in an arbitrary context. As such, it is the narrow-range rules that bear the burden of delineating the precise sets of linguistic judgments that give rise to Baker's paradox.

Recognizing that a set of narrow-range rules must be created before productive generalizations can be made is straightforward; the child need only determine that the broad-range semantic change is not correlated with the presence of an affixing operation. But acquiring the exact semantic operations of narrow-range rules is a surprisingly difficult learnability problem. Let me first consider two approaches that do not work.

6.4.1 Why Lexical Abstraction Doesn't Work

It is easy to see that Lexical Abstraction—which is basically a version of traditional category formation, applied to lexical semantic structures—is logically incapable of creating the narrow conflation classes that define narrow-range rules. Consider just these two problems.

First, the distinction between a feature that is *specified in different ways* across the exemplars of a subclass, and a feature that is *not specified at all* across the exemplars of a class, is crucial. Upon hearing *He shouted that John left; She murmured that she was in love; They screamed that they needed help*; and so on, the child should not conclude that because there is no consistent manner specified, the definition of the class appearing with sentential complements says nothing about manner. Rather, the child should conclude that each of the verbs must specify *some* manner, *any* manner, so that he or she could exclude *tell*. That is, meaning components must be *parameterized* (e.g., MANNER = X), not discarded, in forming class definitions from verb definitions.

Second, the child cannot simply look for the most inclusive definition that encompasses all the verbs sharing an argument structure. The reason is that this would at best result in a broad-range class, which is too coarse, rather than a narrow-range class. The simplest definition that would fit with all the dativizable verbs (e.g., the *tell* verbs and the *throw* verbs) would have to mention no more than that the verbs involved causation of abstract change of possession. But this would include the nondativizable *scream*-type and *pull*-type verbs as well, bringing back Baker's paradox. At the level of existence-predicting rules, the child must be impelled to hypothesize a set of small and moderately complex classes rather than a single large and simple class.

6.4.2 Clustering Algorithms and Classwise Indirect Negative Evidence: Would They Work?

What could impel the child to hypothesize anything other than a simple, broad class? It is instructive to consider possibilities that are capable of working even on logical grounds. One possibility is that any overly broad class will falsely predict that many verbs should appear in the child's lexicon in (say) the double-object form, verbs that in fact are not listed in the double-object form because they have never been heard in the double-object form in the input. That is, the problem with "cause a change of possession" as a definition for dativizable verbs is that it falsely predicts that the double-object form for verbs like *shout* and *pull* should be lying around in the child's lexicon. The child could detect that a partition of his or her lexicon into finer-grained classes (distinguishing possession of ideas from possession of objects, specified from unspecified manners, and ballistic from accompanied motion) can account in an economical way not only for the verbs that are known to dativize but for the verbs that are not known to dativize. First, the nondativized verbs are excluded by a sufficiently narrow class. Second, they themselves could be succinctly defined with a set of their own narrow, but not broad, subclasses. Such a procedure would, in effect, use a form of indirect negative evidence defined over possible narrow classes of verbs rather than over individual verbs. This information would be noisy, of course, because many of the nonobserved entries are actually dativizable and were not witnessed in the double-object form simply because the parent did not get around to using them in the presence of the child.

The way this would work is that the learner would examine the set of verbs occurring in one of the argument structures of a broad-range rule, attempt a variety of partitions of this set using subclass definitions of a variety of sizes, and choose the size that maximally predicts the distribution between witnessed and nonwitnessed forms, while not favoring such a fine class size that there were hundreds of subclasses each spanning one or two words and making productivity impossible. Thus the procedure would try to jointly maximize the simplicity of the class definitions and minimize the inclusion of nonwitnessed verbs. This might be done by having the procedure choose the partition scheme with the greatest product of some accuracy index and some simplicity index. In principle, such intermediate-sized classes could lead to conservatism, if the classes were gerrymandered so as to include all and only the witnessed alternating forms, spuriously excluding the nonwitnessed alternating as well as the nonwitnessed nonalternating forms. However, if there were specific enough constraints on possible class definitions (such as those outlined in chapter 5), this could not happen. That is, the verbs that happen not to have been heard to alternate should be a haphazard sample of the real alternating class, and so there should not be any available hypotheses composed of the notions of manner, path, causality, and so on, that would fortuitously rule them out exactly while ruling in the observed alternators.

Despite the conjecture entertained in Pinker (1989) that this multiple partitioning scheme might provide a discovery procedure for narrow conflation classes,

I now think that it is basically on the wrong track. The problem of how to partition a set of objects, each with a description in terms of feature values, into a set of categories that optimizes some criterion or criteria is well known in Artificial Intelligence research, where it is called "conceptual clustering" (e.g., Michalski and Stepp, 1983; Bobick, 1987). An inherent problem in clustering algorithms is that the number of possible partitions of a set of objects into classes grows explosively with the size of the set and can become computationally intractable even with fairly small sets. Within AI, much of the research in developing these algorithms consists of various ways of pruning the sets of classes to evaluate. In the absence of any hint as to how the child would find the right kinds of candidate class partitionings to begin with, clustering cannot seriously be offered as a possible solution to the learning problem here. Perhaps the problem could be solved, but one would not want to posit a complex ad hoc pruning algorithm just for this task, as it is not the kind of task that the child has any strong need for. The existence of narrow-range classes and rules should be the by-product of some device built to meet other desiderata. They do not pose a major ecological problem that nature has evolved complex special machinery to solve.

Furthermore, the more closely one examines the subclasses that the child must delineate, the less likely it seems that any statistical criterion would favor a correct partitioning drawn from a large set of possible ones and evaluated over the partial lexicon that the child would have acquired at any given point. An inherent property of clustering based on classwise indirect negative evidence is that it requires classes of nonalternating verbs that are large enough to convince the procedure that they really do reflect underlying systematic exceptions rather than accidentally nonwitnessed alternators. The problem is that some of the nonalternating subclasses are fairly small. For example, English does not have many intransitive inherently directed motion verbs (e.g., *come, go, rise, fall*), all of which are noncausativizable, but it does possess a large number of verbs involving motion in general (including manner-of-motion verbs). Verbs of circular arrangement of 1D flexible objects (*wind, coil*, etc.), which are nonlocativizable, number about half a dozen, while verbs that involve caused motion of a nonrigid thing to goal object would be at least three times as numerous. There are a tiny handful of verbs of choosing (nondativizable), but dozens of verbs involving potential benefactive acts. Recall that the subclass definitions that the child must satisfy himself with have to be able to tolerate a fair proportion of no-shows assumed to be temporary gaps corresponding to legitimate alternating verbs. The result is that a variety of overly broad candidate class definitions could easily be accepted that ride roughshod over pockets of nondativizable verbs, which would mistakenly be treated as temporary gaps.[4]

6.4.3 Parameterization of Idiosyncratic Lexical Information

6.4.3.1 Key Facts About Narrow Classes and Rules There are a few key features of narrow classes, as described in the preceding chapter, that provide important clues about the nature of the process that acquires them:

1. Classes can be defined by properties that are obligatorily specified, though specified to a different value in each of the member verbs (e.g., some direction or some manner).

2. The classes can be very, very specific, sometimes specifying individual path-functions, place-functions, or object geometries. In fact, a class definition can specify almost as much information as any of its member verbs; sometimes the class definition is identical to its verb definitions up to specification of idiosyncratic manners (e.g., smearing versus streaking) or object properties (e.g., studs versus spots).

3. Class membership can be arbitrarily small. One locative subclass, as far as I know, is exhausted by the verbs *load, pack*, and *stock*. *Wrap* and *string* may each be a one-word subclass.

4. The semantic properties shared by all the members of a subclass are the "grammatically relevant" ones, that is, the ones that are widespread cross-linguistically, that may be expressed in closed-class morphemes, and so on—for example, the existence of a specific direction of motion, or solid versus liquid, but not the existence of a specific rate of motion, or square versus round, or pertaining to medicine.

5. Classes are rarely if ever delineated by differences in a single semantic substructure. Rather, two classes that differ in syntactic privileges will usually have semantic structures that differ from one another in several ways.

The last point can be illustrated by the *throw* class (dativizable), the *pull* class (nondativizable), and the *bring/take* class (dativizable), which are closest to being minimally contrasting among the classes I have examined. In fact, they differ from one another in several aspects: *throw* verbs differ from *pull* verbs in being achievements rather than activities, and also in specifying that the act precedes the motion in time; the *pull* verbs differ from *bring/take* in that the latter specify no manner, do specify a direction, and require the agent and theme to move together. Similarly, *tell* verbs (dativizable) differ from *shout* verbs (non-dativizable) in lacking a manner of speaking *and* in specifying a 'for/to' property of the communicated message.

6.4.3.2 A Strong Hypothesis for Narrow-Range Rule Formation The simplest learning procedure for narrow conflation classes, then, would be the following. Take a semantic structure for a verb. Replace each idiosyncratic piece of information—any manner, any object property not in the distinguished set in (5.13)—with a parameter. The resulting class then embraces all verbs with the identical semantic structure up to the idiosyncratic, nonlinguistic information, which is free to vary across the members of the class as long as it is specified in some way. This could be represented by a variable or parameter sitting in the same place as the quoted constant in the semantic structure of the original verb. Call this *Narrow Conflation Class Formation by Parameterization of Idiosyncratic Lexical Information*. The effect of possessing such a class would be to equip the speaker with the knowledge that an item sharing the grammatically relevant information of an existing verb, but differing in a manner or idiosyncratic object property, is a possible verb in the language. The speaker would be in a state where he or she could coin just such a verb, or understand such a coinage by others, while still being aware that such verbs *are* new coinages.

A narrow-range *rule* would then be an operation that takes an existing verb form in a narrow class and creates a complete morphological and semantic specification for a new form, perceived as a full-blooded existing member of the language. Upon noticing that a pair of individual verbs are morphologically and semantically related in a way captured by a nonaffixing broad-range rule, the learner would create a rule whose semantic operations mapped the narrow conflation class specification for one onto the narrow conflation class specification of the other. In other words, the generalization that the learner would make would be: if verb *X* alternates, other verbs with the same grammatically relevant semantic structure alternate, too.

The reference to a broad-range rule ensures that completely isolated and accidental alternations exhibited by a single verb are not made into productive narrow-range rules. For example, the alternation *blame the accident on John / blame John for the accident* is unique to the verb *blame* (*pin the accident on John / *pin John for the accident; *criticize the accident on John / criticize John for the accident*). Likewise the verb *rip off* is unique among the possession-deprivation verbs in alternating between loot-object and victim-object forms (*rip off / steal / seize / *rob / *cheat money; rip off / *steal / *seize / rob / cheat John*). Since broad-range rules are formed by abstraction over sets of verbs displaying the same alternation, a single alternating verb will not lead to the creation of a broad-range rule, hence not of a narrow-range rule either. This is simply an example of the insight that narrow-range rules are representations of the actual existence of a possible regularity stated in a broad-range rule. Whether type frequency of exemplification (that is, the number of distinct word pairs that lead to the creation of the same narrow-range rule) should play a role in determining the "strength" of the narrow-range rule directly is an open question. Given the arbitrary size of the domains of narrow-range rules, I suspect its role is relatively minor; perhaps the qualitative distinction between being exemplified by one pair and being exemplified by more than one pair is sufficient.

6.4.3.3   Learning the Variable Ranges of Rules by Focusing on the Changing Arguments   Simply copying lexical semantic structures of alternating verbs, with substitution of variables for idiosyncratic constants, is in fact a bit too stringent. It would make every narrow-range rule equally narrow, basically a near-replica of a single alternating verb admitting only of minor variants of that verb. The classes that undergo causativization and middle formation, for example, appear to be broader than the classes that undergo locativization, and we would not expect that children would have to learn the possibility of *This salt pours easily* in a separate inductive leap from the one that allows *This paint sprays easily*. Furthermore, the narrow classes respected by the various rules can cross-classify one another, as we saw in examining transitive action verbs in section 4.2.

These differences are probably related to the scope of the semantic operation involved in the different rules. The semantic structure carried over from a verb entry to the corresponding narrow-range rule is the structure that is closely associated with the arguments that are altered by the rule. Middle formation affects agent and patient/theme arguments; any other arguments are carried over intact from one structure to another. Causativization, too, affects only the theme or actor argument of the intransitive form. Locativization, however, assigns new semantic roles to the patient/theme and to the location arguments. In the lexical entries, the theme argument is often restricted to having certain geometric or material properties, and the location argument is specified by specific path- and place-functions. Therefore locativization has to look at the entire semantic tree of the verb (recall that the patient is defined in the ACT structure, the theme in the embedded effect-GO substructure, and the location in the further embedded PATH substructure).

These differences in the scope of the argument rearrangements for the different rules may predict the thickness of the narrow-range slices that the rules apply freely to. The fact that the locative rule must process the entire structure of the input verb may explain why the entire grammatically relevant structure of any verb heard to enter into the locative alternation is preserved in the creation of a (very) narrow-range rule. An additional factor that leads the locative to accumulate highly specific context terms in its narrow-range variants is the requirement that some informational source for the creation of a new property in the *with* form be provided. Typically the state is defined by a 'such' or 'for/to' operator in which a copy of the MANNER from the *into/onto* form resides, and as a result the existence-predicting rule requires such information to be stated explicitly, rendering it narrow in range.[5]

The anticausative and middle, in contrast, affect only the agent and the patient/ theme, in ACT and effect-GO structures respectively, leaving any internal constituent of a PATH substructure unaltered, so only the parts of a semantic structure immediately attached to the ACT and GO structure are relevant. The geometric and material properties of moved objects and the place- and path-functions they are moved to or situated at would be defined in embedded layers of structure, so the generalizations of individual middle and anticausative verb forms to narrow-range existence-predicting middle and anticausative rules would be blind to them. Rather, the delineations among their subclasses would be defined in terms of the bits of information surrounding the ACT and GO structures, such as the presence of a state change in a GO subordinated to ACT, the absence of a means structure appended to the ACT, or the presence of a path (though not its internal composition).

Thus the narrow-range rule formation procedure can step back a bit from the entirety of the structure of a single verb heard to alternate, and does not have to copy every twig of their semantic trees. Rather, I propose that narrow-range rules contain the nodes in semantic structure that are either (a) dominated by the same nodes as the open arguments that get remapped by the broad-range lexical rule, or (b) coindexed with such open arguments.[6] The internal structure of more deeply embedded substructures, such as the material/geometric properties of themes of verbs undergoing causativization, would be parameterized by a single symbol that would embrace the entire substructure, whatever its contents. Let me call this process *Narrow-Range Rule Formation by Preservation of Argument-Relevant Parameterized Lexicosemantic Structure*. The logic is similar to that of having broad-range rules built around structures surrounding the alternating open arguments: lexical rules are just those alterations of semantic structure that are involved in causing alterations of argument structures (except that in the case of narrow-range rules, a much richer configuration of information surrounding the changing arguments is preserved). The preservation of only the information that is associated with the remapped arguments is a mechanical implementation of one aspect of the principle that narrow-range rules are "motivated" by the nature of the semantic change captured in the broad-range rule.

There are several theoretical advantages to this theory of the learning of narrow-range classes and rules. First, since narrow-range rules are built from individual alternating verbs, the complexity of the rules is a direct reflection of the complexity of the information needed to know what a verb means. We need not be offended by the positing of some process dedicated to the painstaking construction of intricate class definitions, resulting in narrow-range rules of limited usefulness; narrow rule definitions are just verb definitions, which have to be acquired anyway, generalized a minimal amount. Second, the variable size of the classes is an immediate consequence, not a problem as it would be for a statistically driven procedure: every alternating verb creates its own micro-rule, and any verb sufficiently similar to it (according to the metric implicit in the representation of lexicosemantic structure) is automatically included in the rule. The differences in size among the subclasses included by a rule are epiphenomena of the number of words in the language that happen to be built around a given semantic structure. (The existence of narrow conflation classes to pave particular paths for new coinages is what encourages families of structurally similar words to arise in the first place.) Third, the multiple redundant semantic differences between semantically similar narrow classes that are and are not covered by a rule would be a consequence of principles governing how word meanings are spread out to cover a multidimensional semantic space. Talmy (1983) suggests that sets of word meanings, in effect, tend to be "noncoplanar" in semantic space, corresponding to points that differ in several dimensions at once.

Finally, if what I have been proposing is true, the narrowness of the linguistic generalizations allowed in this domain is not only comprehensible, it is almost inevitable. Grammar is exactly as conservative as it can be, but no more conservative. A grammar can "see" the difference between smearing and pouring, or between shouting and telling, or between going and sliding, or between coating and containing, because all of these distinctions can be stated in terms of the privileged semantic vocabulary that is available to it. Hence if it is designed to be conservative, generalizations between these classes are impossible. However, a grammar cannot "see" the difference between smearing and smudging, between shouting and whispering, between sliding and rolling, or between coating and covering. Hence it is powerless to allow one of these verbs to alternate while preventing the other from doing so; as far as the grammar is concerned, they are indistinguishable.

Let me call this strong hypothesis *Color-Blind Conservatism*: the grammar is basically conservative but cannot see most cognitive distinctions, of which the real-world color of arguments' referents is perhaps the most paradigmatic. If sustainable, it would provide a very satisfying explanation as to why existence-predicting rules are narrowly constrained in the way that they are. Furthermore, Color-Blind Conservatism itself need not be stipulated as an independent restriction. It is an immediate consequence of three principles: (1) conservatism;

(2) grammatically relevant semantic subvocabulary; (3) independence of the principles of morphology from the actual listing of items in the lexicon (see di Sciullo and Williams, 1987). Without this third principle, grammars could be even more conservative, restricting existence to those individual items that have been witnessed in particular argument structures, resulting in the strict itemwise conservatism that was rejected in chapter 1. The reason that languages are *not* that conservative may be that they *can't* be that conservative. That is, lexical rules can't differentiate verbs down to the level of which ones are listed with their idiosyncratic properties. Color-Blind Conservatism, if true, would provide strong support for di Sciullo and Williams's complete separation of listedness and morphological (lexical) rules. I will return to this issue in section 8.5.

6.4.3.4   Other Ways of Preventing the Rules from Being Too Narrow   The effects of Color-Blind Conservatism probably need to be weakened somewhat. Consider the discussions of the representations of sets of verbs belonging to a given subclass that were presented in chapter 5. Ideally, verbs in a class would have identical semantic structures except for idiosyncratic information about manners, properties, states, and so on. But if the classes are of the size I suggested in the preceding chapter, this is not exactly right. While it is true that there is no blocking of productivity based on verbs that differ only in idiosyncratic information, it may not be true that there is inevitably a blocking of productivity based on verbs that differ in grammatically relevant semantic information.   For example, *sell* and *pay*, I suggested, belong to the same class as *give*, but these verbs specify the obligation of a countertransfer, easily statable in the privileged vocabulary, and in an object property (money) that would be parameterized. *Hand* incorporates information about the means of transfer, a kind of information that is not specified by *give*, *sell*, and other putative classmates. Verbs within the classes of obtaining and creation have a variety of instruments, manners, obligated countertransfers, means, and other information associated with them (compare, for example, *buy*, *get*, and *steal*; or *make*, *bake*, *build*, and *sew*). Similarly, in the *spray* and *smear* classes, some verbs seem to specify manners for the causation of motion (e.g., *dab*, *inject*), some for the motion itself (*smear*, *splash*). In causativization, *move* is semantically similar to *roll*, *bounce*, and so on (one-argument GO events without a lexically specified path), presumably explaining why they all happily causativize, but *move* is indifferent as to manner, whereas the others specify one.   Several other examples can be found by reviewing the discussions in the previous chapter of how verbs within a subclass can differ from one another. How can Color-Blind Conservatism be reconciled with the existence of this potentially generalization-blocking detail?

1. *Living with even narrower classes.* There may be a simple solution. Perhaps I have sliced some of the subclasses too thickly. Perhaps *sell, pay,* and *trade* actually belong to their own subclass. The psychological consequence would be that learners would not be able to generalize automatically from the dativizability of *give* to the dativizability of *sell*; they would have to hear *sell* in both forms (though they could then generalize, presumably, from *sell* to *pay* and *trade*). Why, then, would the dativizability of verbs like *sell* intuitively seem so inevitable given the dativizability of *give*? Recall that at the same time as the narrow-range rules are allowing full-fledged generalizations between essentially identically represented verbs, there are broad-range rules for dativization would make the extension of dativization to less similar verbs possible, though they would not be accompanied by intuitions of complete naturalness. Perhaps, then, the broad-range rule makes coinage of many double-object verbs by a speaker extremely likely. They will be perceived, by both speaker and listener, as a bit strange on the first occurrence, like Haigspeak, but as completely comprehensible and as "possible" expressions. Once a learner hears it, he or she will store the item conservatively, and extend the alternation it exemplifies automatically to other verbs sharing its narrow argument-relevant semantic structure. Every child would thus go through the experience of first hearing dativized *sell* as a new form, even if the *give* class had been mastered. Since many of the alternating verbs that have complex semantic structures are high in frequency, and since in the next chapter we will see that children early on acquire a heterogeneous collection of alternating verbs conservatively, the individual conservative mastery of verbs with even minor structural differences may not be too far-fetched. This is simply an empirical issue for which we lack sufficient data.

2. *Ignoring a single semantic difference.* It is possible, too, that some items that do not match a narrow-range rule down to every node are not necessarily excluded. Some kinds of deviation may be considered minor enough that the verbs are basically treated as belonging to a narrow alternating class even though they have some noticeable semantic difference from the definition of the class. I have not discussed the matching function that determines whether a verb is a member of a narrow class, assuming that is simply an exact match up to constants' being substituted for variables, but it may be a bit more flexible than that. First of all, since no two classes differ by a single semantic structure, a match metric that allowed a verb to enjoy the privileges of a class if it matched it exactly *except for one difference* (an object property, a means substructure, an extra coindexing, a difference in whether a manner is attached to an ACT or to a GO) would in fact not do any damage: no nonalternators would be spuriously included, on account of the "scattering" of narrow conflation classes through

multidimensional semantic space. Extending the ophthalmological metaphor, we could refer to the formation of narrow-range rules as being both color-blind and tunnel-visioned, since only information associated with changing arguments is examined, and the matching function as being a bit myopic, ignoring small differences in fine semantic detail.

3. *Ignoring certain kinds of semantic differences.* The matching process may actually be a bit more constrained than that. Some kinds of semantic structure seem more important, on the whole, in drawing boundaries between narrow subclasses than others. Major aspectual differences (e.g., state versus event, accomplishment versus achievement), event type differences (ACT versus GO versus HAVE), major semantic fields (e.g., possessional versus locational), and properties of objects that appear in different positions in the old and new structures (e.g., in a MANNER versus a PROPERTY defined by 'such') all seem to be crucial in blocking productivity.[7] However, a number of semantic structures that can be grammatically relevant in some circumstances may not inevitably be fatal to a verb being considered for admission to some narrow-range rule. Examples are the existence of an object type that is not cross-referenced elsewhere in semantic structure (e.g., the specification of theme types, such as food for *feed* or money for *pay* as opposed to no specification at all for *hand* or *give*); a single isolated goal ('for/to') or a means substructure that does not change role in the alternation; or a temporal ordering of two events that are of the same aspectual type in the verb and the narrow-range rule. If you will allow me to push the metaphor, the matching process would be more astigmatic than merely myopic: it would make finer distinctions along some dimensions than along others.

Thus we have a plausible minor relaxation of Color-Blind Conservatism: a single difference in grammatically relevant structure, or perhaps even multiple differences in the less essential kinds of structure, may result in the natural extension of a narrow-range rule to a verb that does not match its definition exactly. Conceivably, there may also be a continuum of relative acceptability among verbs that fail even this slightly relaxed condition (but obey the broad-range rule), so that the less a verb deviates from an existing narrow-range rule, the less cringing it induces among speakers, and the more likely it is to be added to the language as the basis for its own legitimate narrow class.

In sum, a narrow-range rule is formed by taking the semantic structure of an alternating verb, pruning information that is distant in the tree from the open arguments that alternate, and substituting variables for grammatically idiosyncratic constants. In addition, the set of verbs that can alternate might be expanded somewhat beyond this extremely narrow class by a matching metric that can tolerate small amounts of "minor" structural deviation.

6.5 Summary of Learning Mechanisms

Let me summarize the learning mechanisms I have invoked in this chapter for the structures that play a role in the theory.

Linking rules are not learned at all. Syntactically ergative languages, which constitute the principal exception to the universality of the major linking regularities, are rare, and they may require an adjustment of the linking rules— making the ACT-subject rule pertain only to the argument of monadic ACT, not to the argument of dyadic ACT, so as to maintain consistency with the morphological case system—rather than an abandoning of them.

Lexicosemantic structures are hypothesized by *Event-Category Labeling* under the influence of practical constraints coming from the child's semantic biases, attention to the discourse context, and the Principle of Contrast. The arrangement and composition of these hypothesis structures is influenced by grammatical rules (to the extent that they are known) at several possible levels of specificity by *Syntactic Cueing*: open arguments are posited for each grammatical function in argument structure, reverse linking can constrain the possible roles of those open arguments, and conflation class definitions can fill out characteristic configurations of semantic elements with even greater specificity and accuracy once they are learned. (Possibly, cognitive inferences based on entire sets of related argument structures and their associated linking rules, or so-called *syntactic bootstrapping*, plays a role as well.)

Broad Conflation Classes, defined by the thematic core of the meanings of a set of similar verbs sharing an argument structure, are created as a structure jointly consistent with the universal semantic concomitants of that kind of argument structure, via *Skeleton Building Through Reverse Linking*, and a set of independently acquired lexical entries, via *Conflation Class Completion Through Lexical Abstraction*.

Broad-Range Rule Formation maps one broad-range class onto another by positing a set of basic operations on semantic structure capable of effecting the change and, when possible, by associating them with a morphological operation capable of relating the two words.

Narrow Conflation Classes are created by *Parameterization of Idiosyncratic Lexical Information* (color-blindness) in individual lexical entries belonging to a broad class.

Narrow-Range Rules are formed by *Preservation of Argument-Relevant Parameterized Lexicosemantic Structures*, and the function matching them against individual verbs tolerates mismatches involving small discrepancies in certain kinds of structures.

Chapter 7
Development

Baker's paradox is the simultaneous incompatibility of three assumptions: that learners receive no negative evidence, that the set of verbs that undergo a given rule is arbitrary, and that children use the rules productively. The theory I have outlined was propelled by evidence that the assumptions of no negative evidence and of childhood productivity are true and that therefore the assumption of arbitrariness must be false. Now that I have given some reasons to believe that lexical argument structure alternations are not arbitrary, it is necessary to return to the claim that children are productive, not conservative, users of lexical rules. It is crucial to see whether children use rules in the way that the grammatical and learning theories say they should.

Why is it so crucial? The theory presented in Pinker (1984) and Mazurkewich and White (1984) held that children coin lexical rules that map among syntactic argument structures and then append semantic and morphological conditions to them. This motivated a developmental prediction that children would first use the rules with no semantic constraints. In the theory I have been arguing for here, there is no such thing as a lexical rule mapping from argument structure to argument structure directly, free of semantic considerations; rules inherently involve operations on lexicosemantic structure. Therefore it would be puzzling if children went through a stage in which they formulated rules of fundamentally the wrong type, that is, rules consisting of a direct mapping between one argument structure and another. The prediction that children should not pass through such a stage is thus an important empirical test distinguishing the two theories, buttressing the prior arguments that the new theory wins on grounds of motivation and linguistic accuracy.

Second, if children do create argument structures with an overly broad rule, perhaps a semantically neutral one, it raises the question of how they attain the adult state in which the rules are suitably narrowed and the incorrect entries are expunged. A chief motivation for the new theory is that it seemed implausible that children would be equipped with a mechanism that did nothing but complicate their rules and restrict their expressive power. Given that children's errors do seem to decrease with time, is there a more plausible explanation for why this happens? It is important that some solution to this "unlearning problem" be provided that is consistent with the new theory. If children overgeneralize in a way not predicted by the theory and somehow recover, they would present us with a new version of Baker's paradox.

Finally, the theory predicts very specific interactions between verbs' semantic structures and their argument structures. Children do not know verbs' meanings perfectly when they start to talk. Therefore, changes in children's argument structures should parallel changes in their knowledge of verbs' meanings in some precise ways. Evidence that this occurs would offer strong support for the basic assumption that argument structures are projections of lexicosemantic structures.

7.1   Developmental Sequence for Argument Structure Alternations

Let me begin by reviewing the course of development of argument structure alternations in children. The general pattern is fairly uniform across children and across constructions.

7.1.1   Early Conservative Usage Preceding Onset of Errors

Children first use both of the argument structures involved in an alternation, usually with a relatively small set of verbs and with no evidence of productivity. This is consistent with the assumption that the rule formation process discussed in chapter 6 is triggered by the presence in the lexicon of several verbs with pairs of argument structures, learned conservatively.

Causative. This pattern was first documented for causative verbs by Bowerman (1974, 1982a). The children she studied most intensively, Christy and Eva, used transitive and intransitive verbs correctly for "several months" before the first occurrence of creative causative constructions. Christy, for example, used the words *open, close, break, wet, dry, spill, hurt*, and *pop* in both transitive and intransitive (verb or adjective) phrases by the time she began to overgeneralize the causative relation at age 2;0. Maratsos et al. (1987) report a similar lag in the speech of the senior author's daughter, who used grammatical intransitives and transitives beginning at 1;11 but productive ones beginning only at 2;6.

Locative. Bowerman (1982b) notes a similar pattern in the acquisition of locative forms. Both her daughters correctly used verbs whose objects were locational themes (e.g., *put, pour, spill*) and locational goals (e.g., *touch, cover, hit, bump*) before the age of 2;0. In fact, the two kinds of verbs emerged in each child's speech within weeks of each other (Bowerman, in press). Overextension of the locative alternation in forms like *I'm going to touch it* (her hand) *on your pants* and *Mommy, I poured you. ... Yeah, with water* did not begin until around the third birthday and become frequent only after the fourth.

Passive. In our study of the development of the passive (Pinker, Lebeaux, and Frost, 1987) we found that the first productive passives always came in later than the first nonproductive ones in the spontaneous speech of the three children we examined. Adam uttered his first passive at 3;0 and his first productive passive at 3;3; Eve uttered her first passives at 1;7 and had failed to utter any productive passives by 2;3; Sarah uttered her first passives at 2;5 and her first productive passives at 3;3. It is difficult to tell, or course, to what extent this delayed onset is a sampling artifact stemming from the relative infrequency of productive passives.

Dative. Jess Gropen, Michelle Hollander, and I have examined the development of double-object datives and prepositional datives in the spontaneous speech of Adam, Eve, Sarah, Ross, and Mark (Gropen et al., 1989). The pattern of conservative use of both versions of the alternation with a few verbs, followed by productive extension to new verbs, appeared again. Adam's first overgeneralization of the double-object form occurred at the age of 4;1 (see 1.16 of chapter 1). Before that time, he had used in dative constructions the dativizable verbs shown in (7.1), starting at the ages listed.

(7.1)

	Double-object	Prepositional
bring	3;1	
build		4;0
buy	3;3	4;0
cook		3;2
draw	3;4	
drill		4;0
get	2;4	3;2
give	2;3	2;8
hand	2;6	
leave		3;8
make	3;5	3;0
read	4;2	3;2
send		3;3
show	3;0	2;11
sing	3;0	
tell	3;0	
throw		3;0

Eve's productive use of *write* (meaning *draw*) in double-object constructions at age 2;3 followed her use of the dativizable verbs shown in (7.2), beginning at the ages listed.

(7.2)

	Double-object	Prepositional
bring	1;10	2;3
buy		2;0
find		2;2
get	2;0	2;0
give	1;9	2;2
make		2;2
read	1;8	2;0
show	1;9	

We found no productive double-object forms from Sarah by age 5;1, though many conventional datives of each type were produced by then. The two stages are not clearly demarcated for Ross and Mark, though each boy used some grammatical dative forms before the first appearance of a recognizably productive form. Ross incorrectly used *say* in the double-object form at 2;8; his preceding transcripts show *give* (2;7) being used in the double-object form and *buy* (2;8) being used in the prepositional form. Mark's overextensions of the dative occurred at 3;8 and 4;0; before that he had used the double-object form of *take* at 3;7 and *pour* at 3;8 and the prepositional-dative form of *give* at 3;5.

The sequences for the acquisition of the causative and the locative as studied by Bowerman tend to show larger and more consistent lags between the onset of conventional forms and the onset of overgeneralization than the sequences for the acquisition of the passive and the dative (for Ross and Mark) as studied by my colleagues and me. Since there is no systematic grammatical difference uniting the constructions she studied and differentiating them from ours, the quantitative discrepancy is probably due to the difference in methodology, with her continuous diary data being more sensitive to differences in onset than our biweekly or monthly samples of two hours of speech (or less) apiece.

A salient aspect of the development of dative and locative forms is that neither version of either alternation consistently emerges first. In Pinker (1984) I noted that contrary to a widespread assumption, the prepositional dative does not precede the double-object form in children's spontaneous speech.[1] The first double-object forms of alternating verbs appear before the first prepositional forms for Adam and Eve; they appear in the opposite order for Mark; they appear within a month of each other for Sarah and Ross. The same pattern occurs when we look at individual verbs: of the 28 cases where a child used a verb in both forms, the double-object version came first 16 times, the prepositional object version came first 9 times, and both appeared simultaneously 3 times (each child showed one acquisition order for some verbs, another for other verbs). Furthermore, 22 potentially alternating verbs were used only in the double-object form, and 24 were used only in the prepositional form.

Bowerman (in press) found essentially the same simultaneity in the first appearances of the two versions of *give*, *buy*, and *bring* in Christy's speech. As mentioned, she also found that *put* and *spill*, on the one hand, and *cover*, on the other, which differ in whether the syntactic object corresponds to a locational theme or to a locational goal, emerge within weeks of each other. A related finding is that in simple transitive verbs, there is no consistent acquisition order governing the appearance of verbs whose subjects are themes and whose postverbal arguments are locations or goals, and verbs whose subjects are possessors and whose objects are possessed entities. In Christy's transcripts, *Baby fall down Daddy shirt* and *Toy stay home* appear in the same week as *Cow have ice*, *Daddy have cake*, and *I get spoon*; *BM coming birdie fanny* appears within the same two weeks as *I lost other blanket*. In Eva's transcripts, *Necklace stay purse* appears in the same week as *Ernie got spoon* and *I got necklace*. Given these four examples of simultaneous emergence of verb forms with contrasting mappings between thematic roles and syntactic positions (dative alternation, locative verbs, possessional transitive, locative transitive), Bowerman argues that children in this stage make their lexical entries conform to the argument structures displayed in the input. They show no proclivity to link postverbal arguments with themes as opposed to goals or possessors, or to link subjects with themes rather than with possessors when there is no agent.

Bowerman actually makes a stronger claim: that children do not use innate linking rules at all at any age; the linking rules they use at later ages (see Pinker, 1984) are learned from the input. However, this conclusion is too strong for two reasons. First, as Bowerman herself pointed out in an earlier paper (Bowerman, 1978), the earliest usages of verbs in this age range are often quite restricted, concrete, or context-bound. The more schematized verb meanings that play a role in linguistic generalizations are only in evidence several months after the first usages (see section 7.5.1.3). Thus there is at least a possibility that some of these very early uses may reflect not the lexicosemantic structures and argument structures that theories of linking rules apply to, but some kind of preliminary, relatively unanalyzed placeholder for a word that is given a more abstract and structured semantic representation only later. But there is a more important problem, one that applies regardless of the psycholinguistic status of the first usages. The predictions of acquisition order that Bowerman's data disconfirm are not consequences of innate linking rules in general, but of one theory of linking rules that is probably not viable anyway. Specifically, Bowerman's claim rests on the prediction that only one of the two versions of dative, locative, and location/possession verbs can be generated by linking rules. This is based on the Fillmore theory of thematic roles and linking regularities discussed in chapter 3. However, under the Jackendoff/Rappaport/Levin conception that I have adopted and extended, both versions of the dative and both versions of the locative are consistent with linking rules, since in both versions the patient/theme is linked to syntactic object. Similarly, both possessor-subject and theme-subject verbs are consistent with linking rules, one applying to HAVE states, the other to BE states. In fact, a central tenet of the theory is that all verbs should be consistent with linking rules. Thus the lack of consistent asymmetry in acquisition order for verbs exploiting different sets of the available linking rules is exactly what the theory predicts.

7.1.2 Overapplication of Argument Structure Alternations

In chapter 2 I claimed that at some point children cease being conservative learners of argument structures but apply rules productively. What is the logic behind this conclusion? Any time children use a form that is grammatical in adult English, they could in principle have acquired the form conservatively from the input, so non-English forms of various sorts must be sought as evidence. There are three ways of doing this.

First, experiments can be run in which children are taught novel verbs in one argument structure and given the opportunity to use them in new argument structures. This was the approach of Pinker, Lebeaux, and Frost (1987), Gropen et al. (1989), Gropen et al. (in preparation; see Gropen, 1989), and Gropen, Pinker, and Roeper (in preparation).

Second, one could look for cases where children create a verb that is semantically or morphologically ill formed in the adult language and then use it in an unrelated alternation. For example, Pinker, Lebeaux, and Frost (1987) looked at corpora of children's creative denominal and causative transitive verbs and asked whether children were apt to passivize them; see the tables in (1.14) and (1.15) of chapter 1. For datives, one can look at novel causative verbs involving causation of possession, such as *have*, and ask whether they can be extended to the double-object construction, as in Christy's *Will you have me a lesson?* Similarly, Eve used *write* to mean *draw* as in *I go write a lady for you* and then used it in productive double-object forms such as *Write me a lady.* Morphological errors are another clue that children are not reproducing parental forms: in the passive we get things like Adam's *I want to be shooted* or Sarah's *We got all stuck on each other* or Allison's *These are all bite-ed;* in the causative, we find Christy's *I'm gonna sharp this pencil* or Eva's *Don't tight this 'cause I tight this.*

There is a third kind of evidence for productivity I have cited. If children apply a rule in violation of the criteria that govern the adult version of the rule, we know that they have not reproduced adult usages, because adults presumably obey the criteria themselves in their own speech. Adults do bend the rules in the Haigspeak examples I cited in section 4.5.1, but no one looking at the examples in chapter 1 could possibly suggest that children's errors are reproductions of adults' Haigspeak.

The causative errors shown in (1.17) are the clearest case of children's flouting of criteria. Children causativize verbs of inherently directed motion, such as *come*, *go*, *fall*, and *rise*; verbs of being, such as *stay* and *be*; verbs of going out of existence, such as *die*, *vanish* and *disappear*; verbs of physical action, such as *eat*, *drink*, *sing*, *talk*, *giggle*, *cry*, *swim*, and *climb*; verbs of emission, such as *sweat* and *bleed*; and verbs of psychological activity, such as *remember*, *watch*, *guess*, *feel*, *ache*. In the last three classes, some sense of directness of causation might be violated as well.

Children also extend the dative alternation so as to express purely benefactive or malefactive arguments as surface objects, with no caused or intended change of possession. Examples in (1.16) include the verbs *brush*, *open*, *button*, *pick up*, *fix*, *eat*, *put on*, and *pass*. It is also used fairly frequently for the verb of communication *say* that does not fall into the *tell* class for reasons discussed in chapter 4. A late error with *demonstrate* violates the morphological constraint.

Bowerman's (1982b) examples of overextended locatives, plus the ones in (1.19) of chapter 1, involve assigning the locational theme, rather than the locational goal, to the object argument in several inappropriate classes of verbs: action verbs like *feel*, *touch*, *squeeze*, and *pinch* that are not in the [+motion, +contact, –effect] subclass for which this form (typically with the preposition *against*) is ordinarily licensed; verbs expressing the class of effects involving filling and covering, such as *fill* and *cover*; and a verb of possession deprivation, *rob*. The opposite kind of error, where the locational goal, rather than the locational theme, is assigned to direct object, is overextended to verbs in the classes of enabling gravity to move a substance (*pour*, *spill*), placing flexible objects around a location (*rope*), force exertion (*crash*), manner of image impression (*scribble*), and possession loss (*steal*). In none of these cases is it clear whether the holism meta-constraint is violated. Pinker (1984) suggested that it was in Eva's *Mommy, I poured you. ... Yeah, with water* because her mother was not thoroughly drenched, but since it was pretend water that was being poured, we cannot be sure.

It is much less obvious whether children violate constraints on the passive in their spontaneous speech. Most of the productive forms are due to morphological errors or verbs that are semantically eligible for passivization but happen to be transitive only in the lexicon of the child (e.g., *die*). There were no passives of measure verbs, symmetrical verbs, or verbs of pure possession. Some of the stranded prepositions sound clumsy to adult ears, even if the morphology of the verb is corrected: to be *put things in* and to be *fallen down on* violate a regularity that prepositions can be stranded by passivization only when the verb takes no other postverbal argument (in the seeming adult counterexample *John was taken advantage of*, *advantage* presumably is part of an idiomatic complex verb *take-advantage-of*; see Bresnan, 1982b). For a toilet to be *gone in* sounds somewhat childlike but probably does not violate any constraint (cf. *This toilet has been spat in*).

In sum, children clearly violate adult narrow-range semantic constraints on the causative, the locative, and the dative. They do not seem to violate any constraints on the passive, but given that in the current theory there are no direct narrow-range constraints on the passive in adult English, this is not surprising.

7.1.3 Progression Toward the Adult State

The time course of the *reduction* of children's productive errors as they approach the adult state has not been documented in detail. We know that the stage of overgeneralization errors persists over a span of several years. Incorrect causatives appear over a span of about six years in Christy's speech, from 2;1 to 7;11, and from 2;1 to at least 5;5 in Eva's. Similarly, incorrect locatives last from 3;4 to at least 6;10 for Christy and from 2;11 to at least 7;2 in Eva. According to Mazurkewich and White's examples, ungrammatical double-object datives can occur in children as young as 2;3 (see also the examples from Eve) and as old as 6 (see also Damon Clark's error at 8). Examples of ungrammatical passives span a range from 2;0 to 9;3 in various children, though they may not involve violations of constraints on passivization. A reasonable summary of the data is that overgeneralization errors persist over a long span of time shading into adulthood, diminishing in frequency at different rates for different verbs.

One factor that seems to hasten their demise, at least in the case of causativization, is the strengthening of morphologically unrelated forms that have the same meaning as the ungrammatical derived causative. Bowerman (1982a) notes informally that errors with *go, come, stay, die*, and *fall* ebb as the use of their counterparts *take/send/put, bring, keep/leave, kill*, and *drop/knock down* increase. Some of these (*bring, keep*, and *leave*) had themselves been displaced completely when the overgeneralization errors began to occur. This effect has also been demonstrated experimentally. Hochberg (1986) asked children to listen to two puppets recite different versions of a sentence. On each trial one of them uttered an ungrammatical causative sentence, the other uttered a grammatical version of it. The children were asked to award a gold star to the puppet who spoke better. When intransitive verbs used ungrammatically as causatives were contrasted with their quasi-suppletive forms (*come-bring, fall-drop, stay-keep, be-put, go-take*), children readily chose the puppet uttering the correct quasi-suppletive (78% of the 3-year-olds, 92% of the 4-year-olds). However, for intransitive verbs that lack quasi-suppletives in English (*sing, dance, run, jump, dive*), which were contrasted with periphrastic versions, children were less sure: 3-year-old children chose each puppet equally often, and 4-year-old children preferred the puppet using the grammatical periphrastic form only 68% of the time.

One can imagine a similar progression occurring for pairs such as *rob* and *steal*, but for most of the errors, there are no related forms to displace them. I will return to this issue later in the chapter.

7.2   The Unlearning Problem

As I mentioned at the outset of chapter 5, any speaker who possesses the adult versions of narrow-range rules is immune from Baker's paradox. Conceivably, children could acquire the productive rule in such an adult form as soon as they had any version of it at all. But we have just seen that this is exactly what does not happen. When children become productive, they produce grammatical and ungrammatical structures side by side. This means that Baker's paradox arises in a form that can be called the "unlearning problem": what makes the child abandon his or her overly general grammar?

Of the three kinds of empirical demonstrations of productivity, the first two are innocuous from the point of view of the unlearning problem. In the case of the experiments, we can assume that children simply forget the nonce words they are taught in the lab (at least, that is what I tell the Human Subjects committees that occasionally worry that a generation of Cambridge children will grow up talking about *pilking* this and *floozing* that). For errors involving verbs with incorrect semantic representations, the Semantic Structure Hypothesis Testing procedure discussed in chapter 6 will refine children's semantic representations for the offending verbs and cause them no longer to be eligible to enter into the lexical rules. For morphological errors like *bited* or *to sharp*, the Uniqueness Principle discussed in Pinker (1984)—related to the Blocking Principle of Aronoff (1976)—would drive out the incorrect form once the correct one (and the phonological and morphological principles governing it) had been acquired.

The third kind of error, where the adult constraints are violated, does bring up the unlearning problem. There are two subproblems involved, one fairly easy, the other more serious. The easy problem is what to do with the lexical entries the child has formed containing incorrect argument structures during the time he or she has been overgeneralizing a rule. The answer is that the child must somehow distinguish between forms he or she has heard in the input and forms created using a productive rule. In Pinker (1984) I suggested that the child appended a special "nonwitnessed" symbol ("?") to productively created entries. When the rule was later acquired in its correct form, nonwitnessed entries that violated it would be expunged. The symbol also would be used to let forms like *sharpen* drive out forms like causative *sharp*, rather than vice versa. A logically equivalent scheme would annotate forms with a special symbol if they *have* been witnessed, leaving unannotated forms to be interpreted as having been created by rule. This symbol would capture the notion of an item's being *listed* in the lexicon (see di Sciullo and Williams, 1987). In fact, since the nonwitnessed items are by definition generable by a rule, they can be thrown away as soon as they are used and then be re-created when needed in the future. So the only forms that might need to be listed are the forms that are heard in the input, since they may or may not be generable by a rule. These are the forms that I suggested be specially annotated. Thus we can dispense with either kind of annotation. Verb argument structures that have been witnessed in the input, and only these, are listed in the lexicon, and they are guaranteed to be correct. Incorrect productively formed argument structures, like all productively formed argument structures, can be used once and then thrown away, and so there may be no unlearning problem for them.

The serious problem concerns the sharpening of the rule itself. In Pinker (1984) I noted children's violations of the adult constraints and suggested that children start off with productive rules that are purely syntactic. For example, the symbol for Subject is replaced by the symbol for Object in the causative, or the symbol for Oblique-Object is replaced by the symbol for Object in the dative (e.g., as in Kaplan and Bresnan, 1982; Bresnan, 1982b). Gradually, semantic and morphological constraints are appended to the rule. However, this is the theory that led to the odd picture in which children strive to make their rules more complex and less useful for no apparent reason. In the theory I have been presenting, lexical rules are inherently operations on lexicosemantic structure; there can be no stage in which a purely syntactic operation on argument structures exists. But even if children's early rules are semantically constrained, if they are constrained too broadly, we would need some mechanism that causes them to become narrower as the child grows.

This, then, leaves us with two aspects of the unlearning problem. First, are children really oblivious to the semantic constraints that are alleged consequences of the inherent nature of the lexical rules, and if they are, how could we explain it? Second, regardless of whether children have a productive rule that has no semantic constraints or one that has too few of them, what impels children to add more and more of these constraints so as to approach the adult state and rid us of this lingering piece of Baker's paradox?

7.2.1   A Simple Solution to the Unlearning Problem

In the rest of this chapter I will defend a hypothesis that is so simple that it would be a shame if it wasn't true. The hypothesis, which I will call the "minimalist" solution to the unlearning problem, is stated in (7.3).

(7.3)

Children's overgeneralization errors are due either to the application of broad–range lexical rules or to systematic misconceptions about the meanings of particular verbs.

Let me examine these two purported causes of children's errors separately, starting in this section with broad-range lexical rules.

Recall that broad-range lexical rules that are not associated with affixes are property-predicting, not existence-predicting. They define potential lexical entries that are sensed by speakers as being possible expansions of the language, though not currently part of it. They enter into an individual's linguistic life by giving rise to occasional instances of Haigspeak and by facilitating the acquisition of narrow-range rules, and they influence the history of the language by offering opportunities for new narrow-range rules to arise, presumably at first as Haigspeak.

Note what would happen if children's errors were due to correct broad-range rules. There would be no embarrassment for the theory of argument structure I am proposing, for children would have rules in their heads that are the same as the rules that adults have in their heads. Thus there would be no unlearning problem. Children would just be little Haigs, if you will forgive the unappealing metaphor. They would produce sentences like *Can I fill some salt into the bear?* using the same mechanism that causes adults to write *Take a little of the mixture at a time and fill it into the zucchini.* No developmental change, of course, is the easiest kind of change to explain. It should, I have argued, serve as the null hypothesis in developmental psychology (Pinker, 1984). In the next section I will try to show that several different empirical tests support it, and few or none are inconsistent with it.

Note, too, what the alternative would be. Say that children's errors were due to narrow-range existence-predicting rules that were not yet quite narrow enough in their range, because they were not yet complex enough in their semantic conditions. Development would then have to be driven by some mechanism that split and complicated children's narrow-range rules, from a single too-simple rule to many very complex ones. It is possible to imagine such mechanisms, such as the conceptual clustering algorithms I entertained in chapter 6, but they raise the question of why such a mechanism should exist and whether it would actually work.

Instead, I have suggested that narrow-range rules are low-level generalizations of lexicosemantic representations; their complexity simply reproduces the complexity of verbs' meanings minus the idiosyncratic bits of information that grammar is blind to. In the minimalist developmental theory I am proposing, children would project narrow-range rules from individual lexicosemantic structures during development, on a separate track from their use of broad-range rules. As they got older, they would have more and more narrow-range rules, paralleling their increase in lexicosemantic knowledge and allowing them to make legitimate grammatical generalizations (though these generalizations would be difficult for a psycholinguist to distinguish from conservative usages outside of experimental settings). They would engage in this course of development at the same time as they were using broad-range rules to generate Haigspeak errors. Narrow-range rules would be minor bottom-up generalizations of lexical entries, tracking the development of verb meaning, and most instances of their use in spontaneous speech would be invisible to us because they would be grammatical (to the extent that their individual verb meanings were accurate, an issue I take up in a later section). Broad-range rules would be large top-down generalizations constrained by linking rules and would change minimally during development.

7.2.1.1 Why Children Would Sound Different from Adults Even If the Minimalist Solution Is Correct

At first glance the minimalist theory would seem implausible, as many of the overgeneralizations children make have an unmistakably childlike sound to them and would surely never be found among the kinds of innovative or unconventional usages shown by adults in examples like those presented in section 4.5.1. But this reservation is inconclusive. Children sound childlike for many reasons other than having a bad rule. Here are three important factors that differentiate children from adults and could lead to qualitative differences in the innovations that we would hear from each of them.

1. *Lexical gaps and blocking.* Causative errors with verbs like *be, stay, take, fall, come, go, have, die,* and *eat* are strikingly childlike, and it would be very surprising if an adult ever used them causatively even as a one-shot innovation. Presumably that is because of the existence of *put, make, keep, give, drop, bring, take, give, kill,* and *feed.* I do not think that these are literally suppletive pairs, analogous to *go/went* or *be/was* in the past tense, because causatives, unlike past tense forms, do not form a paradigm in English such that every verb has no more and no less than one lexical causative. Most verbs, like *disappear,* have no lexical

causative; some, like *be* or *have*, have several (e.g., *make* and *put* for *be*, *take* and *give* for *have*; see Miller and Johnson-Laird, 1976, for a review). Nonetheless, if ungrammatical Haigish causatives are produced in response to lexical gaps, that is, in discourse and sentence contexts calling for a lexical causative that is not available, then that situation will simply never arise for verbs like *be* and *come* in the adult state. There will always be a high-frequency word available whose meaning transparently encodes causation of the intransitive meaning, and adult causative errors with these verbs would never occur (see the semantic representations of these verbs in chapter 5).

Clark (1987) has stressed that children are faced with a problem: their vocabulary is laden with gaps, and even the verbs they have acquired may not have been acquired with complete and accurate semantic representations. Therefore, many times when children want to communicate a message, they will lack the adult's means of doing so. As a result, they will stretch their existing vocabulary to fill the gaps, resulting in ungrammatical forms used once and thrown away. As the adult forms are mastered, the child will be in such situations less often and make errors less often. In particular, children may not have causative forms like *bring* and *keep* available and analyzed properly during the period in which they are causativizing the intransitive forms. In section 7.1.3 I reviewed experimental and naturalistic data that suggest that as the transitives are remastered, the ungrammatical causatives drop out. A similar process no doubt accounts for the disappearance of many causativized adjectives with existing lexical causatives (e.g., *sad / sadden*) and for the handful of verbs that have phonologically similar causatives (e.g., *rise / raise*).[2]

2. Metalinguistic Differences. Aronoff (1983) points out that many semiproductive lexical rules (what I would call "property-predicting rules") call attention to themselves when used, and hence can be employed to convey special pragmatic effects, which he collectively calls "foregrounding." For example, the suffixes *-ness* and *-ity* are roughly synonymous ways of converting an adjective to a noun, but only the *-ness* form is fully productive. However, productive uses of the *-ity* form, because they are not automatically generated by an existence-predicting rule, can be used to indicate that the intended meaning is specialized or technical. Thus *relativity* and *productivity* have technical meanings in physics and linguistics that mere *relativeness* or *productiveness* would fail to connote. Aronoff then remarks (p. 167):

> The use of less productive WFP's [word formation patterns] for purposes of foregrounding is pervasive. Technical terms, jargon, highfalutin language, advertising, academese, all use less productive WFP's simply because they are more remarkable. It is also of some interest that young children apparently do not know what is remarkable. Instead (Clark 1978; Berman 1980) they coin words at will, regardless of the productivity of the pattern. Children, in other words, are pure formalists.

The difference between children and adults can be traced to the fact that children's command of their language grows independently of their awareness of it (Sinclair, Jarvella, and Levelt 1978). Awareness comes late, perhaps only after the formal system has developed fully. Since foregrounding depends on awareness, children are incapable of it, as they are incapable of most metalinguistic activities.

Even if the claims about development are somewhat overstated, the overall point is probably right. If so, some of children's errors may seem unlike adults' Haigspeak because they do not exploit the pragmatic nuances that accompany productive use of property-predicting regularities. For example, causativization implies direct unmediated causation, which helps to rule out the causative of action verbs in grammatical English but which may also be exploited creatively to convey the potency of a cause or the passivity of the causee, as when a grandfather says *What's fussing her?* about a crying baby, or when Richard Pryor said *I took acid. It saned me right up.* When an advertisement for an amusement park says *We're gonna splash and we're gonna spin ya. We're gonna scream and we're gonna grin ya,* we sense that the ungrammaticality is excused by—indeed, contributes to—the carefree tone that the brochure seeks to establish. If children are oblivious to these nuances, their errors would be recognizably childlike even if they were caused by a grammatical mechanism that remained unchanged through adulthood.

3. *Incorrect verb meanings.* Much in the theory presented in this book depends on accurate verb meaning representations: conformity of a verb both to broad-range and to narrow-range rules depends on the verb's lexicosemantic structure. If an individual verb has an incorrect semantic structure, it could acquire an incorrect argument structure, even if all the rules that applied were perfectly adultlike. In section 7.5 I will show that many of the errors children make (including ones that actually supplant correct forms) are due to systematic errors and biases in children's acquisition of verb meaning.

My evidence for the minimalist hypothesis consists of three parts: evidence that children's rules of argument structure alternation are always semantically conditioned (section 7.3); evidence that children's overgeneralizations are generally due to the use of property-predicting rules (section 7.4); and, finally, evidence that children's overgeneralizations are otherwise due to incorrect verb meanings (section 7.5).

7.3   Children's Argument Structure Changing Rules Are Always Semantically Conditioned

Two sets of empirical outcomes have disconfirmed the prediction of Pinker (1984) that children initially coin rules of argument structure alternation that operate directly on grammatical functions or structural positions. First, in the

experiments I have run with Jess Gropen, Loren Ann Frost, and others, we failed
to find evidence for any stage at which semantic constraints failed to operate. In
fact, we failed even to find consistent increases with age in children's sensitivity
to those constraints. Second, analyses of children's overgeneralizations show
that they are a sharply constrained subset of the possible errors we would expect
to find if they were really manipulating syntactic argument structures directly.
The evidence, then, is consistent with the hypothesis that from the very start
children use what I have been calling broad-range lexical rules, rules that effect
changes of lexicosemantic structure. I will discuss this evidence separately for
each alternation.

7.3.1   Semantic Constraints on Children's Causatives

7.3.1.1   Experimental Evidence   In Gropen, Pinker, and Roeper (in preparation) we taught children intransitive action verbs and asked them to describe
what was happening when a toy animal caused a second animal to engage in the
action. The causation was shown either by having the first animal directly
manipulate the second, or by having an intervening event in which the first
animal would throw a marble at the second, sending it into the action. Children
in our youngest group were 4 years old, an age at which causative errors are
extremely common in spontaneous speech. Nonetheless, they *never* causativized the intransitive verb to refer to cases of marble-mediated causation, though
they causativized those verbs 55% of the time when referring to direct, unmediated causation. Children in the older group (6 years old) were, if anything, a bit
less mindful of the direct causation constraint: they causativized the verbs 22%
of the time when the causation was mediated, and the magnitude of the difference
between their causativization rates for direct and mediated causation events was
smaller than that for the younger group (44 versus 55 percentage points).

Sensitivity to direct causation in the interpretation of lexical causatives of
existing verbs was shown for even younger children in an experiment reported
in Ammon (1980). In this experiment (the third one she reports), Ammon recited
lexical and periphrastic causative sentences to children and asked them to choose
one out of a set of three pictures that showed the meaning of each sentence. Three
verbs (*bounce, spin,* and *shake*) were presented in lexical causative sentences
each paired with a triplet of pictures. One picture depicted direct stereotypic
causation (e.g., a cartoon character bounces a ball in the usual manner); one
depicted something that could be interpreted as permissive causation (the character watches a ball bounce); and one depicted mediated causation (the character
points a finger at a girl bouncing a ball, as if directing her to do so). The youngest
group of children ranged from 2;8 to 3;4. Despite their tender age they chose the

mediated-causation picture 0% of the time for *bouncing the ball*, 6% of the time for *spinning the globe*, and 8% of the time for *shaking Ernie*. This was not due to a distaste for the picture or to an inability to understand the pictorial conventions, at least for *bounce* and *spin*: the mediated-causation picture was chosen 31% of the time as the best depiction of *let the ball bounce* and 27% of the time as the best depiction of *have the globe spun*. Similarly, the permissive-causation picture was not generally attractive to the young children, who chose it 6% of the time for *bouncing the ball* (while choosing it 56% of the time in connection with *let the ball bounce*).[3] In contrast, the picture showing direct stereotypic causation was chosen 94%, 44%, and 66% of the time by the youngest age group for *bounce, spin*, and *shake*, respectively (chance = 33%). There was some improvement with age: the oldest group, ranging from 5;8 to 6;0, never chose the mediated-causation picture for any of the three verbs and chose the direct causation picture 88%, 88%, and 100% of the time. However, improvement with age in experimental tasks can occur for a variety of reasons, and what is most striking about these data and those from Gropen et al. is that the semantic condition seems to operate, at least probabilistically, in the youngest children tested.[4]

7.3.1.2 Are Productive Transitives in Spontaneous Speech Necessarily Causative? Bowerman has long argued that the appearance of overgenerated causatives in children's spontaneous speech is the product of the child's construing complex verb meanings as having a causal component and adding that component to new verbs whose meanings lack it. In support of this proposal, she notes that her children began overextending the alternation at the same time that they first used periphrastic causatives such as *make it open*, where causation is expressed explicitly. She also notes that when productive causatives appear, they appear simultaneously with intransitive verbs and with adjectives (e.g., *You can't happy me up*) despite the grammatical differences between them, which children otherwise respect. This suggests that the semantic operation of adding a cause element is the crucial step.

Lord (1979) has questioned Bowerman's assertion that children's overextensions necessarily involve the semantic element "cause"; she suggests that they simply involve adding an argument to an intransitive predicate, making it transitive. Lord recorded about two hundred examples of ungrammatical transitives derived from intransitive predicates in her children's speech. She concedes that virtually all of them are consistent with Bowerman's proposal that the child's operation involves adding the notion of causation to the meaning of the intransitive predicate, but emphasizes three examples—shown in (7.4)—where this could not be true.

(7.4) Benjy, 2;8: Did you sound that?! Did you sound that funny guy?! [B hears
      recording of rock singer, comes to see if M heard it too.]

      Benjy, 3;0: I fit these. [B puts on socks; cf. These fit.]

      Jennifer, 4;7: I'm just gonna hold 'em and look at 'em, and, uh, interest
      'em. [They are interesting; J is just going to be interested in them.]

Aside from the fact that productive noncausative transitives are extremely rare
(three out of about two hundred examples in Lord's data; zero out of over a
hundred in Bowerman's), they are almost certainly derived from processes
different from those leading to causative overgeneralizations. If transitive *sound*
is derived from an intransitive form at all, it would have to be from a form like
He sounds funny. However, this could easily be a narrow-range generalization
from alternations displayed in adult English by verbs for the other four senses,
as (7.5) shows.

(7.5) That man looks funny. / I looked at the man.
      Those socks smell bad. / I smelled the socks.
      This cheese tastes awful. / I tasted the cheese.
      This rug feels smooth. / I felt the rug.

Thus they cannot be taken as evidence for a semantics-free rule of transitivization.

As for the other two examples, Bowerman (1982a) suggests that *I fit these* may
be derived not by transitivizing *These fit* but by confusing the roles of the two
arguments in the transitive *These fit me*. Since *fit* encodes a static spatial relation
where the direction of the asymmetry between theme and reference object is not
obvious, its linking with argument structure is unclear, so such a confusion
would not be surprising (indeed, adults occasionally use the verb as Benjy did).
Similarly, Jennifer's use of *interest* cannot be the result of the transitivization of
an intransitive predicate (*These books interest; *These books are interest*) but
could be due to a reversal of the arguments of the transitive verb in *Those books
interest me*. Since English contains perception verbs both with stimulus subjects
and with experiencer subjects (see chapter 4), occasional confusions of this sort
are not unexpected, and Bowerman (in press; see also Bowerman, 1981) reports
I don't appeal to that (= "that doesn't appeal to me") from Christy and eight
errors with the reverse argument assignment (e.g., *I saw a picture that enjoyed
me*) from Christy and Eva in their school-age years. In sum, productive noncausative transitives are vanishingly rare in children's speech, and the few examples
that do occur are not the product of the rule that leads to productive causative
transitives.

Lord also discusses productive intransitive errors, of which she recorded
about fifty-five from her children. The examples she provided are reproduced in
(7.6).[5]

(7.6) *Two–argument verbs:*

    (a) B, 3;1: Come and see what Jenny got today. [B pulls on M's hand, M does not move.] Pull. Pull! Come on!

    (b) B, 3;3: We have two kinds of corn: popcorn, and corn. Popcorn: it crunches. And corn doesn't crunch; it eats!

    (c) B, 3;7: I think I better put it down there so it won't lose.

    (d) B, 3;8: They don't seem to see. Where are they? [B and M are looking for B's sandals.]

    (e) B, 3;9: What does it read about? [The printed dial of a toy blood–pressure gauge]

    (f) B, 3;11: You're bothering me! You keep on talking to her! And that makes me bother!

    (g) J, 2;9: I can't hear it. [Puts clock to ear.] It can hear now. [J hears clock ticking.]

    (h) J, 8;3: Do you think it'll fix? [Father is trying to repair refrigerator.]

    (i) J, 8;5: They attract by the peanuts in the snow. [Squirrels see peanuts in snow, come to porch for more.]

Three–argument verbs:

    (j) B, 2;8: She calls "Fluffy Cat" [= is called].

    (k) B, 2;11: Lunch does *not* call a birthday cake. [At lunch B wants a birthday cake, and when M suggests they pretend his peanut butter sandwich is a birthday cake, he is annoyed.]

    (l) J, 2;10: I wanna take it out so it can't put on my nose. [J wants to take ice cream out of cone so that it won't get on her nose as she eats it.]

Bowerman questions how common the error pattern is, as she failed to find many in the speech of her children or in adult innovations. However, Lord notes that intransitivization errors are not as noticeable to an observer as transitivization errors and that once she started listening for them, she heard them frequently. I suspect that this is true. Since I started recording adults' argument structure innovations I have found that innovative intransitives are as common as innovative transitives (see (4.46) and (4.47) in chapter 4). Furthermore, ungrammatical intransitives are not really that hard to find in most children's speech. Bowerman herself (1978) reproduces one example from her daughter (without calling attention to the intransitive error): *You put a place for Eva to put in* (= "You should make a place for Eva to be put in"). Maratsos et al. (1987) provide *It's not losing* (a balloon tied to a stroller) from the senior author's daughter and note that she produced eleven others within a six-month span. Recently a street urchin of about 6 or 7 demanded a dollar from me after running a squeegee across my car's windshield. Vigilant consumer that I am, I pointed to a large squashed bug still stuck to the glass. "That don't take off," he said.

Bowerman (1982a) finds such examples, many of which are not derived by the subtraction of a "cause" element from the transitive verb, "more difficult to explain away." But an examination of the grammar of adult English eliminates the difficulty. Recall that English contains at least two rules of intransitivization (other than passivization) that result in the deletion of the transitive subject and the promotion of the object to intransitive subject. As shown in sections 3.3.4.3 and 4.2, anticausativization is the inverse of causativization; it subtracts the ACT causal superstructure, making the verb express an event whose cause is nonexistent or unspecified. It is restricted to subclasses of verbs whose semantic structures contain an effect substructure pertaining to change of state or undirected manner of motion and that lack a manner or means appended to the ACT superstructure. Hence one can say *The glass broke* or *The ball bounced* but not *The package brought* (directed mannerless motion) or *The bread cut* (means of causation specified). Some of the examples in (7.6) can clearly be interpreted as the result of a broad-range application of anticausativization that is unmindful of the narrow classes it is restricted to in adult English, such as the sentences with *pull, fix, put*, and *lose*. Anticausativization is also a likely source for the examples with *eat* (which clearly entails a specific causal effect on the food argument) and *bother* (which has close relatives that do undergo a causativization/anticausativization alternation in adult English: *John angered / cheered up / saddened Bill; Bill slowly angered / cheered up / saddened*).

English also has a rule of intransitivization that does not involve the subtraction of a causal superstructure. Keyser and Roeper (1984) and Hale and Keyser (1987) discuss the middle construction (see sections 3.3.4.3 and 4.2) which converts a transitive predicate "*X* verbs *Y*" into an intransitive predicate "*Y* verbs," whose meaning is not "*Y* undergoes the event denoted by the verb but with an unspecified or nonexistent cause" but rather "*Y* is such that the event denoted by the verb is doable to *Y* with degree of ease *Z*," where *Z* is expressed by any of several devices. Most typically, it is an adverbial phrase, as in (7.7a), but it can also be a negative polarity element (7.7b) or markers of certain nonindicative modalities such as imperative syntax or exclamative stress (7.7c, d).

(7.7) (a) This bread cuts easily.
       (b) This bread won't cut (it's frozen).
       (c) Cut, damn you!
       (d) Wow, this bread CUTS!

As mentioned in earlier sections, the narrow-range rules of middle formation apply more broadly than those for anticausativization (e.g., they apply to *cut* and *bribe*), but they do not apply to just any transitive predicate (*These birds watch easily; *?The wall slaps easily*), only those with specified effects. However, the presence of an effect is part of the narrow-class definition only. The broad-range rule of middle formation does not need a causing event to subtract, and indeed it does not generally refer to an event at all: it is a generic, quasi-stative predication of the patient. This allows for the use of middle formation (as a broad-range rule) to derive intransitives from verbs that were not causative to begin with (see, for example, some of the Haigspeak sentences in (4.47)). When we look back at Lord's data, we see that most of her examples that are not anticausatives are almost surely overextended middles, both on semantic grounds, because they express a stative predication of a patient rather than an event description, and on grammatical grounds, because they contain grammatical devices indicating ease of acting on the patient. In (7.6a), we have *pull* in the imperative (cf. (7.7c)); in (b), *eat* is in an exclamation (cf. (7.7d)); in (c), *lose* is negated and in future tense (cf. (7.7b)); in (d), *see* is negated; in (g) and (i), there are quasi-generic predications using modal and instrumental items that are also middle-like (cf. *This bread will cut now (it's thawed out); ?This bread will cut only with a very sharp knife*).

Of the remaining examples in (7.6), (e) (and possibly (d) and (g) as well) could easily be the inverse of Benjy's error with *sound* in (7.4), based on a narrow generalization from the alternation displayed by *smell, taste, feel*, and *look (at)*. This leaves (j) and (k) as the only examples of children's productive intransitives that cannot be explained as the application of broad but semantically conditioned rules of anticausativization, middle formation, or sensory verb alternation. (Even here, it is not implausible that the errors stem from the fact that the correct target expression such as *She is called Fluffy Cat* is a passive that is perhaps higher in frequency than its corresponding active and not transparently derived from it, leading the child to misanalyze it.) Entirely absent are errors such as *I just saw* (= "Someone just saw me"), *I'm slapping!* (= "Someone is slapping me"), *I don't want to tickle!* (= "be tickled"), and so on, where neither anticausativization (because of the lack of effect) nor middle formation (because of the temporally specified event) can be the source.

7.3.1.3 Choice of Causativized Predicates and Arguments in Causative Errors
Let me discuss another way in which causative errors in children's spontaneous speech are subject to semantic constraints similar to those governing broad-range causativization in adults. In chapters 4 and 6 I showed how broad-range rules might serve several functions: constraining the form of narrow-range rules, defining possibilities for expanding the stock of alternating verbs and narrow-range rules in the language, delimiting the amount of a verb's semantic structure that is reproduced in a narrow-range rule, and motivating which narrow subclasses of verbs were most likely to submit to an alternation in history and in one-time usages. The notion of direct causation, inherent in the

definition of the broad-range rule of causativization, makes it likely that classes of verbs of physical motion or physical change of state will be lexically causativizable in a language and far less likely that verbs of voluntary activity will be (Nedyalkov and Silnitsky, 1973). Some verbs may fall into a gray area vis-à-vis direct causation, and languages may be expected to differ in terms of whether causativization is permitted. For example, for verbs of involuntary activity, such as changes of mood (e.g., *sadden, cheer up*), verbs typically involving nonhuman, hence semivolitional, actors (e.g., *trot, gallop*), and verbs involving inherently directed motion (e.g., *rise, exit*) or emission of entities (e.g., *sweat, shine*), it is neither obvious that the events are directly causable by an external agent nor obvious that they have internal causes that would make any external prodding indirect. English allows the causativization of a subset of the first class and the second class, but not the third and fourth, though other languages differ in this regard.

If children's overcausativization results from a broad-range rule based on a semantic structure whose cognitive content involves causation by unmediated acting upon, their errors should mirror the cross-linguistic patterns; not all verbs would have an equal chance of yielding ungrammatical causatives in their speech. Verbs that are uncausativizable by virtue of the subtle linguistic criteria that delineate narrow subclasses in English should be causativized more often than verbs that are uncausativizable by virtue of being cognitively incompatible with the notion of direct unmediated causation. For example, we might expect children to be especially prone to errors resulting from a failure to distinguish between verbs of manner of motion and verbs of direction of motion, or from a failure to distinguish verbs of changing state from verbs of being in a state or from verbs of going out of existence. Conversely, they should be unlikely to produce ungrammatical lexical causatives for verbs of voluntary activity, even though opportunities for producing such errors are rampant: parents forcing, threatening, inducing, preventing, or allowing children to do things, and children enticing or badgering their parents or siblings to do things, have to be among the most common events involving some notion of causation that children are likely to think about or comment on. This could in principle lead to a variety of errors such as *She's always washing me up* (= making me wash up); *She played me outside*; *He's cooking her* (= making her cook); *I'm leaving him me alone*; *I'm trying to run her away*; *Stop talking me in front of people all the time* (= making me talk), and so on.

To test this prediction, I examined the 106 sentences listed by Bowerman (1982a) that involved children's use of causatives of noncausativizable verbs (i.e., the verbs derived from adjectives were excluded). They break down as shown in (7.8).

(7.8)

Subclass	Verbs	# of Sentences	
Directed motion	come, go, fall, rise, drop	30	(28%)
Going out of existence	die, disappear, vanish	12	(11%)
Being/staying	stay, be, spell, sound, wait	16	(15%)
Possession	have, take	13	(12%)
Psychological	remember, watch, guess, wish, feel, ache, learn	12	(11%)
Involuntary emission	sweat, bleed	3	(3%)
Internally caused state change	bloom	1	(1%)
Semivoluntary expression of emotion	laugh, cry, giggle	5	(5%)
Voluntary action		14	(13%)
	eat, drink	6	(6%)
	sing, talk (inanimate causee)	5	(5%)
	swim (inanimate causee)	1	(1%)
	climb	2	(2%)

Of these subclasses, the first five are clearly eligible for broad-range causativization, since classes of morphologically unrelated verbs conflating causation with the kind of event expressed by these verbs exist in English. For directed motion we have *bring, take, put, drop, raise, lower*; for going out of existence we have *kill, destroy*; for being/staying we have *keep, make*; for possession we have *have* and *take*;[6] for psychological verbs we have *remind, show, hurt, teach*. These sentences, each of which involves a legitimate semantic conflation class with an illegitimately assigned stem, account for 77% of children's causative errors in the examples provided by Bowerman. Another 9 sentences (9% of the sample) do not have causative counterparts in modern English but involve events that have enough of an involuntary component that direct causation is not inconceivable, and indeed there are causative verbs that are not entirely unrelated to causation of these events: *bleed* (as in what barber-surgeons used to do to patients), *grow* (what one does to plants), *amuse, upset*, and *tickle*. (In fact, the sentence *Don't giggle me!* may even have been a malapropism in which the child confused the stems *giggle* and *tickle*. She was being tickled at the time, and intrusions of words that are phonologically and semantically similar to a target are not uncommon in children's speech. Pinker and Prince (1988) report *grained* for *ground, fulled* for *filled*, and *brecked* for *wrecked*, for example.)

This leaves 14 sentences (13%) seemingly involving voluntary actions. But closer examination reduces this number still further. *Eat* was used to mean *feed*, and indeed may have been a malapropism rather than a causativization error. Note that *feed* does not mean "cause to eat" in adult English. It really means something like "give food to" (actually, "give food to so that the recipient may eat"; see section 5.6.1), as its participation in the dative alternation would suggest. For example, one does not *feed a child* by approaching him in the high chair with his food already in front of him and then bribing or threatening him; and one does not *feed a rat* by surgically removing the ventromedial nucleus of its hypothalamus or by electrically stimulating the lateral nucleus of its hypothalamus, though these events cause it to eat, rather directly in the latter case. Whenever there is *feeding*, however, there *is* giving of food. The child's ungrammatical use of *drink* may be exactly the same; indeed historically the English verb *drench* was morphologically related as a kind of causative of *drink* (Curme, 1935), though causation of voluntary action was never part of its meaning. Thus these examples are not really cases of "causing to act."

Of the remaining 8 action verbs, 6 were used to refer to toys. This leaves 2 sentences out of a total of 106 that involve voluntary action by a real-world animate agent.

Thus a classwise analysis of causativization errors reveals a striking pattern: the majority of such errors denote events where direct causation, without the mediation of a voluntary agent, can be carried out, and the ungrammaticality of the sentences is due to the semiarbitrary delineation of narrow-range causativizable classes in English. Only 2% clearly involve causation of activity by an animate causee, which the notion of direct causation that is grammaticized into the causative semantic structure rules out. This suggests that children's rule of causativization involves such a structure.

7.3.1.4 Causativization of Transitive Verbs
If causativization simply added an external argument to a predicate, we would expect that some transitive verbs should be converted to double-object (ditransitive) verbs. Note that it is unlikely that adult English has a rule capable of doing this. For one thing, there are very few English verbs that alternate between transitive and double-object forms with the subject of the transitive demoted to the first object of the double–object form and the object of the transitive demoted to second object of the double-object form (even ignoring the question of whether the added argument is a cause).[7] That is, there are no alternations like *John ate the apple / *I ate John the apple*; *The dog entered the room / *He entered the dog the room*; and *The explosion destroyed the house / *I destroyed the explosion the house*. Furthermore, if there were, and if they were the consequence of a rule that added an argument to an arbitrary argument structure (which would serve as a variable in the operation),

the process could then apply to three–argument verbs, yielding *I handed John Bill the ball* (= "I caused John to hand Bill the ball") or *Merrill Lynch earned that investment me a lot of money*. It could even apply recursively, generating *She entered him the dog the room*, *The storm entered her him the dog the room*, and so on. This supports the claim that the causative rule does not simply add an argument to a variable standing for an argument structure, but adds a causal superstructure onto specific configurations of semantic structure. This is true not only in English but cross-linguistically. Nedyalkov and Silnitsky's (1973) survey shows that although some languages can causativize transitive verbs to yield three-argument causatives, four-argument causatives are extremely rare and five-argument causatives do not exist at all. Thus the rule of causativization universally does not iterate.[8]

If this is right, we get the prediction that children should not treat the causativization rule as a pure argument-addition operation, increasing the valence of arbitrary verbs, even if the added argument was invariably a cause. There are a few cases where children do extend two-argument verbs to become three-argument double-object verbs. Lord reproduces three clear examples (she mentions that productive three-argument sentences were produced for five other verbs, but it is not clear how many were ditransitive). In the sample that Bowerman provides, I found fourteen (counting immediate repetitions as a single example).[9] The seventeen examples are reproduced in (7.9).

(7.9) From Lord (1979):
   (a) B, 4;7: Take me a piggyback ride! [B wants a piggyback ride on father.]
   (b) J, 3;8: You can drink me the milk [feed, help to drink].
   (c) J, 4;8: I'm trying to guess Aunt Ruth what I have. [J wants Aunt Ruth to guess what she has in her hand.]

   From Bowerman (1982):
   (d) Rachel, 2;0: Don't eat it me. [As M feeds R cottage cheese]
   (e) C, 4;0: Will you have me a lesson? [Request to adult friend in swimming pool]
   (f) C, 4;6: Would you like me to ... have ... you some? [Re: piece of gingerbread C is holding, to M]
   (g) C, 3;8: You feed me. Take me little bites. Give me little bites.
   (h) Robert, 11+: We took him a bath yesterday and we took him one this morning. [Reporting on bathing baby brother]
   (i) Julie, 5+: When we go home I'm gonna take you a bath with cold water. [To her doll]
   (j) Hilary, 4+: C'mon, Mama, take me a bath. C'mon, David, Mama's gonna take us a bath.

(k) C, 3;9: You better not take me a quiet time, you better take me a quiet time. [C paraphrasing for D's benefit a protest she'd made earlier when M said she should have a nap: "You better not give me a quiet time, you better give me a quiet time." Note the change from *give* to *take*. After original sentence she laughed when she realized she'd made a mistake, intending to say, "You better not give me a *nap*, you better give me a quiet time."]

(l) C, 3;5: A nice nurse lady took me a ride. [Reporting that nurse in hospital had pushed her in a wheel chair]

(m) Hilary, 4+: David, let's take Mama a ride. [M: Oh, you're gonna give me a ride?] Yes, we're gonna take you a ride, Mama.

(n) Rachel, 4;6: I want you to take me a camel ride over your shoulders into my room.

(o) Jaime, 5;10: I'm taking my babies a walk. [Pushing dolls in buggy around house]

(p) C, 4;3: Andrea. I want you to watch this book. Andrea. I want to watch you this book. [Shortly:] I just want you to watch this book. [C trying to get A's attention so she will look at the book]

(q) C, 6;11: Remember me what I came in for.

These data show a uniform pattern. Without exception, all the productive two-object forms involve a notion of possession akin to that expressed in existing English double-object forms. Ten of the seventeen forms involved *take* in idioms that require *give* in adult English (*a ride*, four times; *a bite*; *a bath*, three times; *a nap* / *"quiet time"*; *a walk*). These idioms also involve a sense of metaphorical possession that is transparent enough to support use of the verb *have*: *I already had a ride* / *a bite*/ *a bath* / *a nap* / *a walk*. Two involved *have* outright, playing the role of *give*. Two were analogous to *feed* (*eat* and *drink* once apiece), which participates in the dative alternation and means roughly *give food to* (see the preceding subsection). Finally, *watch*, *guess*, and *remember* are being used in senses very close to *show*, *ask*, and *tell*, respectively, all dativizable verbs that exploit the widespread communication-as-possession-transfer metaphor. (The children were simply ignoring the extra attribution of cognitive activity on the part of the recipient of communication that bars these verbs from causativizing in adult English.) A similar pattern has been noted by Maratsos et al. (1987), who remark that in the speech of Maratsos's daughter, *eat* was the only transitive verb to be causativized.

This is a striking finding, one that offers strong support to the the centrality of thematic cores in the current theory. Before looking at the data, we might have expected any verb to gain an argument through the child's application of the cause-adding operation (e.g., *She killed me the bug* = "caused me to kill the bug").

This should be expected even more strongly for the optionally transitive verbs that children do occasionally turn into causative transitives—since children say *I'm singing him*, they could also say *I'm singing him a song*, meaning "causing him to sing a song"; since they say *Climb me up there*, they could also say *Climb me the tree*, meaning "Help me climb the tree." Instead, we find that 100% of the productive double-object utterances involved verbs that in adult English are associated as a semantic class with literal or metaphorical change of possession, a notion which embraces all existing double-object forms in English and which tends to characterize double-object forms in other languages as well. However, in few of these cases could the errors be derived by dativization—none of the verbs is grammatical in the prepositional form for the adult, and only a few appeared in that form in the children's speech. The finding thus supports the hypothesis that rules that change argument structures are mappings among thematic cores, where these thematic cores have an independent identity in the lexicon as definitions of the possible verb meanings underlying a given kind of argument structure. In English and many other languages, the dative rule maps stems underlying prepositional-object forms onto that thematic core; apparently, for children the causative rule is another route to the same type of structure, revealing the existence of that structure independent of the various rules that map onto it.

But the clincher comes from cross-linguistic evidence. Nedyalkov and Silnitsky (1973) observe that if a causative morpheme in a language is unproductive for transitive verbs but admits of a few exceptions, these exceptions are either psychological verbs, like "see/show," "remember/remind," or "understand/explain," or verbs pertaining to the giving of something to be consumed, such as "eat/feed," "drink/give to drink," or "suck/suckle." Of course these are just the kinds of transitive verbs that English children overgeneralize the causative rule to. Apparently universally, causative ditransitive structures are attracted to conflations of causation with literal or metaphorical possession. Convergences like this should give comfort to anyone who likes to think of language acquisition as a form of hypothesis testing. The sentences in (7.9) show that English-speaking children are entertaining a correct hypothesis about causativization; it's just that the languages that the hypothesis is correct in happen not to include English.

7.3.2 Semantic Constraints on Children's Datives

7.3.2.1 Experimental Evidence In Gropen et al. (1989), we examined children's willingness to utter productive double-object datives for verbs involving specific instruments of transfer, as a function of the kind of target of the transfer. We hoped to exploit the fact that when a toy was transferred to an inanimate object (such as a book), the child would be unlikely to perceive it as the "possessor" of the transferred toy, but that when the child himself or herself was the destination, a change of possession would be a natural interpretation. When a toy animal was the destination, the likelihood of a possessional interpretation should be somewhere in between. If so, and if children use the dative rule to generate semantic structures encoding change of possession, they should be most likely to say *You're mooping X the marble* when X refers to the child, less likely when X refers to an animal toy, and least likely when X refers to an inanimate place. This is what we found: the three percentages were 52%, 37%, and 32%, respectively, and both differences were statistically significant. Although the youngest group of children we tested was from 5;8 to 7;6, dative errors in spontaneous speech still occur during that age range. Thus it was interesting that the effect of type of recipient on frequency of productive double-object utterances held in that age group (whose means were 54%, 40%, and 34% in the three respective conditions) and the size of the effect was no larger in the older age group of 7;6 to 8;11 (whose means were 51%, 34%, and 30%). So we fail to find an age range in which children use a rule free of the notion of possession change, which is at the heart of the broad-range dative rule, and we fail to find an age-related increase in the degree to which this notion affects productive usage.

7.3.2.2 Spontaneous Speech   In (1.16) in chapter 1, I reproduced twenty-six productive double-object forms (not counting repetitions within a recording session) from Gropen et al. (1989). They break down as follows.

One was a morphological violation involving the Latinate verb *demonstrate*. Four involved the use of *put* to mean *give* (see Bowerman, 1978), which is illegitimate in adult English because *put* specifies a 'to' path and selects for a place (Jackendoff, 1987a), which cannot be satisfied by a word denoting a person. Since the children also used *put* in the prepositional-dative form in sentences such as *You put the pink one to me* (Christy) and *We're putting our things to you* (Eva), this appears to be the result of a general tendency to substitute *put* for *give* on occasion, perhaps with the dative rule applied to the prepositional form. In either case, the resulting double-object form clearly is intended to signal change of possession. Five sentences involved the verb *say*. As discussed in section 4.4.1, *say* is a verb of communication taking a transparent propositional argument that makes it fall outside the narrow class of verbs of illocutionary communication embracing *tell*, *pose*, and so on, but otherwise involves the same sense of causation of possession of a message that motivates the dativizability of the *tell* verbs. Five sentence types from one child involved *write* used as a synonym for *draw*; used in this way as a verb of creation, its dativizability is not surprising. One more involved the substitution of *keep* for *do* in the double-object idiom *do me a favor*.

Seven of the usages involved a pure benefactive interpretation, in which a conversion of the sentence to the *for*-prepositional form would render it grammatical in adult speech, but in which no literal possession change occurs. The verbs *brush, button, finish, fix, open, pass*, and *pick up* were used in this way. Interestingly, in chapters 4 and 5 I reviewed a range of evidence (much of it from Green, 1974) suggesting that the benefactive relation can be subsumed under the thematic core used to represent prospective possession, where the beneficiary is treated as "possessing" an advantageous object, opportunity, or offering due to the exertions of the agent. The developmental evidence suggests that this metaphoric extension is quite natural in the mind of the child.

Two examples from the MacWhinney boys show the same parallelism but with the opposite affective polarity, namely malefactive. The sentences have meanings that conflate the malefactive relation with the notion of "prospective loss of possession," ordinarily encoded in English verbs such as *bet, envy, cost, begrudge*, and *spare* that appear only in the double-object form. *You ate me my cracker* clearly involves loss of possession and also suggests bad fortune, as if *You ate my cracker on me* was the target.[10] *Ross is gonna break into the TV and is gonna spend us money* is an example of causativization of a transitive leading to a double–object form that involves change of possession, as in section 7.3.1.4, only in this case the change of possession is away from the causee. Indeed, *cost* substituted for *spend* in Mark's sentence almost makes it acceptable.

Adam's sentence *I gon' put me all dese rubber bands on* is difficult to classify. The context of the utterance in the Brown transcripts shows clearly that Adam was putting rubber bands not on himself, but onto a board on which the colored rubber bands could form designs. Thus the sentence was not derived from *I gon' put all dese rubber bands on me* or *I gon' put all dese rubber bands to me*. The immediate discourse context is shown in (7.10).

(7.10) Adam: I gon' put each ... all of the rubber bands on dere?
        Ursula: You can put them in all different directions.
        Adam: I got me another one. I gon' put me ... I gon' put me all dese rubber
        bands on. I can make a direction with dis.

Some kind of perseveration or priming from *I got me another one* might be occurring; if it is not an outright speech error it might be a kind of reflexive benefactive form of the sort discussed in chapter 4 that appears in colloquial American speech (e.g., *Robert played himself one heck of a ballgame*).

Thus all of the children's errors that can be classified involve either literal change of possession (concrete or communicative) or the benefactive/malefactive relation, which may be an extension of possessional structures to a more abstract semantic field. A skeptic may worry that it is possible to shoehorn virtually any example into the category of possession change. However, this suspicion can be falsified by even the briefest consideration of the kinds of errors that could have been produced if the children had analyzed the dative alternation as a purely syntactic rule. (For starters, one can simply note that all of the first objects in children's errors refer to humans, a prerequisite to those arguments' denoting possessors, though they needn't have turned out that way on syntactic or logical grounds.) In (7.11) and (7.12) I list some constructions involving "V NP *to* NP" and "V NP *for* NP" that do not involve possession transfer or benefaction and hence fall outside the broad range of the dative rules. The (a) forms in each set could occur if the child was doing a phrase-by-phrase analysis of the alternations; the (b) forms would be possible if the child was a bit more structure-sensitive, insisting that alternations apply to sets of a verb's arguments but was otherwise insensitive to the thematic structure that I have been emphasizing. None of the children's errors are of either type and I predict that none should be found.

(7.11) (a) Amy took the road to Chicago. / *Amy took Chicago the road.
         Custer fought the Indians to the last man. / *Custer fought the last man the Indians.

(b) Betty threw the ball to the fence. / *Betty threw the fence the ball.
    Jimmy drove the car to the top. / *Jimmy drove the top the car.
    Sally brought roses to the cemetery. / *Sally brought the cemetery roses.
    Alex put a gun to his head. / * Alex put his head a gun.
    Sheila finally put pencil to paper. / * Sheila finally put paper pencil.
    They blew the building to smithereens. / *They blew smithereens the building.

(7.12) (a) Hildy wiped the case for her typewriter. / *Hildy wiped her type-writer the case.
         Babs took a trip for fun. / *Babs took fun a trip.
         Jane planted the trees for six hours. / * Jane planted six hours the trees.

(b) Bill bought a car for $6000. / *Bill bought $6000 a car.
    God punished Tex for all those sins. / *God punished all those sins Tex.
    John programmed the autopilot for Chicago. / *John programmed Chicago the autopilot.

Errors of this ilk are not in the realm of science fiction. Jane Grimshaw told me that the child she studied, Lisa, once said *That's you some tea*, which seemed to mean "That's some tea for you." This is presumably not an error in the argument structure of *be* but a mistaken noun phrase structure. A phrase like *make some tea for you* can be parsed either as [make [some tea] [for you]] or as [make [some [tea for you]]]. Lisa must have heard a sentence that should have been parsed as [make [you] [some tea]] and given it the analogous parse [*make* [*you some tea*]]. This is a rare kind of error, I believe, but it shows that misanalyses are possible. If children were able to allow such surface misanalyses to be built into incorrect argument structures associated with verbs, resulting in frequent errors like those in (7.11) and (7.12), it would count as evidence against the present hypothesis. As I have shown, children's argument structure overextensions are in fact not of that sort but appear to be the result of adultlike thematic generalizations.

7.3.3 Semantic Constraints on Children's Locatives

7.3.3.1 Experimental Evidence   Jess Gropen (Gropen, Pinker, and Goldberg, 1987; Gropen, 1989; Gropen et al., in preparation) tested children's sensitivity to the regularity that the verbs involving moving things select as their direct objects the entity that is affected in some salient verb-specific way. Specifically, a verb may express the goal of the motion as its surface object only if the goal changes state as the result of the addition of the theme of motion; if the referent action involves no state change, but instead a distinctive manner of motion, it is the moving thing that is expressed as surface object. This regularity is a consequence of the linking rule for objects. It is reflected in the thematic cores for the *into/onto* and *with* forms of the locative alternation, and in the broad-range rule underlying the alternation, which converts a goal of motion into a theme of a state change. It is expected to constrain children's use of the two forms of the locative to events involving a possible state change or a distinctive motion, respectively.

Two similar experiments were run in which children were presented with a novel verb in an intransitive gerundive form ("This is pilking"), paired with a demonstration of motion of a theme entity (e.g., a sponge) to a goal (e.g., a square of cloth) that either had a distinct manner (e.g., hopping or zigzagging) and resulted in no distinctive end state, or that had no distinctive manner and did result in a distinctive end state (e.g., the goal object changed color when the theme was moved to it). The experiment is described in more detail in section 7.5.3.3. In each experiment forty-eight children participated, sixteen 3-year-olds, sixteen 5-year-olds, and sixteen 7-year-olds. In addition, sixteen adult control subjects were given the task. The results are shown in (7.23) and (7.24) in section 7.5.3.3. The relevant data are the differences between the number of goal-as-surface-object sentences uttered in response to actions with a distinctive manner and the number of such sentences uttered in response to actions with a distinctive end state. If children are sensitive to the constraint, there should be more of the latter, and the difference shown in the tables should be positive.

Two patterns are noteworthy. First, even children in the youngest age group were sensitive to the constraint. Second, there was no consistent age trend going from the 5-year-old group to the 7-year-old group to the adult group: the effect sizes for frequency of goal-as-direct-object ("pilk the cloth") responses, averaged over the two experiments, were 47 percentage points, 42 percentage points, and 45.5 percentage points, respectively. (There was, however, a quantitative difference between the 5-and-over's and the 3-year-olds, whose effect size was only 23.5 percentage points.) Note that the errors in using locative alternation verbs in spontaneous speech come from children between the ages of 2;11 and 7;2 (Bowerman, 1981, 1982b). Thus for the locative alternation, as for the dative and causative alternations, the experiments fail to find a stage at which error-prone children are insensitive to the constraint embodied in the broad-range rule, and fail to show a developmental trend in the degree to which children respect the regularity during most of the period in which errors are made.

7.3.3.2 Spontaneous Speech Bowerman (1982b) has already considered the question of whether children's locative errors reflect a rule that operates directly on surface roles (demoting a direct object to an oblique object and promoting an oblique object to direct object) or a rule that is restricted to thematic relations involving locational themes and goals (she uses Talmy's terms "figure" and "ground"). She notes that all the errors she has recorded (reproduced in (1.19) of chapter 1) involve physical motion and an associated figure-ground relation. She reports failing to find syntactically similar errors of the sort shown in (7.13), involving the locativization of communication, perception, and instrumental relations, in her data.

(7.13) I read a book to Mary. / *I read Mary with a book.
　　　 He read a poem out of (from) the book. / *He read the book of a poem.
　　　 Mother saw (called) Johnny from the window. / *Mother saw (called) the window of Johnny.
　　　 I ate my pudding with a spoon. / *I ate a spoon against (on, into) my pudding.
　　　 I opened the door with my key. / *I opened my key against (on, into) the door.

I can add several other kinds of examples of generalizations that are syntactically parallel to the locative alternation but that have not been, and should not be, observed in children's speech; they are shown in (7.14). They involve changes of identity, accompanied nonagentive motion, changes of circumstance, comitative relations, abstract antagonistic relations, and others difficult to classify.

(7.14) The fairy turned the frog into a prince. / *The fairy turned the prince with
        a frog.

I followed him into the room. / *I followed the room with him.

She turned his friend against him. / *She turned him with his friend.

She helped him with his homework. / *She helped his homework onto
him.

She saw Paris with him. / *She saw him into Paris.

She fought a battle with him. / *She fought him into a battle.

I reminded her of her brother. / *I reminded her brother from her.

7.3.4 Semantic Constraints on Children's Passives

7.3.4.1 Experimental Evidence   Pinker, Lebeaux, and Frost (1987) ran five experiments in which children were taught verbs with different semantic properties in either the active or passive voice and encouraged to utter them either in the voice taught or in the other voice. Unlike the other alternations we have discussed, the passive relates two forms one of which is significantly later acquired, more difficult, and more pragmatically specialized than the other. Because we wanted to disentangle difficulty in using the passive from the difficulty in generalizing to the passive, we measured the effects of verb semantics by examining the size of the 2×2 interaction between verb semantics (more or less canonical for the passive) and voice taught (passive, requiring no productivity, versus active, requiring a generalization). The magnitude of this interaction, which we called the Relative Passivizability Index (RPI), is simply a difference between differences: for each type of verb, one subtracts the probability of uttering a passive when it was taught in the active from the probability of uttering a passive when it was taught in the passive, and then subtracts this difference for one verb type from the corresponding difference for the other verb type.

Four experiments allowed between-subjects examinations of age trends in the effect of verb semantics on passivizability. In the first, we compared actional verbs (meaning "to back into" and "to slide down the back of") with two verbs denoting static spatial relations ("to suspend" and "to contain"). The effect size was .125 for the 3-to-$4\frac{1}{2}$-year-old children, and it was .125 for the $4\frac{1}{2}$-to-$5\frac{1}{2}$-year-old children. In the second experiment, we compared action verbs whose subjects were agents and whose objects were patients with difficult "anticanonical" action verbs whose subjects were patients and whose objects were agents. The effect size for the 5-to-6-year-old children was .31; for the 7-to-8-year-old children it was .375. Though the Verb Semantics × Voice Taught interaction capturing this effect was significant, the three-way interaction including Age Group was not. Furthermore, when the scores were adjusted to eliminate trials in which the child failed to learn the anticanonical verbs, the effect of verb semantics remained for both age groups, but the difference in the magnitude of this effect between the older and younger children reversed: for the younger children it was .44; for the older children it was .12. The third experiment was a replication of the second. High error rates made it mandatory to eliminate trials where the anticanonical verb had not been learned; when this was done the effect of verb semantics was .35 for the 5-to-6-year-olds, and .11 for the 7-to-8-year-olds. In the fourth experiment, we compared verbs of spatial relations that conformed to Jackendoff's Thematic Hierarchy Condition (e.g., "to have at one's center," where the subject is a location and the object is a theme) with verbs that violated it (e.g., "to be at the center of," where the subject is a theme and the location is an object). In their elicited productions, the 5-to-6-year-old children showed the effect (RPI = .375) and the 7-to-8-year-old children did not (RPI = 0). In a separate sentence-judgment task, where both kinds of passives were judged by the children as to whether they sounded "good" or "no good," the effect was shown both by the younger children (RPI = .125) and by the older children (RPI = .25).

In sum, in the five independent sets of data allowing age comparisons, we find that the effect of verb semantics on productive passivizability in the right direction can be detected in the younger of the two age groups in all five cases. Furthermore, the effect was stronger for the older group in one of the comparisons, stronger for the younger children in two of the comparisons, equal in the two groups in a fourth, and stronger for either the older or younger age groups, depending on how the effect was calculated, in a fifth.

7.3.4.2 Spontaneous Speech As mentioned in section 7.1.2, there were no good examples of children violating adult broad-range constraints on the passive. However, in the case of the passive, there may be even better evidence that children respect the broad constraints than for the other alternations: they may respect it *more* than adults do. Recall that the adult broad-range rule for the passive incorporates a predication effect, whereby the patient argument was the theme of a BE predication, and an agency or authorship effect, whereby what was asserted of this theme was that it had been acted upon or caused to be in its current state by an agent. This statement is abstract enough that no specific effect need be predicated of the theme other than that an agent had acted upon it (thus embracing *hit* and *touch*), but if the patient is being treated as a theme, it would be natural for a more concrete state or motion to be predicated of it as well as its circumstance of being the target of an agent's act; this would be the canonical way of representing a theme. (In fact, this is the dominant pattern in most languages; Keenan, 1985.) Thus it is conceivable that children's broad range rule for the passive incorporates the predication effect and the agency effect, but the predication effect may be more concrete in requiring a specific change or motion.

A conclusion very much along these lines has been suggested for children's passives in their semispontaneous speech (elicited descriptions of pictures) by Horgan (1978). She suggested that for a child, a passive is used as an "after-the-fact observation on the state of things." Borer and Wexler (1987) make a similar observation and use it to argue that for preschool children, only the adjectival passive exists, not the verbal passive. Pinker, Lebeaux, and Frost (1987) show that these claims are too strong. For example, they presented a set of passives in Adam's spontaneous speech, reproduced in (7.15), that are not after-the-fact observations on the states of things. However, there is a weaker version of the Horgan-Borer-Wexler observation that can be substantiated. Every single one of these passives involves a verb with a specific effect (i.e., the active verb would have both a patient and a theme, or in the scheme used in chapter 5, an 'effect' link to a GO substructure). Passives of common actional verbs, like *slap*, *hit*, *touch*, *kiss*, and *feel*, are entirely absent, as are passives of less concrete verbs such as verbs of perception. For Eve and Sarah, the pattern is even stronger, as all of their spontaneous passives were ambiguous between stative adjectives and verbal passives. It is clear that children are nowhere near pushing the outside of the envelope surrounding the broad class of passivizable verbs in adult English.

(7.15) 3;2: So it can't be cleaned?

  3;3: When I get hurts, I put dose one of dose bandage on.

  3;3: Mommy, its will be cooked ... in de minute. Yeah. It will be cooked in de minute.

  3;4: He gon' get apared.

  3;7: I don't want the bird to get eated.

  3;8: I want to be shooted.

  3;10: Why he gon' be locked in a cage?

  3;10: Saw the cows being milked [repetition of Mother's "And saw the cows being milked?"].

  3;10: How could it go up if its not ... if it's not flyed? [a wheel of an airplane].

  3;11: You don't like to be rolled into clay.

  4;0: Mommy, de cow gonna get locked up. Now de cow gonna get locked up.

4;2:   Oh he got killed.

4;2:   Is dat where I was borned?

4;7:   I don't want my animals get killed.

4;8:   I wanna get something fixed.

4;9:   De top might get killed.

4;11: I'm gonna ask Mommy if she has any more grain ... more stuff that
       she needs grained.

4;11: They gonna get cut and cut [talking about crackers being ground
       up].

4;11: It needs some paint to be painted.

4;11: Mommy, Paul wants to be chained.

4;11: You better sit down before you get killed.

5;2:   I don't care if my table gets messed up.

5;2:   He's not fixed yet.

7.3.5   Summary of Semantic Constraints on Children's Lexical Rules

We have examined teaching experiments and spontaneous speech errors for four
argument structure alternations. The results are highly consistent. First, there is
no stage at which the effects of semantic constraints cannot be measured in the
experiments. Second, there is no measurable age trend in the size of the effects
of verb semantics (with one minor exception in the case of the locative) during
the years in which children are prone to overgeneralization. Third, in children's
spontaneous speech, their overgeneralization errors are not due to treating the
alternations as manipulations of phrase structures or even of purely syntactic
argument structures; the errors always fall within fairly well-defined semantic
boundaries that betray the use of a rule mapping among semantic structures, in
each case very close to what I have proposed for broad-range rules for adults.

There are highly surprising findings. Age trends in experiments with children
are as inevitable as death and taxes, and the experiments were all designed with
the intent of finding them, based on the predictions of Pinker (1984). The absence
of age trends cannot be attributed to insensitivity of the measures, as the semantic
effect itself was detectable in the predicted direction in every case and statistically significant in most of them. Furthermore, the results of the spontaneous
speech corpora run completely counter to beliefs held by many developmental
psycholinguists (though never by me) that children's generalizations are the
result of distributional analyses of surface regularities in the input.

This pattern, then, is one important pillar of support for my solution for
Baker's paradox, which stems from the inherent lexicosemantic nature of the alternations, and for my explanation for the developmental version of Baker's
paradox, namely that children's overgeneralization errors are the result of a

mechanism that does not disappear and that undergoes little modification during development.

7.4 Do Children's Errors Have the Same Cause as Adults'?

What I have been trying to avoid is needing a process that progressively splits and narrows a rule from the broad-range one that appears to be the cause of children's errors to the set of narrow-range ones that delineate the alternation in the adult language, because there is no way to make sense of such a process. Rather, I have posited parallel pathways toward development of the adult state: a broad-range rule that does not change, and a set of narrow-range rules copied from lexicosemantic structures in the child's lexicon and changing in synchrony with them as word meanings are refined. To support this simple parallel-tracks view, I must show that children's errors are due either to incorrect lexicosemantic structures for particular verbs (which I take up in the section 7.5) or the use of a broad-range rule to generate sentences directly. As mentioned, adults occasionally use broad-range rules in that way in the phenomenon I call Haigspeak; the question is whether I can show that many of the errors children make reflect the same mechanism.

There are two criteria that tell us that for adults, *What's fussing her?* and *He squeezed the fish with lemon juice* and *Can you reach me that book?* are one-shot innovations rather than the product of existence-predicting rules. First, they are far rarer than usages such as *What's bothering her?* and *He covered the fish with lemon juice* and *Can you get me that book?* Second, the majority of speakers with a comparable linguistic background, and perhaps even the speaker himself or herself, would judge the sentences as sounding odd. In the next two subsections, I show that by both of these criteria, many of children's overgeneralization errors can be shown to have the same genesis as adults' errors.

7.4.1 Overall Tendency Toward Conservativism

A key empirical assumption of the entire argument in this book, from chapter 1 on, has been that children are not conservative recorders of adult argument structures, and there is much evidence to support the assumption of productivity over "strict itemwise conservatism." However, the theory developed herein allows only highly circumscribed productive mechanisms: use of broad-range rules as form-predicting constraints (except for rules that add affixes), and extensions of conservatively acquired pairs of argument structures to small numbers of similar verbs in narrow conflation classes. Against these limited processes we require a pervasive background tendency of conservatism. We should find that in children broad-range productivity indeed occurs, but conservatism is the rule.

7.4.1.1   Experimental Evidence for Conservative Tendencies   Experimentally, a tendency toward conservatism can clearly be seen in the experiments of Gropen et al. (1989), in which children were taught different verbs in the prepositional and double-object dative forms. When children heard a verb in the prepositional form, they used that verb in the prepositional form 68.5% of the time when answering questions about similar events and used it in the double-object form 31% of the time. However, when children heard a verb in the double-object form, they used it in the prepositional form only 44% of the time, using the double-object form 54% of the time.

In Gropen, Pinker, and Roeper (in preparation), transitive forms were elicited more often when the verb had been modeled in transitive clauses than when it had been modeled in intransitive clauses, and intransitive forms were elicited more often when the verb had been modeled in intransitive clauses than when it had been modeled in transitive clauses. Maratsos et al. (1987), in their study eliciting productive use of a novel action verb, obtained similar results. Subjects who heard the verb used in a causative transitive form themselves used the verb in a causative transitive form (or the same form with the object deleted) on 98% of the opportunities for doing so in various production tasks. However, children who had heard the verb in an anticausative or middle intransitive form used it in a causative transitive only 26% of the time.

Although in the experiments of Pinker, Lebeaux, and Frost (1987) children passivized novel active verbs readily, they passivized verbs that they had heard in the passive even more readily. In every experiment, for every age range, and under every condition, we were more successful in eliciting a sentence containing a particular voice when the verb had been taught in that voice than when the verb had been taught in the other voice, an effect that reached statistical significance in every case. Gordon and Chafetz (1986) also demonstrated a verb-specificity effect in the acquisition of the passive in a test-retest experiment. They found that children were consistent from one week to the next in which verbs they found difficult to comprehend in the passive.

7.4.1.2   Conservative Tendencies in Spontaneous Speech   From the errors reported in (1.14)–(1.19) in chapter 1, one might think that children use productive rules in many of the cases where they need a verb in a given argument structure, and that examples of such errors can be amassed simply by listening to children speak for a while, much like overgeneralizations of past-tense morphology. This is quite untrue. While the errors are "common" in the sense that

virtually all children make them and in the sense that enough tokens can be gathered per child for us to know that they are not freak events or random word strings, they are quite uncommon considered as a proportion of the child's total speech or as a proportion of the child's sentences involving the particular argument structures. Let us first consider dative errors, putting aside for now the question of the source of these errors, and treat them as if they were all the product of a productive dativization rule, even though some are surely the result of substituting the wrong stem for a conservatively acquired double-object verb (this issue will be discussed at length in the next section). Here are some figures that put the frequency in perspective.

Datives. For the productive dative constructions shown in (1.16), 22 of the errors come from an analysis that Jess Gropen, Michelle Hollander, and I performed on the speech of five children: Adam, Eve, and Sarah from Brown (1973), and Ross and Mark, whose speech Brian MacWhinney recorded and contributed to the ChiLDES project (MacWhinney and Snow, 1985). We believe that these sentences contain all, or nearly all, of the clear productive double-object datives in the transcripts of their speech residing in the ChiLDES files. How large was the pool of utterances from which these errors came? Adam produced a total of 22,303 utterances in the transcripts; Eve produced 9,482; Sarah produced 26,913; Ross produced 19,591; Mark produced 8,043. Obviously many of these sentences were from stages in which utterance lengths were too short to support double-object sentences, or were in contexts where potentially dativizable verbs were not called for, but a rate of one double-object form every 4,111 sentences (.0002) gives one an idea of how rare these errors are. (Recall that the double-object form is a common construction in casual speech.)

Furthermore, the vast majority of the child's double-object forms were grammatical usages with a few common verbs in forms that were used by their parents. In (7.16) we see that the number of productive (ungrammatical) double-object forms was a small percentage of the number of grammatical double-object forms that could have been picked up from parental speech. In fact, virtually all of the

(7.16)

| | Ungrammatical | | Grammatical | | Grammatical |
	Tokens	Types	Tokens	Types	types also used by adults
Adam	5	3	118	13	11
Eve	11	1	11	5	5
Sarah	0	0	73	12	10
Ross	3	2	172	13	11
Mark	3	2	36	8	7

children's grammatical double-object forms actually did appear in that form in adults' speech in their transcripts, as the last column shows (and others undoubtedly appeared in their speech outside the recording sessions).[11]

Thus on the average, about 95% of a child's double-object sentences (tokens), and about 86% of the verbs the child uses in double-object sentences (types), could have been based on argument structures acquired conservatively from adult speech. This is by no means an obvious result; given that children are prone to using double-object forms to express benefactive relations, the pool of possible double-object forms includes every transitive verb in their vocabulary. Furthermore, only a small number of the verbs that are dativizable in adult speech were actually used in the double-object form by the children. Knowing only how often children use grammatical double-object forms, and that they are capable of productively using it for benefactives, it would be natural to predict that the children's ungrammatical double-object forms would outnumber their grammatical ones, contrary to what we find.

Locatives. Productive use of the locative alternation is even rarer. I searched through the transcripts of Adam, Eve, Sarah, Ross, and Mark for several classes of high-frequency verbs for which the locative alternation in either direction would be natural, though ungrammatical, in English. Specifically, I looked at all sentences involving verbs in the *coil* and *pour* classes, which are grammatical only with locational theme objects, and verbs in the *fill*, *block*, and *soak* classes, which are grammatical only with locational goal objects. This search turned up a total of four clear errors out of the 86,000 sentences in the database. (In addition, Pinker, Lebeaux, and Frost, 1987, noted two errors in which theme and goal were confused, each uttered twice, involving the verbs *crash* and *scribble*.) In comparison, there were hundreds of sentences in which verbs involving themes or goals were used with the correct direct object, including verbs in these classes and verbs in the prominent alternating classes (*splash* verbs, *smear* verbs, *stuff* verbs, *load* verbs, and *pile* verbs). Bowerman reported sixteen errors involving theme-goal reversal with locative verbs and verbs of contact in her 1982b paper, representative of a somewhat larger corpus of errors (size unreported) that she has gathered, from a database that one can roughly estimate as being on the order of a million sentences per child.[12] She notes that "at no time did one or the other 'rule' completely take over. Most of the time, the various verbs were handled in the conventional way (only one Pattern G [object = goal] verb per child—*touch* for Christy and *fill* for Eva—appears to have been completely reinterpreted as a Pattern F [object = theme] verb for a time)" (p. 342). (Even these consistent reversals, we shall see in section 7.5 of this chapter, may be attributed to processes other than productive rule application.) Thus overgeneralization of the locative alternation is a fairly uncommon event, and correct usage of the adult argument structure seems to be the norm.

Causatives. How frequent are overgeneralizations of the causative? In proportional terms, the number of productive causative utterances reported in Bowerman (1982a)—about 125, depending on what is included—is fairly small, considering that they come from seventeen different children, including Bowerman's two daughters, whose diary data may comprise on the order of a million sentences apiece (see note 12). (However, the list provided is not exhaustive.) Furthermore, the number of grammatical causative verbs that children use surely dwarfs the number of productive ones—most of children's transitive verbs have a causative component, either with (e.g., *break*) or without (e.g., *cut*) an intransitive counterpart. Virtually any page of a transcript of a child's speech will contain a causative transitive verb; finding a productive one requires considerable patience.

On the other hand, there are some cases where productive causative verbs outnumber conservative usages. Bowerman (1982a) notes that Christy passed through a stage in which she used *come* and *stay* in transitive sentences, completely replacing *bring*, *keep*, and *leave*. This phenomenon, like the preponderance of incorrect usages of *fill* and *touch* noted earlier, runs against the general pattern of children's conforming to adult argument structures in the vast majority of their utterances involving the relevant argument structure. It calls out for a distinct explanation, which I try to provide in section 7.5.

Passives. Recall that since passivization is marked by a productive affix, the theory does not predict the kind of narrow-class-based conservatism we saw for the other three alternations. Indeed, Pinker, Lebeaux, and Frost (1987) noted that productive passivization is not a rare phenomenon: 18 of the 72 passives we found in Adam's transcripts (25%) and 7 of the 32 we found in Sarah's (22%) could not have been based directly on parental speech. Even the child (Allison) who produced only two passives in all produced one that was productive. Passives were also frequent in the examples of productive transitive verbs reported by Clark (1982) and Bowerman (1982a), neither of whom looked for passives in particular. Granted, for most of these forms we could only be certain that they were productive in morphology, not in argument structure, because the verbs did have a grammatical passive participle in adult speech, such as *I don't want the bird to get eated* or *His mouth is splitted*. But it seems unlikely that in every one of those cases the child heard the passive in adult speech, remembered the passive argument structure, and forgot its surface form.

In sum, productive generalization of argument structures is robust in the sense that virtually all children do it and that they do it systematically enough that random causes can be ruled out. However, the experiments show that children find it easier to use a verb in an argument structure they have heard it in than in a new argument structure that alternates with it, and the spontaneous speech data show that (with the exception of the passive and a handful of particular verbs in the locative and causative alternations) the large majority of children's usages of the argument structures related by an alternation are with verbs that take those argument structures in adult speech. Apparently children are wired to be very sensitive to the combinations of verbs and argument structures they hear in the input, and to stick to those combinations most of the time.

7.4.2 Evidence That Children Are Ambivalent About Their Own Errors

According to the minimalist theory of the source of children's errors, the errors (other than passives) should have the same status with respect to children's grammars as Haigspeak does with respect to adults' grammars: they should be the product of property-predicting but not existence-predicting rules. For adults, this relation is one that leads to intuitions that the novel usages are odd or unusual. Therefore, the theory makes the strong prediction that children should find their own errors odd-sounding as well. Of course this is very hard to demonstrate. The metalinguistic ability to make judgments of well-formedness is notoriously underdeveloped in preschool children. Furthermore, many of the errors children make are seamlessly woven into their discourse, giving an observer no reason to think that anything in their heads is causing them to balk or have second thoughts. Therefore, I will not be able to show that *all* of children's argument structure errors occur without their grammar's full seal of approval. However, there is evidence that *many* of their argument structure errors are of a form that is not fully acceptable to the very children who are prone to making them.

Bowerman (1982a) noted an intriguing phenomenon in Christy's speech. By a certain age, Christy began to show metalinguistic awareness that some causatives are not grammatical in English. She began to correct herself in midsentence and to judge her own and other speakers' productive causative utterances to be ill formed. Examples are presented in (7.17).

(7.17) (a) 3;8: I have to be—have it up! [Tugging on sock]

(b) 3;8: And go—put it like that. [As M puts C's socks on; telling M to turn tops over in a certain way]

(c) 4;7: She won't sit me—let me sit next to her during reading time. [Complaining about friend's behavior in school.]

(d) 4;10: C: Bigger my band. [To M, as request for M to loosen sports band on her glasses. Intonation suggests she recognizes something odd about the word.] M: Is that a real word? C: No. "Smaller my band ... small my band ..." [Contemplative, trying these out] M: If I said "I'm going to bigger your band"—does that sound like something I would say? C: No, because it's not a real word. M: How would I say it? C: "I'm going to bigger—I'm going to make your band bigger today."

(e) 5;3:   C: You almost made me fall down [to M]. M: I almost fell you down. C: [Grins broadly.] M: Can you say that? C: No! You almost made me fall down![13]

(f) 5;4:   I'm not going to pick up the Cheerios that I fall—that I drop on the floor.

(g) 5;11: [Has been begging for friend to be allowed to stay for dinner; M has said she thought friend's family needed her later on.] They're not gonna need her! We' eat' her'! [Emphatic stress on each word. Then claps hand over mouth and smiles sheepishly, recognizing error.]

(h) 6;2:   Say "rabbits ears cooking on the stove" [a family formula for making unwilling child laugh] and see if you can laugh— [breaks off, pauses] ... make me laugh.

(i) 6;3:   E: Will you learn me how to read that book? [to M]. C: [Also to M, with pointed scorn] "Learn" you? What does she mean, "learn" you?

(j) 6;8: E: Christy, you fell me into the car! C: [Laughs and repeats E's error for M's benefit, with pointed emphasis on word *fell*.]

One might think that the recognition that overgeneralized causatives were deviant would coincide with the beginning of the end of the use of these causatives in the child's own speech. That is not so. The first evidence that Christy recognized that not all verbs can be causativized came at 3;8. Though this is over a year after she started to make causative errors, a full four years later (7;11) she was still making them. In fact, 57% of the 62 novel causatives reported for Christy in Bowerman (1982a) occurred during or after the month at which she started to correct herself and others, occupying 73% of the age range at which causative errors were recorded. Thus most of Christy's causative errors occurred during a time at which she was aware that these types of error were ungrammatical.[14]

Hochberg (1986) ran a grammaticality judgment experiment whose results are consistent with that picture. Children awarded a gold star to one of two puppets for speaking "better." When one puppet uttered an ungrammatical lexical causative with *come, fall, stay, be,* or *go* and the other used a correct version containing *bring, drop, keep, put,* or *take,* the correct version was chosen by 78% of the children in the 3;4–3;10 age group, and by 92% of the children in the 4;1–5;5 age group. The majority of Bowerman's (1982) spontaneous speech errors involving these verbs occur in children within this age range, including many errors by children 4 and older. Again, children both make errors and realize that such forms are errors.

The situation is more complicated for the voluntary action verbs *sing, dance, run, jump*, and *dive*, which were uttered in a lexical causative form by one puppet and in a periphrastic sentence by the other puppet. The older children chose the grammatical periphrastic form 68% of the time. As I showed in (7.8), these verbs appear in a small minority of children's errors, so it is difficult to verify whether they are produced during the age range at which they are judged ungrammatical. Nonetheless we do find *cry, watch*, and *remember* used causatively by children over the age of 4, as I would predict. The behavior of the younger children, however, does not fit into the picture I have been painting. Their preferences in the task were at chance (52%), and children of that age are prone to making causative errors with action verbs in their spontaneous speech. However, there is a confounding factor here. Periphrastic causatives are syntactically complex, involving an embedded clause. Ammon and Slobin (1979) showed that 3- and 4-year-old English-speaking children comprehend them poorly, about 70% of the time. In contrast, children learning languages that express causatives in a single clause act them out nearly perfectly by age 4. Single-clause active sentences with English action verbs are also comprehended near-perfectly by 3- to-5-year old children; see, for example, Pinker, Lebeaux, and Frost (1987), table 6. Thus children may have failed to reject ungrammatical lexical causatives involving action verbs in part because the only available alternative—periphrastic causatives—were not easily parsed as natural-sounding sentences.

7.4.3 Summary of Differences Between Children's Errors and Adults'

I have been trying to explain why children speak differently from adults. Too big a difference is an embarrassment: if adults' productivity is due to a complicated rule and children's to a simple version of that same rule, we need to invoke a seemingly useless rule-complication procedure. A more elegant theory is that adults are productive in two ways, one involving a simple rule, one involving a complex rule, and that children's errors are due to their use of the same simple rule. If so, children's errors should resemble adults' errors. I have shown two ways in which this is true. First, children's spontaneous errors are far rarer than their correct usages, and in experiments they have a strong tendency to behave in a way that would make errors impossible: they like to reproduce the argument structures in which they hear a novel verb used. Second, most of the errors children make occur at ages at which they are demonstrably capable of judging such sentences to be ungrammatical. In this regard they demonstrate the same double standard as adults who occasionally bend the language and realize that they are doing so.

7.5   Acquisition of Verb Meaning and Errors in Argument Structure

It is probably difficult to maintain that all of children's productive usages are the product of broad-scale rules used as one-shot innovations. In at least two cases, ungrammatical forms displaced grammatical counterparts during development: Christy's abandonment of *bring*, *keep*, and *leave* in favor of transitive *come* and *stay*, and the systematically incorrect choice of direct object for the verb *touch* by Christy and *fill* by Eva. Clearly, the innovative use of a broad-range rule on an ad hoc basis should not lead to the elimination of a correct form. Moreover, Bowerman cites a datum—reproduced in (7.18)—showing that it is possible for a child to overextend an argument structure in *comprehension*, not just production.

(7.18)   M: Simon says, "Touch your toes."
             C: To what? [Interprets toes as Figure, is looking now for Ground]
             [A moment later]
             M: Simon says, "Touch your knees."
             C: To what?

Such an error would not seem to be the result of a temporary innovation; surely not even the cookbook writer who told her readers to fill the mixture into the zucchini would interpret *fill the glass* as meaning "put the glass into something." Rather, there is a persistent error of some kind here. Perhaps it has something to do with the child's interpretation of the meaning of the verb *touch*.

The cornerstone of the thematic core theory is that lexical rules effecting argument structure alternations involve manipulations of a verb's lexicosemantic structure. The choosiness of an alternation stems from the compatibility of the semantic operation with the existing semantic structure, assessed by either cognitive compatibility (for the use of broad-range rules) or detailed correspondence of semantic structure (for the use of narrow-range rules). Now if children had correct lexical rules but incorrect lexicosemantic representations, they should utter some ungrammatical sentences. Take an extreme case: if children thought *touch* meant *move*, they could say *Touch your hand to that*; if they thought *fill* meant *pour*, they could say *Fill salt into the bear*, even if the rest of their grammars were identical to those of adults. Furthermore, outright verb-for-verb confusion is not a prerequisite for this kind of error: if children thought that *fill* had a meaning that was structurally identical to that of *pour* except for some difference that was not grammar-relevant, such as a different manner of motion or manner of acting upon, its grammatical privileges would be identical to those of *pour*. I will try to show that this chain of events can and does occur in development. To the extent that it does, children will utter errors that sound as if they come from a bad rule but in fact come from a bad word meaning—the errors would essentially be malapropisms with syntactic consequences. For those errors, there is no need to explain how the rule changes, because it doesn't.

In this section I will do two things. First, I will review the literature on the development of verb meaning, which shows that errors in verb semantics are pervasive in young children. Second, I will show that children's meaning errors can be, and often are, the cause of their argument structure errors. Specifically, I will show that systematic biases and errors in the acquisition of verb meaning lead to predictable kinds of errors in argument structure.

7.5.1 The Development of Verb Meaning

Slobin (1985), in his extensive review of cross-linguistic patterns in language acquisition, suggests that children seek the linguistic means of expressing certain kinds of conceptual gestalts. The most prominent of these gestalts or "scenes" are the "manipulative activity scene," where an agent acts on a patient and causes a change, and the "figure-ground scene," where an object moves with respect to a reference frame. These of course are the same as the ACT-THING-THING (agent-patient) relation and the GO-THING-PATH relation that constitute the basic semantic substructures out of which verb meanings are composed in the current theory. Slobin invokes these schemas to explain a variety of cross-linguistic evidence showing contrasts between early acquisition of some forms and errors with others in acquisition, many of them involving closed-class morphemes. Interestingly, children's verb errors do not generally seem to involve confusions about these basic elements: the agency and motion/change components of verbs are virtually always respected in spontaneous speech and in the experiments on comprehension of verb meaning to be discussed below. The distinction between punctual events and ongoing processes or states, which is represented as a point/region distinction on the time line, the third major tier of lexicosemantic representations, is also attended to early and consistently by children cross-linguistically (Slobin, 1985; Bickerton, 1981). Thus the basic semantic structures underlying verb meanings—agency/force, motion/change, and time—are salient, easily acquired notions for the child, as their centrality in the representational theory would predict.

However, most verb meanings involve specific patterns of conflation involving combinations of these and other semantic structures. At the beginning of

chapter 5, especially section 5.3, I showed that many of the structures representing particular verb meanings had to be learned by the child. This was necessary
because many syntactic distinctions were explained by appealing to detailed
properties of semantic structures, and those semantic structures were distinct
from conceptual categories and varied from language to language. Since the
learning mechanisms for specific verb meanings proposed in chapter 6 cannot
succeed in a single trial for any verb that is not simply a label for a cognitive event
category, but requires the accumulation of evidence over situations, we would
expect children to make errors with verb meanings. This would show up in their
producing or accepting verbs in situations that would be inappropriate in the
adult language. A great deal of evidence suggests that children do that.

7.5.1.1 Later Onset and Slower Rate   Gentner (1982) presents extensive
evidence that at the beginning of the acquisition process, children in a variety of
language communities acquire their first verbs later than their first nouns, and acquire verbs at a slower rate than nouns. She demonstrates that this asymmetry is
not explainable in terms of frequency (verbs have higher token frequencies than
nouns) nor in terms of serial position, phonological transparency, or other
potentially confounding factors. She proposes that most nouns that children hear
correspond to tightly interconnected representations for object categories that
children's perceptual and conceptual systems assemble automatically, uniformly, and independently of language. Verb meanings, in contrast, consist of
representations whose exact conflations of semantic components are more
cognitively and perceptually arbitrary and more variable across languages.
Hence the proper semantic structures must be assembled by the child as part of
learning the language; they cannot simply be retrieved from a store of preexisting concepts and assigned a morpheme. This learning would correspond to
the Semantic Structure Hypothesis Testing mechanism outlined in chapter 6.

7.5.1.2 Underspecified meanings   One of the ways in which a child could
have a defective verb meaning before learning is complete is that semantic substructures could be missing from a lexicosemantic representation. Gentner
(1975) provides evidence that this occurs in the acquisition of transfer-of-
possession verbs, whose semantic structures have overlapping components.
Give and *take* are the simplest verbs in this group, involving the causation of a
transfer of possession. *Pay* and *trade* contain this conflation as a substructure of
their meanings; on top of that, *pay* contains the selection restriction that the
transferred object is money and *trade* contains the provision of a countertransfer.
Buy, *sell*, and *spend* are the most complex, specifying causation of possession

transfer, the selection restriction involving money, and a countertransfer. Gentner asked children between the ages of $3\frac{1}{2}$ and $8\frac{1}{2}$ to act out sentences involving these verbs with dolls and toys. Children's success rates in acting out the verb meanings as an adult would were related to the verbs' semantic complexity. *Give* and *take* were acted out best, followed by *pay* and *trade*, followed by *buy*, *sell*, and *spend*. Errors generally consisted of omitting the countertransfer or the selection restriction: *buy* was acted out as if it meant *take*; *sell* was acted out as if it meant *give*.[15] This suggests that children's early representations of the meanings of verbs like *buy* and *sell* have only a part of the semantic structures that the verbs have in the adult language.

Ammon (1980) has also demonstrated children's failure to respect all the components of a verb's meaning. She presented children with eleven sentences involving verbs of causation of motion (*hand, throw, hook, lock, skate, drive, shovel, scratch*, and *pinch*). Each sentence was paired with three pictures, two of which were inappropriate by virtue of having an incorrect instrument, body part, manner of causation of motion, or path of motion. Children between the ages of 2;8 and 6 were tested. In almost all cases, performance improved markedly with age. A number of semantic distinctions were particularly difficult for younger children. The youngest children were insensitive to the distinction between *hand* and *throw* that requires proximal physical transfer for one and ballistic motion over a path for the other. They also had trouble with verbs incorporating specific object types into their meanings, assigning them the role of patient/theme rather than instrument. Specifically, they often chose a depiction of throwing a skate for *skating*, merely moving a hook or lock for *hooking* or *locking*, and pushing a car for *driving*.

Other studies have also shown children acquiring parts of the meanings of verbs, causing earlier acquisition of simpler verbs in families such as *come, go, bring*, and *take* (Clark and Garnica, 1974) and *ask, promise*, and *tell* (Chomsky, 1969).

7.5.1.3 Overspecified meanings Cases where a child has too much semantic structure in a verb-meaning representation are harder to detect than when the child has not enough semantic structure, because they result in the child's failing to use a verb in certain situations rather than using it incorrectly. However, there is some evidence that young children at first restrict verbs to small subsets of their permissible contexts. Bowerman (1978, p. 982) notes:

Christy and Eva's first uses of *put, take*, etc., were restricted to relatively specific, and different contexts. For example, they initially used *put* in the context of donning clothing, placing small objects onto surfaces or into containers ("put on," "put in"), returning things to an original location ("put back"), or storing things out of sight ("put away"). In contrast, they used *take* for the removal of clothing from the body or small objects from surfaces or containers ("take off," "take out"), for requests to be taken outside ("take outside"), and for asking that something be removed or protesting its removal ("take away"). A child who is quite capable of choosing the correct word in contexts like these ... may be at a loss when she wants to refer to a new act that does not fit clearly into any of these categories, such as sticking her thumbs up.

There is, of course, no contradiction between the observation that children's verb meanings can either be underspecified (causing overly general usages) or overspecified (causing overly specific usages). It is plausible that children may carve events into categories at a "basic level" of specificity, as they seem to do for object categories (Brown, 1958; Rosch, Mervis, Gray, Johnson, and Boyes-Braem, 1976), and label these categories with verbs in the language they are acquiring. However, high-frequency verbs, unlike high-frequency nouns, do not in general seem to map onto basic event categories, and thus we would expect children to make errors for verbs whose meanings are more specific or less specific than those basic event categories.

7.5.1.4 Biases in Semantic Development   Children not only acquire verb meanings piecemeal but also show biases in *which* aspects of events they like to encode into verb meanings. Gentner (1978) noted that a common pattern in the development of noun meaning was for preschool children to attend to the perceptual appearance of objects, sometimes ignoring information about an object's function. She reasoned that an analogous bias in the acquisition of the meanings of action verbs might manifest itself as a sensitivity to manner of motion and an insensitivity to specific change of state. In particular, she considered the verbs *mix*, *stir*, *beat*, and *shake*. According to her analysis, *mix* specifies a particular change of state ("an increase in homogeneity") but is noncommittal about the kind of action that effects it. The other three verbs, in contrast, are noncommittal about the resulting state of the patient, but each requires a particular manner of motion: rotary motion, medium rate, for *stir*; elliptical motion, rapid rate, for *beat*; oscillating motion for *shake*. Children aged 5 to 9 and adults were asked to describe six kinds of events and to verify whether each of the four verbs was appropriate to them: a stirring, beating, or shaking motion performed on salt and water (which could "mix") or on cream (which, already being a homogeneous substance, could not). Verbs encoding manners of motion posed no problem for the children: 97% of the 5-to-7-year-olds and 93% of the 7-to-9-year-olds paired the correct manner-of-motion verb with the appropriate manner of motion. However, the end-state requirement of *mix* was poorly grasped: the 5-to-7-year-olds used *mix* on 48% of the trials where the patient was mixable and on 46% of the trials where it was not. (The 7-to-9-year-olds and adults were more discriminating, though not invariably so, perhaps because they sensed that water is more aptly described as dissolving salt than mixing with it or because of their knowledge that milk products are separable suspensions.) Gentner notes that the indiscriminate use of *mix* was due to a verb meaning distorted so as to encode manner rather than end state, not to a general unfamiliarity with the verb itself: in a separate, unpublished experiment, she showed that children understand *mix* as an action verb similar to *stir* by the age of $3\frac{1}{2}$.

Other phenomena reported in the literature may be related to this bias. Huttenlocher, Smiley, and Charney (1983) observe that when children use verbs to refer to other people's actions, they use manner-of-motion verbs like *walk* before change-of-state verbs like *open*. Furthermore, manners are salient enough to children that they easily conflate them with motion-path structures in ways not sanctioned by their language. Bowerman (1981) notes that Christy and Eva occasionally conflated postures or emotional expressions with motion, resulting in errors such as *He laughed all the way down the hill and he laughed on top of the other people* (Eva, 3;11), *OK, then I'm frowning out the door* (Eva, 5;0), and *We crouched down the hill* (Christy, 10;5). Even in Spanish, a language that never allows manner of motion to be conflated with translation along a path in the verb system (Talmy, 1985), children seem to think that manners are possible components of complex meanings; Slobin (1985) cites errors such as *correr abajo* (run down).

7.5.1.5 Substitution Errors If children's representations of verb meanings are incomplete, biased, or in flux, this should be manifest in their using them in inappropriate situations in spontaneous speech. Since some English verbs form families of minimally differing members, such errors will often consist of using one verb where adult English calls for a different verb. Menyuk (1969) was the first investigator I know of to document incorrect verb usages in spontaneous speech. She noted errors such as those shown in (7.19) in her sample of 152 children between the ages of 3 and 7.

(7.19) They'll close him in jail.
   I want to say in the microphone.
   He does instruments.
   She has to make a lot of work.
   I didn't see at the other patients.

She also noted that substitution errors involving the verbs listed in (7.20) were common.

(7.20) *go* for *do*   *tell* for *say*
       do for *will, can, make*   *ask* for *tell*

make for *do, play, have*	*speak* for *say*
have for *get*	*see* for *look*
get for *become*	*look* for *see*
take for *get, keep, put*	*sit* for *stay*
put for *take*	*stay* for *sit*
close for *put*	*hang* for *fall*
say for *tell,* spea*k*	*fall* for *hang*

Bowerman (1978; see also 1981, 1982c) provides a large number of verb substitution examples accompanied by the full sentence and the age of the child who produced them. Representative examples of each type of substitution, including the earliest examples provided for each of the two children, are given in (7.21). The semantic distinctions being flouted are locational versus possessional transfer (*put* versus *give*), locational versus state changes (*put* versus *make*), active versus permissive causation (*let* versus *make*), and paths of motion distinguishing the path-functions 'to' and 'from' and the deictic place-constants 'here' and 'there' (*put* versus *take* versus *bring*).

(7.21) *put* for *give*

      C 3;3:   You put me just bread and butter.

      C 3;4:   You put the pink one to me.

      E 2;2:   I go put it to Christy.

     give for *put*

      C 4;4   Whenever Eva doesn't need her towel she gives it on my table and when I'm done with it I give it back to her.

      E 2;7:   Give some ice in here, Mommy. Put some ice in here, Mommy.

      E 2;10: Don't give those next to me.

     put for *make*

      C 3;1:   You put a place for Eva to put in. [Wants M to make a depression in a pillow in doll carriage so E can ride]

      C 3;9:   But never ever put the door locked.

      E 2;10: I want to put it tight. [Wants M to let her tighten nipple on her bottle]

      E 4;7:   I'm not going to put it too long. [E cutting pieces of yarn for a doll's hair]

     make for *put*

      E 2;2:   I make some butter my sandwich. [As E puts butter on bread]

      E 3;0:   Make them back up. [Wants M to put/set tiny dolls back onto table; they'd just fallen off]

     let for *make*

      C 3;3:   I don't want Sandra to say good night. So don't let me.

C 3;11: Don't ever ever let me stay in my bedroom until I go to bed. [As M starts getting C ready for bed without officially ending C's stay in her room for naughtiness]

make for *let*

C 3;6: But usually puppets make—let people put their hands in. [After M had called dolls with toilet-paper-roll bodies "puppets"; C disagreeing]

C 3;9: Make me watch it. [Wants father to let her watch a TV show]

put for *take, bring, drop, make go*

C 2;2: I hafta put these off so I can do it better. [Trying to take rings off her fingers]

E 2;1: I go put rubber band off. [Starting to take rubber band off deck of cards]

take for *bring, put*

C 2;1: Daddy take his pants on.

C 2;2: Hey, I take this at home. [Finding doll she had brought home earlier]

E 2;0: I take it up. [Putting bowl up onto shelf in cupboard]

bring for *take, put*

C 2;1: Let bring this out. [Wants to take cooked bacon out of pan on stove]

E 2;9: I'm bringing it back to my pocket. [Putting a piece of gum back in her pocket]

For many of these examples the mental mechanisms causing the errors are difficult to identify uniquely. There are three areas of indeterminacy. First, for verbs that appear in an argument structure that is inappropriate for that verb in adult English, it is unclear whether the child had an impoverished, distorted, or mislabeled verb meaning that was fed into a correct rule of argument structure alternation, or a correct verb meaning that was fed into an overly broad rule of argument structure alternation, or both. For example, *They'll close him in jail* could reflect either the child's using *close* with a meaning similar to *put* or the child's applying an overly broad locative rule to *close the jail*. Similarly, when Christy used *put* in a double-object structure in *You put me just bread and butter*, it could be because she used *put* as if it meant *give*, or because (for whatever reason) she already had a prepositional-dative argument structure for *put*, as in her utterance *You put the pink one to me*, and applied the dative alternation to it (see Pinker, 1984, for a general discussion of this methodological problem). However, in some cases lexical rules can be ruled out: for verbs that appear in an argument structure that is grammatical for adults but in a context that is semantically inappropriate, as in *I'm bringing it back to my pocket* or *Don't ever ever let me stay in my bedroom until I go to bed*, it is clear that the verb meaning itself was inappropriate.

A second open question is whether the errors reflect a stable but incorrect semantic representation for the verb, or a correct representation that is incompletely or improperly processed during the on-line computations involved in speech production. In her 1978 paper Bowerman suggests that on-line processes are the culprit: the child used the verbs correctly for a period of time before the errors began to appear, and correct usages outnumbered errors at all stages. Larry Rosen and I corroborated the rarity of these errors in two ways. We extracted from the transcripts of Adam, Eve, and Sarah all sentences containing verbs that seemed likely to be used in errors involving confusions of locational, stative, and possessional verbs, like the ones reported in Bowerman (1978, 1982c, 1983b): *become, bring, force, give, go, has, hold, is, keep, make, put, stand, stay, stick, take,* and *turn*. The four examples reproduced in (7.22a) were the only ones we found. Second, in an unpublished experiment, we asked children to describe pictures involving changes of state and possession, such as a mother giving a ball to a girl or a boy coloring a piece of paper. We stacked the deck in an effort to elicit substitution errors by explicitly telling the child to use the typically intrusive verb. For example, we said, "Can you tell me what she's doing, using the word *put*?"—hoping for an occasional *He's putting the paper blue*. Thirty children each described nineteen pictures, for a total of 570 invitations to make an error. However, when children used the target verb, they did so by exercising their option to use it correctly, as in *He put water on him*; the four utterances shown in (7.22b) were the only clear-cut errors produced.

(7.22) (a) A 3;1: I goin' put de door open.

A 4;4: Now I think I take the whole crayoned. [Coloring in a picture]

A 4;5: It's gonna stay raining.

E 2;3: He put his bread and butter folded over.

(b) 3;3: Mother takes ball away from boy and puts it to girl. Square go big.

3;11 Boy puts flowers to girl.

4;7: Square went bigger.

Although we have evidence that verb substitutions are in some ways like one-time speech errors, in a later unpublished paper Bowerman (1983c) points out some differences between the substitution errors and ordinary slips of the tongue of the sort adults make. First, children's errors involve systematic patterns of substitution that recur within and between children (in fact, they are systematic enough for Rosen and me to have replicated the existence of some of her exact error patterns in several other children), whereas any *particular* substitution in an adult's speech is likely to be a random, extremely rare event. Second, adults' substitution errors rarely involve verbs (approximately 3% of adults' substitution errors; 81% involve nouns), whereas children's substitution errors virtually never involve nouns. Third, adults' errors are usually self-corrected, whereas these childhood errors were not. In addition, I doubt that adults make many substitution errors of the kind displayed in (7.21) or (7.22); I have never heard one during the period of time I have been listening for argument structure errors in adults' speech (see section 4.5.1). These considerations lead me to suggest that children's substitution errors cannot be explained completely by the properties of the mechanisms that generate adults' slips of the tongue. The children's representations of verb meanings themselves must be shifting or poorly consolidated compared to those of adults.

A third open question is whether the substitution errors, assuming they result from transient processes, result from the child's looking for one stem during the word-finding process and incorrectly fetching a stem for a related verb, or from the child's representing one entry incorrectly and applying it to a situation that happens to be more aptly described by an independent entry in the adult language, with that other entry playing no causal role. The fact that most of the errors can be rendered more grammatical by substituting another verb suggests at first that it is simply the word-finding process that has gone astray. However, the semantic space defined by causation of motion and possession is fairly well filled in English, so the fact that we can think of a verb that would be more appropriate than the one the child used does not mean that the child was trying to retrieve that verb. In fact, for many of the errors it is questionable whether the child was in fact aiming for a distinct target word. For example, the sentence *They put Dorothy different than in the book* (after watching "The Wizard of Oz" on television) and *He put his bread and butter folded over* can be classified as "*put* for *make*" substitutions, but *make* is not quite right either in adult English, so it is not obvious that the child was seeking it. And in a small number of errors, the prepositions are appropriate for the verb the child actually used, not the verb that adults would use (e.g., *I'm bringing it back to my pocket*), suggesting that the child wanted to use that verb but did not know it was inappropriate, rather than wanting to use a different verb and failing to retrieve its stem. Thus either or both processes could be occurring in the errors.

Despite these indeterminacies for the psycholinguist interested in underlying mechanisms, one thing is clear. Something about children's semantic structures is different from those of adults. Even when children know enough about a verb's meaning to use it correctly most of the time, the pieces are not consolidated firmly enough to prevent occasional errors, of predictable kinds, from occurring. And, of course, adults do not show the kinds of systematic errors in experimental tasks that children do. With converging evidence from a variety of sources that children have difficulty with verb meanings, we can turn to the question of whether these semantic difficulties can be lawfully and causally related to children's syntactic errors.

7.5.2   Relations Between the Development of Verb Meaning and the Development of Argument Structure

Children make errors with verbs' argument structures, and they make errors with verbs' meanings. Can their errors with meanings sometimes be the cause of their errors with argument structures? The theory says that this should happen. Every time it does, the minimalist solution to the unlearning problem has one less datum to explain; as the child's verb meanings become increasingly tuned to the adult state by the situation-sensitive mechanisms discussed in chapter 6, some of the sources of the argument structure errors disappear.

In this section I discuss three correlational linkages between semantic structure and argument structure in language development. As always, causal relations are more difficult to establish, requiring experimental interventions. I will end the chapter by discussing experiments designed by Jess Gropen (Gropen, Pinker, and Goldberg, 1987; Gropen, 1989; Gropen et al., in preparation), which represent important strides in this direction.

7.5.2.1   Onset of Errors   The first link I discuss is only a correlation, but it is an intriguing one. In her discussion of errors in verb semantics, Bowerman notes that children initially use the error-prone verbs *put*, *give*, *make*, and *let* accurately, though in restricted sets of contexts. Furthermore, when errors begin to occur, they are not random substitutions but represent a subtle analysis of verb meanings into abstract notions such as change and causation, exactly as the Thematic Relations Hypothesis of Gruber (1965) and Jackendoff (1972) would predict. That is why *put* (cause a change of location) and *make* (cause a change of identity or state) are interchanged, why *put* is interchanged with *give* (cause a change of possession), and why *make* (actively cause) is interchanged with *let* (permissively cause).[16] Further evidence that these errors stem from the child's performing a thematic analysis comes from the fact that similar errors occur in the domain of prepositions and nouns involving a spatial metaphor for time, such as *Can I have any reading behind the dinner?* or *Do we have room before we go to bed for another reading?* (Bowerman, 1982c). In the prepositional system, some languages have different prepositions (e.g., analogous to the English *to*) for

changes of location and possession; children often confuse them (Slobin, 1985). However, substitutions of verbs and prepositions that are not related by shared thematic substructures are rare or nonexistent.

The fact that these errors do not occur at the onset of use of the relevant verbs suggests that the early verb meanings are not properly built around the basic thematic notions of cause, change, and so on, but may have been more undifferentiated schemas for specific kinds of events. (This could correspond to the verbs' being ad hoc labels for gestalts corresponding to interesting kinds of events, bypassing the representational structures for semantic structure altogether, or to the representations' being temporarily cluttered by so many extraneous substructures for situation-specific manners, object properties, 'for/ to' goals, and so on, that similarities among verbs are obscured.) In either case, a change in the representations of verb meanings seems to occur that makes the similarities among thematically related verbs more salient to the child, presumably because they are more explicitly represented in the verbs' entries.

An initial period of correct use followed by overextensions to ungrammatical cases is, of course, the familiar sequence of development for argument structure alternations as well. Recall from section 7.3 that children's ungrammatical argument structures are never the result of pure syntactic rearrangements, but at all stages betray the application of semantic operations manipulating notions like causation, possession, motion, and state change. Until children analyze verb meanings as containing these notions, they will be unable either to abstract the broad-range rule from conservatively acquired verb pairs or to apply it productively to verbs acquired in one version of the alternation. The suggestion, then, is that the reanalysis or abstraction process that leads to the appearance of verb substitution errors is a prerequisite for the formation and application of lexical rules affecting argument structure.

Some of the age milestones for various verb uses in the speech of Christy and Eva are at least roughly consistent with there being a correlation between semantic and syntactic changes. As mentioned, the first uses of periphrastic causatives involving *make* are synchronous with the onset of lexical causative errors in their speech and in the speech of several other children noted in Bowerman (1982a). For Eva, early examples of the correct use of *put, give, make,* and *let* run from 1;11 to 2;0; errors in verb choice begin at 2;1, and her causativization errors begin at 2;2. For Christy, correct use of the four verbs are documented for the age range 2;0–2;3; verb selection errors begin at 2;1, and her causative errors also begin at 2;1. Naturally one would not want to make too much of these rough correlations, but they are consistent with the picture of related developments in lexical semantics and argument structure syntax.

7.5.2.2   Argument Structures in Verb Substitution Errors   In chapter 1 I presented a large number of spontaneous speech forms that demonstrate nonconservative use of verbs in argument structures. These errors could have resulted from any of three processes: applying a lexical rule too broadly; having the right verb in mind and retrieving the wrong stem (a speech error or one-time malapropism); or having a distorted or partially acquired semantic representation of a verb that spuriously allows it to match a lexical rule (a stable malapropism). Distinguishing these processes is possible for some of the errors, not for others. If for a given error no other English verb would be appropriate in that argument structure, if the semantics of the verb used was appropriate in the context, and if the thematic core of the broad-range rule also fit the context, it was probably overapplication of a rule that was the cause. *Brush me my hair*, *Button me the rest*, and *Can you climb me up there?* are examples. However, if the verb-argument structure combination that would have been the input to the lexical rule does not exist in adult English, if one can think of an existing English verb that would be syntactically and semantically perfect if substituted in the sentence, and if the meaning components uniquely possessed by the verb used were not appropriate to the context, incorrect stem retrieval would have to be the cause. An example of this kind is *Keep me a favor*; cf. **Keep a favor for me; *Keep a favor*. (*Write me a snowman* is similar, but as mentioned in chapter 1, Eve actually used sentences like *Write a lady for me* but never used sentences like *Draw me a lady*, so both a stable lexicosemantic error and the use of a rule are implicated.) The telltale signs of errors caused by relatively stable mislearned verb meanings would consist of verb use whose meaning was appropriate neither to the adult version of that verb nor to the adult version of any other verb. This kind of error is best detected through experiments, which I will discuss in the next section.

A large number of the argument structure errors reported in chapter 1 are ambiguous. For example, many of Bowerman's causative errors could have been the result of seeking a noncausative stem and retrieving its causative counterpart because of the meaning components they share: *come* where *bring* or *take* would be appropriate, *go* where *take*, *put*, or *send* would be appropriate, *stay* for *keep* or *leave*, *fall* for *drop*, *die* for *kill*, *eat* for *feed*, *remember* for *remind*, *rise* for *raise*, *have* for *take* or *give* (especially in idioms), and *be* for *put*, *make*, or *keep*.

Causative-for-noncausative malapropisms may be the source of some of the causativization errors in languages like Hebrew (Berman, 1982) and Hungarian (Slobin, 1985), in which few or no words appear in identical form with both causative and noncausative argument structures; morphological differences always distinguish such pairs in the language. The fact that 2-to-3-year-old children make these errors is puzzling because the children could not simply be overgeneralizing a regularity in the input—there is none—at least not if they are attending to morphology at all. However, if they mistakenly pair the stem for a verb with a causative meaning with a distinct, noncausative, verb, the errors would result. The fact that many of the verbs cited by Berman as being overgeneralized have nonhomophonous lexical causative forms in the child's vocabulary supports this account. But this is not true in all cases (Berman, personal communication), so not all of the errors can be due to problems in retrieving stems for a known verb. Children may also create causative verb meanings for which they lack stems, and may borrow the stem for the noncausative verb that represents the effect event, resulting in an error. In either case, the syntactic error could be traced to a deviant pairing of stem and meaning, not to an overly broad rule.[17]

Among the errors with double-object verbs, we find many uses of *put* rather than *give*, but since the child also said *You put the pink one to me*, a lexical rule could have been the proximal cause. The use of *say* where an adult would use *tell* is ambiguous, as is *spend us money*, which probably came from causativization of *spend* resulting in a possession-loss verb, but conceivably could have been an intrusion of *spend* where *cost us money* was the target. In general, *say* is a very common intruder in children's speech. Aside from several substitutions for *tell* in (1.16) in chapter 1, we see it used for *talk* or *speak* in (7.19), and it was used to mean *call* at least three times by Ross MacWhinney in "V NP_{object} $NP_{complement}$" structures that resemble the double-object form (e.g., *Him said me twerp; You said me a Skywalker*). Ross also used *tell* in the double-object form for *ask* (*Don't tell me any more questions*) and for *read* (*No, tell me Siegfried first*).

Among the locative errors, some can be characterized as directly substituting *steal* for *rob* and vice versa; for most of the others, the misused word does seem fully compatible in meaning with the context, though we cannot completely rule out the possibility that *cover* was used for *put* or *fill* for *pour*.

In sum, an unknown proportion of children's argument structure errors, greater than zero but less than 100%, are malapropisms caused by stem intrusions from semantically similar verbs. Overapplied lexical rules were discussed in the previous section, and the effects on argument structure of systematically miscon-strued verb meanings will be discussed in the next section, but is there anything to be learned from stem intrusion errors themselves? In this subsection I would like to make a small point, but one that is not obvious and perhaps not insignificant. That is that the phenomenon of stem intrusions shows that children link argument structures tightly to details of verbs' semantic structures, as the theory requires.

Say the child seeks verb V_1 which has meaning M_1, argument structure A_1, and stem S_1. Instead, his retrieval mechanism gives him stem S_2 from verb V_2, because of the similarity of its meaning, M_2, with M_1. Now the question is: will the argument structure used by the child be A_2, because the stem is S_2, or A_1, because the meaning is M_1? Another way of putting it is, when a stem and a meaning part company, does the stem get its way in choosing the argument structure, or does the meaning? The empirical answer is that when A_1 and A_2 are different, we usually find A_1, the argument structure belonging to the target meaning, being used. Children say *Put Eva the yukky one first*, or *You put the pink one to me*, not *Put the yukky one into/onto Eva first*. Conversely, they say *Give some ice cream in here*, not *Give some ice cream to here*. There are a very small number of exceptions, such as Eva's *I'm bringing it back to my pocket*, where *bring* wins out over the possible target *put* and enforces the choice of *to* over *into*, and many ambiguous cases, such as *Write me a snowman*, where A_1 and A_2 are the same (*Draw me a snowman, Write me a letter*). But it is significant that we observe argument structure errors accompanying apparent verb substitution errors at all.

Is this too obvious to mention? I don't think so. The view that argument structures are arbitrarily and conventionally paired with verbs directly and on a verb-by-verb basis, with no consistent contribution from lexical semantics other than specifying the number of arguments, would predict that an intruding verb should carry its own argument structure along with it; the fact that the child had a different meaning in mind would be irrelevant.

Furthermore, it cannot be assumed that a verb's meaning is in some sense the "most important" part of its lexical entry, so that in hybrid stem-meaning pairings that are the result of processing errors, the meaning wins out in determining all other parts of the lexical hybrid entry merely because of its importance or centrality. Pinker and Prince (1988) point out that meaning plays no systematic role in the formation of the past tense in English. Irregular verbs like *come, go, do, have, set, get, put*, and *stand* each have dozens of meanings, especially in combination with particles like *in, out, up*, and *off*. But each of the verbs has the same irregular past tense forms in all of their semantic incarnations. This occurs even when these stems appear in combination with meaningless prefixes—*stood/understood, got/forgot, came/overcame*. Conversely, synonyms need not have the same kinds of past tense forms: compare *hit/hit* with *strike/struck* with *slap/slapped*, which have similar meanings but different kinds of past tenses. Thus past-tense morphology is sensitive to stems, not to meanings. Children, of course, very frequently overgeneralize past-tense regularities, but interestingly, the generalizations follow the lines of morphology and phonology—we find

errors like *brang* for *brought* and *bote* for *bit* (cf. *sing/sang* and *write/wrote*)—
but children never, as far as I know, follow the lines of semantics: they are not
tempted to say *hit/hut* because of the semantic similarity of *hit* to *strike/struck*,
or *run/rane* on the analogy of semantically similar *come/came*, or *write/wrew*
because of *draw/drew*. As far as children are concerned, verb entries have not just
more or less "important" parts for generalization, but different kinds of information that are relevant to different kinds of generalization. Thus it is noteworthy
that regardless of what causes them, errors with argument structures are associated with the meaning that the child had in mind, and are not generally suppressed
by the stem he or she used.

7.5.2.3 Relations Between Biases in Acquiring Verb Semantics and Re-
curring Errors in Argument Structures   A third suggestive correlation be-
tween errors in verb semantics and errors in argument structure is the fact that we
can use the nature of the biases in acquisition of lexical semantics to predict the
nature of the persistent argument structure errors in spontaneous speech. Among
the verb biases that have been demonstrated experimentally are a sensitivity to
manner of causation of motion combined with an undersensitivity to the end state
(Gentner, 1978) and a tendency to interpret certain arguments (e.g., instruments
and themes of means events) as primary patient/themes of caused motion (Ammon, 1980).   Among the argument structure errors that are not one-time
innovations but actual stable replacements for the correct argument structure
over a period of time are Christy's use of *touch* with its theme of motion as direct
object and/or its goal of motion as oblique (as in *Touch your toes ... To what?*)
and Eva's use of *fill* in the same way (e.g., *Can I fill some salt into the bear?*).
Interestingly, the biases in acquiring verb semantics, if they tainted the semantic
representations of *touch* and *fill*, would directly lead to the persistent argument
structure errors, according to the current theory. The thematic core of the *into/
onto* locative form consists of X causing Y to move to Z, and most verbs in the
broad class have a manner attached either to the causation of the motion or to the
motion itself. If a child mistakenly thought that *touch* meant "cause X to move
into contact with Y" rather than "cause a body part to be in contact with Y," as the
moving-theme/patient bias would predict, *touch* would fit the thematic core of
the *into/onto* locative form. Likewise, if a child mistakenly thought that *fill* meant
"pour X into Y, making Y more full" rather than "cause Y to be full," here again
the thematic core of the *into/onto* locative is satisfied and incorrect use of its argument structure should ensue. Many other possible semantic biases could result
in argument structure errors as well, but these are particularly interesting cases
because the semantic bias has been demonstrated in independent experiments
and the associated syntactic errors are particularly persistent (and thus cannot be

explained by occasional innovative use of broad-range rules). In the next section I discuss experimental evidence demonstrating that this intriguing correlation probably has a causal basis.

7.5.3 Experimental Evidence Showing That Semantic Biases Affect Argument Structures

Fill the water-type errors are among the most persistent argument structure errors, supplanting correct *fill the glass*-type usages in the speech of at least one child and occurring in at least four different children whose speech we have examined (Christy, Eva, Adam, and Ross). There is a semantic bias in acquiring verb meaning, Gentner's manner-over-end-state bias, that could account for the error if the current theory is correct. Jess Gropen and I thus chose errors of this kind as a case study for the theory's prediction that argument structures are projections of lexicosemantic structure and that some of children's argument structure errors are the result of errors in verb semantics. What has to be demonstrated is that (a) the manner-over-end-state bias actually taints children's understanding of the meaning of *fill*, causing it to denote something like pouring, filling by means of pouring, or increasing the contents by means of pouring; (b) children who have an incorrect meaning for *fill* also have a tendency to say *fill the water*; (c) acquiring a verb with a given semantic representation is *sufficient* to lead to the use of a particular argument structure.

7.5.3.1 Errors in Understanding *Fill*-type Verbs

The first task assessed children's understanding of verbs like *fill* and *empty*, which require the locational goal/source or "container" as direct object,[18] and of verbs like *pour* and *dump*, which require the locational patient/theme or "content" as direct object. (The verbs *stuff* and *splash*, which alternate, were also tested.) The task required children to decide which of two sequences, each consisting of a before-and-after pair of drawings, corresponded to the verb in question. To familiarize children with the drawing conventions, we first presented a sequence of drawings that was consistent with both pouring and filling; these sequences were constructed so as to provided no information to the child as to what either *pour* or *fill* means, and could be used prior to the testing of either verb. For example, in the first frame, a woman pours water from a pitcher to a glass in a sink, and in the second frame, the glass is shown full of water in the sink. Children were told: "Look at this [first frame] ... there's a woman, a pitcher, water, and a glass; look at this [second frame] ... there's the glass and the water; now look at both of them ... when the woman does this [pointing to first frame] and it ends up like that [pointing to second frame], it's called 'pouring'" (or "filling," depending on which verb we were about to test with that set of pictures for that child.) Then the child was shown two test sequences, each preserving one of the two frames from the demonstration sequence. In one sequence, the first frame showed the woman pouring water from the pitcher to the glass, but the second showed the glass empty, with pools of water lying in the sink. In the other sequence, the first frame showed the woman filling the glass by lifting the faucet handle, which we thought would be a less prototypical manner of pouring than use of a pitcher, and the second frame showed the glass full of water. For both sequences, the question was: "Which of these two sets of pictures is 'pouring'?" (or "filling", if that was the verb being tested). The "correct" answers we had in mind were the pitcher-empty sequence for pouring and the faucet-full sequence for filling. (When we administered the task to a group of sixteen adult subjects, they made those exact choices in every case but one.) Each verb was tested twice, the second time with a new set of pictures depicting a different set of participants. Each sequence of pictures was used to test *pour* for half the children and *fill* for the other half. Similar triplets of sequences were constructed for the other verbs. All the usual factors were counterbalanced. Three groups with sixteen children in each group were tested: ages 2;6–3;5, 3;6–4;5, and 4;6–5;5. The primary dependent measure was the number of children who chose the sequence appropriate to the adult verb meaning on both trials.

The results showed that the manner-over-end-state bias indeed affects the acquisition of the meanings of verbs in these classes. For the manner–specific verbs *pour* and *dump* (which take the theme/patient or content as direct object), children in all three age groups chose the sequence depicting the correct manner and incomplete effect for both picture sets in numbers significantly above chance (thirteen of the sixteen 2-to-3-year-olds, fourteen of the sixteen 3-to-4-year-olds, thirteen of the sixteen 4-to-5-year-olds; chance = 25% = four out of sixteen children). In contrast, children, unlike adults, did not insist that the end-state-specific verbs *fill* and *empty* apply to sequences depicting full or empty containers at the end: in none of the three age groups did the children choose the correct sequences in numbers significantly greater than chance. Moreover, for some children in the oldest group, there was actually a preference for the typical but semantically irrelevant manner associated with filling containers: for *fill*, half the children chose the sequence depicting pouring from a pitcher and an empty glass on both opportunities, a proportion that is at the statistical above-chance threshold ($p = .05$), and a similar though weaker bias was in evidence for *empty*.

7.5.3.2 Semantic and Syntactic Errors with *Fill*-type Verbs in the Same Children A second task was presented to the same group of children to verify that they, like the children whose spontaneous speech errors have been reported in the literature, were prone to making *fill the water*-type syntactic errors. After children chose a sequence as depicting a given verb (which had always been presented to them in the argumentless gerund), they were asked to describe what was happening. The dependent measure was whether the theme/patient/content or the source/goal/container was used as the verb's direct object. All the adult control subjects but one expressed the content as the direct object of *pour* and *dump* and the container as the direct object of *fill* (responses were split for *empty*, presumably because the verb can alternate in adult English when the preposition *from* is used).

Virtually all of the children's uses of the verbs *pour* and *dump* with direct objects were adultlike, with the content argument appearing in the object position; in fact, there was no statistical difference between the children and the adults. However, for *fill*, the (incorrect) content argument was expressed as the direct object about as frequently as the (correct) container argument was, a proportion significantly different from that of adults. The responses were as follows: for the 2-to-3-year-olds, 17% content, 15% container; for the 3-to-4-year-olds, 17% content, 14% container; for the 4-to-5-year-olds, 10% content, 18% container. Responses for *empty* were also split, though this result is harder to interpret given that it can alternate in adult speech.

The asymmetry in syntactic errors, with *fill* being used incorrectly far more often than *pour* and *dump*, is consistent with the data from spontaneous speech. Bowerman reports eleven errors with container-object (*fill*-type) verbs, but only three errors with content-object (*pour*/*dump*-type) verbs. And it is consistent with the manner-over-end-state bias in the interpretation of the verbs shown in the previous task: children of all ages knew that *pour* and *dump* specify a particular manner; at no age did they consistently demonstrate knowledge that *fill* and *empty* require a particular end state; and some of them may have mistakenly thought that *fill* specifies a particular manner.

Can this correlation be extended even further, to individual children? If we consider only rough age trends, we do not see a correlation: the tendency to misinterpret *fill* as meaning something like *pour* peaks in the oldest group, but the tendency to make syntactic errors is stronger for the two younger groups. More insight can be gained, however, by focusing on patterns of correlation across individual children, particularly the children in the oldest group, half of whom seemed sensitive to a spurious manner correlate of *fill*. In order to see whether individual children who misinterpret *fill* as specifying a pouringlike manner are also more prone to uttering errors like *fill the water*, we constructed a 2×2 contingency table, with each child contributing one data point. On one dimension, a child was scored as "semantically biased to manner" if he or she chose the pouring-from-pitcher/empty-glass type of sequence on both trials, "semantically sensitive to end state" if he or she chose the lifting-faucet-handle/ full-glass type of sequence on both trials. On the other, a child was scored as "syntactically error-prone" if he or she uttered at least one ungrammatical sentence with the theme/content as direct object, and "not syntactically error-prone" if he or she never did so. Given the noise in the two tasks and the fact that four children gave inconsistent responses in the semantic test and had to be excluded, this is a very demanding test, but a trend is visible: nine children were either manner-biased and error-prone or end-state-sensitive and not error-prone, and three displayed one of the converse patterns; X^2 (1) = 3.09, p < .08.[19]

7.5.3.3 Effects of the Semantics of Newly Learned Verbs   The most powerful evidence that children's representations of verb meaning cause their choices of argument structures must come from experiments where one attempts to manipulate their semantic representations of verbs they learn there and then. Only in such cases can we be confident that children represent meanings in a particular way, and that properties of the meaning representation affect the verbs' argument structures rather than vice-versa.

Gropen (1989) reasoned that although children may have an overall bias to attend to manner of motion over change of end state, there are situations in which one or the other may be so salient that the child would naturally encode it as the main event of the verb's meaning. After all, we hypothesize that the child's linking rule for direct object specifies that objects are patients (or patients and themes), a rule that is neutral as to whether the patient/theme is defined within the field of physical location or physical state. Children should be equipped to map either kind of patient/theme onto syntactic objects; Gentner's manner bias is simply a greater tendency to construe the moving entity as the patient/theme than the changing entity. (In fact, the simultaneous emergence of verbs like *put* and verbs like *cover* suggest that children are capable of noticing either kind of change.) If we could arrange situations in which either the motion or the state change was distinctive, we should be able to affect which entity children construe as the patient/theme. And if the theory is correct, this in turn should affect their choice of which entity to express as the syntactic object—even if they had no linguistic evidence to go on whatsoever.

As described in Gropen (1989), two experiments were run in which children were taught new verbs in the argumentless gerund form: "This is pilking." In each case children were taught two new verbs pertaining to an action in which a thing (the theme) was moved to a place (the goal). The actions came in two versions: one involved a distinctive manner of motion of the theme with no distinctive change of state of the goal; the other involved a distinctive change of state of the goal with no distinctive manner of motion of the theme. The two versions of each action were counterbalanced across children, as was order of presentation.

In one experiment, a handful of pennies or marbles was moved to a piece of cloth that was suspended like a hammock. The experimenter either moved the pennies into the hammock in a hopping motion, or moved them in a straight path but moved enough of them that the hammock collapsed under their weight. In the second experiment, the experimenter moved a small cotton ball or piece of sponge saturated with liquid over to a larger square of wet cloth. Either the sponge was moved in a zigzag path, or it was moved over directly and the cloth changed color as the result of a chemical reaction.[20] In both experiments, children were then shown the action and were asked, "Can you tell me what I'm doing?" Based on children's spontaneous speech and pilot experiments, we did not expect that the children would invariably provide a third, oblique argument, especially the *with*-object that encodes the theme when the goal is direct object, and so we simply scored whether the direct object was the theme or goal. If no object was provided, we followed up the initial query with "Can you tell me what I'm pilking?"

The results are summarized in (7.23) and (7.24). The difference between the response frequencies for "manner" and "end state" conditions are listed in each case. Positive values indicate that subjects were sensitive to the regularity that the specifically affected entity (the one displaying a distinctive change, either in motion or in state) is encoded as the direct object.

(7.23)

Age	Condition	Goal=object responses	Theme=object responses
3	Pennies hop (manner)	.06	.94
	Cloth sags (end state)	.22	.75
	Difference	.16	.19
5	Pennies hop (manner)	.03	.97
	Cloth sags (end state)	.22	.78
	Difference	.19	.19
7	Pennies hop (manner	.16	.84
	Cloth sags (end state)	.41	.56
	Difference	.25	.28
Adult	Pennies hop (manner)	.19	.75
	Cloth sags (end state)	.44	.56
	Difference	.25	.19

(7.24)

Age	Condition	Goal=object responses	Theme=object responses
3	Sponge zigzags (manner)	.47	.53
	Cloth changes (end state)	.78	.16
	Difference	.31	.37
5	Sponge zigzags (manner)	.25	.75
	Cloth changes (end state)	1.00	.00
	Difference	.75	.75
7	Sponge zigzags (manner)	.25	.75
	Cloth changes (end state)	.84	.16
	Difference	.59	.59
Adult	Sponge zigzags (manner)	.34	.66
	Cloth changes (end state)	1.00	.00
	Difference	.66	.66

The first thing that is apparent in the pennies experiment is a manner-over-end-state bias: most of the utterances had the theme as object in both conditions, especially for the younger children. We suspect that this effect was accentuated by the fact that the change of state of the goal in this action—a collapsing of the hammocklike cloth—was accompanied by a distinctive path of motion of the theme (downward), so that the experimenter's placing of pennies in the hammock could have been construed as forcing or stuffing the pennies, making the manner of their motion or the manner of causation of their motion to be salient even in the condition in which we hoped it would be "neutral." Nonetheless, superimposed on this bias is the effect we predicted: all age groups were more apt to encode the goal as the object if the manner of motion was nondescript and the goal underwent a distinctive state change. The second experiment, involving a goal entity that changed color, was designed to minimize the manner-over-end-state bias. And in fact, for all age groups subjects were more likely to have the object encode the goal than the theme when the goal changed state, and more likely to have the object encode the theme than the goal when the theme moved in a distinctive manner.

The experiments, therefore, strongly confirm the prediction that children's verb meanings constrain their argument structures. Arguments serving as theme/patients in a verb's semantic representation are mapped onto object. Either a moving object or a changing object can be encoded as a theme/patient of the verb's main event. The choice of which entity is encoded as theme/patient depends on whether the manner of motion (or manner of causation of motion) or the change of state is distinctive, superimposed with an overall bias to encode the moving object and its manner as the main event.

7.6 Some Predictions About the Acquisition of Narrow-Range Rules

I have said little about the acquisition of the narrow-range rules that license unqualified productive extensions of verbs to new argument structures for nonaffixing alternations in the adult language. Children may not be forthcoming with the kinds of subtle judgments that would distinguish possible but nonlicensed generalizations from possible and licensed generalizations (e.g., *squeeze the fish with lemon juice* versus *brush the fish with lemon juice*). Therefore it is difficult to tell whether their generalizations are licensed narrow-range ones; I have provided indirect evidence that their *over*generalizations are in fact due to broad-range rules. Moreover, if the child does use narrow-range rules and they are properly formulated, the outputs will be grammatical and hence indistinguishable from conservatively learned argument structures in spontaneous speech. A final methodological problem is that young children generally do not possess entire families of verbs with linguistically equivalent semantic representations; they generally master only a few verbs in each narrow subclass. (For example, the five children whose dative forms we examined used between one and three verbs of obtaining, and from zero to three verbs of creation. For the locative, the narrow classes were even more sparsely represented, with most classes having between zero and two exemplars in the young children's vocabulary.) This might make the question of narrow-range rules moot at this stage; there could be few or no verbs in their vocabulary for the rule to apply to that lack the argument structure in question.

However, the evidence reviewed in this chapter shows that many of the pieces are in place for children to make narrow-range generalizations from a known verb to a semantically similar verb once they begin to acquire sets of related verbs and need to extend them to new argument structures. We know that argument structures are very tightly tied to lexical semantics for children: when verb A is maximally similar to verb B—when it is confused with it—B inherits the argument structure ordinarily belonging to A. Thus it is not implausible that when word A is merely similar (in the right way) to B, it would also get to use B's argument structures. As verb meanings become more accurate and stable, existence-predicting argument structure generalizations should become more adultlike. It seems quite likely, then, that narrow-range rules would track the child's increasingly refined semantic representations, so that once larger numbers of lower-frequency verbs are acquired, correct narrow-range rules would be in place. The empirical prediction is that children, especially older children, should spontaneously and freely generalize new argument structures to newly acquired verbs when the grammatically relevant parts of their semantic representations are similar to verbs that already alternate in their vocabulary. Conversely, if they hear a couple of examples of verbs of a new kind alternating, they should freely generalize to verbs that are semantically similar to it in the relevant ways, and only to such similar verbs.

The experiments I have run on the dative offer some support for this prediction. Although in the two experiments I have mentioned (Gropen et al., 1989) we were successful at eliciting productive double-object forms from children, this success did not come easily. In a pilot experiment (originally reported in Wilson, Pinker, Zaenen, and Lebeaux, 1981, and summarized in Gropen et al., 1989), children produced *no* double-object forms at all, not even for the verb *give*. The two subsequent experiments owe their success to some fairly strong measures we took to make the double-object construction salient (even for existing verbs like *pass*). Basically, we demonstrated similar kinds of actions while using double-object sentences (of course, never with the verbs we later tested), we had the child repeat the sentences, and we called attention to the form itself as a way of describing the event. In hindsight, we can see why these measures were necessary. It was not because children had not yet mastered the double-object form at all; we knew that their spontaneous speech contained many double-object forms. Rather, the actions that we had hoped children would describe using the double-object form, such as to transfer an object to a recipient using a clothesline, conflated a manner and instrument of motion with causation of a change of possession. But when we later analyzed the subclasses of verbs that dativize in adults' and children's speech, we learned that certain kinds of manner-of-causation-of-motion verbs (continuous causation verbs, such as *pull* and *carry*) do not dativize even for adults, and that the manner-of-causation-of-motion verbs that do dativize (ballistic motion verbs such as *throw*, *toss*, and *slide*) were *never* used in the double-object form in the children's spontaneous speech. Children simply had not acquired any narrow-range dativization rule that applies to verbs of manner of causation of motion; all their double-object forms were from other subclasses of verbs. The effect of our pretraining measures, then, may have been to provide children with evidence that manner-of-causation-of-motion verbs can dativize. With this knowledge under their belts, the children freely generalized the double-object form to the semantically similar novel verbs we taught in the main conditions of the experiment. If this interpretation is correct, it would confirm the prediction that children freely dativize verbs only with prior evidence that other verbs within that narrow semantic subclass exist in the double-object form in adult speech.

7.6.1 A Speculation About the Role of Maturation I would like to offer another prediction about the acquisition of narrow-class rules, though it does not fall out of the theory. It is a speculation that I have a strong hunch about but would not care to defend extensively at this point. The prediction is that an adult's narrow-class rules correspond to the verbs that happen to alternate in his or her lexicon at a maturationally determined critical point, presumably around puberty or shortly thereafter. Such a hypothesis has been suggested by Ritchie (1985) for the dative alternation in English, based on the fact that many of the Latinate nonalternating verbs are part of the learnèd vocabulary that might be acquired relatively late in life. The analyses of spontaneous speech reported in section 4.4.1.1 are consistent with this hypothesis: we found no Latinate-sounding verbs in five children's dative constructions, and only one in the speech of their parents.

Why do I find this speculation about maturation plausible? For one thing, the minimal requirement, namely that at least one alternating verb in each narrow class be mastered by children, seems likely to be met. Each of the alternating sub-classes has at least one or two verbs of high enough frequency that children would likely have acquired them by early adolescence. For example, each of the dativizable subclasses (except for the somewhat unusual denominal verbs denoting creation or communication with the use of a named instrument) was exemplified by at least two verbs in the pooled vocabularies of the five children we studied, the oldest of whom was only $6\frac{1}{2}$. Furthermore, I have the impression that narrow-range constraints are among the subtle points of grammar that even very successful adult learners of foreign languages frequently err on.

But what is most striking to me is my own language development, or, more specifically, lack of it. I have been working on Baker's paradox for over eight years. During that time I have read, pondered, rehearsed, said to myself, proofread, and pronounced out loud hundreds, perhaps thousands, of tokens of ungrammatical combinations of verbs and argument structures. I have also attended to them in the natural speech and writing of others, finding several dozen examples which I have examined many times since first noting them. And yet, the ungrammatical sentences—*He donated the museum a painting, *He squeezed the fish with lemon juice, *She filled water into the glass, *What's fussing her?*—sound as awful to my ears today as they did on the day I first read Baker's article, no matter how subtle or puzzling the criteria that rule them out.

True, I consciously knew that each of the ungrammatical sentences sounded ungrammatical to me and other speakers on first hearing, and thus always entertained them in my mind as violations, but it seems unlikely that this high-level cogitation (for example, knowing what the notational convention of an asterisk next to a sentence means) could penetrate down to the unconscious mechanisms that acquire vocabulary and syntax. Rather, I suspect that I am simply beyond the age at which hearing both versions of an alternating verb can affect my narrow-range lexical rules.

This comes as a surprise to many people, who suspect that "after you listen to enough of those sentences, they all start to sound good." Indeed this happens to me (and frequently to audiences I am talking to) in the short term, over a span of minutes, probably because of a syntactic analogue of the phenomenon of "semantic satiation"—when you say a word over and over again, it momentarily seems to lose its meaningfulness. But when this habituation wears off and I confront the examples anew, their subjective grammaticality remains unchanged. Jane Grimshaw has commented to me on a similar phenomenon. Apparently it is common lore among linguists that the best informants for linguistic judgments in an area of language—the people that have the most stable and discriminating reactions to sentences—are usually other linguists working in the same area. This is true even when the other linguist's pet theory makes no prediction, or a different prediction, about which sentences *should* sound grammatical, and so it is not just a case of observer bias. If people learn language throughout their lives through exposure to positive exemplars, this phenomenon is puzzling. It should be just those speakers that hear the ungrammatical sentences most often that have the weakest negative reactions to them. But if anything, the subjective discriminations become crisper with increasing exposure.

7.7 Summary of Development

The goal of this chapter was to resolve the developmental version of Baker's paradox: that children overgeneralize argument structure alternations even beyond the boundaries of adult productivity, yet grow into adults without the benefit of negative evidence. In particular, I sought to explain their overgeneralizations and unlearning of them without invoking an ad hoc mechanism that did nothing but take simple rules and make them needlessly more complicated. The following hypothesis was proposed: children's errors are of two kinds. The first consists of one-shot innovations based on broad-range rules and thus have the same status as adult innovations, requiring no specific unlearning. The second is due to childhood malapropisms: semantic representations that are incorrect for that stem (transiently or over a sustained period) in ways that cause incorrect argument structures to be paired with them. The source of the syntactic errors thus disappears as an automatic consequence of the fine-tuning of the verbs' semantic representations.

The hypothesis was supported by a wide range of data that are consistent across experimental and naturalistic methodologies, and consistent across the four alternations I have been focusing on (apart from differences in productivity stemming from the fact that the passive is signaled by an affix). Three findings support the essential continuity between children's errors and adults' broad-range rules. First, children's overgeneralizations are always consistent with the semantic constraints that characterize the adult broad-range rule. Second, children's overall tendency is toward conservatism; overgeneralization errors are the exception. Third, children can be capable of displaying metalinguistic judgments in which they detect overgeneralization errors at the same time that they make them in their own speech. And three findings support a causal role for children's undeveloped verb semantics in their production of ungrammatical sentences. First, there is independent evidence that children's lexicosemantic representations are often incomplete, distorted, or unstable, often in specifiable ways that would directly lead to the argument structure errors we hear them make. Second, there are correlations between semantic errors and syntactic errors across individual children, ages, and verbs. Third, experimental efforts to manipulate children's verb meanings, with no syntactic evidence available to the children, cause them to make predictable choices for the verbs' argument structures when they use the verbs.

Chapter 8
Conclusions

No one can do sustained research on the psychology of language without an inordinate fondness for linguistic detail. Still, I would not have written a four-hundred-page explanation of why the sentence *He donated us a book* sounds funny if I did not think it would shed light on psychological questions of some generality. In this chapter I first provide a succinct summary of the resolution of the learning paradox introduced in the first chapter, since the solution could easily have been lost sight of during the intervening discussions. Then I will spell out some nonobvious conclusions about language and mind that this solution entails, and discuss some of their broader implications.

8.1 A Brief Summary of the Resolution of the Paradox

The acquisition of argument structure poses a learnability paradox: without the benefit of negative evidence, children learn a grammar in which lexical rules allow productive generalizations of many verbs to new argument structures, while excluding other verbs that are otherwise syntactically indistinguishable ("Baker's paradox," chapter 1). The solution I have proposed, in a nutshell, is as follows:

• Children and adults use rules productively but respect semantic and morphological criteria determining which verbs they can apply to. ("Criteria-governed productivity," chapter 2.)

• Criteria arise from an interaction between the nature of lexical rules and verbs' inherent meanings. Argument structures are projections (via linking rules) of verbs' semantic structures; lexical rules are operations that change semantic structures. The semantic change will be more compatible with some verbs' meanings than others. Thus the lexical rules will apply more naturally to some verbs than to others. ("Thematic cores," chapter 3.)

• In a given language, the verbs that undergo a nonaffixing lexical rule most freely fall into numerous narrow classes with similar meanings and forms. ("Narrow conflation classes," chapter 4.)

• Verbs' meaning representations are built around a distinctive set of semantic structures corresponding to aspects of motion, location, force, causation, time, and object type. Other kinds of information can also be represented in designated slots provided by these structures but are ignored by grammar. ("Grammatically relevant subsystem," chapter 5.)

• Verbs' meanings are learned through an interplay of assigning verbal labels to preexisting conceptual categories, tuning these representations by noting the situations in which each verb is used by adults, and maximizing their consistency with existing linguistic knowledge. The narrow classes of verbs affected by a rule are learned by retaining parts of the grammatically relevant portions of the semantic structures of verbs heard to undergo the rule and parameterizing the grammatically irrelevant portions. ("Color-blind conservatism," chapter 6.)

• Children's lexical rules at all stages are formally similar to those of adults. The main developmental mechanism that makes them sound more like adults as they grow up is the acquisition of more and more accurate meanings for more and more verbs. ("Minimalist hypothesis" and "childhood malapropisms," chapter 7.)

The actual content of the book consisted of making each of the following notions in that capsule description explicit and reviewing the relevant evidence: "semantic structures," "linking rules," "operations on semantic structure," "compatibility with verb meanings," "applying naturally," "narrow classes," "similar in meaning and form," "interplay of processes," "acquisition of accurate verb meanings," and "children sounding more like adults." In the next few sections I will explore some of the interesting implications of these specific hypotheses.

8.2   Argument Structure as a Pointer Between Syntactic Structure and Propositions: A Brief Comparison with a "Connectionist" Alternative

These days it is hard to talk about argument structure among psychologists, computer scientists, and philosophers without hearing that a radically new approach to the topic can solve problems that have beset the classical linguistic treatment. The work I have presented falls squarely within that classical tradition, and it is important to see why there is no reason to abandon it.

Work on argument structure in contemporary linguistics treats it as an interface between lexical semantics and sentential syntax (see, e.g., di Sciullo and Williams, 1987; Grimshaw, in press; B. Levin, 1985; Rappaport and Levin,

1986). Linking rules generate argument structures out of semantic representations, but the information in the argument structure is all that the syntax sees. Argument structures function in sentence interpretation essentially by *copying* the representations of words and phrases found in argument positions in the sentence (see section 5.5.2). If the sentence has the noun phrase *Colorless green ideas* in subject position, then the semantic representation for colorless green ideas is copied into the open argument slot for the verb of the sentence, say, *sleep*, no matter how unusual or implausible. When the representations of verb and arguments are fused, conflicts between the two, if any, will give rise to a sense of anomaly. This sense of anomaly may be reduced at times by selecting from among a range of possible meanings left open by the words, or by embroidering the interpretation of the sentence so as to define a scenario in which it can be interpreted as true. But it cannot be resolved by rewriting the representations of the argument terms to make the sentence more plausible.

McClelland and Kawamoto (1986) assume a radically different mechanism in their model of argument structure assignment, which falls within the "connectionist" or "parallel distributed processing" framework. In their model, arguments' representations are not copied; the operation of copying, because it consists by definition of dissociating a pattern from the hardware it is instantiated in, is not a natural operation within connectionist architectures (see Pinker and Prince, 1988). Rather, there is a trainable network of associations between an input vector of features each of which represents properties of the verb or of the phrasal arguments, and an output vector of features each of which represents a combination of a property of the event and a property of the semantic role that one of the arguments plays in the event. The associations are strengthened through training sessions in which a "teacher" provides both input sentences and their output interpretations. For example, a verb could pair the input features [subject is soft and medium-sized], [object is food and female], and [verb is intense and causes a chemical change] with the output features [agent of causal event is round], [patient of no-change event is compact], and [instrument of shredding-event is soft]. (These are actual examples of features used in the model, drawn from a set of 1,052 input features and 2,500 output features. The reason that each input feature represents a pair of attributes rather than a single attribute is that it provides a partial remedy for the problem that standard connectionist architectures have difficulty binding arguments, objects, and attributes properly.)

An immediate problem that the model faces is that since there is no mechanism forcing the semantic properties of input phrases to be copied into the representation of the sentence as a whole, very unnatural verbs are easily learnable. For example, the network would have no trouble learning a verb that always interprets a human male subject as a female nonhuman patient and a hard food subject as an agent consisting of a soft tool. In practice, the contingencies of the world train the model to build more reasonable associations. But since the constraints come from the world and not from the linguistic representation, the result is a massively knowledge-driven process of sentence interpretation in which the actual contents of the sentence play a small role, merely activating preexisting associations of what typically happens in the world. McClelland and Kawamoto give the examples shown in (8.1) of how their model assigns arguments to predicates during sentence comprehension. (I have recast the examples into the form of a dialogue but have otherwise left the interpretation arrived at by the model unchanged.)

(8.1) Q: The plate broke. What broke?
       A: A vase or a window.

       Q: The boy broke. What broke?
       A: A piece of furniture.

       Q: The wolf ate a chicken. What did it eat?
       A: Cooked chicken meat.

       Q: The bat broke the window. What happened?
       A: A bat (animal) broke the window using a baseball bat.

       Q: The pillow broke the window. What broke the window?
       A: Something hard.

       Q: John touched Mary. What did he do?
       A: He hit her.

McClelland and Kawamoto treat this behavior as support for their model, showing that one man's reductio ad absurdum is another man's universal principle. McClelland and Kawamoto are seeking to solve the problem of how knowledge can disambiguate two argument structures that are identical on the surface, such as *John ate the pasta with the clams / with the fork*. Thus they are impressed with how their model brings background knowledge to bear on sentence interpretation. But what they have done is collapse *ambiguity* with *vagueness*, and thus they failed to distinguish the use of background knowledge to *select from a set of candidate meanings* from the use of background knowledge to *create a single meaning*. Affectionate John, falsely accused of beating his wife, is a victim of this collapsing. A related problem, common in connectionist models of language (Pinker and Prince, 1988), is the lack of distinct representations for distinct lexical entries sharing a sound, which are blended in a single "distributed" representation. The result is the bat-wielding *Vespertilio pipistrellus*.

Efforts like the McClelland-Kawamoto model are instructive in showing how even the most basic assumptions about linguistic representation can be powerful psychological hypotheses. The computational role of argument structure as a pointer between lexically specified roles and their syntactically specified fillers is a basic design feature of human language. It allows us to compose descriptions of possible and imagined events and to expect that the descriptions can be interpreted literally, no matter how implausible or unexpected (as in the famous newspaper headline "Man Bites Dog," or the record album by Norman Greenbaum, *The Eggplant that Ate Chicago.*) In this book I have concentrated on one aspect of the formal nature of argument structures, namely, their demand that a particular number of argument slots be filled by phrases of specific types. But above and beyond the subtleties of which verbs make which such demands, the fact that they demand fillable slots to begin with, rather than serving as conduits of association between sentence positions and frequently cooccurring kinds of events and participants, is a significant aspect of the psychology of language.

8.3   The Autonomy of Semantic Representation

A central claim of the theory is that lexical rules involve operations on semantic structure, and accordingly I have emphasized the semantic properties of verbs and semantic development in children as key explanatory factors in language structure and development. I do so with some apprehension, as the claim is easily misunderstood. The temptation is to equate lexicosemantic structure with conceptual structure. This equation is made quite explicitly by Jackendoff (1983) and by Hale and Keyser (1986, 1987), who call it Lexical Conceptual Structure. Given how heavily I rely on such structures, I fear that the "semantics = concepts" equation will arouse a variety of prejudices that will cause readers to accept or reject the current theory for entirely wrong reasons.

The idea that argument structure is based on conceptual structure is appealing to theorists who reject the possibility that linguistic knowledge is part of an autonomous mental faculty and who want to base it directly on nonlinguistic cognitive representations (e.g., Lakoff, 1987). It is also appealing to theorists holding the completely opposite view, who want to segregate as many messy cognition-related language phenomena as possible from the language faculty, the better to portray that faculty as consisting only of autonomous formal principles (e.g., Hale and Keyser, 1986). Another class of theorists sharing this overall philosophy might nonetheless find the current proposals *unappealing*, as they seem to trivialize the essentially formal nature of linguistic regularities by glibly relegating them to an ad hoc, unexplained, and all-powerful conceptual component.

So let me immediately withdraw any comfort or consternation provided to these theorists by denying the premise that semantic representations are the same as conceptual representations. Everything I have discussed about constraints on lexical rules has pointed to the conclusion that verbs' semantic structures constitute an autonomous level of linguistic representation, not reducible to syntax or cognition. Like other linguistic representations, they contain semiarbitrary language-particular features while obeying formal and substantive universals. The argument for this distinction is fairly simple: the lexical representations that govern the applicability of argument-changing rules are not syntactic, and they are not conceptual. Let me consider each in turn.

There are two ways in which syntactic distinctions do not succeed in distinguishing alternating from nonalternating verbs. First, the syntactic vocabulary in which argument structures themselves are couched—internal versus external argument, direct versus indirect argument, argument versus adjunct, obligatory versus optional argument—simply don't do the job if we use standard syntactic evidence for when they are applicable. (Of course they could always be made to do the job in a useless sense, by discarding the syntactic content that motivates these criteria and simply equating their presence with susceptibility to the alternation in question, but that would explain nothing.) Furthermore, the criteria that do distinguish alternating from nonalternating verbs are not meaningless formal symbols but have cognitive content. That is, they can interface with conceptualizations of situations so as to yield intuitions about the kinds of situations that we feel the verb could be applied in, independent of the verb's syntactic properties. For example, the distinction between *Spray the flowers with water* and **Pour the flowers with water* hinges on a property of the verbs that *also* leads us to feel that we would not use the verb *spray* in connection with a measuring cup nor the verb *pour* in connection with a water pistol. Any proposal about the lexical representations relevant to argument structure that fails to posit representations of this kind—"semantic representations"—is simply at odds with the semantic choosiness of rules that alter argument structure.

But the view that the syntactically relevant semantic features of lexical entries are simply copies of preexisting conceptual categories for kinds of events and states fares no better. The problem here is that the *semantic* distinctions can be so specific to the speaker's particular language or dialect, and so poorly motivated by independent principles of cognitive organization, that equating linguistic semantic representations with the conceptual categories underlying nonlinguistic thought is tantamount to a very strong and implausible Whorfian claim.

Consider some of the semantic distinctions I have appealed to regarding the dative alternation. The distinction between *Give the ball to him* and *Give him the ball* derives from the distinction between "causing *Y* to go to *Z*" and "causing *Z* to have *Y*." This distinction is necessary to motivate the pattern of choosiness of the dative alternation, which favors verbs that can be interpreted as denoting a change of possession, and it helps explain why the constructions have the grammatical functions they do, why they resemble certain nonalternating verbs, some of the pragmatic differences between the two dative forms, some restrictions on idioms, and the changing interpretation of verbs like *teach*. But despite the linguistic importance of this semantic distinction, its independent cognitive importance is negligible. Consider the following phenomena:

1. The two constructions are usually so cognitively interchangeable that speakers and writers often cannot decide which to use, and many linguists have simply assumed that there is no semantic difference between them. If the semantic structures simply consisted of the cognitive structures representing the content of someone's communicative intentions, then as soon as a speaker knew what he wanted to say, he would know which argument structure to use to say it.

2. There are dialectal and idiolectal differences in dativizability. As I have mentioned, Georgia Green (1974), for example, finds *I carried / dragged / hauled / pulled / pushed him the box* to be grammatical, but I do not. I would explain this in terms of these verb entries having different sets of semantic representations in her dialect than mine. Among the versions of *drag* in her lexicon is one that has the rough meaning "*X* causes *Y* to have *Z* by causing *Z* to move in a dragging manner with *X* to *Y*"; my lexicon lacks such an entry and cannot attain it with any of my lexical rules. Yet surely Green and I do not have different conceptions of what dragging is.

3. Languages differ in the range of verbs that analogous alternations can apply to. Even in a language as closely related to English as Dutch, the equivalents of *say* and *suggest* are grammatical in the closest translations of the double-object form. Nonetheless it seems unlikely that the Dutch conceive of the acts of saying or suggesting differently from us, except at the moment that they have to express them in words. Since all of the alternations examined show cross-linguistic variation in the exact sets of words they apply to, examples can easily be multiplied. For example, in Hebrew there are lexical causatives corresponding to action verbs like *dance* and *write*, but surely Hebrew speakers do not conceive of humans as will-less automata.

4. Any attempt to relate these linguistic differences to stable cultural differences among language communities is surely doomed to failure. For example, one of the most widely discussed interactions among verb semantics and argument structure involves motion verbs and their complements, which Talmy

has shown to fall into three patterns: conflation of motion and direction, conflation of motion and manner, and conflation of motion and object type. Aronoff (1987) points out that it is hard to find any cultural unity among the groups of languages that obey each one: Romance, Semitic, Polynesian, and Nez Perce follow the first pattern, Chinese, English, and Caddo follow the second, and Navajo and American Sign Language follow the third.

5. The narrow subclasses of verbs that do or don't alternate are based on criteria that would be unlikely to divide event categories into subclasses that have anything important in common with respect to reasoning. In fact, the criteria are so cognitively subtle that even linguists who have studied the alternations have mostly not noticed the nature of the subclasses and have asserted, incorrectly I claim, that they are semantically arbitrary. For example:

• The three-way distinction between *handing*, *carrying*, and *taking* is unlikely to be as cognitively salient as the distinction between, say, *throwing*, *kicking*, and *rolling*, yet as far as the dative is concerned, each of the first three belongs to a different class while the latter three belong to the same class.

• The English language, but not its speakers when they are not speaking, must consider *telling* to be a different kind of activity than *saying*, *shouting*, *talking*, or *speaking*, but the same kind of activity as *quoting*, *leaking*, *asking*, *posing*, or *writing*. Conversely, *shouting* is no more similar to *yelling* or *screaming* than it is to *whispering* and *murmuring*.

• *Baking a cake* has to be construed as similar to *building a house* and *writing a letter of recommendation* but as dissimilar to *warming a cake*, *burning a cake*, or *reheating a cake*.

• *Betting* has to be represented as being like *envying*, *sparing*, and *begrudging* but unlike *selling*, *paying*, or *trading*.

Clearly it would be hard to claim that the English language is following the natural lines of fracture of event concepts into psychological natural kinds, and it would be even harder to do so after other languages were examined. But at the same time, the crucial distinctions are decidedly semantic, in that they can be related to sets of situations in the world where the verbs could be used, and not syntactic, as none of the available syntactic properties of arguments makes the right cuts. Therefore semantic representations of words, and by extension sentences, are distinct from cognitive or conceptual representations of categories, events, scenes, propositions, and so on (though they may be built out of overlapping primitive vocabularies). When children learn the semantic representation of a verb with a given argument structure, they must arrive at a meaning representation that is mutually consistent with the situations in which the verb can be used and with the semantic concomitants of the argument structure that the language pairs with that verb, using learning mechanisms with properties like those outlined in chapter 6.

The meaning of a sentence is not a rich knowledge structure for a particular event or state or for a typical kind of event or state. Rather, it is a highly schematic construal of an event or state, an austere idealization into a structure built of foundational notions such as causation, motion, and change. The same situation, even the same state of knowledge about a situation, must first be mapped onto one of the many possible idealizations of it before it can be described in words: *spraying* can be causing water to move or causing a wall to be wet, *giving* can be causing a book to go or causing a person to have. One's particular language spells out which of those possible idealizations are available for linguistic encoding. Whorf was surely wrong when he said that one's language determines how one conceptualizes reality in general. But he was probably correct in a much weaker sense: one's language does determine how one must conceptualize reality when one has to talk about it.

8.4   Implications for the Semantic Bootstrapping Hypothesis

It is widely recognized both that syntax is correlated with semantics and that syntax is not reducible to semantics. In other work I have used this observation to try to explain a fundamental problem in language acquisition: how the child uses perceptual input (sounds and situations) to hypothesize grammatical structures (grammatical categories and relations, phrase structures, lexical entries) at the outset of the language acquisition process (Pinker, 1982, 1984, 1987). The suggestion is that children innately expect syntax and semantics to be correlated in certain ways in the speech that they attend to, can derive the semantic representation by nongrammatical means (attending to the situation, making inferences from the meanings of individually acquired words), and can thereby do a preliminary syntactic analysis of the first parental utterances they process. For example, if children know that a word refers to a thing, they can infer that it is a noun; if they know that X is a predicate and Y is its argument, they can infer that X is the head of a phrase that includes Y; if they know that a phrase is playing the role of agent, they can infer that it is the subject of the clause. With some grammatical rules under their belts, children would now be equipped to handle sentences violating these correlations as they start to be relaxed in the input speech they process (e.g., passives, where the subject is not an agent, or deverbal nouns, which do not refer to things). They can do this by classifying these nonbasic words in terms of their distribution within the grammatical structures that they are now capable of analyzing. For example, a child could now infer that Z must be a noun because it is in a noun position.

Some version of this "semantic bootstrapping hypothesis" appears to be helpful in explaining how language acquisition gets started, but it is not without problems (see Pinker, 1987, for discussion). First, like most explicit theories of language acquisition (see Pinker, 1979), it assumes that children can accurately encode from context the adult's intended meaning. Second, if the correlations between syntax and semantics are not universal, we need a special explanation for how children learn languages that violate them. Third, if the correlations are only probabilistic even in the most cooperative of languages, we need to assume either that parents filter the noncorrelated structures (passives, deverbal nouns, etc.) out of their own speech, or that children can filter them out of parents' speech using some independent criterion such as complexity or nonstandard illocutionary force. These are strong assumptions.

In constructing the semantic bootstrapping hypothesis, I pretty much equated semantic structures with conceptual structures. This was an expedient step because I was trying to show how language acquisition got started, and so I could only allow input information that the child could possess before he or she knew a thing about the particular target language. The flow of information, and idealized assumptions about the correspondences between structures, are shown in (8.2).

(8.2)

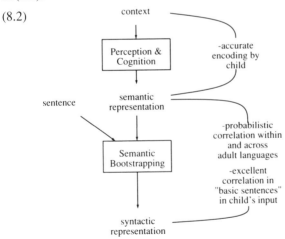

However, the argument I just provided for the autonomy of semantics changes the picture somewhat, making it simpler in one way and more complex in another. Since semantic representations are linguistic representations that are partially specific to a language, they cannot be inferred from context before language acquisition has started. Rather, it must be a separate conceptual structure that is created from context. The assumption that children can accurately encode the meaning of an input sentence from context would be replaced by two assumptions. First, there is the innocuous assumption that children's perceptual and cognitive mechanisms are enough like adults' (at least in situations in which they interact with their parents) that they construe the world in pretty much the same way that the adults speaking to them do. Second, there is a somewhat stronger assumption: that in parent-to-child speech, the parent uses words whose semantic representations correspond closely to the child's conceptual representation for that situation, so that event-category labeling and analogous processes for other grammatical entities will generally be accurate. Something like that assumption was behind the success of the Gropen et al. experiments in which we were able to predict (on fairly common-sense assumptions about distinctiveness) that children would set up the semantic representation for one event in terms of a state change and the semantic representation for another as a kind of motion, even though logically either encoding would have been possible for either event. Then semantic bootstrapping can take place, using syntax-semantics correspondences like the linking rules invoked throughout this book. The new picture is shown in (8.3).

(8.3)

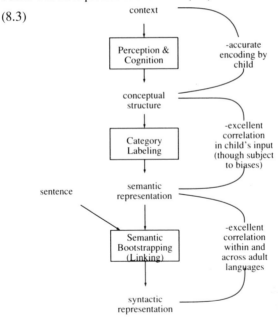

This new picture is more complicated in that it involves one extra link in the chain between perceptual input and grammatical output, and hence one more thing that can go wrong. However, its linguistic and psychological assumptions are simpler and more reasonable. First, the correspondences between syntax and semantics are no longer probabilistic correlations that the child exploits heuristically. Rather, they are the product of formal grammatical linking principles that may be universal and exceptionless (except for rare adjustments like those in syntactically ergative languages). This comes at the cost, of course, of making the semantic representations more abstract and language-particular and much more loosely tied to conceptual categories. Second, the assumptions about the child's effective input (or "intake," as it is sometimes called) are different: rather than parents having to use only syntactic structures that respect syntax-semantics correlations (or the child having to filter out the violations that slip through), the parents would have to use only semantic structures that correspond to the child's conceptual encoding of the situation. Though in many individual cases the assumptions would be equivalent, the revised picture is more plausible on the whole. Heuristic correlations between perceptually derivable conceptual/semantic categories and syntax are both undesirable formally and difficult to defend empirically, compared to linking regularities between syntax and an abstract semantics. (See Langacker, 1987, for an extensive attempt to link syntax to semantic categories that are highly abstract yet potentially interfaceable with nonlinguistic conceptual structure.) Furthermore, it is easier to swallow the psychological assumption that parents use words and constructions that they think their children will understand in the same way they do than that they use words and constructions that belong to a specially well-behaved subset of grammar. In fact, a main defense of the earlier version of the bootstrapping hypothesis was the hope that in many cases these two assumptions would be identical; it is clearly the former assumption that is the untendentious one.

In concrete terms, the difference would run as follows. In the simplified two-box version in (8.2), the child assumed that agents of physical actions were subjects, and parents avoided sentences in which agents of physical actions weren't subjects (e.g., passives). In the more realistic three-box version in (8.3), the child assumes that the first argument of an ACT semantic structure, or the first argument of a BE structure if there is no ACT structure, is a subject, and parents avoid sentences in which the child would not be likely to construe the meaning as involving an ACT or BE relation (thus they would be free to use passives in contexts in which the child was likely to realize that something was being predicated of the patient). Similarly, in the older view, the child would assume that patients of physical motion were objects, and parents would have to avoid verbs like *fill* where that is not true. In the newer view, children would assume that entities serving as the second argument of ACT and the first argument of GO were objects, and parents would have to avoid verbs whose objects were not motional patients only if the child would fail to construe that situation as involving a change of state of the motional goal. Again, note that the Gropen et al. experiments suggest that children's construals of such events can be fairly predictable by adults.

In sum, an autonomous semantics separate from conceptual structure allows the acquisition theorist to continue to exploit a correlation between syntax and the child's conception of the world, but to break up that correlation into a formal and nearly exceptionless grammatical linkage between syntax and semantics and a more probabilistic cognitive correlation between semantics in parental speech and childlike concepts. Obviously this does not eliminate the many complexities and unknown quantities in getting acquisition started on the right foot, but it involves shifting some of the burdens of explanation onto subtheories that are better able to bear them.

8.5   Conservatism, Listedness, and the Lexicon

A crucial part of my resolution of Baker's paradox for nonaffixing alternations is that a verb-argument structure combination can have three kinds of psychological status:

• Verbs witnessed in the input with a particular argument structure will be listed directly in the lexicon as having that argument structure, and speakers will judge the combination as sounding perfectly natural.

• Verbs witnessed in the input with one argument structure but not with another can be fed into a broad-range lexical rule relating those two argument structures. The resulting combination of an old verb with a new argument structure will be perceived as a "possible form," not as an "actual" form, and will not sound fully grammatical.

• Verbs witnessed in the input with one argument structure but not with another, and whose meanings are similar to (perhaps "grammatically indistinguishable from") listed verbs that have been heard in both argument structures, may be fed into narrow-range rules relating those two argument structures. The resulting combination of an old verb with a new argument structure will be perceived as an actual form and will sound fully grammatical.

As I discussed at the end of chapter 4, at the heart of this three-way distinction is a fundamental conservatism. Though people possess powerful and lawful generators of possible forms, the only forms they readily accept as a natural part of their language are forms that they have heard or forms that are semantically very similar to forms that they have heard. Grammars define paths of lexical generalization but allow them to be taken only very grudgingly. I suggested that this is related to the fact that the connection between meanings and words, or at least word roots, is conventional and hence must be treated psychologically as an irreversible brute-force memorization. Because there can be a linguistically unpredictable chemistry between the inherent meaning of a verb and the meaning change effected by a broad-range lexical rule, the sense of conventionality and the requirement for memorization from the input is extended to inhibit the creation of new verb-meaning pairings as well (except for words highly similar in the relevant ways to those already listed in memorized pairs, or when an affix clearly signals the change of meaning.)

This implies a sharp dissociation between the phenomenon of "formation by a rule" and the phenomenon of "acceptance as an actual form." Di Sciullo and Williams (1987) offer an insightful discussion of the distinction and its implications for the relation between syntax, morphology, and the lexicon. They consider the following three concepts: "listed objects" or "listemes" (entities that are included as items in the lexicon), "morphological objects" (words formable by the rules of morphology), and "syntactic objects" (phrases or sentences formable by the rules of syntax). The traditional equation, they note, is between "listeme" and "morphological object": the lexicon is a structured list of words. They then summarize arguments that this equation is wrong. Many syntactic objects, such as idioms and verb-particle combinations, have properties that are not predictable by any rule of syntax, and so must be listed in the lexicon. Conversely, many morphological objects cannot be listed: recursively formed families of words like *anti-anti-missile-missile missile*, words in agglutinating languages each of which may have ten thousand forms, freely formed compounds such as *China report*. They suggest that the link between morphology and the lexicon (or between morphology and unproductivity or listedness) be severed: syntax and morphology are both productive systems, building complex objects of different kinds out of different sets of "atoms" using different kinds of rules. The lexicon is simply a list of objects of *any* type whose properties cannot be predicted by the rules of formation. They write: "If conceived of as the set of listemes, the lexicon, is incredibly boring by its very nature. ... The lexicon is like a prison—it contains only the lawless, and the only thing that its inmates have in common is their lawlessness" (p. 3; commas as in original). Di Sciullo and Williams note that there is one principled exception to the dissociation between morphology and the lexicon: the "atoms" of morphology, namely word roots, all must be listed, because of the arbitrary nature of the meaning-sound relation.

However, there is another thread that di Sciullo and Williams may not have succeeded in severing. One of the original motivations for the equation of morphology and the lexicon is speakers' sense of actual versus possible forms. Lexical (morphological) rules of all sorts, not just the argument structure changing rules that I have examined here, can generate lawful forms that speakers nonetheless perceive to be ungrammatical: *gracious*/*graciosity*, *gold*/ *golder*, and so on. However, novel syntactic forms generated by rule are perceived as grammatical. Therefore the necessary conditions for actuality or grammaticality would seem to be either (a) being a syntactic form generated by rule, or (b) being a morphological form listed in the lexicon (memorized conservatively). Unlisted rule-generated morphological forms, then, are not automatically perceived as grammatical. Di Sciullo and Williams argue against such a linkage, pointing out that some unlisted rule-generated morphological objects are perceived as actual, and some rule-generated syntactic objects are perceived as potential but not actual. The difference is one of degree, not kind, they suggest:

> Linguistic theory defines a hierarchy of units where each unit is defined in terms of the previous one:
>
> (17) morpheme > word > compound > phrase > sentence [P. 14]
>
> ... The explication of the intuitions about actual/potential would then be this: speakers have an extreme intuition about actual versus potential morphemes; they have a strong intuition about actual and potential words ... ; they have a weak intuition about actual versus potential compounds; they have little intuition about actual versus potential phrases; and they have no sense of a difference between actual and potential sentences. [P. 18]

Di Sciullo and Williams have saved their dissociation of morphology and the lexicon, but at the cost of having no explanation whatsoever of why some forms at a given level of the hierarchy are perceived as actual and others as merely potential. The distinction cannot be identified with the morphology-syntax boundary (the boundary between compounds and phrases, in this hierarchy), nor can it be identified with the listed/unlisted distinction, nor with a conjunction of the two. The licensing of "actual" forms in the face of form-generating rules is simply left unexplained, though it is an important phenomenon in the logical problem of language acquisition, at the heart of Baker's paradox and many other fundamental aspects of acquisition.

Let me point out in passing that even the listedness of the morphemes of a language, and the corresponding psychological hypothesis that sound-meaning pairings are learned conservatively, is not a trivial fact—it is, like gravity, the kind of phenomenon that is obvious until one starts to think about it. A speaker's competence includes phonological rules that define a "possible word" in the language. It is not terribly taxing for a speaker to make up new roots that obey these rules (as my collaborators and I do every time we need nonce forms like *pilk*, *moop*, *keat*, or *flose* for a developmental experiment). But we take it for granted that the vast majority of children's utterances consist of words based on adult phonological forms. This is true even though it is conceivable that in language development each child might invent an idiosyncratic inventory of phonologically possible roots (subsequently learned by his or her parents to maintain communication), which the child would gradually replace with the conventional forms, perhaps when he or she started playing with friends or going to school. (Many parents can provide anecdotes of this happening, but that only underscores the fact that it is the exception.) Similarly, it is interesting that in the history of languages lexical roots rarely appear ab initio. Most roots either can be traced back as far as there are historical records for the language or its ancestors and neighbors, or are formed by a limited set of manipulations of existing roots; Bauer (1983) found only six words in all of English that appear to have come out of the blue (see also Aitchison, 1987). Even creole languages, whose syntax and morphology are allegedly created out of thin air by the first generation of children that speak them, seem to be constrained to borrow their lexical roots from a superstrate language including some approximation or vestige of their meanings (Bickerton, 1981). There are obvious functional reasons why speakers of a language must end up with the same stock of morphemes, of course. But this end state is generally not a mosaic reached by piecemeal compromise among a Babel of speakers (child and parent, child and child, adult and adult) but rather the product of conservative learning of roots in any situation where this is at all possible. The conservative learning of lexical roots (what Clark, 1987, calls The Principle of Conventionality) is a powerful constraint built into language acquisition, an aspect of the psychology of the learner that is not at all obvious given the existence of rules of lexical well-formedness.

The licensing into existence of forms that *are* generated by rules is a problem whose solution is much more obscure. However, the conclusions I have reached in the preceding chapters may suggest something about the nature of the principles involved. We have seen that the generation of "actual" or "existing" lexical argument structures depends on rules that require extreme similarity between a verb considered for generalization and a verb already known to alternate. This kind of generalization is basically a structure-sensitive analogy (see Gentner, 1983), familiar in other domains of psychological generalization. Indeed, I suggested that it might be seen as a minor extension of conservatism or actualness-based-on-listedness: a form is perceived to be grammatical (actual) if it is listed or sufficiently similar to a form that is listed. Of course, the basis for the analogy, the definition of "sufficiently similar," cannot be found in ordinary notions of conceptual relatedness that might be lifted from cognitive psychology. Instead, it must come from the privileged set of grammaticizable semantic elements and ways of structuring them, and a metric that requires the base and target forms in the analogy to have identical configurations of such semantic structures (at least, in the portions of those semantic structures attached to the alternating arguments) while tolerating arbitrary variation in conceptual elements outside that set. This "color-blind conservatism" is one novel kind of explanation of the distinction between actual rule-generated forms and potential rule-generated forms.

Some preliminary comparisons to another system. Alan Prince has noted several properties of the past-tense system in English that raise intriguing questions about the general relation between lawfulness and grammaticality. (Pinker and Prince, 1988). The English regular past-tense rule (*walk/walked*) is an existence-predicting rule. It can apply regardless of the phonology or semantics of the stem, and it outputs a form that is invariably as natural-sounding as the stem that serves as its input. *Genuflected* sounds as natural as *genuflect*; *fleeched* sounds as natural as *fleech* (even if one has never heard *fleech* before and has no idea what it means). Similarly, *She crooked her finger* sounds as natural as *She crooks her finger* even if the verb *crook* is highly idiomatic. (The only exception is when there exists an irregular counterpart blocking the regular form: *go/went/*goed*.) The English irregular past tense subregularities (e.g., *hit/hit, cut/cut, put/put; bear/bore, tear/tore, wear/wore; sting/stung, sling/slung, fling/ flung*), though lawful in some ways, are not existence-predicting. Generally, irregular verbs have to be heard in their past-tense form to be accepted as sounding natural. For example, some irregular yet partially lawful past forms are of marginal grammaticality (e.g., *tread/?*trod* and *kneel/?knelt* in American English). Some idioms with irregular past-tense forms do not inherit the naturalness either of the present tense form of the idiom or of the nonidiomatic past-tense form (e.g., *I don't know how she ?*stood / could stand the bastard; I don't know how she ?*bore / could bear the bastard*). Sometimes when an irregular past-tense regularity applies perfectly and exclusively to a low-frequency stem, the result is nonetheless ungrammatical: *?*I forwent the pleasure of reading student papers last night.*

At this point one might want to say that past-tense subregularities are simply unproductive, which is how they have traditionally been characterized: the irregulars constitute a list, the list must be memorized during language acquisition, and in this domain "actual = listed." But that is not quite right. If the irregulars were nothing but a list, they should be as lawless as the inmates in di Sciullo and Williams's metaphorical prison. But in fact the 180 irregular past tense forms fall into about a dozen families of similar forms. The subregularities are psychologically strong enough that at some points in the history of English new words were assimilated to them; *quit* and *cost*, for example, were recently borrowed from French. Furthermore, if a nonce form is similar enough to the prototype of a family of related irregulars, it can be assigned the subregular form. When asked for the past tense form of *skring*, for example, virtually everyone provides *skrung*, presumably because of its similarity to *spring/sprung*, *string/strung*, *sting/stung*, and so on (Bybee and Moder, 1983). Generalizations of the subregularities are also seen in speech errors (Bybee and Slobin, 1982) and, of course, in children's speech (e.g., *brang*).

Prince and I suggested that the English past tense subregularities have a peculiar status that is very different from the existence-predicting productivity of the regular rule but not as stubbornly unproductive as the members of a list of memorized exceptions. Rather, a stem that is similar to a cluster of related irregulars is perceived as potentially having that past-tense form, and if its similarity is extreme enough (and if certain formal conditions are met), the judgment of the goodness of the form approaches "actualness." The dimensions of this psychological similarity are linguistic ones, however: global morphophonological properties like alliteration, rhyme, and monosyllabicity. Semantic similarity plays no role, as we saw in the last chapter; nor does pure phonological similarity independent of morphological analysis (see Pinker and Prince, 1988, for details).

Thus there may be a suggestive common strand in the phenomena of speakers' senses of "existence," "grammaticality," or "actuality" in irregular past-tense regularities and in nonaffixing argument structure alternations. A regularity defines possible forms; a sense of actualness is bestowed only on the basis of analogy with listed forms, where the dimensions of similarity are defined over a particular kind of grammatical structure. It appears, then, that linguistic objects come to be deemed "actual" parts of one's language in three ways: (1) by being generated by existence-predicting rules, including most rules of syntax and some rules of morphology (such as the regular past-tense rule and the rule of passive participle formation); (2) by being acquired conservatively and listed in the lexicon; and (3) by being generated by property-predicting rules *and* being similar along the right linguistic dimensions to listed alternating forms. The analogy is by no means exact, though; the narrow-range rules appear to be far more freely inclusive when a word is similar in the right way to existing alternators, and far more fussy when it is not, than the graded generalizations of irregular inflection patterns.

Why are some well-formed linguistic objects grammatical only if they are listed or are similar to objects that are listed, whereas other linguistic objects are acceptable automatically, by virtue of their form? Most obviously, morphological operations that yield completely predictable output forms transparently composed of a stem and affix (e.g., regular past tenses and passives) are existence-predicting, whereas those whose output forms are morphologically unchanged or unpredictable in form (e.g., irregular past tenses and causatives) are merely property-predicting (see Aronoff, 1976, who makes a similar point). But this correlation only raises the question of why some operations are accompanied by predictable affixation and are productive whereas others have nondetectable or irregular changes that lead to semiproductivity. The causative alternation could be (and in other languages is) signaled by a regular affix; the *feel/felt* alternation could be (and in Old English, may have been) a rule applying to any verb with the right phonological properties; so why aren't they in modern English? Perhaps it has something to do with the distinction between operations whose effects are additive with the properties of the objects they apply to, and operations whose effects lead to nonadditive interactions or "mental chemistry" with the properties of their inputs. Nonadditive semantics would lead to restrictions of a rule to narrow classes; nonadditive phonology would lead to irregularity. I can offer only some vague speculative examples. In lexical semantics, turning an assertion of an action into an assertion of a circumstance defined by that action (the semantic operation accompanying passivization) interacts minimally with the inherent nature of the action itself (e.g., the distinction between an event of cutting and a circumstance of being cut has little to do with anything specific to the nature of cutting). But expressing an event or state as having been caused does interact with the kind of event or state, since some events are more causable than others (e.g., the distinction between breaking and being caused to break is very different from the distinction between walking and being caused to walk). In inflectional morphology, adding syllabic -*ing* to a stem does not affect its sound pattern; adding subsyllabic -*t/d* to a stem (some of which already end in *t* or *d*), or ablauting its vowel, does. One can speculate that this has something to do with why lexical irregularity and its concomitant partial productivity is associated with the rule that adds -*t/d* but not with the rule that adds -*ing*. Further exploration of these issues is critical to understanding the structure and acquisition of linguistic regularity.

8.6   Spatial Schemas and Abstract Thought

The use of a physical "metaphor" to express abstract relations (the Thematic Relations Hypothesis) is ubiquitous in language. The choice of prepositions, verbs, idioms, and argument structures, and the patterns of broad-range generalizations among them in a variety of abstract fields, are based on a mapping of those fields onto a small number of schemas based on space, force, and time. This parallelism is not just historical; children's speech shows that the metaphor is grasped by the age of two. In fact, if my theory of lexicosemantic structure is not too procrustean, most verb meanings are built around combinations of a non-Euclidean geometry of "things," "places," and "paths" (Talmy, 1983), and a non-Newtonian physics of forceful antagonists, resistant agonists, and chunks of time packaged into instants and intervals (Talmy, 1988).

The discovery that conceptions of space, force, and time lie at the foundation of the lexical semantics of more abstract relations has an intriguing, Kantian flavor, and certain theorists aware of the discovery have thought it to be rather profound. Among them are linguists of a variety of theoretical persuasions (e.g., J. M. Anderson, 1971; Jackendoff, 1972, 1982, 1983; Lakoff, 1987; Langacker, 1987; Talmy, 1983, 1988), psycholinguists (Clark, 1973; Slobin, 1985; Wexler, 1970), perceptual psychologists (Shepard and Cooper, 1982), and neuroscientists (O'Keefe and Nadel, 1978). To the occasional perplexity of these people, the rest of the cognitive science community has been largely unaware or unmoved. Let me explain why I count myself among the impressed.

A fundamental puzzle in the study of the mind is how evolution could have produced a brain capable of intricate specialized achievements like mathematics, science, and art given the total absence of selection pressure for such abstract abilities at any point in history. The problem has two parts, a phylogenetic one and an ontogenetic one: what was the evolutionary path that led to the human brain's special abilities, and what allows these abilities to be extended to completely novel kinds of problems in the lifetime of an individual? According to Gould (1980), Alfred Russel Wallace, codiscoverer with Darwin of the theory of natural selection, was so struck by this problem that he denied that selection could explain the evolution of human intelligence at all and invoked divine intervention. More recent thinkers who have pondered the problem have stopped short of this desperate move but have come to a conclusion no less pessimistic: that the problem is simply not scientifically tractable at present. For example, Chomsky (1975) terms the evolution of abstract cognition a "mystery." Fodor (1983) suggests that abstract thought processes are so unconstrained that one can't even characterize them in an interesting scientific theory.

Utter pessimism may be premature. There are precedents for explaining the emergence of novel capabilities in evolution: old parts can be recruited to new uses. Phylogenetically, swim bladders become lungs, heat-exchange panels become wings, wrist bones become crude thumbs. Ontogenetically, wings are used to block out reflections on water; the bridge of the nose is used to hold up eyeglasses. Rozin (1976), Lieberman (1984), Shepard and Cooper (1982) and others have suggested that neural circuits could also be converted to new uses in evolution. Copies of brain structures originally selected as motor programs, higher perceptual analyzers, or coordinators of complex behavior sequences could be freed from their ties to peripheral sensory and motor systems and applied to more abstract tasks that are partially isomorphic in computational structure to the one exerting the original selection pressure.

From this perspective, the interest of the Thematic Relations Hypothesis is obvious. Cognitive structures that evolved to represent the locations and paths of movable objects may have been co-opted in hominid evolution to represent abstract states and changes; structures that represented exertion and resistance of physical force could have come to be useful for representing more abstract forms of causation, agency, and responsibility. In phy'ogeny, physical and spatial schemas may have been extended to fields such as possession and circumstance that are deeply encoded in many human languages. Tl·ey may also be extendible by individuals in their own lifetimes to more specific fields in analogies, metaphors, and internal and external spatial models such as mental images or charts and graphs (Gentner, 1983; Shepard and Cooper, 1982; Pinker, 1981b).

But it is not just that we can think of an evolutionary story into which the Thematic Relations Hypothesis fits; stories of that sort are all too easy to come by. Rather, the study of thematic relations contacts a wide-ranging, often highly precise empirical database: syntactic and lexical regularities in the grammar of English and other languages, historical linguistics, experimental studies of adult perception and cognition, developmental psycholinguistics, and perhaps even comparative cognitive psychology. There is no reason why such data could not be used to push speculations about the nature and evolution of the "language of thought" underlying abstract cognition in the direction of greater specificity and testability than one usually associates with such proposals. I have an example of such a nonobvious proposal in mind, based on the conclusion outlined in this chapter and in chapter 4 that lexical semantic structure is an autonomous level of representation.

One striking property of the spatial metaphor in language is that it is a highly abstract and simple idealization. In this regard it contrasts with "frames" and "scripts," which are rich knowledge structures that summarize characteristic properties of events for use in common-sense probabilistic reasoning. When I think about a man filling a glass, many bits of knowledge about the participants come to mind: his goals and intentions, the typical kinds of physical manipulation and instruments he may use (e.g., a faucet), the path, rate, and shape of the water as it moves, what a typical glass looks like, and so on. But when I talk about the event, my grammatical choices are governed by a much more skeletal abstraction. The possibility of my saying *He poured water into the glass* hinges on a conceptualization of an undifferentiated mass following a trajectory characterized as downward and terminating at a place in the object, which itself is characterized only as something that has a cavity; its state before and after the motion are unspecified. On the other hand, in order to assemble *He filled the glass*, I must undergo a gestalt shift in which the glass shrinks down to a dimensionless point changing "position" in state space (from not full to full), with no concept of the physical motion of the water or the relation of its path to the geometric layout of the glass playing any role. A single script which listed defaults for both the typical effect on the glass and the typical motion of the water in a filling-scenario fails to make the distinction; we know that people are not confined to consulting such a script, because they do not say *pour the glass or *fill the water.

The ability to adopt one of a set of cross-clarifying schemas, each involving a sparse, precisely-structured idealization in which knowledge not schematized is simply not entertained, no matter how well-correlated or cognitively salient, is a crucial part of the logic of lexical semantics and generalization that resolved the learnability paradox considered in this book. I suspect that it is also a crucial property of the cognitive processes that allow such achievements as folk science and formal science, kinship and social structure, music and mathematics, ethics and law, notwithstanding the current enthusiasm in cognitive science for massive networks of probabilistic bits of real-world knowledge. But that is a story for another day.

References

Aitchison, J. (1987) *Words in the mind: An introduction to the mental lexicon.* New York: Basil Blackwell.

Allan, K. (1977) Classifiers. *Language* 53: 285–311.

Ammon, M. S. H. (1980) Development in the linguistic expression of causal relations: Comprehension of features of lexical and periphrastic causatives. Ph.D. dissertation, University of California, Berkeley.

Ammon, M. S. H. and Slobin, D. I. (1979) A cross-linguistic study of the processing of causative sentences. *Cognition* 7: 3–17.

Anderson, J. M. (1971) *The grammar of case: Towards a localistic theory.* New York: Cambridge University Press.

Anderson, S. R. (1971) On the role of deep structure in semantic interpretation. *Foundations of Language*, 6, 197–219.

Anderson, S. R. (1977) Comments on the paper by Wasow. In P. Culicover, T. Wasow, and A. Akmajian, eds., *Formal syntax.* New York: Academic Press.

Armstrong, S. L., Gleitman, L. R., and Gleitman, H. (1983) What some concepts might not be. *Cognition* 13: 263–308.

Aronoff, M. (1976) *Word formation in generative grammar.* Cambridge, Mass.: MIT Press.

Aronoff, M. (1980) Contextuals. *Language* 56: 744–758.

Aronoff, M. (1982) Potential words, actual words, productivity, and frequency. In S. Hattori and K. Inoue, eds., *Proceedings of the XIIIth International Congress of Linguists.* Tokyo: CIPL.

Aronoff, M. (1987) Review of J. L. Bybee's "Morphology: A study of the relation between meaning and form." *Language* 63: 115–129.

Atkins, B. T., Kegl, J., and Levin, B. (1986) Explicit and implicit information in dictionaries. Lexicon Project Working Papers #12. Cambridge, Mass.: MIT Center for Cognitive Science. Also to appear in *Advances in lexicology: Proceedings of the Second Conference of the Centre for the New OED.* Waterloo, Ontario: University of Waterloo.

Baker, C. L. (1979). Syntactic theory and the projection problem. *Linguistic Inquiry* 10: 533–581.

Baker, C. L., and McCarthy, J. J., eds. (1981) *The logical problem of language acquisition.* Cambridge, Mass.: MIT Press.

Baker, M. (1985) Incorporation: A theory of grammatical function changing. Ph.D. dissertation, MIT.

Baldi, P., Broderick, V., and Palermo, D. (1985) Prefixal negation of English adjectives: Psycholinguistic dimensions of productivity. In J. Fisiak, ed., *Historical semantics and historical word-formation.* New York: Mouton.

Bauer, L. (1983) *English word formation.* New York: Cambridge University Press.

Belletti, A., and Rizzi, L. (1986) Psych-verbs and theta-theory. Lexicon Project Working Papers #13. Cambridge, Mass.: MIT Center for Cognitive Science.

Berman, R. A. (1980) Child language as evidence for grammatical description: preschoolers' construal of transitivity in the verb system of Hebrew. Unpublished manuscript, Tel Aviv University (cited by Aronoff, 1982).

Berman, R. A. (1982) Verb-pattern alternation: The interface of morphology, syntax, and semantics in Hebrew child language. *Journal of Child Language* 9: 169–191.

Berwick, R. C. (1986) *The acquisition of syntactic knowledge.* Cambridge, Mass.: MIT Press.

Berwick, R. C., and Weinberg, A. (1984) *The grammatical basis of linguistic performance.* Cambridge, Mass.: MIT Press.

Bickerton, D. (1981) *The roots of language.* Ann Arbor: Karoma.

Bobick, A. (1987) Natural object categorization. Ph.D. dissertation, MIT.

Bohannon, J. N., and Stanowicz, L. (1988) The issue of negative evidence: Adult responses to children's language errors. *Developmental Psychology* 24: 684–689.

Bolinger, D. (1971). *The phrasal verb in English.* Cambridge, Mass.: Harvard University Press.

Bolinger, D. (1977a) Transitivity and spatiality: The passive of prepositional verbs. In A. Makkai, V. B. Makkai, and L. Heilmann, eds., *Linguistics at the crossroads.* Lake Bluff, Ill.: Jupiter Press; Padua, Italy: Liviana Editrice.

Bolinger, D. (1977b) *Meaning and form.* London: Longman.

Borer, H., and Wexler, K. (1987) The maturation of syntax. In T. Roeper and E. Williams, eds., *Parameter-setting and language acquisition.* Dordrecht, Netherlands: Reidel.

Bowerman, M. (1974) Learning the structure of causative verbs: a study in the relationship of cognitive, semantic and syntactic development. Papers and Reports on Child Language Development, 8. Stanford, Calif.: Stanford University Department of Linguistics.

Bowerman, M. (1978) Systematizing semantic knowledge: Changes over time in the child's organization of word meaning. *Child Development* 49: 977–987.

Bowerman, M. (1981) The child's expression of meaning: Expanding relationships among lexicon, syntax, and morphology. In H. Winitz (Ed.), *Native language and foreign language acquisition.* New York: New York Academy of Science.

Bowerman, M. (1982a). Evaluating competing linguistic models with language acquisition data: Implications of developmental errors with causative verbs. *Quaderni di Semantica* 3: 5–66.

Bowerman, M. (1982b) Reorganizational processes in lexical and syntactic development. In E. Wanner and L. R. Gleitman, eds., *Language acquisition: The state of the art.* New York: Cambridge University Press.

Bowerman, M. (1982c) Starting to talk worse: clues to language acquisition from children's late errors. In S. Strauss, ed., *U-shaped behavioral growth.* New York: Academic Press.

Bowerman, M. (1983a). How do children avoid constructing an overly general grammar in the absence of feedback about what is not a sentence? Papers and Reports on Child Language Development, 22. Stanford, Calif.: Stanford University Department of Linguistics.

Bowerman, M. (1983b). Hidden meanings: The role of covert conceptual structures in children's development of language. In D. R. Rogers and J. A. Sloboda, eds., *The acquisition of symbolic skills.* New York: Plenum.

Bowerman, M. (1983c) Theses for "Dealing with Trouble in Language" workshop. Unpublished manuscript, Max Planck Institute for Psycholinguistics, Nijmegen, Netherlands.

Bowerman, M. (1987a) Commentary: Mechanisms of language acquisition. In B. MacWhinney, ed., *Mechanisms of language acquisition.* Hillsdale, N.J.: Erlbaum.

Bowerman, M. (1987b) The 'no negative evidence' problem: How do children avoid constructing an overly general grammar? In J. A. Hawkins, ed., *Explaining language universals.* Oxford: Basil Blackwell.

Bowerman, M. (1989) Learning a semantic system: What role do cognitive predispositions play? In M. L. Rice and R. L. Schiefelbusch, eds., *The teachability of language.* Baltimore: Paul H. Brookes.

Bowerman, M. (in press) Mapping thematic roles onto syntactic functions: Are children helped by innate "linking rules"? *Journal of Linguistics.*

Braine, M. D. S. (1971) On two types of models of the internalization of grammars. In D. I. Slobin,, ed., *The ontogenesis of grammar: A theoretical symposium.* New York: Academic Press.

Bresnan, J., ed. (1982a) *The mental representation of grammatical relations.* Cambridge, Mass.: MIT Press.

Bresnan, J. (1982b) The passive in lexical theory. In J. Bresnan, ed., *The mental representation of grammatical relations.* Cambridge, Mass.: MIT Press.

Bresnan, J. (1982c) Polyadicity. In J. Bresnan, ed., *The mental representation of grammatical relations.* Cambridge, Mass.: MIT Press.

Bresnan, J. (1982d) Control and complementation. In J. Bresnan, ed., *The mental representation of grammatical relations.* Cambridge, Mass.: MIT Press.

Brown, R. (1958) How shall a thing be called? *Psychological Review* 65: 14–21.

Brown, R. (1973) *A first language: The early stages.* Cambridge, Mass.: Harvard University Press.

Brown, R., and Hanlon, C. (1970) Derivational complexity and order of acquisition in child speech. In J. R. Hayes, ed., *Cognition and the development of language*. New York: Wiley.

Burzio, L. (1986) *Italian syntax: A Government-Binding approach*. Dordrecht, Netherlands: Reidel.

Bybee, J. L. (1985) *Morphology: A study of the relation between meaning and form*. Philadelphia: Benjamins.

Bybee, J. L., and Moder, C. L. (1983) Morphological classes as natural categories. *Language* 59: 251–270.

Bybee, J. L., and Slobin, D. I. (1982) Rules and schemas in the development and use of the English past tense. *Language* 58: 265–289.

Carey, S., and Bartlett, E. (1978) Acquiring a single new word. Papers and Reports on Child Language Development, 15. Stanford, Calif.: Stanford University Department of Linguistics.

Carter, R. J. (1976a) Some constraints on possible words. *Semantikos* 1: 27–66.

Carter, R. J. (1976b) Some linking regularities. Unpublished manuscript, University of Paris VIII, Vincennes. In B. Levin and C. Tenny, eds.,(1988), On linking: Papers by Richard Carter. Lexicon Project Working Papers #25. Cambridge, Mass: MIT Center for Cognitive Science

Chomsky, C. (1969) *Acquisition of syntax in children from 5 to 10*. Cambridge, Mass.: MIT Press.

Chomsky, N. (1965). *Aspects of the theory of syntax*. Cambridge, Mass.: MIT Press.

Chomsky, N. (1975) *Reflections on language*. New York: Random House.

Chomsky, N. (1981) *Lectures on government and binding*. Dordrecht, Netherlands: Foris Publications.

Chomsky, N. (1982) *Some concepts and consequences of the theory of government and binding*. Cambridge, Mass.: MIT Press.

Chomsky, N. (1987) *Knowledge of language: Its nature, origin, and use*. New York: Praeger.

Chomsky, N., and Halle, M. (1968) *The sound pattern of English*. New York: Harper and Row.

Chomsky, N., and Lasnik, H. (1977) Filters and control. *Linguistic Inquiry* 8: 425–504.

Clark, E. V. (1978) Discovering what words can do. *Papers from the parasession on the lexicon*. Chicago: Chicago Linguistics Society, University of Chicago (cited by Aronoff, 1982).

Clark, E. V. (1982) The young word maker: a case study of innovation in the child's lexicon. In E. Wanner and L. R. Gleitman, eds., *Language acquisition: The state of the art*. New York: Cambridge University Press.

Clark, E. V. (1987) The Principle of Contrast: A constraint on language acquisition. In B. MacWhinney, ed., *Mechanisms of language acquisition*. Hillsdale, N.J.: Erlbaum.

Clark, E. V., and Carpenter, K. (in press) Where do oblique agents and causes come from? *Journal of Linguistics*.

Clark, E. V., and Clark, H. H. (1979) When nouns surface as verbs. *Language* 55: 767–811.

Clark, E. V., and Garnica, O. (1974) Is he coming or going? On the acquisition of deictic verbs. *Journal of Verbal Learning and Verbal Behavior* 13: 559–572.

Clark, H. H. (1973) Space, time, semantics, and the child. In T. E. Moore, ed., *Cognitive development and the acquisition of language*. New York: Academic Press.

Comrie, B. (1978) Ergativity. In W. P. Lehmann, ed., *Syntactic typology*. Austin: University of Texas Press.

Comrie, B. (1985) Causative verb formation and other verb-deriving morphology. In T. Shopen, ed., *Language typology and syntactic description*. Vol. 3: *Grammatical categories and the lexicon*. New York: Cambridge University Press.

Crain, S., Thornton, R., and Murasugi, K. (1987) Capturing the evasive passive. Paper presented at the Twelfth Annual Boston University Conference on Language Development, Oct. 23–25.

Culicover, P. W., and Wilkins, W. (1986) Control, PRO, and the Projection Principle. *Language* 62: 120–153.

Curme, G. (1935) *A grammar of the English language*. Vol. 2: *Syntax*. Boston: Barnes and Noble. 1983 ed: Essex, Conn.: Verbatim.

Davison, A. (1980) Peculiar passives. *Language* 56: 42–66.

de Villiers, J. G., Phinney M., and Avery, A. (1982) Understanding passives with non-action verbs. Paper presented at the Seventh Annual Boston University Conference on Language Development, Oct. 8–10.

Demetras, M. J., Post, K. N., and Snow, C. E. (1986) Feedback to first language learners: The role of repetitions and clarification questions. *Journal of Child Language* 13: 275–292.

Denny, J. P. (1976) What are noun classifiers good for? *Papers from the Twelfth Regional Meeting*. Chicago: Chicago Linguistics Society, University of Chicago.

di Sciullo, A. M., and Williams, E. (1987) *On the definition of word*. Cambridge, Mass.: MIT Press.

Dixon, R. M. W. (1972) *The Dyirbal language of West Queensland*. New York: Cambridge University Press.

Dowty, D. R. (1979a) Dative "movement" and Thomason's extensions of Montague Grammar. In S. Davis and M. Mithun, eds., *Linguistics, philosophy, and Montague Grammar*. Austin: University of Texas Press.

Dowty, D. R. (1979b) *Word meaning and Montague grammar*. Dordrecht, Netherlands: Reidel.

Dowty, D. R. (1982) Grammatical relations and Montague Grammar. In P. Jacobson and G. K. Pullum, eds., *The nature of syntactic representation*. Dordrecht, Netherlands: Reidel.

Dowty, D. R. (1987) Thematic proto roles, subject selection, and lexical semantic defaults. Paper presented at the Linguistic Society of America Colloquium.

Dresher, E. B., and Hornstein, N. (1977) On some supposed contributions of artificial intelligence to the scientific study of language. *Cognition* 4: 321–398.

Dryer, M. S. (1986) Primary objects, secondary objects, and antidative. *Language* 62: 808–845.

Elliott, N., and Wexler, K. (in press) Principles and computations in the acquisition of grammatical categories. *Linguistic Inquiry.*

Erteschik-Shir, N. (1979) Discourse constraints on dative movement. In T. Givon, ed., *Syntax and Semantics.* Vol. 12: *Discourse and Syntax.* New York: Academic Press.

Fauconnier, G. (1984) *Mental spaces: Aspects of meaning construction in natural language.* Cambridge, Mass.: MIT Press.

Fiengo, R. (1981) *Surface structure: The interface of autonomous components.* Cambridge, Mass.: Harvard University Press.

Figueira, R. A. (1984) On the development of the expression of causativity: A syntactic hypothesis. *Journal of Child Language* 11: 109–128.

Fillmore, C. J. (1967) The grammar of hitting and breaking. In R. Jacobs and P. Rosenbaum, eds., *Readings in English transformational grammar.* Waltham, Mass.: Ginn.

Fillmore, C. J. (1968) The case for case. In E. Bach and R. J. Harms, eds., *Universals in linguistic theory.* New York: Holt, Rinehart, and Winston.

Fodor, J. A. (1970) Three reasons for not deriving "kill" from "cause to die". *Linguistic Inquiry* 1: 429–438.

Fodor, J. A. (1975) *The language of thought.* New York: T. Y. Crowell.

Fodor, J. A. (1981) The present status of the innateness controversy. In J. A. Fodor, *Representations.* Cambridge, Mass.: MIT Press.

Fodor, J. A. (1983) *Modularity of mind.* Cambridge, Mass.: MIT Press.

Fodor, J. A., Fodor, J. D., and Garrett, M. F. (1975) The psychological unreality of semantic representations. *Linguistic Inquiry* 6: 515–531.

Fodor, J. A., Garrett, M. F., Walker, E. C. T., and Parkes, C. H. (1980) Against definitions. *Cognition* 8: 263–267.

Fodor, J. D. (1985) Why learn lexical rules? Paper presented at the Tenth Annual Boston University Conference on Language Development, Oct. 25–27. Written up as "The procedural solution to the projection problem," unpublished manuscript, City University of New York.

Fodor, J. D., and Crain, S. (1987) Simplicity and generality of rules in language acquisition. In B. MacWhinney, ed., *Mechanisms of language acquisition.* Hillsdale, N.J.: Erlbaum.

Foley, W. A., and Van Valin, R. D. (1984) *Functional syntax and universal grammar.* New York: Cambridge University Press.

Foley, W. A., and Van Valin, R. D. (1985) Information packaging in the clause. In T. Shopen, ed., *Language typology and syntactic description.* Vol. 1: *Clause structure.* New York: Cambridge University Press.

Fukui, N., Miyagawa, S., and Tenny, C. (1985) Verb classes in English and Japanese: A case study in the interaction of syntax, morphology, and semantics. Lexicon Project Working Papers #3. Cambridge, Mass.: MIT Center for Cognitive Science.

Gaulding, J. (1988) The acquisition of argument structure: Towards a computational model. Unpublished manuscript, MIT.

Gazdar, G., Klein, E., Pullum, G. K., and Sag, I. A. (1985) *Generalized phrase structure grammar*. Cambridge, Mass.: Harvard University Press.

Gee, J. P. (1974) Jackendoff's thematic hierarchy condition and the passive construction. *Linguistic Inquiry* 5: 304–308.

Gentner, D. (1975) Evidence for the psychological reality of semantic components: The verbs of possession. In D. A. Norman and D. E. Rumelhart, eds., *Explorations in cognition*. San Francisco: W. H. Freeman.

Gentner, D. (1978) On relational meaning: The acquisition of verb meaning. *Child Development* 49: 988–998.

Gentner, D. (1981) Some interesting differences between verbs and nouns. *Cognition and Brain Theory* 4: 161–178.

Gentner, D. (1982) Why nouns are learned before verbs: Linguistic relativity vs. natural partitioning. In S. A. Kuczaj II,, ed., *Language development*. Vol. 2: *Language, thought, and culture*. Hillsdale, N.J.: Erlbaum.

Gentner, D. (1983) Structure-mapping: A theoretical framework for analogy. *Cognitive Science* 7: 155–170.

Gentner, D. (1988) Cognitive and linguistic determinism: Object reference and relational inference. Paper presented at the Thirteenth Annual Boston University Conference on Language Development, Oct. 21–23.

Gergely, G., and Bever, T. G. (1986) Relatedness intuitions and the mental representation of causative verbs. *Cognition* 23: 211–277.

Gleason, J. B., Goodglass, H., Obler, L., Green, E., Hyde, M., and Weintraub, S. (1980) Narrative strategies of aphasic and normal subjects. *Journal of Speech and Hearing Research* 23: No. 2.

Gold, E. M. (1967) Language identification in the limit. *Information and Control*, 16, 447–474.

Gonsalves, R. J. (1988) For definitions: A reply to Fodor, Garrett, Walker, and Parkes. *Cognition* 29: 73–82.

Gordon, P. (in press) Learnability and feedback: A commentary on Bohannon and Stanowicz. *Developmental Psychology*.

Gordon, P., and Chafetz, J. (1986) Lexical learning and generalization in passive acquisition. Paper presented at the Eleventh Annual Boston University Conference on Language Development, Oct. 17–19.

Gould, S. J. (1980) Natural selection and the human brain: Darwin *vs*. Wallace. In S. J. Gould, *The panda's thumb*. New York: Norton.

Green, G. M. (1973) A syntactic syncretism in English and French. In B. B. Kachru, R. B. Lees, Y. Malkiel, A. Pietrangeli, and S. Saporta (Eds.), *Issues in linguistics: Papers in honor of Henry and Renee Kahane*. Urbana: University of Illinois Press.

Green, G. M. (1974) *Semantics and syntactic regularity*. Bloomington: Indiana University Press.

Grimshaw, J. (1979) Complement selection and the lexicon. *Linguistic Inquiry* 10: 279–326.

Grimshaw, J. (1981) Form, function, and the language acquisition device. In C. L. Baker and J. J. McCarthy, eds., *The logical problem of language acquisition*. Cambridge, Mass.: MIT Press.

Grimshaw, J. (1985) Remarks on dative verbs and universal grammar. Paper presented at the Tenth Annual Boston University Conference on Language Development, Oct. 25–27.

Grimshaw, J. (1987) Unaccusatives— An overview. *Proceedings of the North East Linguistics Society* 17.

Grimshaw, J. (1989) Why we bother to get the dative alternation right. In I. Laka and A. Majahan, eds., MIT Working Papers in Linguistics. Cambridge, Mass.: MIT Department of Linguistics and Philosophy.

Grimshaw, J. (in press) *Argument structure*. Cambridge, Mass.: MIT Press.

Grimshaw, J., and Pinker, S. (in press) Positive and negative evidence in language acquisition. (Commentary on D. Lightfoot's "The child's trigger experience: 'Degree-0' learnability.") *Behavioral and Brain Sciences*.

Grimshaw, J., and Prince, A. (1986) A prosodic account of the *to*-dative alternation. Unpublished manuscript, Brandeis University.

Gropen, J. (1989) Learning locative verbs: how universal linking rules constrain productivity. Ph.D. dissertation, MIT.

Gropen, J., Pinker, S., and Goldberg, R. (1987) Constrained productivity in the acquisition of locative forms. Paper presented the Twelfth Annual Boston University Conference on Language Development, Oct. 23–25.

Gropen, J., Pinker, S., Hollander, M., and Goldberg, R. (in preparation) Syntax and semantics in the acquisition of locative verbs. Manuscript in preparation, MIT.

Gropen, J., Pinker, S., Hollander, M., Goldberg, R., and Wilson, R. (1989) The learnability and acquisition of the dative alternation in English. *Language, 65*.

Gropen, J., Pinker, S., and Roeper, T. (in preparation) The role of directness of causation in children's productive lexical and periphrastic causatives. Manuscript in preparation, MIT.

Gruber, J. (1965) Studies in lexical relations. Ph.D. dissertation, MIT. Reprinted, 1976, as *Lexical structures in syntax and semantics*. Amsterdam: North-Holland.

Guerssel, M. (1986) On Berber verbs of change: A study of transitivity alternations. Lexicon Project Working Papers #9. Cambridge, Mass.: MIT Center for Cognitive Science.

Haider, H. (1987) Argument-structure: Linking and bootstrapping. Paper presented at the symposium "The Structure of the Simple Clause in Language Acquisition." Max Planck Institute for Psycholinguistics, Nijmegen, Netherlands, Nov. 9–13. To appear in *Journal of Linguistics*.

Hakuta, K. (1981) Grammatical description versus configurational arrangement in language acquisition: The case of relative clauses in Japanese. *Cognition* 9: 197–236.

Hale, K., and Keyser, S. J. (1986) Some transitivity alternations in English. Lexicon Project Working Papers #7. Cambridge, Mass.: MIT Center for Cognitive Science.

Hale, K., and Keyser, S. J. (1987) A view from the middle. Lexicon Project Working Papers #10. Cambridge, Mass.: MIT Center for Cognitive Science.

Hale, K., and Laughren, M. (1983) *Warlpiri Lexicon Project: Preface to dictionary entries of verbs.* Unpublished manuscript, MIT.

Hall, R., and Friends. (1984) *Sniglets (snig' let): any word that doesn't appear in the dictionary, but should.* New York: Macmillan.

Hamburger, H., and Wexler, K. (1975) A mathematical theory of learning transformational grammar. *Journal of Mathematical Psychology* 12: 137–177.

Harrison, G. B. (1968) *Shakespeare: The complete works.* New York: Harcourt, Brace, and World.

Higginbotham, J. (1988) Comments on Dowty's "Thematic proto roles, subject selection, and lexical semantic defaults." Paper presented at the Center for Cognitive Science Seminar, MIT, November 1.

Hirsh-Pasek, K., Treiman, R., and Schneiderman, M. (1984) Brown and Hanlon revisited: Mothers' sensitivity to ungrammatical forms. *Journal of Child Language* 11: 81–88.

Hochberg, J. (1986) Children's judgments of transitivity errors. *Journal of Child Language* 13: 317–334.

Hochberg, J., and Pinker, S. (1989) Syntax-semantics correspondences in parental speech. Unpublished manuscript, Northwestern University.

Hopper, P. J., and Thompson, S. A. (1980) Transitivity in grammar and discourse. *Language* 56: 251–299.

Horgan, D. (1978) The development of the full passive. *Journal of Child Language* 5: 65–80.

Hust, J., and Brame, M. (1976) Jackendoff on interpretive semantics. *Linguistic Analysis* 2: 243–277.

Huttenlocher, J., Smiley, P., and Charney, R. (1983) Emergence of action categories in the child: Evidence from verb meanings. *Psychological Review* 90: 72–93.

Jackendoff. R. S. (1972) *Semantic interpretation in generative grammar.* Cambridge, Mass.: MIT Press.

Jackendoff, R. S. (1975) Morphological and semantic regularities in the lexicon. *Language* 51: 639–671.

Jackendoff, R. S. (1977) *X-bar syntax: A study of phrase structure.* Cambridge, Mass.: MIT Press.

Jackendoff, R. S. (1978) Grammar as evidence for conceptual structure. In M. Halle, J. Bresnan, and G. Miller, eds., *Linguistic theory and psychological reality.* Cambridge, Mass.: MIT Press.

Jackendoff, R. S. (1983) *Semantics and cognition.* Cambridge, Mass.: MIT Press.

Jackendoff, R. S. (1987a) The status of thematic relations in linguistic theory. *Linguistic Inquiry* 18: 369–411,

Jackendoff, R. S. (1987b) Adjuncts. Unpublished manuscript, Brandeis University.

Jackendoff, R. S. (1987c) Some further thematic functions for space. Unpublished manuscript, Brandeis University.

Jackendoff, R. S. (1987d) *Consciousness and the computational mind.* Cambridge, Mass.: MIT Press.

Jespersen, O. (1938) *Growth and structure of the English language.* Oxford: Basil Blackwell. Tenth ed., 1982, Chicago: University of Chicago Press.

Kaplan, R. M., and Bresnan, J. (1982) Lexical-functional grammar: A formal system for grammatical representation. In J. Bresnan, ed., *The mental representation of grammatical relations.* Cambridge, Mass.: MIT Press.

Katz, J. J., and Fodor, J. A. (1963) The structure of a semantic theory. *Language* 39: 170–210.

Keenan, E. O. (1976) Towards a universal definition of "subject." In C. Li, ed., *Subject and topic.* New York: Academic Press.

Keenan, E. O. (1985) Passive in the world's languages. In T. Shopen, ed., *Language typology and syntactic description.* Vol. 1: *Clause structure.* New York: Cambridge University Press.

Keil, F. C. (1979) *Semantic and conceptual development: An ontological perspective.* Cambridge, Mass.: Harvard University Press.

Keyser, S. J., and Roeper, T. (1984) On the middle and ergative constructions in English. *Linguistic Inquiry* 15: 381–416.

Kiparsky, P. (1987) Thematic rules and grammatical relations. *Proceedings of the North East Linguistics Society* 17.

Kuczaj, S. A. II, and Maratsos, M. (1979) The initial verbs of *yes-no* questions: A different kind of general grammatical category. Presented at the symposium "The Child's Formulation of Grammatical Categories and Rules," Biennial Meeting of the Society for Research in Child Development, San Francisco, March.

Lakoff, G. (1971) On generative semantics. In D. Steinberg and L. Jakobovits, eds., *Semantics: An interdisciplinary reader in philosophy, psychology, linguistics, and anthropology.* New York: Cambridge University Press.

Lakoff, G. (1977) Linguistic gestalts. In *Papers from the Thirteenth Regional Meeting of the Chicago Linguistics Society.* Chicago: Chicago Linguistics Society, University of Chicago.

Lakoff, G. (1987) *Women, fire, and dangerous things: What categories reveal about the mind.* Chicago: University of Chicago Press.

Lakoff, G., and Johnson, M. (1980) *Metaphors we live by.* Chicago: University of Chicago Press.

Lakoff, R. (1971) Passive resistance. In *Papers from the Seventh Regional Meeting of the Chicago Linguistics Society.* Chicago: Chicago Linguistics Society, University of Chicago.

Landau, B., and Gleitman, L. R. (1985) *Language and experience*. Cambridge, Mass.: Harvard University Press.

Langacker, R. W. (1987) Nouns and verbs. *Language* 63: 53–94.

Larson, R. K. (1988) On the double object construction. *Linguistic Inquiry* 19: 335–391.

Lasnik, H. (1988) Subjects and the theta-criterion. *Natural language and linguistic theory* 6: 1–17.

Lasnik, H. (in press) On certain substitutes for negative data. In W. Demopoulos and R. May, eds., *Learnability and linguistic theory*. Dordrecht, Netherlands: Reidel.

Laughren, M., Levin, B., and Rappaport, M. (1986) What's behind theta-roles: What syntax tells us about lexical representation. Unpublished manuscript, Center for Cognitive Science, MIT.

Levin, B. (1985) Lexical semantics in review: An introduction. In B. Levin, ed., Lexical semantics in review. Lexicon Project Working Papers #1. Cambridge, Mass.: MIT Center for Cognitive Science.

Levin, B., and Rappaport, M. (1986) The formation of adjectival passives. *Linguistic Inquiry* 17: 623–661.

Levin, L. (1985) Operations on lexical forms: Unaccusative rules in Germanic languages. Ph.D. dissertation, MIT.

Li, C., and Thompson, S. A. (1976) Subject and topic: A new typology of language. In C. Li, ed., *Subject and topic*. New York: Academic Press.

Lieber, R. (1979) The English passive: an argument for historical rule stability. *Linguistic Inquiry* 10: 667–688.

Lieberman, P. (1984) *The biology and evolution of language*. Cambridge, Mass.: Harvard University Press.

Light, M. (1988) The acquisition of argument structure: Towards a computational model. Unpublished manuscript, MIT.

Lightfoot, D. (1981) The history of noun phrase movement. In C. L. Baker and J. J. McCarthy, eds., *The logical problem of language acquisition*. Cambridge, Mass.: MIT Press.

Lord, C. (1979) "Don't you fall me down": Children's generalizations regarding cause and transitivity. Papers and Reports on Child Language Development, 17. Stanford, Calif.: Stanford University Department of Linguistics.

MacWhinney, B. (1985) Hungarian language acquisition as an exemplification of a general model of grammatical development. In D. I. Slobin, ed., *The crosslinguistic study of language acquisition*. Vol. 2: *Theoretical issues*. Hillsdale, N.J.: Erlbaum.

MacWhinney, B. (1987) The competition model. In B. MacWhinney, ed., *Mechanisms of language acquisition*. Hillsdale, N.J.: Erlbaum.

MacWhinney, B., and Snow, C. (1985) The Child Language Data Exchange System. *Journal of Child Language* 12: 271–296.

Major, D. (1974) *The acquisition of modal auxiliaries in the language of children*. The Hague: Mouton.

Maling, J. (1983) Transitive adjectives: A case of categorial reanalysis. In F. Heny and B. Richards, eds., *Linguistic categories: Auxiliaries and related puzzles.* Dordrecht, Netherlands: Reidel.

Marantz, A. P. (1982) On the acquisition of grammatical relations. *Linguistische Berichte: Linguistik als Kognitive Wissenschaft* 80/82: 32–69.

Marantz, A. P. (1984) *On the nature of grammatical relations.* Cambridge, Mass.: MIT Press.

Maratsos, M. P. (1986) On the roles of input and tabulation. Paper presented at the Eleventh Annual Boston University Conference on Language Development, Oct. 17–19.

Maratsos, M. P. (1988a) Metaphors of language: Metaphors of the mind? (Review of G. Lakoff's "Women, fire, and dangerous things.") *Contemporary Psychology.*

Maratsos. M. P. (1988b) Crosslinguistic analysis, universals, and language acquisition. In F. Kessel, ed., *The development of language and language researchers: Essays in honor of Roger Brown.* Hillsdale, N.J.: Erlbaum.

Maratsos, M. P., and Abramovitch, R. (1975) How children understand full, truncated and anomalous passives. *Journal of Verbal Learning and Verbal Behavior* 14: 145–157.

Maratsos, M. P., Fox, D. E., Becker, J. A., and Chalkley, M. A. (1985) Semantic restrictions on children's passives. *Cognition* 19: 167–191.

Maratsos, M., Gudeman, R., Gerard-Ngo, P., and DeHart, G. (1987) A study in novel word learning: The productivity of the causative. In B. MacWhinney, ed., *Mechanisms of language acquisition.* Hillsdale, N.J.: Erlbaum.

Maratsos, M. P., Kuczaj, S. A., II., Fox, D. E., and Chalkley, M. (1979) Some empirical studies in the acquisition of transformational relations: Passives, negatives, and the past tense. In W. A. Collins (Ed.), *Minnesota Symposium on Child Psychology,* Vol. 12. Hillsdale, N.J.: Erlbaum.

Marchand, H. (1951) The syntactical change from inflectional to word order systems and some effects of this change on the relation "verb/object" in English: A diachronic-synchronic interpretation. *Anglia* 70: 70–89.

Marin, O. S. M., Saffran, E. M., and Schwartz, M. F. (1976) Dissociations of language in aphasia: Implications for normal functions. *Annals of the New York Academy of Sciences* 280: 868–884.

Marr, D., and Vaina, L. (1982) Representation and recognition of the movements of shapes. *Proceedings of the Royal Society of London* 214: 501–524.

Mazurkewich, I., and White, L. (1984) The acquisition of the dative alternation: Unlearning overgeneralizations. *Cognition* 16: 261–283.

McCarthy, J. J., and Prince, A. (in preparation) *Prosodic morphology.*

McCawley, J. D. (1968) The role of semantics in a grammar. In E. Bach and R. T. Harms, eds., *Universals in linguistic theory.* New York: Holt, Rinehart and Winston.

McCawley, J. D. (1971) Prelinguistic syntax. In R. J. O'Brien, ed., *Linguistics: Developments of the Sixties—Viewpoints for the Seventies. 22nd Annual Georgetown University Round Table on Languages and Linguistics.* Washington, D.C.: Georgetown University Press.

McClelland, J. L., and Kawamoto, A. H. (1986) Mechanisms of sentence processing: Assigning roles to constituents of sentences. In J. L. McClelland, D. E. Rumelhart, and The PDP Research Group, *Parallel distributed processing: Explorations in the microstructure of cognition.* Vol. 2: *Psychological and biological models.* Cambridge, Mass.: MIT Press.

McNeill, D. (1966) Developmental psycholinguistics. In F. Smith and G. Miller, eds., *The genesis of language.* Cambridge, Mass.: MIT Press.

Menyuk, P. (1969) *Sentences children use.* Cambridge, Mass.: MIT Press.

Miceli, G., Mazzucchi, A., Menn., L., and Goodglass, H. (1983) Contrasting cases of Italian agrammatic aphasia without comprehension disorder. *Brain and Language* 19: 65–97.

Miceli, G., Silveri, M. C., Villa, G., and Caramazza, A. (1984) On the basis of the agrammatic's difficulty in producing main verbs. *Cortex* 20: 207–220.

Michalski, R. S., and Stepp, R. E. (1983) Learning from observation: Conceptual clustering. In R. S. Michalski, J. G. Carbonell, and T. M. Mitchell, eds., *Machine learning: An artificial intelligence approach.* Palo Alto, Calif.: Tioga.

Miller, G. A., and Johnson-Laird, P. N. (1976) *Language and perception.* Cambridge, Mass.: Harvard University Press.

Morgan, J. L. (1986) *From simple input to complex grammar.* Cambridge, Mass.: MIT Press.

Morgan, J. L., and Travis, L. L. (in press) Limits on negative information in language learning. *Journal of Child Language.*

Nedyalkov, V. P., and Silnitsky, G. G. (1973) The typology of morphological and lexical causatives. In F. Kiefer, ed., *Trends in Soviet theoretical linguistics.* Dordrecht, Netherlands: Reidel.

Newport, E. L., Gleitman, L. R., and Gleitman, H. (1977) Mother, I'd rather do it myself: Some effects and non-effects of maternal speech style. In C. E. Snow and C. A. Ferguson, eds., *Talking to children: Language input and acquisition.* New York: Cambridge University Press.

Nwachukwu, P. A. (1987) The argument structure of Igbo verbs. Lexicon Project Working Papers #18. Cambridge, Mass.: MIT Center for Cognitive Science.

Oehrle, R. T. (1976) The grammatical status of the English dative alternation. Ph.D. dissertation, MIT.

Oehrle, R. T. (1977) Review of *Semantics and syntactic regularity* by G. M. Green. *Language* 53: 198–208.

Oehrle, R. T., and Ross, J. R. (n.d.) Brevity is the soul of everything. Unpublished manuscript, MIT.

O'Keefe, J., and Nadel, L. (1978) *The hippocampus as a cognitive map.* Oxford: Oxford University Press.

Osherson, D. N., Stob, M., and Weinstein, S. (1985) *Systems that learn.* Cambridge, Mass.: MIT Press.

Ostler, N. D. M. (1980) A theory of case linking and agreement. Unpublished manuscript, Indiana University Linguistics Club, Bloomington.

Penner, S. (1987) Parental responses to grammatical and ungrammatical child utterances. *Child Development* 58: 376–384.

Perlmutter, D. (1978) Impersonal passives and the unaccusative hypothesis. *Proceedings of the Berkeley Linguistics Society* 4: 157–189.

Perlmutter, D. (1980) Relational grammar. In E. Moravcsik and J. Wirth, eds., *Syntax and Semantics*. Vol. 13: *Current Approaches to Syntax*. New York: Academic Press.

Perlmutter, D., and Postal, P. (1984) The 1-advancement exclusiveness law. In D. Perlmutter and C. Rosen, eds., *Studies in relational grammar*. Chicago: University of Chicago Press.

Perlmutter, D., and Rosen, C., eds. (1984) *Studies in relational grammar*. Chicago: University of Chicago Press.

Pinker, S. (1979) Formal models of language learning. *Cognition* 7: 217–283.

Pinker, S. (1981a) Comments on the paper by Wexler. In C. L. Baker and J. J. McCarthy, eds., *The logical problem of language acquisition*. Cambridge, Mass.: MIT Press.

Pinker, S. (1981b) A theory of graph comprehension. Center for Cognitive Science Occasional Papers #15. Cambridge, Mass.: MIT Center for Cognitive Science.

Pinker, S. (1982) A theory of the acquisition of lexical interpretive grammars. In J. Bresnan, ed., *The mental representation of grammatical relations*. Cambridge, Mass.: MIT Press.

Pinker, S. (1984) *Language learnability and language development*. Cambridge, Mass.: Harvard University Press.

Pinker, S. (1986) Productivity and conservatism in language acquisition. In W. Demopoulos and A. Marras, eds., *Language learning and concept acquisition: Foundational Issues*. Norwood, N.J.: Ablex.

Pinker, S. (1987) The bootstrapping problem in language acquisition. In B. MacWhinney, ed., *Mechanisms of language acquisition*. Hillsdale, N.J.: Erlbaum.

Pinker, S. (1989) Resolving a learnability paradox in the acquisition of the verb lexicon. In M. L. Rice and R. L. Schiefelbusch, eds., *The teachability of language*. Baltimore: Paul H. Brookes. Also appeared as Lexicon Project Working Papers #17. Cambridge, Mass.: MIT Center for Cognitive Science, 1987.

Pinker, S., Lebeaux, D. S., and Frost, L. A. (1987) Productivity and constraints in the acquisition of the passive. *Cognition* 26: 195–267.

Pinker, S., and Prince, A. (1988) On language and connectionism: Analysis of a Parallel Distributed Processing model of language acquisition. *Cognition* 28: 73–193.

Pustejovsky, J. (1987) On the acquisition of lexical entries: The perceptual origin of thematic relations. *Proceedings of the Association of Computational Linguistics*. Stanford, Calif.: Stanford University.

Pustejovsky, J. (in press) A theory of lexical semantics for concept acquisition in natural language. *International Journal of Intelligent Systems*.

Pye, C. (in press) The ergative parameter. *Journal of Linguistics*.

Quirk, R., Greenbaum, S., Leech, G., and Svartvik, J. (1971) *A grammar of contemporary English*. London: Longman.

Randall, J. H. (1980) -ity: A study of word formation restrictions. *Journal of Psycholinguistic Research* 9: 523–534.

Randall, J. H. (1987) Indirect positive evidence: Overturning overgeneralizations in language acquisition. Unpublished manuscript, Indiana University Linguistics Club, Bloomington.

Rappaport, M., and Levin, B. (1985) A case study in lexical analysis: The locative alternation. Unpublished manuscript, MIT Center for Cognitive Science.

Rappaport, M., and Levin, B. (1988) What to do with theta-roles. In W. Wilkins, ed., *Thematic relations*. New York: Academic Press.

Rappaport, M., and Levin, B. (in press) -er nominals: Implications for the theory of argument structure. In E. Wehrli and T. Stowell, eds., *Syntax and Semantics 24: Syntax and the lexicon*. New York: Academic Press.

Rappaport, M., Levin, B., and Laughren, M. (1987) Levels of lexical representation. Lexicon Project Working Papers #20. Cambridge, Mass.: MIT Center for Cognitive Science. Also to appear as Niveaux de representation lexicale, *Lexique*.

Ritchie, W. C. (1985) Word-formation, learnèd vocabulary, and linguistic maturation. In J. Fisiak, ed., *Historical semantics and historical word-formation*. New York: Mouton.

Roeper, T. (1981) On the deductive model and the acquisition of productive morphology. In C. L. Baker and J. J. McCarthy, eds., *The logical problem of language acquisition*. Cambridge, Mass.: MIT Press.

Rosch, E., Mervis, C. B., Gray, W. D., Johnson, D. M., and Boyes-Braem, P. (1976) Basic objects in natural categories. *Cognitive Psychology* 8: 382–439.

Rosen, C. (1984) The interface between semantic roles and initial grammatical relations. In D. Perlmutter and C. Rosen, eds., *Studies in relational grammar*. Chicago: University of Chicago Press.

Ross, J. R. (1972) Act. In D. Davidson and G. Harmon,, eds., *Semantics of natural language*. Dordrecht, Netherlands: Reidel.

Rozin, P. (1976) The evolution of intelligence and access to the cognitive unconscious. In L. Sprague and A. N. Epstein, eds., *Progress in psychobiology and physiological psychology*, Vol. 6. New York: Academic Press.

Saksena, A. (1982) Contact in causation. *Language* 58: 820–831.

Salkoff, M. (1983) Bees are swarming in the garden. *Language* 59: 288–346.

Schank, R. C. (1973) Identification of conceptualizations underlying natural language. In R. C. Schank and K. M. Colby, eds., *Computer models of thought and language*. San Francisco: W. H. Freeman.

Selkirk, E. O., and Dell, F. (1978) On morphologically governed vowel alternations in French. In S. J. Keyser, ed., *Recent transformational studies in European languages*. Cambridge, Mass.: MIT Press.

Shepard, R. N., and Cooper, L. A. (1982) *Mental images and their transformations*. Cambridge, Mass.: MIT Press.

Shibatani, M. (1976) The grammar of causative constructions: A conspectus. In M. Shibatani, ed., *Syntax and semantics*. Vol. 6: *The grammar of causative constructions*. New York: Academic Press.

Shopen, T., ed. (1985a) *Language typology and syntactic description*. Vol. 1: *Clause structure*. New York: Cambridge University Press.

Shopen, T., ed.. (1985b) *Language typology and syntactic description*. Vol. 3: *Grammatical categories and the lexicon*. New York: Cambridge University Press.

Sinclair, A. R., Jarvella, J., and Levelt, W. J. M. (1978) *The child's conception of language*. Berlin: Springer-Verlag (cited by Aronoff, 1982).

Slobin, D. I. (1985) Crosslinguistic evidence for the language-making capacity. In D. I. Slobin, ed., *The crosslinguistic study of language acquisition*. Vol. 2: *Theoretical issues*. Hillsdale, N.J.: Erlbaum.

Smith, C. S. (1973) On causative verbs and derived nominals in English. *Linguistic Inquiry* 3: 136–138.

Steele, S. (with Akmajian, A., Demers, R., Jelinek, E., Kitagawa, C., Oehrle, R., and Wasow, T.) (1981) *An encyclopedia of AUX: A study of cross-linguistic equivalence*. Cambridge, Mass.: MIT Press.

Stemberger, J. P. (1982) Syntactic errors in speech. *Journal of Psycholinguistic Research* 11: 313–345.

Storm, P. (1977) Predicting the applicability of dative movement. In *The book of squibs*. Chicago: Chicago Linguistics Society, University of Chicago.

Talmy, L. (1976) Semantic causative types. In M. Shibatani, ed., *Syntax and semantics*. Vol. 6: *The grammar of causative constructions*. New York: Academic Press.

Talmy, L. (1983) How language structures space. In H. Pick and L. Acredolo, eds., *Spatial orientation: Theory, research, and application*. New York: Plenum.

Talmy, L. (1985) Lexicalization patterns: Semantic structure in lexical forms. In T. Shopen, ed., *Language typology and syntactic description*. Vol. 3: *Grammatical categories and the lexicon*. New York: Cambridge University Press.

Talmy, L. (1988) Force dynamics in language and cognition. *Cognitive Science* 12: 49–100.

Tenny, C. (1988) The aspectual interface hypothesis. *Proceedings of the North East Linguistics Society* 18.

Tversky, A. (1977) Features of similarity. *Psychological Review* 84: 327–352.

Vendler, Z. (1957) Verbs and times. *Philosophical Review* 66: 143–160.

Visser, F. T. (1963) *An historical syntax of the English language*. *Part One: Syntactical units with one verb*. Leiden: Brill.

Wanner, E., and Maratsos, M. (1978) An ATN approach to comprehension. In M. Halle, J. Bresnan, and G. A. Miller, eds., *Linguistic theory and psychological reality*. Cambridge, Mass.: MIT Press.

Wasow, T. (1977) Transformations and the lexicon. In P. W. Culicover, T. Wasow, and A. Akmajian, eds., *Formal syntax*. New York: Academic Press.

Wasow, T. (1981) Comments on the paper by Baker. In C. L. Baker and J. J. McCarthy, eds., *The logical problem of language acquisition*. Cambridge, Mass.: MIT Press.

Wasow, T., Sag, I., and Nunberg, G. (1983) Idioms: An interim report. In S. Hattori and I. Inoue, eds., *Proceedings of the XIIIth International Congress of Linguists*. Tokyo: CIPL.

Wexler, K. (1970) Semantic structure: Psychological evidence for hierarchical features. Paper presented at the Research Workshop on Cognitive Organization and Psychological Processes, sponsored by the Council on Basic Research in Education, Huntington Beach, Calif., Aug.

Wexler, K., and Culicover, P. (1980) *Formal principles of language acquisition.* Cambridge, Mass.: MIT Press.

Whorf, B. (1956) *Language, thought, and reality.* Cambridge, Mass.: MIT Press.

Williams, E. (1980) Predication. *Linguistic Inquiry* 11: 203–238.

Williams, E. (1981) Argument structure and morphology. *Linguistic Review* 1: 81–114.

Wilson, R., Pinker, S., Zaenen, A., and Lebeaux, D. (1981) Productivity and the dative alternation. Paper presented at the Sixth Annual Boston University Conference on Language Development, Oct. 9–11.

Zaenen, A. (1986) Are there unaccusative verbs in Dutch? *Proceedings of the North East Linguistics Society* 16.

Zubizaretta, M. L. (1987) *Levels of representation in the lexicon and syntax.* Dordrecht, Netherlands: Foris.

Zwicky, A. (1971) In a manner of speaking. *Linguistic Inquiry* 2: 223–233.

Notes

Chapter 1: A Learnability Paradox

1. These alternations are treated by different kinds of mechanisms in different theories. In early versions of Transformational Generative Grammar (e.g., Chomsky, 1965) and in Generative Semantics (e.g., Lakoff, 1971), they were treated as transformational rules applying to phrase structures. They are treated as being the products of lexical rules in Bresnan's Lexical Functional Grammar (LFG, Bresnan, 1982a, b; Pinker, 1984) and in most versions of the Extended Standard Theory of generative grammar, such as Chomsky's Government and Binding framework (GB, Chomsky, 1981). This is true even for the passive, which involves the "move a" transformation: it is a special property of the participle, namely failure to assign accusative case, that triggers the movement rule, and the conversion of a verb into a passive participle is accomplished by a lexical rule. In Gazdar, Klein, Pullum, and Sag's (1985) Generalized Phrase Structure Grammar (GPSG), they consist of "metarules" that derive new phrase structure rules from old ones; in Perlmutter's Relational Grammar (RG; Perlmutter, 1980; Perlmutter and Rosen, 1984), they consist of rules that operate on lists of symbols representing grammatical relations. The learnability paradox applies to all these formulations.

2. Furthermore there are flaws in both of the statistical tests purported to establish the difference in the Hirsh-Pasek et al. study. The t-test showing that mothers repeat their 2-year-old children's ungrammatical sentences more often than their grammatical ones was significant only at a one-tailed significance level, whereas a two-tailed test is the appropriate one. It is the availability of information to children that is at issue, not the exact form of parents' behavior, so consistent differential repetition of ungrammatical over grammatical sentences *or vice versa* would serve as negative evidence. Indeed, the later studies which differentiated verbatim from corrected repetitions found that verbatim repetitions followed grammatical utterances *more* often. In addition, Hirsh-Pasek et al.'s other analysis, a sign test, pooled the responses of the different mothers, rather than treating each mother as a unit, violating the assumption of independence of observations. Thus the test could have magnified the behavior of a single mother or small subsample of mothers into a significant overall result.

3. I thank my sister, Susan Pinker, for providing the example from the speech of her daughter, Eva Boodman.

4. In much of the GB literature "ergative" is used as a synonym of "unaccusative," and "intransitive" is used as a synonym of "unergative." I will avoid this ambiguous terminology.

5. Often abstract deep-structure configurations are motivated by certain binding phenomena, for example, the fact that *Pictures of each other impressed the men* is grammatical whereas **Pictures of each other absolved the men* is not. It is assumed that binding principles are sensitive only to phrase structure configuration (Chomsky, 1981), so configurations are proposed that preserve the validity of the binding principles. If binding is not exclusively governed by configuration, though (see, e.g., Grimshaw, in press), the motivation for the abstract deep-structure configurations diminishes. See also Culicover and Wilkins (1986), which makes a similar point regarding control.

6. Of course, there is a trivial way in which syntactic criteria could differentiate alternating from nonalternating verbs. For example, one could say that any verb appearing in the frame *What did John <verb>?* is causativizable. It is trivial because *wh*-question formation is orthogonal to causativization, so object-questions are simply variants of the transitive argument structure that we are worried about to begin with. We are simply left with a minor variant of conservatism. This is the problem with Borer and Wexler's suggestion that the child uses the appearance of passives as a cue to the causativizability of a verb, for example.

7. Furthermore, some of these generalizations may apply to different kinds of lexical alternations than the ones discussed here, such as category-changing rules (e.g., the formation of adjectival passives; Levin and Rappaport, 1986). See also section 3.3.

Chapter 2: Constraints on Lexical Rules

1. The extension of the Grimshaw-Prince account that is designed to handle schwa-initial verbs does not work perfectly. Some schwa-initial verbs do not dativize: **I announced him my plans; *He arranged me a party; *They abandoned the vandals the car; *She admitted me her faults (cf. She advanced me the money)*. Some verbs beginning with an unstressed syllable that is more than a schwa do dativize: *He referred me a patient; They reserved me a seat*. In chapter 4 I return to these examples.

2. We found no such difference for the *for*-dative verbs. I will discuss a possible reason for this in chapter 4.

Chapter 3: Constraints and the Nature of Argument Structure

1. I am using the term "predication" in its traditional sense, not the technical sense introduced by Williams (1980).

2. The English preposition *on* is itself probably a homonym for at least two distinct location functions: roughly, "at the top of," as in *an apple on the table*, and "contacting the outer surface of," as in *a blister on the sole of your foot*. See Bowerman (1989) and Talmy (1983) for discussion.

3. This predicts that the holistic effect should apply to the object of the in*to*/*onto* forms as well. This seems right: *I loaded the hay into the wagon* does entail that all the hay being referred to was loaded, and *I piled a place setting onto the table* ordinarily entails that all parts of the place setting were moved, in contrast to *I piled rice onto a place setting*, which

is compatible with the outcome that only one piece of the place setting ended up with rice on it. At first glance there might seem to be counterexamples: *I loaded hay into the wagon* does not seem to mean that I loaded *all* the available hay. The apparent failure of the holistic interpretation, however, is the result of an interaction with the interpretation of an indefinite mass or plural noun, and applies in the *with* variant as well: *She loaded wagons with hay* does not mean that every wagon in the farm has hay in it. But all the wagons that did get hay were completely filled, just as in the *into* sentence all the hay that did get moved ended up in the wagon. See Dowty (1987) and Foley and Van Valin (1984).

4. In the next chapter I consider a variant of this proposal which does not invariably require the double-object form to involve literal change of possession.

5. The first argument of passives can also be the subject or object of *get*, the object of *have*, or unexpressed in appositives, but these are also realizations of the theme role.

6. Syntactically ergative languages, at first glance counterexamples to this generalization, will be discussed in chapter 6.

Chapter 4: Possible and Actual Forms

1. It was Whorf (1956) who first called attention to the fact that certain constructions are restricted to narrow classes of verbs defined by subtle criteria; he called them "crypto-types."

2. More specifically, we would have to assume that the relevant definition of *at* would allow it to pertain to the patient that an act is intended to involve in the usual way, but does not necessarily succeed at so doing.

3. There are several other subclasses of motion verbs participating or failing to participate in this alternation that I will not discuss. See Dowty (1987) for an extensive list of these verbs.

4. This is somewhat different from Lakoff's own position. Lakoff introduced the concept of motivated categories in discussing the family of senses connected with a polysemous word. He claims that these families reflect the nature of human categories, which presupposes that the motivations are grasped by all speakers. Maratsos (1988a) questions this claim, noting that many motivations for categories may play a role diachronically but may be opaque to many speakers in a given generation. I share Maratsos's doubts. Judgments of the well-formedness or ill-formedness of class members are often much more discriminating than the best "motivation" one can discover. When we examine the narrow verb classes, we will see that speakers reject many putative members that are as well motivated as those already in a category. Furthermore, motivations cannot be predicted in advance—not by the linguist, and therefore presumably not by the learner. Thus motivated classes must be learned as lists at least part of the time.

5. I have not found a detailed analysis of these verbs in the linguistic literature. They seem to be similar to verbs of incorporated themes, discussed by Rappaport and Levin (1985), Jackendoff (1983, 1987b), and Clark and Clark (1978), such as to *butter* or *to paint*. They have similar paraphrases based on the associated noun: *to butter X* = "to cause butter to go on *X*"; *to reward / credit / supply X* = "to cause a reward / a credit / supplies to go to *X*." They both take *with*-objects, usually optionally: *He buttered the bread (with unsalted margarine); He rewarded her (with a kiss)*. And the semantic properties of the *with*-object must stand in a certain relation to those of the incorporated nominal, basically adding

nonredundant information: *?He buttered the bread with butter*; *?He rewarded her with a reward*; *?He credited her with a credit*.

6. The prepositional-dative form of *ask* is not perfectly acceptable to many speakers with the preposition *to*, although it improves with the preposition *of*: *??I already asked that question to him / ?I already asked that question of him*. I have heard, however, *I don't know if you're the right person to ask this to, but ...*

7. Green (1974) finds *shout* and *whisper* to be dativizable to her and proposes that they encode the *means* of communication rather than the *manner*. The difference can be seen in the contrast between *Using a whisper / shout, he gave her a word of encouragement* and **Using a mumble / mutter / mention, he gave her a word of encouragement*.

8. Food-preparation usages, which are quite productive, may seem to fall into a different class, but I think that careful analysis of their semantics would lump them with the verbs of creation. At first glance, usages such as *I poured her some coffee*, *She boiled me a lobster*, and *She fried me some chicken* appear to be counterexamples, since nothing is created and therefore only a benefactive relation holds. However, a closer look shows that this is not quite right. These cases involve food terms that are ambiguous between a raw material or source and a unit or kind of item fit for consumption. Thus the verbs seem to entail creation of the edible product prior to the act of giving. This predicts that the referent of the second object must denote only the edible product or unit created, not the original material acted upon, and the prediction seems correct. First, consider the case where someone pours coffee from a pot. It is much better to say *Can you pour me a cup of coffee / a cup of that coffee / some of that coffee?*, where the relevant part is created by the action, than to say *Can you pour me that coffee / a pot of coffee / that pot of coffee?* (unless the entire pot is to be consumed). Second, when edible products have names distinct from their sources, the former are much more natural in the double-object construction. Compare, for example, *She cooked a pig / some pork for me* with *She cooked me some pork / *a pig*; *She tossed me a salad* with **She tossed me some lettuce, tomatoes, and carrots*. Third, when one of the verbs is used with an object that only changes state, rather than turning into a new kind of object, the double-object form is blocked: *Dave baked the Plexiglas panel for me / *?baked me the Plexiglas panel*. Finally, Green (1974) notes that *a baked cake* is vaguely redundant, and *an unbaked cake* vaguely contradictory, which suggests that *bake* means "create," not "prepare" or "change the state of," when used with food objects.

9. Beth Levin has called my attention to discussions in Bolinger (1971), Dowty (1979b), and Green (1973) of the general ability of particles to add an effect meaning component to a verb, similar to "resultatives" such as *She hammered the metal flat*.

10. Line from Bob Dylan's *Highway 61 Revisited*.

11. The semiproductive causative morphology operated only in Old English and did not change the vowel directly but simply added the suffix *-jan*; the vowel change was just a phonological adjustment. When the Old English suffixes eroded, only the vowel change survived (Visser, 1963).

12. *Sprinkle* is a borderline case. Prototypically the motion of the particles is caused by downward applied force (as in using a salt shaker). Downwardness meets the criteria of class 5; force causing a motion in a certain spatial distribution along a trajectory meets the criteria of class 3. The involvement of force seems to allow it to enter class 3 and alternate.

However, *shake* is similar but is confined to class 5. A possible cause is the fact that *shake*, unlike *sprinkle* and most of the other alternating verbs, has a homophonous counterpart that does not require a masslike theme, hence the *with* form would contain a garden path: **shake the table with flour*. A completely different possibility for the locativizability of *sprinkle* that I will not explore further is its phonological similarity to *spatter, splash, splatter, spray,* and *squirt* and perhaps also *slather, smear, smudge, spread,* and *streak,* all in alternating classes and all somewhat onomatopoeic.

13. Might be in Class 1 of the into/onto verbs, both syntactically and semantically: ?I *dappled paint onto the canvas*.

14. A nice example of how the choice of locative form is governed by the geometry of the content and container, with a nonholistic distribution leading to the content-oriented *into/onto* form, comes from an article in the food section of the *Boston Globe* of March 23, 1988. In it, Jane and Michael Stern invent a new locative verb, use the verb in the *into* form, and state the relevant principle themselves: "In some Grape-Nuts puddings we've sampled, the cereal is mixed throughout the custard. In Brandy Pete's, it is ribboned into the custard as a distinct separate area."

15. Their different syntax, according to the theory, should nonetheless be associated with subtly different meanings that can be exploited in discourse, poetry, and rhetoric. Because the only difference between *rob* and *steal* is that one is "done to" people and the other is done to" possessions, the Beatles could sing *She could steal but she could not rob* (in "She Came in Through the Bathroom Window") to suggest that the subject of the song was motivated to obtain objects but not to hurt people.

16. Perhaps subsumed within this class are verbs of posture incorporating particles, which alternate: *stand up, sit down, bend over, lay down* (in informal American speech), *lean against*, and so on.

17. Thus the verb *climb* is ruled out doubly: as an action verb (*He climbed across the rubble*) it is a verb of volition; as a pure spatial verb (*The airplane climbed*) it is a verb of inherently directed motion.

18. It is necessary to differentiate these verbs, which pertain to objects, from verbs that pertain to aspectual properties of events, which do alternate, such as *start, begin, continue, end, finish*.

19. A few emotion-experiencing verbs incorporating the suffix *-en* or the particle *up* seem to alternate: *The boy saddened / gladdened / cheered up / perked up; They saddened / gladdened / cheered up / perked up the boy with the news*.

20. There are a number of harmless positive exceptions to these generalizations— harmless both because they *are* positive, hence learnable, and because one can show that they are not pure causative verbs meaning simply "cause to *verb*" but contain idiosyncratic meaning elements specific to the transitive version, so they must be learned individually. One can *rattle* something, but only by shaking it, not by, say, driving a car over a bump. Secrets, but not water, can be *leaked*; pipes, but not poorly dyed clothing, can be *bled*; cigarettes and ham can be *smoked* (in two different specific senses) but firewood and butter cannot. Transitive *shine* can only mean "polish" (as in shoes) or "direct a beam" (as in flashlights), not "put in sunlight," "coat with high-gloss paint," and so on.

21. Note also that there are scattered positive exceptions in both directions, usually accumulating bits of idiosyncratic meaning in one of the two forms, such as *She burped the baby* / *The baby burped; He fed the baby* / *The baby fed; He dropped the ball* / *The ball dropped; Bill drowned* / *John drowned Bill*; see also section 3.3.4.3 and note 18 above. Basically, the class of transitive verbs for which anticausativization appears to be productive consists of verbs of causing something to change physical state or causing something to move in some manner, as long as there is no lexical specification of direction, manner of causation, or motion of an instrument. In other words, anticausativization applies only to causative verbs that could have been formed from a causativization rule to begin with.

22. Recall that this principle would also apply to the alternative treatment of constraints on passivizability I discussed, according to which the passive would be a purely syntactic rule operating on any transitive argument structure. On this account, the thematic properties of verbs would determine whether they have argument structures that are genuinely transitive, that is, with a real syntactic object, or that only resemble transitive structures, with some other kind of unmarked postverbal argument.

23. For double-object forms that are not derived from the *to* prepositional form (that is, *for*-datives and *begrudge*-type verbs), the situation is slightly different, though it fits the overall pattern. Unlike what happens in *to*-datives, it is not clear that the first object in the double-object forms of these verbs is in any way a patient. For example, it is very hard to think of Bob as a patient of Sam's action in *Sam stole Bob a watch*; Bob may have nothing to do with the theft. Likewise, if *Sam begrudges Bob his good looks*, Bob and Sam do not stand in any clear agent-patient relation. This would predict that these forms should not passivize, and indeed they do not seem to do so easily: *?Bob was stolen a watch by Sam*; *Bob was begrudged his good looks by Sam* (see also Dowty, 1987, who makes similar observations). A full treatment of these cases, however, will have to wait until section 5.6.1, where precise representations for these verb forms are examined.

24. In most of these cases, however, the antagonist is the stronger body as well. In some verbs, the agonist is stronger, and it can be mapped onto the subject function, as in *The wall resisted the wind*. Thus the most common subjects are stronger antagonists, but weaker antagonists and stronger agonists are possible as well. I know of no cases of weaker-agonist subjects of transitive verbs.

25. There are other reasons for wondering whether the passives of *frighten* verbs are invariably adjectives. Grimshaw's observations show that they *can be* adjectives, but they do not show that they *cannot* be verbal participles; this is a general problem in the differentiation of adjectival from verbal passives. For example, most of the passives cannot be prefixed with *un-* (*unfrightened*, *unscared*, *undelighted*, etc.), but all of them can take the preposition *by*. Furthermore, many of the *fear* verbs display the same kinds of behavior as the *frighten*-verbs with respect to the passive in the progressive (e.g., *John was coveting* / *craving* / *enjoying Bill's wife* / *??Bill's wife was being coveted* / *craved* / *enjoyed by John*), though they should be bona fide verbal passives according to the account. This suggests that stativity itself, and not only adjectivehood, taints progressive passives, including the progressive passive of the the stative sense of *frighten*. Interestingly, its other, eventive sense may not take the progressive passive for a different reason. It seems likely that aspectual operations (e.g., the "zooming in" on the intermediary component of an event for the progressive aspect) apply to the temporal properties

of the role played by the surface subject argument. For many verbs it may be much more difficult to expand the temporal unfolding of the change of state undergone by the patient than of the action performed by the agent. This would make the progressive of any verb denoting an instantaneous state-change, whether or not it is a psychological like *frighten*, better in the active than in the passive. For example, compare *John was bursting the balloon* with *?The balloon was being burst by John*, or *Bill was swatting a fly* with *?A fly was being swatted by Bill*.

26. In addition, many languages use a locational analysis that is more familiar from the work of Jackendoff and Gruber, whereby the experiencer is a goal to which ideas "move."

27. There is also a sense of *contain* that implies counteracting an object's tendency to escape: *Moshe Dayan contained the Egyptian army; The force field contained the superhot plasma. Contain* used in this sense passivizes—*The army was contained by Dayan*—and it also passes the other tests to be outlined that the purely geometric version of *contain* fails. Thus it is not a counterexample.

28. One form of *have* does passivize. The following are examples I have heard or read: *A splendid time was had by all; A wonderful day was had; A more interesting measure of how well the system is doing can be had by making use of the trigram decoding scheme discussed above ...* . In all three the implicit argument is an experiencer, suggesting that there is a version of *have* that falls into the *fear* class of psych-verbs.

29. The speaker was from a rural, predominantly black area of Louisiana; I do not know whether this is standard in his dialect.

30. Katarina Rice has pointed out to me that there is an an alternative, grammatical reading that the writer may have intended: "make those eyes eyes that the person will find unforgettable."

31. Gregory continues the story. A hostile crowd of onlookers warned him, "Whatever you do to that chicken, we're going to do to you." So he picked up the piece of chicken and kissed it.

Chapter 5: Representation

1. I ignore the deictic directional component of *go* for now.

2. I also ignore other senses of *put* such as that used in *I put the book at the corner of the desk* (which specifies a place, not a path) and *He put a gun to his head* (which specifies an 'against' place; see Jackendoff, 1987a).

3. A similar account may be justified for the selection of the phrasal categories of arguments. Although verbs can select for NPs versus Ss, holding semantics roughly constant (e.g., *I asked what the time was / I asked the time* versus *I wondered what the time was / *I wondered the time*), in the vast majority of cases the selection of the syntactic category of an argument is predictable from its semantic properties (see Grimshaw, 1981). Furthermore many cases of putative selection of syntactic categories turn out to be selection for kinds of semantic categories. For example, *seem* seems to select for APs but not PPs—*John seems happy / *John seems in the room*—but it is perhaps better characterized as selecting for "properties," since *John seems in trouble / in the dumps* is grammatical; see Maling (1983).

4. Another typical, though perhaps not necessary, condition on these incorporated arguments may be that they occur in verbs whose roots come from or are related to nouns for the argument types (e.g., *butter*).

5. I omit a few categories and distinctions that are not as widespread cross-linguistically and not important in the English verb system; see Allan (1977).

6. Jackendoff (1987c) suggests that boundedness and formedness may be separate object qualities; I will collapse them for simplicity's sake.

7. Jackendoff appends the field specifier to the GO function, but since the choice of field affects the interpretation not only of the type of function but also of all its participants—for example, a THING in the locational field must be a physical object, but in the psychological field it is an idea—it seems more transparent to append it to the dominating category type.

8. Of course, *know* must be distinguished from other epistemic verbs, such as *believe*, by the property that a speaker using *know* must himself or herself believe in the truth or existence of the idea. This lexical difference, an example of the "factivity" information that Talmy finds cross-linguistically, has sentence-scope consequences in English, such as in "neg-raising" sentences like *I don't think he's very bright*. The distinction might be captured in a feature that distinguishes things or propositions from their representations in pictures, narratives, or other people's minds; see Jackendoff (1983) and Fauconnier (1984).

9. In fact, there is certainly even more complexity in semantic representations than I have depicted. The list of place-functions and path-functions, for example, must be defined in terms of more basic notions such as boundaries, directions, dimensionality, and so on (see Talmy, 1983; Jackendoff, 1987c).

10. There is also a nonpossessional version of pass, as in *Pass the part down the assembly line*, but this appears to be fairly specialized.

11. B. Levin's (1985) syntactic criteria discussed in section 4.2 are roughly consistent with this analysis: *John touched / chose; *She touched at / chose at John*, and **Handsome men touch / choose easily*. Somewhat less clear are the examples *She touched John on the face / *She chose John on the face / *?She chose John on his face / She chose John on his merits*.

12. It may be that translation in a specified direction is more important than mannerlessness in killing the possibility of causativization. Verbs like *soar* and *swoop*, which do have a manner but also have a direction, do not causativize; the verb *move*, which lacks a manner and a direction, does causativize. The correlation between directionality and mannerlessness probably occurs because if a verb of motion does not specify a manner, it must specify a direction or else it would be synonymous with *move*, violating the Principle of Contrast which generally rules out synonymity (see Bolinger, 1977b; Clark, 1987). Another possibility, however, is that *soar* and *swoop* imply self-powered motion and hence are represented as ACTs, like *run*.

13. The verb *sink* might appear to be a counterexample because it exists in both transitive and intransitive forms but specifies a direction of motion (downward). However, it is easy to see that transitive *sink* is not the product of a causativization rule at all: *Bill sank the bird / his fishing line / John's spirits / the feather*. Rather, it is an independent verb

specifying a means of causation as well as the fact of causation; roughly, to cause to sink in water by means of causing to be full of water. Thus it is like *cut*, which specifies an effect and a means, not like *break*, which specifies only an effect.

14. Jackendoff (1987b), in his discussion of similar verbs, suggests that the change is specified using an inchoative (INCH) function representing the bringing into being of a state wherein the substance was ALL IN or ALL ON the surface. For example, *smear* might be defined as "cause to become X all-on Y." There are two problems with this representation. First, it stipulates the holistic effect using complex place-functions involving the new symbol ALL, rather than allowing it to be a direct consequence of the interpretation of the surface as undergoing a change of state. Second, it does not allow a straightforward way of defining the idiosyncratic spatial distribution of the substance on the surface that these verbs require.

15. The rule would probably specify 'mass', which would embrace aggregates such as sand and jimmies as well as liquids and semisolids.

16. Note that although the actor can act on the liquid at the same time as some liquid hits a surface, as in *spraying*, that need not be the case, and it is literally different individual bits of matter that leave the agent and that arrive at the goal at a given instant in time, as the representation would lead us to expect. This differs from the *smear* verbs, where the stuff the agent is pushing is the exact same stuff that is moving along the surface at any instant.

17. Although the receptacle has the property of being designed to contain the moved object, in this form of the verb there is no constraint that the moved objects have the property of being appropriate to the location: *Biff loaded his gun with jellybeans* is a natural sentence. However, when the *with*-object is absent, an "appropriateness" interpretation ensues: *Biff loaded his gun* strongly implies that bullets, not jellybeans, were inserted. This phenomenon is similar to the effects of the rule of unspecified object deletion applied to transitive verbs, whereby *Sal ate* implies that food, not pencils, were consumed, even though *Sal ate the pencils* is not ungrammatical. This would be represented by appending a property on the substructure representing the "suppressed" (non-open) object, defined in terms of the 'for/to' operator adjacent to a replica of the superordinate action structure. Hence X *ate* = "X ate something with the property of being intended for eating."

18. ACTs in the efficacy field can either be states in which it is asserted that one entity in a relationship is responsible for the circumstance of a second, or events in which one entity actually exerts its causal efficacy to bring about a state change of a second; this is responsible for the ambiguity of S*now covered the ground*.

19. I suggest that a similar account can apply to another semantic field in which HAVE is defined, namely that applying to wholes and their parts. The English verb *have* can express this relation (*Canada has ten provinces*), and other transitive verbs that express it more specifically also do not passivize: **Biff's name is included by the list; *Ten provinces are comprised by Canada*.

Chapter 6: Learning

1. Of course, many closed-class morphemes, such as those sensitive to gender or declensional class, do not have perceptual correlates. The acquisition of such morphemes is discussed in Pinker (1984).

2. In addition, the verbs like *butter* that are most specific about properties of their references often make this idiosyncratic information morphologically transparent by the similarity of the verb to a related noun, as I pointed out in chapter 4.

3. I have not dealt with the aspectual or time-line representation in discussing these procedures, but I assume that broad-range and narrow-range rules include them, perhaps with only a coarse point/region distinction for the former.

4. A related problem is that the verbs that the child is likely to hear in both forms of an alternation may not be a random sample of the ones in the alternating class. For example, the nonwitnessed verbs may have more complex definitions. If any legitimate semantic structure statistically correlates with the sample the child is likely to hear, a clustering procedure could exclude the nonwitnessed ones, preventing productive extension of the alternation to them.

5. In terms of information content, geometric and material properties could be attached either to a patient in an ACT structure or to a theme in a GO structure, as they will be coindexed. However, specifications of shapes and materials for locative verbs are inherently more interdependent with their path and destination as they move than with the agent that acts on them—for example, the properties of an object *loaded* into a container are such that the object be of a size and shape appropriate to the container; the fact that *sprayed* stuff is liquid is intimately related to the shape it assumes as it is moving, and so on. I will use these cognitive considerations to motivate a constraint, necessary for the current learning account to work, that object properties of locative verbs are in fact attached to the theme argument in the GO structure and not to the patient argument in the ACT structure.

6. A possible problematic case involves the *stuff* verbs. In analyzing their semantic structures—see (5.63)—I suggested that the state of the *with* variant was related to the manner of the *into* variant not by virtue of copying identical structures, but by a kind of cognitive inference: inserting the contents against resistance in the *into* form is related to the container's being overfull in the *with* form. It is not clear if this is really necessary or if there is actually a set of common symbols mentioned in both the resistance and the overfull specification. If the former, the rule-creation process would also have to include in the rule not only the parts of the input structure that are coindexed with alternating arguments but also any parts that are necessary premises for the inference of structures in the derivation of the second form.

7. The importance of aspectual differences is consistent with the spirit of Tenny's (1988) proposal that aspect is a key interface between lexical semantics and syntax.

Chapter 7: Development

1. The asymmetry occurs only in comprehension experiments, probably because the pair of adjacent unmarked NPs taxes the child's parser, as it does the adult's. You can clearly feel this in trying to understand a sentence like *The horse sent the tiger the elephant.* See Pinker (1984, p. 398) and Gropen et al. (1989) for discussion.

2. Clark and Clark (1979) suggest that some innovative transitive verbs might be blocked by homonymity with existing verbs. If so, errors like *I'm singing him* might be blocked by *I'm singing the song* when the latter argument structure is consolidated in the child's lexicon.

3. The permissive-causation picture was never shown for s*hake*; for *spin* it was chosen 42% of the time in connection with the lexical causative, perhaps because a globe can spin long after the causing event has taken place, making the permissive-causation picture consistent with past direct causation as well. For *let the globe spin* it was chosen 46% of the time.

4. Ammon used three other verbs as well, but her nonorthogonal design does not allow the relevant comparisons to be made for them. *Squirt* was not paired with a picture triplet contrasting direct and indirect causation. *Open* was never presented in a lexical causative form. *Pour* was depicted with a genie who worked magic in one of the pictures, making the permissive-causation picture also construable as involving magic and hence highly ambiguous.

5. Lord and Bowerman discuss at length the fact that the appearance of novel intransitives is inconsistent with the notion of a unidirectional causativization rule deriving transitives from intransitives (see also Hochberg, 1986). But this is orthogonal to the question of whether either such rule operates on lexicosemantic structure (adding, or subtracting, a "cause" superstructure) or on syntactic argument structure (adding, or subtracting, an external argument), and thus is not relevant to that issue.

6. Strictly speaking, verbs of being and having do violate the broad-range rule for adult English as I stated it in (5.54) in chapter 5, which excludes the <–dynamic> predicates BE and HAVE. Possibly this bit of overgenerality in the child's rule is the result of the indeterminateness of Reverse Linking; Lexical Abstraction would eventually trigger the slight narrowing that would be needed to bring the child's broad-range rule into conformity with the adult's.

7. The only exception I know of is for some verbs of obtaining where a phrase denoting an abstract cause can be added: *John earned considerable fame / Perseverance and talent earned John considerable fame* (also *get, win, gain, ?attain*).

8. Perhaps, it might be suggested, the principles governing compatibility between argument structures and sentential syntax would filter out iterated causation if a lexical rule permitted it: LFG contains a universally available OBJ2 function, but no OBJ3, OBJ4, and so on, and GB would have to struggle for a mechanism to assign the later arguments case given their non-adjacency to the verb or to any preposition. However, it is not clear how the solutions adopted to handle second objects (such as the OBJ2 function in LFG, or verb-object incorporation or various special forms of case marking in GB), which were somewhat ad hoc to begin with, would be prevented from extending naturally to handle a third or fourth object.

9. I exclude the example *Spell this "buy"* (where Christy is asking her mother to rotate the blocks on a toy until the word "buy" is formed), because a verb with a quoted argument is not generally a double-object form. Most likely, it is an object-predicate complement construction, as in *She calls him "Hoss"; They deemed him a fool; We elected him president*; and *I spell "relief" "R, O, L, A, I, D, S"*.

10. Green (1974) notes that malefactive arguments colloquially expressed using *on* as in *She played a trick on us* can dativize: *She played us a trick*. This example is marginal to me, however, and others are even worse: *The car snapped a fan belt on us / *snapped us a fan belt*.

11. Usages of the prepositional forms of dativizable verbs in these children's speech also closely mirrored the adult input: 79% of the dativizable verbs (types) appearing in the prepositional form in the children's speech also appeared in the prepositional form in the speech of adults in that child's transcripts.

12. Adam and Eve produced sentences at a rate of about two hundred per hour, and four hours a day is a rough estimate of the amount of time in which a linguistic error from the child would have been noticed. At a conservative estimate of ten months a year, six years of speech from Christy (age 2–7) would amount to about 1.4 million utterances and four years of speech from Eva (age 2–5) would amount to .96 million utterances.

13. Bowerman notes that apart from the two examples in (d) and (e), she virtually never called attention to Christy's errors or discussed them with her.

14. Bowerman does not discuss whether this phenomenon also occurred with Eva. However in the data she reports, there is a self-correction by Eva at 5;0 (*Be a hand up your nose.* [M: *What?*] *Put a hand up your nose*), and five other causative errors that occurred at that age or later, the latest at 5;5 (which is roughly as far as the diaries for Eva went at that point).

15. Katarina Rice has told me that when she gets cash from an automatic teller machine, her 2-year-old son asks, "Are we buying money now, Mom?"

16. Interestingly, *make* and *give* are not interchanged with each other. This confirms that location is the base domain which can be extended to possessional or state/circumstance fields, rather than there being a completely content-free coordinate system that can be instantiated variously as location, possession, or state/circumstance.

17. I thank Ruth Berman for generously sharing her findings and interpretations surrounding this phenomenon.

18. *Empty* can also occur with the theme as direct object if a *from*-object is included, as in *empty water from the glass*, but in a simple transitive form it is the source or container that must be the object: **empty the water*.

19. In a second experiment testing only the word *fill* (Gropen, 1989; Gropen et al., in preparation), we have replicated the semantic manner bias, the content-as-object syntactic errors, and the weak contingency between these two error types across individual children.

20. For the curious: Boil small pieces of purple cabbage in water, then drain, and let the purple liquid cool. If you add a base to it (e.g., baking soda), it will turn green; if you add an acid to it (e.g., lemon juice), it will turn pink. The cabbage juice sold in supermarkets is red because vinegar has already been added. Thanks go to Jess Gropen for this explanation.

Index